LIST OF MAPS

NEW ORLEANS

Greater New Orleans   45
New Orleans
   Accommodations   56–57

New Orleans Dining   86–87
New Orleans
   Attractions   130–131

NEW ORLEANS WALKING TOURS

The French Quarter   159
The Garden District   167
The Lower Garden District   171

Esplanade Ridge   175
A Streetcar Tour   177

EXCURSION AREAS

Plantations Along the Great
   River Road   211

Cajun Country   227

W9-ASW-610

FROMMER'S

COMPREHENSIVE TRAVEL GUIDE

NEW ORLEANS '95

Garden Dsst

Cannons - ceasar salad,

Cheesecake Bistro

Deanis - seafood,

Pat O'Brians
         piano Kwor
nextto : JAZZ music
     looks like a all-
Preservation Hall

2. Madewood
       P. 213

? Kent a Car
   1 day ?

3. Cajun Swamp Tour
       P. 229

Jackson Square

MACMILLAN • USA

About the Author:

Lisa Legarde was born in New Orleans and graduated from Wellesley College with a B.A. in English. She has traveled extensively in Europe and North America and is author or co-author of 12 Frommer Guides.

Macmillan Travel
A Prentice Hall Macmillan Company
15 Columbus Circle
New York, NY 10023

ISBN 0-671-88375-5
ISSN 0899-2908

Design by Robert Bull Design
Maps by Geografix Inc.

SPECIAL SALES

Bulk purchases (10+ copies) of Frommer's Travel Guides are available to corporations at special discounts. The Special Sales Department can produce custom editions to be used as premiums and/or for sales promotion to suit individual needs. Existing editions can be produced with custom cover imprints such as corporate logos. For more information write to: Special Sales, Prentice Hall, 15 Columbus Circle, New York, NY 10023.

Manufactured in the United States of America

CONTENTS

1 INTRODUCING NEW ORLEANS 1

1. Geography, History & People 3
2. Culture 8
3. Famous New Orleanians 13
4. Food & Drink 16
5. Recommended Books & Recordings 19

SPECIAL FEATURES
- What's Special About New Orleans 2
- Dateline 3

2 PLANNING A TRIP TO NEW ORLEANS 23

1. Information & Money 23
2. When to Go—Climate & Events 24
3. What to Pack 27
4. Getting There 28

SPECIAL FEATURES
- What Things Cost in New Orleans 24
- Calendar of Events 25
- Frommer's Smart Traveler: Airfares 28

3 FOR FOREIGN VISITORS 30

1. Preparing for Your Trip 30
2. Getting To & Around the U.S. 33

SPECIAL FEATURES
- Fast Facts: For the Foreign Traveler 34
- The American System of Measurements 38

4 GETTING TO KNOW NEW ORLEANS 41

1. Orientation 41
2. Getting Around 46
3. Networks & Resources 50

SPECIAL FEATURE
- Fast Facts: New Orleans 48

5 NEW ORLEANS ACCOMMODATIONS 52

1. In the French Quarter 53
2. Outside the French Quarter 72

SPECIAL FEATURE
- Frommer's Smart Traveler: Hotels 59

6 NEW ORLEANS DINING 81

1. In the French Quarter 82
2. Downtown 101
3. Central Business District 103
4. Uptown (including the Garden District) 106

SPECIAL FEATURE
- Frommer's Smart Traveler: Restaurants 97

5. Metairie   110
6. Lake Pontchartrain   111
7. Nearby Dining   112
8. Specialty Dining   113
9. Restaurants By Cuisine   117

7   WHAT TO SEE & DO IN NEW ORLEANS   120

1. Suggested Itineraries   121
2. The Top Attractions   123
3. More Attractions   125
4. Cool for Kids   141
5. Organized Tours   142
6. Mardi Gras & Other Festivals   145
7. Sports & Recreation   156

SPECIAL FEATURES
● *Did You Know . . . ?   121*
● *Frommer's Favorite New
   Orleans Experiences   126*

8   STROLLING AROUND NEW ORLEANS   157

1. The French Quarter   157
2. The Garden District   165
3. The Lower Garden District   169
4. Esplanade Ridge   173
5. A Streetcar Tour   177

9   SAVVY SHOPPING   181

1. The Shopping Scene   182
2. Shopping A to Z   183

10   NEW ORLEANS NIGHTS   192

1. The Performing Arts   192
2. The Club & Music Scene   194
3. The Bar Scene   200
4. More Entertainment   202

SPECIAL FEATURE
● *The Major Concert/
   Performance Halls   193*

11   EASY EXCURSIONS FROM NEW ORLEANS   204

1. The Plantations Along the Great River Road   204
2. Cajun Country   221

INDEX   239

ABOUT THIS FROMMER GUIDE

What is a Frommer City Guide? It's a comprehensive, easy-to-use guide to the best travel values in all price ranges—from very expensive to budget. The one guidebook to take along with you on any trip.

WHAT THE SYMBOLS MEAN

 FROMMER'S FAVORITES—hotels, restaurants, attractions, and entertainments you should not miss

 SUPER-SPECIAL VALUES—really exceptional values

 FROMMER'S SMART TRAVELER TIPS—hints on how to secure the best value for your money

IN HOTEL AND OTHER LISTINGS

The following symbols refer to the standard amentities available in all rooms:

A/C air conditioning   TEL telephone   TV television
MINIBAR refrigerator stocked with beverages and snacks

The following abbreviations are used for credit cards:

AE American Express   DISC Discover   JCB Card (Japan)
CB Carte Blanche   ER enRoute   MC MasterCard
DC Diners Club   V Visa

TRIP PLANNING WITH THIS GUIDE

Use the following features:

What Things Cost In . . . to help you plan your daily budget

Calendar of Events . . . to plan for or avoid

Suggested Itineraries . . . for seeing the city

What's Special About Checklist . . . a summary of the city's highlights—which lets you check off those that appeal most to you

Easy-to-Read Maps . . . walking tours, city sights, hotel and restaurant locations

Fast Facts . . . all the essentials at a glance: emergencies, information, safety, taxes, tipping, and more

OTHER SPECIAL FROMMER FEATURES

Cool for Kids—attractions

Did You Know . . . ?—offbeat, fun facts

Impressions—what others have said

INVITATION TO THE READERS

In researching this book, I have come across many wonderful establishments, the best of which I have included here. I'm sure that many of you also will come across appealing hotels, inns, restaurants, guesthouses, shops, and attractions. Please don't keep them to yourself. Share your experiences, especially if you want to comment on places that have been included in this edition that have changed for the worse. You can address your letters to:

Lisa M. Legarde
Frommer's New Orleans '95
c/o Macmillan Travel
15 Columbus Circle
New York, NY 10023

A DISCLAIMER

Readers are advised that prices fluctuate in the course of time, and travel information changes under the impact of the varied and volatile factors that affect the travel industry. Neither the author nor the publisher can be held responsible for the experiences of readers while traveling. Readers are invited to write to the publisher with ideas, comments, and suggestions for future editions.

SAFETY ADVISORY

When you're traveling in an unfamiliar city or country, stay alert. Be aware of your immediate surroundings. Wear a moneybelt and keep a close eye on your possessions. Be particularly careful with cameras, purses, and wallets, all favorite targets of thieves and pickpockets.

CHAPTER 1

INTRODUCING NEW ORLEANS

- **WHAT'S SPECIAL ABOUT NEW ORLEANS**
1. **GEOGRAPHY, HISTORY & PEOPLE**
- **DATELINE**
2. **CULTURE**
3. **FAMOUS NEW ORLEANIANS**
4. **FOOD & DRINK**
5. **RECOMMENDED BOOKS & RECORDINGS**

There's no other place quite like it in our country. Call it the "Crescent City," because it sits along a deep bend of the Mississippi River; call it the "City That Care Forgot"; call it "America's Most Interesting City"—by any name, New Orleans is truly unique among American cities.

It also holds, I'm quick to confess, first place in my affections. I've never been able to put my finger on exactly why this should be so. Maybe it's the intriguing architecture of the French Quarter; or the Old South appeal of the Garden District; or the food—so special that the mere memory of it can make me homesick when I'm far away; or the uninhibited gaiety of Bourbon Street; or the joyous jazz of Preservation Hall. Certainly all of these things are part of the city's irresistible charm, but I think perhaps it was really the *people* of New Orleans who first won my heart many years ago and have held it captive ever since. Although I grew up in the tradition of hospitality that is the hallmark of the South, I've found over the years that the word "hospitality" takes on richer meaning in this city. It isn't only that you're warmly welcomed—it's that New Orleanians seem *overjoyed* that you've chosen to come, and they seem always to go to great lengths to make sure you enjoy your stay! Tales abound of those who have come on a "passing-through" basis and remained to join the ranks of residents. It's unlikely you'll escape a similar inclination, even after only a day or two.

Some of the most exciting and colorful chapters in American history have been played out in and around New Orleans—it has been a haven for swashbuckling privateers, such as Jean Lafitte; was courageously defended by Andrew Jackson and his men in the War of 1812's spectacular Battle of New Orleans; was a capital of the great Mississippi riverboat industry that Mark Twain wrote about; and was an elegant zenith of antebellum Southern society. As you walk the narrow streets, lined with well-kept centuries-old buildings that are flush with fancy ironwork, the city's past will seem palpably alive—it's hard not to imagine that the frock-coated gentlemen and hoop-skirted ladies of bygone days are strolling the sidewalks beside you or taking their leisure in the elegant courtyards and restaurants.

WHAT'S SPECIAL ABOUT NEW ORLEANS

Monuments
☐ Jackson Square Monument, in the heart of the French Quarter.

Buildings
☐ St. Louis Cathedral, on the edge of Jackson Square.
☐ The Old U.S. Mint, on Esplanade Avenue behind the old French Market.

Museums
☐ The New Orleans Historic Voodoo Museum, one of the only places like it in the United States.

Parks/Gardens
☐ Audubon Park, across from Tulane and Loyola Universities, just off the streetcar line.
☐ City Park, with a wealth of activities as well as natural beauty.

Events/Festivals
☐ Mardi Gras, one of New Orleans's biggest and most spectacular events.
☐ Jazz Fest, hosting thousands of musicians every year.

Religious Shrines
☐ The tomb of the 19th-century voodoo queen Marie Laveau, a religious shrine to countless admirers who visit yearly.

Food/Drink
☐ Creole, Cajun, Italian, and many other kinds of restaurants—a number of which are among the best in the country.

Nightlife
☐ Music — New Orleans is the birthplace of jazz, which remains a nightclub staple, along with equally vibrant traditions of Cajun, zydeco, and rhythm-and-blues music.
☐ Bourbon Street, the famous 24-hour, 7-days-a-week, 365-days-a-year party.

Great Neighborhoods
☐ New Orleans's historic French Quarter, or Vieux Carré.
☐ The beautiful Garden District, with its old Southern plantation homes.

But don't for one instant imagine that you'll be stuck in New Orleans's past. The world-famous brassy jazz sound of New Orleans that fills the streets is very much of the 20th century. A look across Canal Street from the French Quarter will show you that the city is indeed keeping up with the times—skyscrapers, once thought impossible to build on this swampy site, share the skyline with skeletonlike frameworks of others yet to come. The Louisiana Superdome is the city's focal point for large-scale sports and entertainment events, while the towering International Trade Mart and the sprawling Rivergate Exhibition Center serve the interests of commerce. And the rejuvenated riverfront has come alive with shops, eateries, and entertainment.

Then there are the people. Artists "on the fence" around Jackson Square; musicians sitting in at jazz clubs or Preservation Hall; shopkeepers displaying exquisite imports alongside inexpensive souvenirs; taxi drivers hopping out to open doors (unheard of in most places nowadays); natives happily sharing tables with tourists at the Café du Monde for an any-hour café au lait and beignets (more about these later)—New Orleanians display a startling occupational, ethnic, and linguistic variety. The population "stew" that comes from this marrying of flavors is a natural result of New Orleans's long history, a past that has seen widely differing groups gather here, opposing one another in the beginning, but learning to join hands in mutual self-interest in the end.

1. GEOGRAPHY, HISTORY & PEOPLE

GEOGRAPHY New Orleans, the largest city in Louisiana and one of the chief cities of the South, is situated strategically at the mouth of the great drainage basin of North America, the Mississippi-Missouri system. The "Crescent City"—coextensive with Orleans Parish ("county")—covers an area of 364 square miles along a deep bend of the Mississippi, 110 miles from its mouth. The city is bounded by Jefferson Parish and the Mississippi to the west, Lake Pontchartrain to the north, Lake Borgne to the east, and St. Bernard Parish and the Mississippi to the south.

The Vieux Carré, the oldest part of New Orleans, was built on some of the highest ground to be found close to the mouth of the Mississippi and the Gulf of Mexico—elevations rise to all of 12 feet above sea level. But many parts of the modern city are located as much as 6.5 feet *below* sea level, and thus the city relies on an extensive and ingenious system of levees, canals, and water pumps to protect against flooding.

Although this carefully engineered system prevents floods, the fact remains that the city is built on rather marshy ground. Until fairly recently, this circumstance served as a natural barrier to the sort of towering skylines found in other American cities—it was expensive and laborious to lay foundations that would support tall buildings. New construction methods have, however, allowed New Orleans to build some skyscrapers.

To the south, to the west, and to some degree to the north of New Orleans are Louisiana's lowlands and bayous—this area, home to one of the most unique and scenic ecosystems in the United States, is definitely worth a look.

HISTORY In 1718 a Canadian-born Frenchman, Jean-Baptiste Le Moyne, Sieur de Bienville, set out to find a suitable location for a settlement to protect France's holdings in the New World from British expansion. His brother, Pierre Le Moyne, Sieur d'Iberville, had planted a cross at the great bend of the Mississippi River in 1699, and de Bienville found this place a strategic point for his "city." Although it

DATELINE

- **1718** City founded by Jean-Baptiste Le Moyne, first governor of Louisiana
- **1726** Capuchin monastery erected
- **1730** Ursuline *(continues)*

DATELINE

convent completed

1762 Louis XV secretly cedes New Orleans and all of Louisiana west of the Mississippi to Spain

1783 Treaty of Paris confirms Spanish possession

1788, 1794 Fire destroys much of the city; new brick buildings replace wood

1795 Treaty of Madrid opens port to Americans; trade thrives

1800 Louisiana again becomes French possession

1803 United States purchases Louisiana

1812 The *New Orleans*, a steam vessel, arrives from Pittsburgh

1815 Battle of New Orleans

1834 Medical College of Louisiana founded, forerunner of Tulane University

1838 First Mardi Gras festival

1840 Antoine Alciatore, founder of Antoine's, arrives from Marseilles. New Orleans is by this point the fourth-largest city in the United States, second only to New York as a port

1850 Commerce booming; cotton accounts for 45% of total commerce; city

(continues)

was almost 110 miles inland from the Gulf of Mexico by river, the city had an easy portage route to a little stream (Bayou St. John) that provided easy water transportation directly into Lake Pontchartrain. From a military standpoint, this was a convenient "backdoor" for defense or escape, should the fortunes of war turn against the French. And, of course, it was a perfect trade route inland to the nearby Native American villages and their fabled gold, which de Bienville's superiors in France were convinced would soon be shipped to them from Louisiana.

Following the plan of a late French medieval town, a central square (the Place d'Armes) was laid out, with streets forming a grid around it. A church, government office, priest's house, and official residences fronted the square and earthen ramparts dotted with forts were built around the perimeter. In honor of the Duc d'Orléans, then the Regent of France, the little town was named New Orleans.

Today we know this section of the city as the Vieux Carré (it means "Old Square" and is pronounced "View Ka-*ray*") and the Place d'Armes as Jackson Square. Rude huts of cypress filled in with moss and clay were erected, and a tiny wooden levee was raised against the mighty river, which persisted in flooding periodically to turn streets into rivers of mud.

The fabled Native American gold turned out to be just that, a fable. But there were furs aplenty, and de Bienville needed settlers to work as trappers, to run farms to feed the colony, and to fight off hostile Indians. The French government saw this as a perfect opportunity to rid itself of all its misfits at home and sent to New Orleans the dregs of its prisons, some bonded servants, and slaves from French Caribbean settlements. They were the first ingredients of New Orleans's population "stew." Among them were "fallen women" who somehow managed to leave no direct descendants, if you can believe today's New Orleanians: Almost everyone proudly traces his or her ancestry to French or Spanish nobility and the respectable "casket girls" brought over by Ursuline nuns in 1727 (carrying all their worldly goods in casketlike trunks), with never a mention of those earlier women of the streets.

Lured by the first real estate scam in this country's history (a flamboyant speculator named John Law painted the appealing picture of a virtual paradise on earth in the new settlement), wealthy Europeans, aristocrats, merchants, exiles, soldiers, and a large contingent of German farmers arrived to find only mosquitoes, a raw frontier existence, and swampy land that resisted all but the most heroic efforts to put it to productive use. But the Europeans stayed on, and as they tamed the land, the colony prospered and attracted more and more members of the aristocratic class. Social life began to take on the complexion of European court life. By 1763 yet another seasoning was added to the pot—Acadians from Nova Scotia fleeing British rule. You'll find their descendants living a little to the west of New Orleans, still engaged in farming and trapping, still speaking their unique brand of French, and proudly calling themselves "Cajuns."

French to the core from the very beginning, New Orleanians were horrified to learn in 1764 that Louis XV had secretly given their city to his cousin, Charles III of Spain. Their resentment forced the first Spanish governor to leave, and it wasn't until Don Alexander O'Reilly, known as "Bloody O'Reilly," was dispatched by the Spanish Crown with 3,000 soldiers in 1769 that revolutionary ideas were firmly squelched (after the execution of five French patriots) and Spanish rule was accepted as a reality. With a Gallic shrug, French aristocracy mingled with Spanish nobility, intermarried, and created a new "Creole" culture.

Tragic fires struck in 1788, when more than 850 buildings were destroyed, and again in 1794 in the midst of rebuilding. From the ashes emerged a completely new city, dominated by the proud Spanish style of brick-and-plaster buildings replete with arches, courtyards, balconies, and, of course, attached slave quarters. Even today you'll see tile markers giving Spanish street names at every corner in the "French" Quarter.

The new city was much coveted by both the English and the Americans. France, recognizing its blunder in giving the city away, wanted it back. Control of the lucrative trade conducted along the Mississippi River was at stake, and with all sorts of plots

DATELINE

becomes greatest slave market in the country

- **1853–55** Yellow fever epidemic
- **1861** Louisiana secedes from the Union
- **1862** City captured by Adm. David Farragut
- **1865–77** Reconstruction; carpetbaggers swarm into the city
- **1871** Audubon Park created
- **1880** Railroad arrives
- **1882** Canal Street illuminated by electric light
- **1884** Cotton Centennial Exposition (World's Fair)
- **1885** Joe "King" Oliver born
- **1890** Jelly Roll Morton born
- **1892** First electric streetcar operated along St. Charles Avenue
- **1897** Sidney Bechet born
- **1900** Louis Armstrong born
- **1906** Barney Bigard, clarinetist/tenor saxophonist, born
- **1911** Razzy Dazzy Spasm Band performs in New York, where its name is changed to Razzy Dazzy *Jazz* Band
- **1917** Original Dixie Land Jazz Band attains height of popularity

(continues)

DATELINE

- **1921** Arnaud's established
- **1927** Levee at Poydras erected.
- **1938** Tennessee Williams arrives in New Orleans; Huey P. Long Bridge built over Mississippi River
- **1939** French Quarter Residents Association formed, an agent for preservation
- **1956** Lake Pontchartrain Causeway completed
- **1960** Public schools integrated
- **1969** Bacchus krewe organized
- **1973** Parades banned in the Vieux Carré
- **1975** Superdome opens
- **1977** Ernest N. "Dutch" Morial becomes first black mayor
- **1984** Louisiana World Expo

flying about, Governor Carondelet reinforced the wall around the city and armed its five forts with cannons pointing outward to fend off invaders and inward to ward off any internal uprising. France finally regained possession in 1800, with a surprisingly quiet transfer of ownership, and held on for three years while Napoleon negotiated the Louisiana Purchase with the United States for the paltry (as it turned out) sum of $15 million. To the Creole society, this was almost as appalling as Spanish rule had been to the French settlers, for they considered all Americans barbarians who would surely bring about the end of the sophisticated Vieux Carré lifestyle.

Shunned by existing New Orleans society, the newly arrived Americans settled across Canal Street (so named because a drainage canal was once planned along its route, although it was never actually constructed) and set about showing the "downtown" snobs that they were no strangers to culture. Splendid mansions rose in what is now the Garden District, and a segregated social life took shape. But not for long. Yankee commercialism (which made "uptown" into a boomtown) brought industry and wealth much needed by the downtowners, and the vitality of warm-blooded downtown society drew uptowners like a magnet. Besides, both were forced to join forces against hurricanes, yellow fever epidemics, and floods. Such a spirit of unity grew between the two sections that when Andrew Jackson needed volunteers in 1814 to protect New Orleans against British attack, some 5,000 citizens responded—from both sides of Canal Street. Even the infamous (but much revered in New Orleans) privateer Jean Lafitte joined in, supplying cannons and ammunition that swung the balance in favor of the Americans. Ironically the Battle of New Orleans—which left some 2,000 British casualties as opposed to only a small number of American dead and wounded—took place on January 8, 1815, two weeks *after* a peace treaty had been signed, unbeknownst to either side at New Orleans.

From then until the Civil War, New Orleans gloried in a prosperity unmatched anywhere in the country. Wealthy cotton and sugar planters left upriver mansions from time to time to occupy luxurious town houses and to attend festivals, opera, theater, banquets, parades, and spectacular balls (including "Quadroon Balls," where beautiful mulatto girls were displayed to the male gentry as possible mistresses). Hardworking Irish and German immigrants arrived in vast numbers to add their own dash of spice to the already exotic culture. Canals and levees were built to keep the city alive and a little drier; steamboats plied the river serving the cotton trade and pleasure-seeking passengers; politics and gambling became passionate pastimes; and there was a lively trade in the slaves who supported the plantation economy on their oppressed backs. Federal troops put an end to all that when they marched in in 1862 during the Civil War and stayed until 1877, through a bitter Reconstruction period. New Orleans would never again be quite so flamboyant, but it was far from dead.

Like the rest of the defeated South, the city went about the business of rebuilding its economic life without the dependency on slavery that had been its downfall. By 1880 port activity had begun to pick up and industrial activity drew from the business world more and more visitors, many of whom became residents. And a new group of immigrants, Italians, came to put their special mark on the city. Through it all there survived an undiminished enthusiasm for fun. Gambling again thrived in over 80 establishments, there were almost 800 saloons, and scores of "bawdy houses" openly engaged in prostitution (illegal but uncontrolled). New Orleans was earning a reputation for open vice, and there were some who felt that something should be done to counteract such publicity.

Alderman Sidney Story, in 1897, thought he had the answer. He moved all illegal (but highly profitable) activities into a restricted district along Basin Street, next door to the French Quarter. Quickly nicknamed "Storyville," the district boasted fancy "sporting palaces" with elaborate decor, musical entertainment, and a variety of ladies of pleasure. Visitors and residents could purchase a directory (the "Blue Book"), which listed alphabetically the names, addresses, and races of more than 700 prostitutes, ranging from those in the "palaces" to the poorer inhabitants of wretched, decaying shacks called "cribs" on the blocks behind Basin Street. African American musicians came into their own when they moved from the streets into ornate bordellos to entertain patrons with the music we know as jazz. Although jazz itself predates Storyville, here it gained the popularity that sent it upriver and into this country's musical heritage. When the secretary of the navy decreed in 1917 that our armed forces should not be exposed to so much open vice (without, it might be added, any visible support from the troops), Storyville closed down and disappeared without a trace.

In recent years, New Orleans has built its port into the largest in the United States and the second busiest in the world. (Amsterdam is first.) It ranks near the top in tourism in this country (conventions alone bring in close to one million visitors each year) and is one of the top travel destinations in the United States for foreign visitors. Drainage problems have been conquered by means of high levees, canals, pumping stations, and great spillways, which are opened to direct floodwater away from the city.

IMPRESSIONS

"I will hold New Orleans in spite of Urop and all hell."
— ANDREW JACKSON, 1812

Outside the French Quarter, the city's face has changed considerably over recent years. The 1984 World's Fair left a legacy of high-rise luxury hotels and a reconstructed waterfront on the fair's site, in what was a derelict warehouse district. New Orleans's emergence as a major financial center (with more than 50 commercial banks) has brought with it the construction of soaring office buildings, mostly in the Central Business District.

Yesterday lives on in the architecture and lifestyle of the French Quarter, Garden District mansions, and colorful steamboats ferrying fun-loving passengers around the harbor—and, as always, it joins hands happily with today's Yankee entrepreneurs in a friendly, heart-warming collaboration that makes New Orleans an exciting travel experience not to be missed.

THE PEOPLE New Orleans is Louisiana's largest city and is one of the principal cities of the American South. It is not, however, a typical southern metropolis. The city's history as a pawn in the territorial struggles between Spain, France, and later, the United States has imparted to it a distinctly cosmopolitan flavor. It is home to significant populations of African Americans, French, Spanish, Irish, Germans, Anglos, Cubans, and Cajuns.

The French and Spanish were the first to arrive, and their descendants call themselves Creoles; their cuisine of highly spiced French and Spanish dishes has become internationally famous. Another major part of the cultural mix was introduced when large numbers of Acadians, expelled by the British from Atlantic Canada in 1763, settled in the Bayou Country to the west of New Orleans; today they proudly call themselves Cajuns and retain one of the nation's most distinctive cultures.

Well over 50% of New Orleanians are African American; unlike in many of the south's major cities, race relations here have always been characterized by at least a degree of harmony. In antebellum days, free people of color constituted an important minority, and today the city has sizable African American upper- and middle-class populations.

2. CULTURE

MUSIC Most people, when they think New Orleans, think jazz—specifically Dixieland jazz, or "trad" jazz as they call it in Europe.

IMPRESSIONS

"What little I have seen of this I like perhaps better than any town in the Union. There are pictures on the Quays: there are old French houses: there are streets which look for all the world like Harvre — the sweet kind of French tongue is spoken in the shops. . . . There is capital ordinaire Claret for dinner — The faces are not Yankee faces with their keen eager narrow eyes, there are many fat people — these are interesting facts."
—W. M. THACKERAY, LETTER TO ANNE AND HARRIET THACKERAY, 7–10 MARCH 1856.

In fact, New Orleans is considered the birthplace of jazz—one of the more remarkable American cultural contributions to western culture—which spread from the Crescent City to such centers as Chicago, New York, Kansas City, and the West Coast and eventually became popular throughout the world.

Jazz developed in the late 19th century from the work songs, spirituals, and blues that the African Americans sang; all of these were rooted in the rhythms and sounds they brought from their homeland. As still often happens with popular music today, jazz did not enter the mainstream until it was played and recorded by white bands such as the New Orleans Rhythm Kings and the Original Dixie Land Jazz Band, which first brought jazz north; much later, in the 1930s, jazz's popularity was boosted further by racially mixed bands, led by such figures as Benny Goodman, that performed at such major venues as Carnegie Hall.

The earliest jazz bands were called "spasm" bands; they played outside the theaters, saloons, and brothels of the city. They employed a makeshift group of instruments—cigar-box fiddles, old kettles, cowbells, pebble-filled gourds, harmonicas, bull fiddles constructed of half a barrel, and various whistles and horns. Equally colorful were the names of the players—ranging from Stalebread Charley to Warm Gravy. One of these groups, the Razzy Dazzy Spasm Band, actually played New York in 1911, and there its name was changed to the Razzy Dazzy *Jazz* Band.

Jazz is improvisational music, and as a result no performance is ever the same—each depends on the personalities, musicianship, and inspirations of the individual players. New Orleans jazz is played by small bands, usually featuring cornet or trumpet; clarinet; trombone; and a rhythm section that includes bass, drums, guitar or banjo, and sometimes piano. When the bands march, as they often do at festivals and funerals, the bass and piano are replaced by a tuba. The difference between the original New Orleans style and the many incarnations of jazz that have followed lies primarily in the New Orleans emphasis on counterpoint and ensemble—the contrapuntal, improvisational melodic flow between the three lead instruments and the rhythm section. In the big bands of the 1920s and 1930s, for example, emphasis had shifted to a single melodic line played by a virtuoso performer.

Let's now return to the birth of jazz. In the 19th century, New Orleans was one of the nation's great trading ports, and its society was a lively ethnic mix of Creole, Spanish, and African American with a Catholic culture that was more relaxed and fun-loving than the typical American Protestant culture. Storyville, New Orleans's red-light district with its brothels, honky-tonk saloons, and gambling dens, was an ideal environment for the growth of jazz. The pioneer African American New Orleans jazz band led by Buddy Bolden had been formed in the 1890s, but it was not until the all-white Original Dixieland Jazz Band made its first record in 1917 that jazz became widely popular. As long as Storyville existed New Orleans was the center of the jazz world, but when it closed in 1917 many of the musicians left for northern cities, such as Chicago, bringing the New Orleans traditional sound with them. Kid Ory, King Oliver, Louis Armstrong, Jelly Roll Morton, Barney

Bigard, and Johnny Dodds carried the New Orleans torch to Chicago, New York, and elsewhere, eventually evolving distinct sounds of their own.

Gradually the New Orleans style was modified, and a single melodic line with star performer replaced the ensemble approach to music. With each decade jazz evolved as new performers improvised and experimented, producing new styles of jazz for each generation. In the late 1920s *swing* originated in Kansas City and Harlem, promoted by the big bands of jazz giants Duke Ellington and Count Basie, as well as by groups led by Fletcher Henderson, Glenn Miller, Benny Goodman, Jimmy Lunceford, Artie Shaw, and Tommy Dorsey.

In the late 1930s and 1940s the big bands were replaced by bebop with more elaborate rhythms and more convoluted melodies—a beautiful, fiercely improvisational music whose premier exponents were Charlie Parker, Dizzy Gillespie, and Thelonius Monk.

Cool jazz was exactly that—rooted in bebop, but bluesier and with a loping tempo. It was developed in the late '40s and early '50s by such seminal figures as Miles Davis, John Coltrane, Lester Young, Stan Getz, and pianist Dave Brubeck. New trends have followed ever since—the neo-bop of Sonny Rollins and Art Blakey; the third-stream combination of classical music and jazz of Charles Mingus and George Lewis; the avant-garde sounds of Ornette Coleman, Archie Shepp, and Roland Kirk; and the various marriages of jazz to Latin, rock, and practically everything else being played.

But New Orleans started it all, and many of the original performers were born in the Crescent City, like the two early giants of jazz, Louis Armstrong and Sidney Bechet. Louis Armstrong learned to play cornet in the Waif's Home in New Orleans. He started playing with Kid Ory's band and made several trips between 1918 and 1921 with a Mississippi riverboat band. In 1922 King Oliver lured him to Chicago to play second trumpet behind him, but soon Louis was building a reputation as a brilliant virtuoso soloist. He organized several bands of his own and appeared on Broadway as well as in several American and foreign films. The great clarinetist and soprano saxophonist Sidney Bechet was born in New Orleans and began his musical career with his brother's band in 1911. He also played with King Oliver's band but made his greatest name abroad in Europe, where he settled for the last 20 years of his life.

Pianist/composer Jelly Roll Morton, born Ferdinand Joseph La Menthe in Gulfport, Mississippi, began his career in Storyville. A colorful figure whose moods and cantankerous personality led many to disparage him, he was nevertheless one of the great composers of early jazz, the creator of such great tunes as "Dead Man Blues," "Jelly Roll Blues," "King Porter Stomp," "Sidewalk Blues," and "Wolverine Blues."

King Oliver, born in Abend, Louisiana, began playing in the Onward Brass Band in 1904 and established himself as a leading cornet player in New Orleans. He left in 1918 to form his own band in Chicago, and from 1920 to 1923 led the Creole Jazz Band there, popularizing the New Orleans sound in Chicago and elsewhere in the North. Other famous New Orleans jazz artists have followed—Al Hirt and Pete Fountain, to name two.

There's still a flourishing jazz scene in the city, but don't expect to hear jazz emanating from every club on Bourbon Street as was once the case. Sadly, rock and roll, country, and rhythm and blues have replaced jazz on Bourbon Street, so that there are only one or two places to hear jazz in the French Quarter today—the foremost being Preservation Hall. The other serious jazz clubs are outside the quarter, like Pete Fountain's in the Hilton Hotel. Jazz, however, is still played—and young New Orleanian musicians such as Wynton and Branford Marsalis are among those pushing the music into the future. Although the invitation to stroll down Bourbon Street may not produce as much jazz as it once did, the sound is still cherished in the city.

VOODOO To some, voodoo is synonymous with New Orleans. That's no surprise, really, since voodoo has been practiced widely in New Orleans for almost 200 years.

It is said that voodoo originated in the African kingdom of Dahomey and was then called Vodu. The Africans believe in the god Zombi, who was said to have been a snake that granted sight to the first people on earth—thus the presence of snakes in voodoo ceremonies. Rather than the harbinger of evil that snakes are in the Judeo-Christian tradition, the serpent in voodoo is held to be an omnipotent force that performs acts of good. When large numbers of Africans from the kingdom of Dahomey were transported into the French West Indies as slaves, they took voodoo with them and the mystical religion lived on.

By the early 19th century, thousands of African slaves had been brought to the state of Louisiana from the French West Indies, and again their religion remained with them. Voodoo so terrified an 18th-century Spanish governor of Louisiana that he refused to allow any more slaves to be imported from that area of the world, but his decree was in vain as many French planters (who came from the Caribbean) settled in New Orleans and brought their slaves with them.

Voodoo has a history of being matriarchal, and it is believed that the first organized voodoo ceremony took place in an abandoned brickyard on Dumaine Street and was presided over by Sanite Dede, one of the great voodoo queens. It is interesting to note that the voodoo queens were always free women of color, never slaves. Because police constantly raided the voodoo ceremonies, they moved around from one location to another. Voodoo ceremonies were eventually deemed illegal, except on Sunday. Congo Square in today's Armstrong Park was one of the places in which the voodoo ceremonies were allowed to take place. Many people used to go to Congo Square on Sunday to watch the singing, chanting, and dancing. It is thought, however, that what went on in

IMPRESSIONS

"It is the most congenial city in America that I know of and it is due in large part, I believe, to the fact that here at last on this bleak continent the sensual pleasures assume the importance which they deserve . . . ."
—HENRY MILLER, *THE AIR-CONDITIONED NIGHTMARE*, 1945.

that particular public meeting place was nothing like the serious voodoo ceremonies that took place in secret.

Witnesses to one such ceremony, held on one of voodoo's most important nights, June 23 (St. John's Eve), claimed that they saw naked dancers almost flying in a whirling frenzy around a bonfire and a cauldron, in which they threw live chickens, snails, frogs, black cats, and, of course, snakes. (Some thought that the voodooists stole white babies and sacrificed them during their ceremonies, but this has never been substantiated.) The voodoo queen would dance with the snake while others beat rhythmically on tom-toms. They became like animals—throwing each other to the ground; clawing and biting at each other; having mad, frenzied sex as if in a trance; and ending in an exhausted heap of sweaty, bloodied, naked bodies.

Today, one of the most famous names in voodoo around New Orleans is Marie Laveau, a legendary 19th-century voodoo queen. She lived in a house at 1022 St. Ann Street, and her voodoo powers were much sought after, even by the city's respectable Catholic families. Their most common request was for succor in turning errant lovers and husbands into ardent and attentive slaves; Marie sold love potions and charms that were purported to work such wonders. There were actually two Marie Laveaus—a mother and daughter. The original Marie Laveau was said to have had exceptional beauty, even up to her death, but some believe that when the first got too old to continue as voodoo queen her daughter took over, pretending to be her mother. Regardless of when the first gave way to the second, people were terrified of Marie Laveau's powers. It is said that she got rid of other queens through her "gris-gris" (gree-gree), killing them with her voodoo powers. Due to the fear that Laveau instilled in local politicians, she became one of the great political forces of her day.

The presence of voodoo in New Orleans today is not nearly as large as it was during the time of the reign of Marie Laveau as voodoo queen, but it does still exist—there's a voodoo shop on Bourbon Street, a museum and shop on Dumaine Street, and people still come from all over to leave gifts and offerings on what is thought to be Marie Laveau's tomb.

LANGUAGE The language is English, of course—but it may come in tones, accents, and pronunciations that surprise you. Don't expect to hear a lot of "you-alls" or other Deep South expressions; be prepared instead for a sort of southern Brooklynese. Unless you stick to the Garden District and university campuses, you should know before you come that *erl* means "oil," *toin* translates to "turn," and even the most cultured downtowner is likely to slip in *de* for "the." There are, of course, all sorts of dialects around town, as you'd expect from the variety of ethnic backgrounds represented in New Orleans, but somehow they *all* seem to have developed a little bit along the lines of speech in New York's Brooklyn. Various theories have been raised to explain this phenomenon: that the same ethnic groups immigrated to both cities in the 1800s, that both are seaports, or that *most* foreigners who learn English later in life adopt this kind of talk (although I have my doubts about that). Whatever the reason, it seems to be a permanent part of the New

Orleans scene, and believe it or not, it's actually part of the city's charm.

As for the pronunciation of certain rather ordinary street names and other commonly used words, there is simply no explanation—except that New Orleanians seem to have decided that that's the way they're said in New Orleans. To help you sound less like a "foreigner" as you move around town, here are some words that are given the native twist:

bayou	BY-you (a marshy, sluggish stream, usually feeding into a river or lake; also, the swamplands of southern Louisiana)
banquette	ban-KET (a French word for bench that means "sidewalk" in New Orleans, since early wooden sidewalks were elevated above muddy streets)
Vieux Carré	View Ka-RAY
Conti Street	CON-teye
Burgundy Street	Bur-GUN-dee
Carondelet Street	Car-ONDE-let (not "lay")
Calliope Street	CAL-i-ope (not "Cal-i-opee")
Chartres Street	Charters
Dauphine Street	Daw-FEEN
Iberville Street	EYE-bur-vill
Bienville Street	Bee-EN-vill
Orleans Street	Or-LEENS
	but
New Orleans	Noo OR-lyuns (or, better yet, *Nor*-luns)

You're sure to hear others that sound peculiar—but don't question, just follow the lead of those who live there.

3. FAMOUS NEW ORLEANIANS

Louis Armstrong (1900–71). One of the all-time jazz greats, "Satchmo" spent part of his boyhood singing in a quartet on the streets of New Orleans. He learned the cornet at the Colored Waif's Home and went on to become perhaps the greatest of all jazz trumpeters. He joined King Oliver's band in Chicago, then headed for New York and Fletcher Henderson's Orchestra. He became an international star and also appeared in such films as *Pennies from Heaven*. He died in Corona, Queens.

Sidney Bechet (1897–1959) As a young man, this clarinetist and soprano saxophonist played with the great musicians of New Orleans before moving to Chicago to join the orchestra of Will Marion Cook, with whom he traveled to Europe. He made headlines in London and later returned to play with Duke Ellington and others in New York along 52nd Street. In 1949 he moved to Paris permanently and died there.

Ernest J. Bellocq (ca. 1880–ca. 1945) A commercial photographer in New Orleans during the early decades of this century,

Bellocq made a series of portrait photographs, discovered only after his death, of Storyville "ladies of the evening"; they capture with unusual clarity the romantic legend of New Orleans as a city of unbridled sensuality.

George Washington Cable (1844–1925) His first book, *Old Creole Days*, was successful and was followed by a number of local genre novels, including *The Creoles of Louisiana* (1884), *Bonaventure* (1888), *The Cavalier* (1901), and *The Flower of the Chapdelaines* (1918).

Truman Capote (1924–84) With *In Cold Blood* (1966), a fictionalized account of a Kansas mass murder, he pioneered the genre of the nonfiction novel. He also wrote *Other Voices, Other Rooms* (1948), *Breakfast at Tiffany's* (1958), and other works, but *In Cold Blood* is considered his masterpiece. His later life was largely destroyed by drugs and alcohol and a constant round of socializing to the detriment of his talent.

Pete Fountain (b. 1930) This clarinetist and saxophonist began his career in New Orleans in the 1940s playing with Monk Hazel's Band, the Junior Dixieland Band, and others. His great success came when he teamed with Lawrence Welk in 1957, and he went on to TV and radio stardom during the 1960s; during these years he also opened his club on Bourbon Street. Today he performs regularly at his club in the New Orleans Hilton.

Louis Moreau Gottschalk (1829–69) This pianist and composer was the first American composer to achieve recognition in Europe. Among his piano pieces are "Polka de Salon," "La Savane," "Bamboula," "Souvenir de Porto Rico," and "Ojos Criollos." He also composed songs and orchestral works.

Shirley Ann Grau (b. 1929) Grau, a writer, was born in New Orleans. Her stories of life in the South were first published in *The New Yorker, The Saturday Evening Post,* and *Mademoiselle*. Later, her books *The Black Prince* and the Pulitzer Prize–winning *Keepers of the House* were published to wide critical acclaim.

Bryant Gumbel (b. 1948) A native of New Orleans, Gumbel started his career in TV as a sportscaster, was a regular on the show "Games People Play," and for the past 15 years has hosted NBC's popular "Today" show.

Lafcadio Hearn (1850–1904) Most often associated with Japan, he lived in New Orleans for 10 years beginning in 1877. Among the works he wrote about the city are *Chita* and *Gombo Zhebes*, the latter a book of Creole proverbs.

Lillian Hellman (1905–84) This playwright's first stage success, *The Children's Hour* (1934), a drama about a child accusing two teachers of lesbianism, caused a sensation. Other successes followed, like *The Little Foxes, Watch on the Rhine*, and the film *Julia*, which was adapted from her autobiography, *Pentimento*. Politically sympathetic to Communism, she was subpoenaed to appear before the House Committee on Un-American Activities and became even more famous when she refused to testify about others, saying, "I can't cut my conscience to fit this year's fashions." She wrote several volumes of autobiography and became embroiled in a feud with rival Mary McCarthy.

Al Hirt (b. 1922) He took up the trumpet at eight and went on to a career with the New Orleans Philharmonic in addition to playing clubs. He became a major recording star, with such hit singles as "Java."

Mahalia Jackson (1911–72) This gospel singer and civil rights worker learned to sing in the church choir before moving to Chicago in 1927. After making her first recording in 1934, she went on to achieve wide attention with "Move On Up a Little Higher" (1945) and to debut at Carnegie Hall in 1950. She was dedicated to devotional songs and refused to sing the blues.

George Lewis (1900–68) This clarinetist/alto saxophonist was working in brass bands by 1919. Unlike many other jazz musicians, he stayed in New Orleans and led various bands playing regularly at Manny's Tavern in the 1940s. In the 1950s he played Bourbon Street.

Wynton Marsalis (b. 1961) A member of a true jazz family (father Ellis is a fine musician and composer, and brother Branford is an up-and-coming saxophonist), Wynton Marsalis is living proof that jazz is alive and well in New Orleans. A prodigiously talented trumpeter—in 1986 he won a brace of Grammy Awards for classical and jazz musicianship—he is known for his virtuosic solos and as an active proponent of traditional modern jazz.

Jelly Roll Morton (1890–1941) A pianist and composer, he was born in Gulfport, Mississippi, but by 1906 was playing piano in Storyville brothels. By 1923 he had moved to Chicago. His most famous recordings are those made with the Red Hot Peppers between 1926 and 1930. Colorful and cantankerous, he claimed to have invented jazz and indeed he did compose some great tunes, including "Jelly Roll Blues" and "Black Bottom Stomp." In the 1930s his personal ensemble style was eclipsed by the big band sound.

Mel Ott (1909–58) Born in Gretna, Louisiana, he was a legendary baseball player, the first to hit 500 home runs in the National League. Ott spent his entire career with the New York Giants and was inducted into the Baseball Hall of Fame in 1951.

Walker Percy (b. 1916) Born in Alabama, this novelist lives in a suburb of New Orleans, and many of his works have the city as background. Among his famous works are *The Moviegoer* (1961), *The Last Gentleman* (1966), and *Love in the Ruins* (1971).

Anne Rice (b. 1941) New Orleans–born Anne Rice has authored a number of best-selling gothic horror novels, including *Interview with the Vampire* and *The Vampire Lestat*.

Sara Walker (1867–1919) Born in Delta, Louisiana, she became famous as Madame C. J. Walker, one of the first successful black female entrepreneurs and philanthropists. She invented a method for straightening hair, established a factory in Indianapolis, and built a major business.

Andrew Young (b. 1932) Most famous for his controversial stint as U.S. ambassador to the United Nations, Young, a New Orleans native, has been active in American politics for 30 years. He was a leader in the civil rights movement, has been a U.S. congressman, was an adviser to Jimmy Carter through the early and mid-1970s, and most recently was a two-term mayor of Atlanta,

Georgia. As ambassador to the UN, Young was an outspoken advocate of Third World nations until he resigned in 1979.

4. FOOD & DRINK

If New Orleans's population is an exciting "stew" of ethnic cultures from far-flung nations, its cuisine is a rich, tasty "gumbo" of French provincial, Spanish, Italian, West Indian, African, and Native American dishes, flavored with a liberal dash of full-fledged Southern cooking. Those who return time after time do so as much for the food as for the jazz, the sightseeing, and Mardi Gras. Indeed, dining out in New Orleans can truly be called entertainment.

Provincial French recipes brought to the New World by early settlers fast took on a subtle twist with the use of native herbs and filé (ground sassafras leaves) from Native Americans. Saffron and peppers arrived with the Spanish somewhat later. From the West Indies came new vegetables, spices, and sugarcane, and when slave boats arrived, landing many a Black woman in the kitchens of white slave owners, an African influence was added. Out of all this came the distinctive "Creole" culinary style unique to New Orleans. Italian immigrants later on added yet another dimension to the city's tables, and, through it all, traditional Old South dishes were retained virtually intact.

MEALS & DINING CUSTOMS Along with their love of exciting combinations of international cooking, the people of New Orleans have inherited an appreciation for fine service in elegant surroundings. Their sense of fun also delights in gourmet dishes that appear in the plainest of settings, as well as in eating the plainest of meals (such as boiled crawfish or red beans and rice) in the fanciest of eateries. Many New Orleanians eat out at least three times a week, and with their nose for an adventurous good time, they may stretch out an evening to include cocktails at a favorite spot, an appetizer (such as oysters Rockefeller) at another, an entree at still another, and perhaps a dessert in a favorite courtyard setting. And for many the evening is not complete without a stop at the Café du Monde for café au lait. In other words, dining out is an occasion, no matter how often it occurs. By all means follow their example

IMPRESSIONS

"The soft, balmy air, with its strange scents of fermenting molasses, semi-baked sugar, green coffee, pitch, Stockholm tar, brine, of mess-beef, rum and whiskey-drippings, contributed a great deal towards imparting the charm of romance to everything I saw. The people I passed appeared to me to be nobler than any I had yet seen. They had a swing of the body wholly un-English, and their facial expressions different from those I had been accustomed to. . . . These people knew no master, and had no more awe of their employers than they had of their fellow-employees."
—Sir Henry Morton Stanley, *Autobiography*, 1909.

and double the number of restaurants you get to sample during even a short stay. Keep in mind, however, that if your evening's itinerary includes the upper-bracket restaurants, men will be required to wear jackets and ties. One way to sample the better spots without breaking your budget is to take your main meals at lunch, when prices are lower and menus are often identical to those at dinner.

THE CUISINE Both *Cajun* and *Creole* have come to mean "New Orleans." What's the difference between the two cuisines? Chiefly it lies in their origins. Cajun cooking came from country folk—the Acadians who left France for Nova Scotia in the 1600s and made their way to the swamps and bayous of rural Louisiana after being expelled from Canada by the British in the 1700s. Their much-loved French dishes traveled with them, but along the way the recipes were adapted to ingredients available locally. Their cuisine tends to be quite robust and hearty, with sausage, duck, poultry, pork, and seafood prepared in a rich roux (a seasoned sauce of fat and flour that lends a distinctive flavor) and served over rice. Creole dishes, on the other hand, were developed by French and Spanish city dwellers. Delicate sauces and attention to presentation are characteristic of "haute Creole," while "low Creole" favorites, such as red beans and rice, are likely to come to table with as little fanfare as Cajun food.

In practice, however, the two cuisines have effected such a happy marriage in New Orleans that it's often difficult to distinguish between them—even the city's leading chefs can't draw the line. Internationally famed Paul Prudhomme, of K-Paul's Louisiana Kitchen, says simply that what has emerged is "Louisiana food." He goes on to say, "Nowhere else have all the ethnic groups merged to combine all these different tastes, and the only way you'll know the difference, honey, is to live 'em!" Suffice it to say that no matter *how* a New Orleans restaurant classifies its culinary offerings, you're bound to find one or two examples of Cajun and Creole cooking on the menu.

As a rule of thumb (but, remember, rules are made to have exceptions), when it comes to New Orleans food, *Creole* means hot and *Cajun* will be spicy. Both can mean hot *and* spicy. The much-loved spices are onions (both green and regular), bay leaf, thyme, parsley, cloves, allspice, cayenne pepper, filé, and Tabasco (a red-hot sauce made of red peppers fermented in brine and vinegar). There is a whole family of sausages: boudin (boo-DAN), which contains onions, spices, pork, and rice and comes in white or red; chaurice (cho-REECE), which is a hard sausage used chiefly for flavoring beans or soups; andouille (ahn-DWE-YE), which is also hard and a bit saltier than chaurice; and delicious smoked sausages. Seafood is everywhere—in fact, I find it next to impossible to order anything else when I'm in town. Oysters on the half shell (usually simply called "raw oysters" in New Orleans) are just the beginning of an oyster feast that includes soups; stews; pies; baked specialties, such as oysters Rockefeller (on the half shell in a creamy sauce, with spinach—so named because that was the only name rich enough for the taste); an oyster loaf (which elevates "sandwich" into the realm of a delicacy); and a host of other creations. Crabs, shrimp, and crawfish are used in imaginative recipes or served plain, hot or cold. Gumbo is a thick soup, always served with rice, usually containing crab, shrimp (sometimes oysters), and okra in a tomato base. Jambalaya is made with meat and seafood combined with rice and seasonings. Beef and veal (you may see either on a menu as *daube,* pronounced "dohb") take on added luster in New Orleans restaurants, as do classic French and Italian dishes. There's also a special quality to the French bread, with its crisp, flaky crust and its insides as light as a feather.

Two mainstays of any native's diet are red beans and rice and "po-boy" sandwiches, which once cost a nickel. This sandwich is made with long, skinny bread loaf and can contain anything from roast beef and gravy; to ham and cheese; to fried fish, shrimp, soft-shell crabs, or oysters, in which case it becomes an oyster loaf. One of the largest (and tastiest) sandwiches you'll ever see is the muffuletta—a mountain of Italian sausages and meats with an un-usual olive salad (consisting of pickled carrots and celery, capers, olives, and other delights) piled onto an 8-inch round Italian "bun."

DRINKS Never let it be said that New Orleanians neglect the li-bations that precede, accompany, and follow a proper meal. As a matter of fact, they lay claim to adding the word "cocktail" to our modern vocabulary: A Monsieur Peychaud, who presided over the bar at 437 Rue Royale in the early 19th century, took to serving small drinks in egg cups—*couquetiers* in French—and Americans took to ordering them using a mangled version of the word. Since then more than a few inspired concoctions have appeared on the scene, among them the Sazerac (bourbon or rye with bitters), the Ramos gin fizz (gin, egg whites, and orange-flavored water), and the Hurricane (rum and passionfruit punch). If you're a cocktail drinker, take my advice and try the local fare. *One note of caution:* Alcoholic drinks are available around the clock, and it's easy to overindulge. If you do, just be sure to walk back to your hotel or take a taxi. The police take a very dim view of drivers who've had one too many, and they are *very* vigilant.

As for coffee, you'll find it strong, hot, and black, with or with-out chicory (which adds a slightly bitter flavor—it was first used to stretch scarce coffee beans during the Civil War). Chicory coffee just might be what the Turks had in mind when they declared that the beverage should be "black as hell, strong as death, and sweet as love." Stouthearted purists drink it black, but most natives mix it half-and-half with hot milk for café au lait. And at least once dur-ing your stay, end a meal with café brûlot (cah-FAY brew-LOW), a lovely mixture of coffee, spices, and liqueurs served in a special cup, with ladle and chafing dish, and flamed at your table.

Restaurants pride themselves on their wine lists. If you are doubtful as to what to order with your entree, don't worry—your waiter will know.

TERMS TO KNOW Here are a few words for your New Or-leans dining vocabulary:

lagniappe	lan-YAP (a little something extra you've neither paid for nor deserve—like the 13th doughnut when you order a dozen)
beignet	bin-YEA (a cross between a doughnut and a cruller, liberally sprinkled with powdered sugar)

dressed	"served with the works"—as when ordering a sandwich
gumbo	a thick, spicy soup, always served with rice
hurricane	a local drink of rum and passionfruit punch
jambalaya	jum-ba-LIE-ya (a jumble of yellow rice, sausage, seafood, vegetables, and spices)
muffuletta	one of the tastiest sandwiches you'll ever have—Italian sausage, deli meats, one or two kinds of cheese, olive salad (pickled olives, celery, carrots, cauliflower, and capers), and oil and vinegar, piled onto a round loaf (about 8 inches in diameter) of Italian bread that is specially made for these incredible sandwiches
pralines	PRAW-lines (a *very* sweet confection made of brown sugar and pecans—they come in "original" and creamy styles)
crawfish	CRAW-fish—a tiny, lobsterlike creature plentiful in the waters around New Orleans and used in every conceivable way in cooking
étouffée	ay-too-FAY (a Cajun dish—a kind of smothered stew served with rice, which may contain crawfish and always contains something very good)
café brûlot	cah-FAY brew-LOW (coffee mixed with spices and liqueurs and served flaming)

COOKING LESSONS Early on during your New Orleans visit, you're likely to develop an itch to duplicate some of the great dishes in your own home. Well, you can scratch that itch by signing up for lunch that comes with a liberal dash of learning at the **New Orleans School of Cooking,** 620 Decatur St., in the Jackson Brewery (tel. 525-2665). It's a great way to learn the secrets of Creole cooking as local Louisiana cooks and chefs conduct entertaining and informative demonstrations of basic techniques, then serve the dishes you've just seen prepared. Groups are limited in number, so reserve as far in advance as possible; if classes are full, inquire about the possibility of special evening courses. The school is in the back of the Louisiana General Store, which is crammed full of cookbooks, Cajun and Creole seasonings, and a host of other New Orleans gift items. The session hours are 10am to 1pm Monday through Saturday. The school also has a free Louisiana gift catalog.

---

5. RECOMMENDED BOOKS & RECORDINGS

BOOKS

FICTION Early fiction that is still worth reading to get a flavor of New Orleans life includes George Washington Cable's stories and novels, the most famous being his *Old Creole Days*, published in 1879. His not-always-flattering portraits of the Creoles was corrected by Grace King in her short stories and her novel *The*

Pleasant Ways of St. Medard (1916). Lyle Saxon and Roark Bradford also wrote books about the legendary figures and tales associated with New Orleans, including Saxon's *Fabulous New Orleans* (1928) and Bradford's Civil War novel *Kingdom Coming,* which contains a lot of information about voodoo. As a riverboat captain, Mark Twain visited the city often, and his *Life on the Mississippi* contains a substantial number of tales of New Orleans and its riverfront life.

William Faulkner lived on Pirates Alley and wrote *Pylon,* which is set in New Orleans, as well as a series of short stories about the city. He penned *Solider's Pay* while living on Pirates Alley. Tennessee Williams was inspired during his brief stay in the city to write his *Streetcar Named Desire; The Rose Tattoo* also is set in the city. Frances Parkinson Keyes lived in the city for more than 25 years on Chartres Street. Her most famous works are *Dinner at Antoine's* and *Madame Castel's Lodger.*

Among the city's best-known contemporary writers are Walker Percy and Shirley Ann Grau. The former's novel *The Moviegoer* (1961) has Carnival Week as a background; the latter's most famous novel, *The Keepers of the House,* won the Pulitzer in 1964. Another Pulitzer also went, albeit posthumously, to John Kennedy Toole's *A Confederacy of Dunces,* a marvelous comic portrait of New Orleans life that you would do well to read before or during your visit. Other nationally recognized contemporary fiction writers that you might want to delve into include Ellen Gilchrist and Anne Rice, who wrote the best-selling vampire chronicles *Interview with the Vampire* and *Queen of the Damned* and several others that are set in New Orleans.

There are several choices in new fiction as well. *Light Sister, Dark Sister,* by Lee Walmsley, is set against a New Orleans background. *With Extreme Prejudice,* by Frederick Barton, is a murder-thriller that takes readers from the mean streets of New Orleans to the picturesque Garden District. For a novel that captures the racial tension of New Orleans, look for *Glass House* by Christine Wiltz. Valerie Martin's *The Great Divorce* is a retelling of Dr. Jekyll and Mr. Hyde set in contemporary antebellum New Orleans.

HISTORY If you're looking to bone up on New Orleans history before you leave, *A Short History of New Orleans* (Lexicos, 1982) by Mel Leavitt will help. *The WPA Guide to New Orleans* also contains some excellent social and historical background and provides a fascinating picture of the city in 1938.

There are many guides to Mardi Gras, including Robert Tallant's *Mardi Gras* and Myron Tassin's *Mardi Gras & Bacchus: Something Old, Something New,* both published by Pelican.

For the definitive account of Storyville, you can't beat Al Rose's *Storyville, New Orleans, Being an Authentic Illustrated Account of the Notorious Redlight District* (University of Alabama Press, 1974).

Other books worth reading include Lyle Saxon's *Fabulous New Orleans* (Pelican, 1988), *New Orleans: Facts & Legends* by Raymond Martinez and Jack Holmes, and *The French Quarter and Other New Orleans Scenes* by Joseph A. Arrigo.

If you're interested in women's history, I'd recommend *Women and New Orleans* by Mary Gehman—it's fascinating and well written.

ART, ARCHITECTURE & ANTIQUES New Orleans is famous for its architecture, and there's an abundance of books available on this subject. *New Orleans Architecture* is a helpful and interesting series—each volume deals with a different area of the city, such as the Garden District, the Lower Garden District, Esplanade Ridge, and the Vieux Carré. The series is published by Friends of the Cabildo, which also published a small book on historical landmarks of New Orleans.

Another book you might want to refer to is *The Great Houses of New Orleans* by Curt Bruce (Knopf, 1977).

Antique lovers will appreciate a little book called *New Orleans Furniture* (The Knapp Press), which has color photographs with descriptive captions that help explain Louisiana antiques.

FOR KIDS The Greater New Orleans Tourist and Convention Commission has just published a guidebook that is specifically for kids, with activities, such as dot-to-dots, and stories so your children can follow along as you sightsee. If you're interested, you should contact them directly at 1520 Sugar Bowl Dr., New Orleans, LA 70112 (tel. 504/566-5011).

MUSIC What follows is only a very short bibliography of what's available:

Boven, John. *South to Louisiana: The Music of the Cajun Bayous.* Gretna, LA: Pelican, 1987.

Carter, William. *Preservation Hall.* New York: Norton, 1991.

Charters, Samuel B. *Jazz: New Orleans 1885–1963.* Jersey City, NJ: Da Capo, 1983.

Chilton, John. *Sidney Bechet: The Wizard of Jazz.* New York: Oxford University Press, 1988.

Feather, Leonard. *The Encyclopedia of Jazz.* Jersey City, NJ: Da Capo, 1965.

Lyttleton, Humphrey. *The Best of Jazz: Basin Street to Harlem 1917–30.* New York: Taplinger, 1982.

Schuller, Gunther. *Early Jazz: Its Roots and Musical Development.* New York: Oxford University Press, 1968.

Shapiro, Nat, and Nat Hentoff. *The Jazz Makers: Essays on the Greats of Jazz.* Jersey City, NJ: Da Capo, 1979.

_____. *Hear Me Talkin' to Ya: The Story of Jazz by the Men Who Made It.* New York: Dover, 1966.

Williams, Martin. *Jazz Heritage.* New York: Oxford University Press, 1987.

_____. *Jazz Masters of New Orleans.* New York: Macmillan, 1967.

_____. *Smithsonian History of Jazz.* New York: Knopf, 1988.

RECORDINGS

New Orleans has been so central to the history of jazz that it would be impossible to list all the great recordings here. There are several books currently available that do just that, provide discographies that cover the history of the music, including Len Lyon's *The 101 Best Jazz Albums: A History of Jazz on Records* (Morrow, 1980), Brian Priestly's *Jazz on Record: A History* (Billboard, 1991), and James McCalla's *Jazz: A Listener's Guide* (Prentice Hall, 1982).

Whether they play jazz, rhythm and blues, or Cajun, New Orleanian musicians have always had a particularly infectious good-time sensibility. Listening to any of the following recordings will help you get a feel for it.

JAZZ Louis Armstrong: *Louis Armstrong and Earl "Fatha" Hines 1928* (Smithsonian); *The Genius of Louis Armstrong* (Columbia). Sidney Bechet: *Bechet of New Orleans* (Columbia); *Jazz Classics Vol. 1 & 2* (Blue Note). Kid Ory: *Kid Ory's Creole Jazz Band* (Folklyric). King Oliver: *The Immortal King Oliver* (Milestone); *King Oliver's Jazz Band 1923* (Smithsonian). Jelly Roll Morton: *Jelly Roll Morton 1923–24* (Milestone); *The Complete Jelly Roll Morton, Vols. 1–4* (RCA).

RHYTHM & BLUES Dirty Dozen Brass Band: *Mardi Gras in Montreux: Live* (Rounder, 1985). Dr. John: *Gris Gris* (Atco, 1968); *Gumbo* (Atco, 1972). Meters: *Cissy Strut* (Island, 1975); *Rejuvenation* (Reprise, 1974). Neville Brothers: *Yellow Moon* (A&M, 1989). Professor Longhair: *New Orleans Piano* (Atco, 1953). Anthologies: *Ace Story, Vol. 1* (Ace, 1981); *New Orleans Jazz & Heritage Festival* (Island).

CAJUN & ZYDECO Balfa Brothers: *J'ai Vu La Lupe, Le Renard et La Belette* (Rounder, 1977). Clifton Chenier: *Bogalusa Boogie* (Arhoolie, 1976); *Classic Clifton* (Arhoolie, 1981). Anthology: *Louisiana Cajun Music Special* (Ace, 1977).

CHAPTER 2

PLANNING A TRIP TO NEW ORLEANS

1. **INFORMATION & MONEY**
   • **WHAT THINGS COST IN NEW ORLEANS**
2. **WHEN TO GO— CLIMATE & EVENTS**
   • **CALENDAR OF EVENTS**
3. **WHAT TO PACK**
   • **FROMMER'S SMART TRAVELER: AIRFARES**
4. **GETTING THERE**

This chapter is devoted to the when, where, and how of your trip—the advance-planning issues required to get it together and take it on the road.

After deciding where to go, most people have two fundamental questions: What will it cost? and How do I get there? This chapter will answer both questions and provide other essential facts, such as when to go and where to obtain more information about New Orleans.

Foreign visitors should also consult Chapter 3, "For Foreign Visitors," for information on entry requirements, getting to the United States, and other matters of importance to foreign travelers.

1. INFORMATION & MONEY

INFORMATION I would advise even the seasoned traveler to write or call ahead to the **Greater New Orleans Tourist and Convention Commission** (GNOTCC) at 1520 Sugar Bowl Dr., New Orleans, LA 70112 (tel. 504/566-5011), for their brochures and information about the city because they're extremely friendly and helpful. While a travel agent can give you some help in planning your trip, you could easily get any information you can't find in this book from the GNOTCC, and with a few phone calls, you're ready to go.

MONEY New Orleans, just like any other place, will seem expensive to some and inexpensive to others, depending on one's place of origin. Prices in the city also vary according to season, so if you're budget conscious, you should try going during an off-season period. You should always have traveler's checks instead of cash if you're carrying all the "cash" you plan to use during your trip. However, if you've got a cash card, there are Automated Teller Machines (ATMs) throughout the city. You might want to check with your bank before you leave home because sometimes it will have a list of ATM locations that will accept your card.

WHAT THINGS COST IN NEW ORLEANS	U.S.$
Taxi from the airport to the Central Business District or French Quarter	21.00
Bus from airport to downtown	1.10
Streetcar fare (one-way)	1.00
Local telephone call	.25
Double at the Hotel Inter-Continental (very expensive)	210–240.00
Double at Place d'Armes Hotel (moderate)	100–140.00
Double at Hotel Villa Convento (inexpensive)	59–85.00
Lunch for one at Port of Call (moderate)	10.00
Lunch for one at Petunia's (inexpensive)	7.00
Dinner for one at Antoine's (expensive)	50.00
Dinner for one at Mike Anderson's Seafood (moderate)	30.00
Dinner for one at the Camellia Grill (inexpensive)	15.00
Bottle of beer	2–5.00
Coca-Cola	1–1.50
Cup of coffee	.50–1.00
Roll of ASA 100 Kodacolor film, 36 exposures	6.50
Admission to New Orleans Museum of Art	6.00
Theater ticket at Le Petit Theatre	18–22.00

2. WHEN TO GO— CLIMATE & EVENTS

CLIMATE The average mean temperature in New Orleans is 70°F, but the thermometer can drop or rise considerably in a single day. The high humidity can make relatively mild temperatures feel uncomfortably cold or uncomfortably warm. The city's climate will be pleasant almost any time of year, but July and August can be exceptionally muggy. If you do come during those months, you'll quickly learn to follow the natives' example and stay out of the noonday sun and duck from one air-conditioned building to another. And even in the rain (an average of 63 inches falls annually), you'll be able to get around without difficulty, mainly because it comes in great downpours that don't last too long.

New Orleans's Average Monthly Temperatures and Days of Rain

	Jan	Feb	Mar	Apr	May	June	July	Aug	Sept	Oct	Nov	Dec
Temp. (°C)	13	14	16	19	23	25	26	26	24	20	15	14
Temp. (°F)	56	58	62	69	76	81	83	83	79	71	61	57
Days of Rain	10	9	9	7	8	10	15	13	10	5	7	10

NEW ORLEANS CALENDAR OF EVENTS

For more information on the major New Orleans events, see "Mardi Gras & Other Festivals" in Chapter 7.

JANUARY

☐ **The USF&G Sugar Bowl Classic** is New Orleans's oldest yearly sporting event (it originated in 1934). The football game is the main event, but there are also tennis, swimming, basketball, sailing, running, and flag-football competitions. Held on New Year's Day.

FEBRUARY/MARCH

✪ *MARDI GRAS,* *the culmination of the two-month-long Carnival season, is the annual blow-out bash that New Orleans is famous for. The entire city stops working and starts partying early in the morning.*

*   ***Where:** All over the city something will be happening. Nowadays, however, the great parades go through the Central Business District instead of the French Quarter. **When:** For 1995 Mardi Gras is scheduled February 28, and in 1996 the date is February 20. Parades begin around 8am and continue into the night. **How:** Contact the Greater New Orleans Tourist and Convention Commission, 1520 Sugar Bowl Dr., New Orleans, LA 70112 (tel. 504/566-5011).*

☐ **The Black Heritage Festival** is a celebration in honor of the African Americans who have made, and are still making, great cultural contributions to New Orleans and have given the city a spirit unlike any other American city. Call 504/861-2537 for more info.

✪ *THE TENNESSEE WILLIAMS LITERARY FESTIVAL* *is a three-day series of events, including theatrical performances, readings, musical events, and literary walking tours dedicated to the playwright.*

Where: Events occur all over the city. *When:* Three days in late March. *How:* Call or write Julia Burke, 2727 Prytania St., New Orleans, LA 70130 (tel. 504/897-9762).

APRIL

✪ *THE FRENCH QUARTER FESTIVAL* is a relatively new event, just over a decade old, and is a celebration of New Orleans's unique history. It's kicked off with a parade down Bourbon Street, and, among other things, you can join people dancing in the streets, learn the history of jazz, visit historic homes, and take a ride on the riverboat.

Where: All over the French Quarter. *When:* The second weekend in April. *How:* Call or write Sandra Dartus, French Quarter Festival, 1008 North Peters St., New Orleans, LA 70116 (tel. 504/596-3419).

✪ *SPRING FIESTA,* which begins with the crowning of the Spring Fiesta Queen, is over half a century old. If you come during this time, you'll be able to go visit some of the city's historic private homes, courtyards, and plantation homes with tours created specially for Spring Fiesta.

Where: Locations throughout the city. *When:* One week in April. Call for current schedule. *How:* Call or write Spring Fiesta, 826 St. Ann St., New Orleans, LA 70116 (tel. 504/581-1367).

✪ *THE NEW ORLEANS JAZZ AND HERITAGE FESTIVAL* is so popular that the city, as it does during Mardi Gras, tends to sell out in terms of lodging, sometimes up to a year in advance. Thousands of musicians, cooks, and craftspeople come together to strut their stuff. If you like jazz, Cajun, zydeco, or New Orleans rhythm and blues with that shuffling, "second-line" rhythm, don't miss this event.

Where: Fair Grounds Race Track and various venues throughout the city. *When:* Ten days, usually the last weekend of April through the first weekend in May. *How:* Call or write Jazz Fest, P.O. Box 53407, New Orleans, LA 70153 (tel. 504/522-4786).

☐ **The Crescent City Classic** is a 10,000-meter road race, sponsored by the *Times-Picayune* and Coca-Cola. The race, bringing an international field of top runners to the city, begins at Jackson Square and ends at Audubon Park. For more information, call or write to: Classic, 8200 Hampson St., Suite 217, New Orleans, LA 70118 (tel. 504/861-8686).

JULY

☐ **Go 4th on the River** is New Orleans's new July 4th celebration. Events begin in the morning at the New Orleans Riverfront and continue into the night, culminating in a spectacular fireworks display. For more information call or write

Anna Pepper, 201 St. Charles Ave., New Orleans, LA 70130 (tel. 504/528-9994).

OCTOBER

□ **The Gumbo Festival.** In a city that loves its food, this festival showcases one of the city's favorites. There are a number of events that highlight Cajun culture, and the entertainment is continuous.

○ **HALLOWEEN** *in New Orleans is said to be even more spectacular than Mardi Gras in terms of the costumes you're likely to see while walking the streets of the French Quarter that night. Events include Boo-at-the-Zoo for children, a number of costume parties, and the Moonlight Witches Run.*

Where: All over the city, but the French Quarter, as always, is one of the major attractions at Halloween. When: October 31. How: Contact the Greater New Orleans Tourist and Convention Commission, 1520 Sugar Bowl Dr., New Orleans, LA 70112 (tel. 504/566-5011).

DECEMBER

□ **Creole Christmas** is a special time in New Orleans, and events include candlelight caroling in Jackson Square and the old New Orleans homes dressed up especially for the occasion. Events held throughout December.

3. WHAT TO PACK

No matter where you go, you should always pack lightly. You'll never wear as many items as you think you will. Travelers tend to get comfortable in a couple of different outfits, and that's all they wear. If you're traveling for a week or more, I'd tell you to bring three different outfits—one for sightseeing and getting dirty; another for going out to dinner in a moderate or inexpensive restaurant; and if you're planning to go out for a more elegant dinner, something a little more dressy.

If you're coming to New Orleans in the dead of summer, T-shirts and shorts are absolutely acceptable (except in the city's finest restaurants). In the spring and fall, bring jeans and a long-sleeve shirt and maybe an extra sweater; in the winter, bring a lightweight coat or jacket. Always bring an umbrella, a raincoat, and your favorite sunscreen and mosquito repellent. A good pair of walking shoes is most important because you'll walk more than you might think—the city is absolutely accessible on foot.

Note: Although sandals are cooler in the summer, I'd strongly advise you to leave them at home—you'll be miserable with the blisters you'll get.

Ⓕ FROMMER'S SMART TRAVELER:
AIRFARES

1. Shop all the airlines that fly to New Orleans.
2. Always ask for the lowest-priced fare, not just a discount fare.
3. Book in advance to take advantage of APEX or other discount airfares.
4. Keep calling the airlines; as your departure date draws nearer, seat prices may go down if the flights are not full.
5. Ask about senior-citizen discounts.

---

4. GETTING THERE

BY PLANE   No fewer than 13 airlines fly to New Orleans International Airport, and among them are **American** (tel. toll free 800/433-7300), **Continental** (tel. 504/581-2965 or toll free 800/525-0280), **Delta** (tel. toll free 800/221-1212), **Northwest Airlines, Inc.** (tel. toll free 800/225-2525), **Southwest Airlines** (tel. toll free 800/435-9792), and **TWA** (tel. 504/529-2585). As we go to press, average round-trip coach fares with no advance booking and no discounts are about $908 from New York, $740 from Chicago, and $1,104 from Los Angeles. With the current yo-yo airline fares situation, these may change, sometimes overnight. And, of course, you should *always* check for **APEX** fares and special promotional packages—New Orleans is a favored destination for seasonal and advance-booking discount rates with some airlines. Be sure to check on what's available when you plan your visit. Twenty-one-day advance purchase might cut your airfare by two-thirds, so plan ahead!

BY TRAIN   **Amtrak** trains reach New Orleans's **Union Passenger Terminal,** centrally located at 1001 Loyola Ave. (tel. toll free 800/USA-RAIL), from Los Angeles and intermediate points; New York, Washington, and points in between; and Chicago and intermediate points. Using the All Aboard America fares, you'll pay $189 from New York, $189 from Chicago, and $269 from Los Angeles. Amtrak, too, frequently offers senior-citizen discounts and other packages, some with a rental car, so be sure to check when you reserve.

Amtrak also does an especially good job with tour packages, which can be arranged through your local Amtrak Tour Desk. Options might range from a ticket with hotel accommodations to an air/rail package—take the train and then fly back to your destination, or choose from eight other combinations of tour packages. Prices will change, of course, during the life of this book, but from past experience it is safe to say that Amtrak tours will be genuine moneysavers.

BY BUS   **Greyhound-Trailways** buses come into the Union Passenger Terminal (call toll free 800/231-2222 for fares and schedules from the New Orleans bus station) from points throughout the country.

BY CAR You can drive to New Orleans via I-10, U.S. 90, and U.S. 61 and across the Lake Pontchartrain causeway on La. 25. Most hotels provide parking, and there are public garages and lots located throughout the city. The **AAA Louisiana Division** is at 3445 N. Causeway, Metairie, LA 70002 (tel. 504/838-7500), and will assist members with trip planning, service aids, and emergency services.

CHAPTER 3

FOR FOREIGN VISITORS

1. **PREPARING FOR YOUR TRIP**
2. **GETTING TO & AROUND THE U.S.**
- **FAST FACTS: FOR THE FOREIGN TRAVELER**
- **THE AMERICAN SYSTEM OF MEASUREMENTS**

Although American fads and fashions have spread across Europe and other parts of the world so that America may seem like familiar territory before your arrival, there are still many peculiarities and uniquely American situations that any foreign visitor to New Orleans will encounter.

1. PREPARING FOR YOUR TRIP

ENTRY REQUIREMENTS

DOCUMENT REGULATIONS Canadian citizens may enter the United States without visas; they need only proof of Canadian residence.

Citizens of the U.K., New Zealand, Japan, and most western European countries traveling with valid passports may not need a visa for fewer than 90 days of holiday or business travel to the United States, provided that they hold a round-trip or return ticket and enter on an airline or cruise line participating in the visa-waiver program. (Note that citizens of these visa-exempt countries who first enter the United States may then visit Mexico, Canada, Bermuda, and/or the Caribbean Islands and then reenter the United States, by any mode of transportation, without needing a visa. Further information is available from any U.S. embassy or consulate.)

Citizens of countries other than those stipulated above, including citizens of Australia, must have two documents: a valid passport, with an expiration date at least six months later than the scheduled end of the visit to the United States; and a tourist visa, available without charge from the nearest U.S. consulate. To obtain a visa, the traveler must submit a completed application form (either in person or by mail) with a 1½-inch-square photo and demonstrate binding ties to the residence abroad.

Usually you can obtain a visa at once or within 24 hours, but it may take longer during the summer rush from June to August. If you cannot go in person, contact the nearest U.S. embassy or consulate for directions on applying by mail. Your travel agent or airline office may also be able to provide you with visa applications and instructions. The U.S. consulate or embassy that issues your visa will determine whether you will be issued a multiple- or single-entry visa and any restrictions regarding the length of your stay.

MEDICAL REQUIREMENTS No inoculations are needed to enter the United States unless you are coming from, or have stopped over in, areas known to be suffering from epidemics, particularly of cholera or yellow fever.

If you have a disease requiring treatment with medications containing narcotics or drugs requiring a syringe, carry a valid signed prescription from your physician to allay any suspicions that you are smuggling drugs.

CUSTOMS REQUIREMENTS Every adult visitor may bring in, free of duty: 1 liter of wine or hard liquor, 200 cigarettes or 100 cigars (but no cigars from Cuba) or 3 pounds of smoking tobacco, and $100 worth of gifts. These exemptions are offered to travelers who spend at least 72 hours in the United States and who have not claimed them within the preceding 6 months. It is altogether forbidden to bring into the country foodstuffs (particularly cheese, fruit, cooked meats, and canned goods) and plants (vegetables, seeds, tropical plants, and so on). Foreign tourists may bring in or take out up to $10,000 in U.S. or foreign currency with no formalities; larger sums must be declared to Customs on entering or leaving.

Foreign tourists to New Orleans can arrange to have a refund check mailed to them on taxes paid on purchases made in the city if they go to the Louisiana Tax Free Shopping Refund Center, located in the New Orleans International Airport. Present the clerk there with sales receipts and vouchers from merchants, your passport, and a round-trip international ticket of less than 90 days. For more information, write to the Greater New Orleans Tourist and Convention Commission, 1520 Sugar Bowl Dr., New Orleans, LA 70112.

INSURANCE

There is no national health system in the United States. Because the cost of medical care is extremely high, we strongly advise every traveler to secure health coverage before setting out.

You may want to take out a comprehensive travel policy that covers (for a relatively low premium) sickness or injury costs (medical, surgical, and hospital); loss of or theft of your baggage; trip-cancellation costs; guarantee of bail in case you are arrested; costs of accident, repatriation, or death. Such packages (for example, "Europe Assistance" in Europe) are sold by automobile clubs at attractive rates, as well as by insurance companies and travel agencies.

MONEY

CURRENCY & EXCHANGE The U.S. monetary system has a decimal base: one American **dollar ($1)** = 100 **cents** (100¢).

Dollar bills commonly come in $1 ("a buck"), $5, $10, $20, $50, and $100 denominations (the last two are not welcome when paying for small purchases and are not accepted in taxis or at subway ticket booths). There are also $2 bills (seldom encountered).

There are six denominations of coins: 1¢ (one cent or "penny"), 5¢ (five cents or "a nickel"), 10¢ (ten cents or "a dime"), 25¢ (twenty-five cents or "a quarter"), 50¢ (fifty cents or "a half dollar"), and the rare $1 piece.

TRAVELER'S CHECKS Traveler's checks denominated in U.S. dollars are readily accepted at most hotels, motels, restaurants, and large stores. But the best place to change traveler's checks is at a bank. Do not bring traveler's checks denominated in other currencies.

CREDIT CARDS The method of payment most widely used is the credit card: Visa (BarclayCard in Britain), MasterCard (EuroCard in Europe, Access in Britain, Chargex in Canada), American Express, Diners Club, Discover, and Carte Blanche. You can save yourself trouble by using "plastic money" rather than cash or traveler's checks in most hotels, motels, restaurants, and retail stores (a growing number of food and liquor stores now accept credit cards). You must have a credit card to rent a car. It can also be used as proof of identity (often carrying more weight than a passport), or as a "cash card," enabling you to draw money from banks that accept them.

Note: The "foreign-exchange bureaus" so common in Europe are rare even at airports in the United States, and nonexistent outside major cities. Try to avoid having to change foreign money, or traveler's checks denominated other than in U.S. dollars, at a small-town bank, or even a branch in a big city; in fact, leave any currency other than U.S. dollars at home—it may provide more nuisance to you than it's worth.

SAFETY

GENERAL While tourist areas are generally safe, crime is on the increase everywhere, and U.S. urban areas tend to be less safe than those in Europe or Japan. Visitors should always stay alert. This is particularly true of large U.S. cities. It is wise to ask the city's or area's tourist office if you're in doubt about which neighborhoods are safe. Avoid deserted areas, especially at night. Don't go into any city park at night unless there is an event that attracts crowds—for example, New York City's concerts in the parks. Generally speaking, you can feel safe in areas where there are many people, and many open establishments.

Avoid carrying valuables with you on the street, and don't display expensive cameras or electronic equipment. Hold on to your pocketbook, and place your billfold in an inside pocket. In theaters, restaurants, and other public places, keep your possessions in sight.

Remember also that hotels are open to the public, and in a large hotel, security may not be able to screen everyone entering. Always lock your room door—don't assume that once inside your hotel you are automatically safe and no longer need to be aware of your surroundings.

DRIVING Safety while driving is particularly important. Question your rental agency about personal safety, or ask for a brochure of traveler safety tips when you pick up your car. Obtain written directions, or a map with the route marked in red, from the agency showing how to get to your destination. And, if possible, arrive and depart during daylight hours.

Recently more and more crime has involved cars and drivers. If you drive off a highway into a doubtful neighborhood, leave the area as quickly as possible. If you have an accident, even on the highway, stay in your car with the doors locked until you assess the situation or until the police arrive. If you are bumped from behind on the street or are involved in a minor accident with no injuries and the situation appears to be suspicious, motion to the other driver to follow you. *Never* get out of your car in such situations. You can also keep a pre-made sign in your car which reads: PLEASE FOLLOW THIS VEHICLE TO REPORT THE ACCIDENT. Show the sign to the other driver and go directly to the nearest police precinct, well-lighted service station, or all-night store.

If you see someone on the road who indicates a need for help, do *not* stop. Take note of the location, drive on to a well-lighted area, and telephone the police by dialing 911.

Park in well-lighted, well-traveled areas if possible. Always keep your car doors locked, whether attended or unattended. Look around you before you get out of your car, and never leave any packages or valuables in sight. If someone attempts to rob you or steal your car, do *not* try to resist the thief/carjacker—report the incident to the police department immediately.

You may wish to contact the local tourist information bureau in your destination before you arrive. They may be able to provide you with a safety brochure.

2. GETTING TO & AROUND THE U.S.

Travelers from overseas can take advantage of the **APEX (Advance Purchase Excursion) fares** offered by all the major U.S. and European carriers. Aside from these, attractive values are offered by **Icelandair** on flights from Luxembourg to New York and by **Virgin Atlantic Airways** from London to New York/Newark.

Some large American airlines (for example, TWA, American Airlines, Northwest, United, and Delta) offer travelers on their transatlantic or transpacific flights special discount tickets under the name **Visit USA,** allowing travel between any U.S. destinations at minimum rates. They are not on sale in the United States and must, therefore, be purchased before you leave your foreign point of departure. This system is the best, easiest, and fastest way to see the United States at low cost. You should obtain information well in advance from your travel agent or the office of the airline concerned, since the conditions attached to these discount tickets can be changed without advance notice.

The visitor arriving by air, no matter what the port of entry, should cultivate patience and resignation before setting foot on U.S. soil. Getting through immigration control may take as long as 2 hours on some days, especially summer weekends. Add the time it takes to clear Customs and you will see that you should make very generous allowance for delay in planning connections between international and domestic flights—an average of 2 to 3 hours at least.

In contrast, for the traveler arriving by car or by rail from Canada, the border-crossing formalities have been streamlined to the vanishing point. And for the traveler by air from Canada, Bermuda, and some places in the Caribbean, you can sometimes go through Customs and Immigration at the point of departure, which is much quicker and less painful.

For further information about travel to and arriving in New Orleans see "Getting There" in Chapter 2 and "Orientation" in Chapter 4.

International visitors can also buy a **USA Railpass,** good for 15 or 30 days of unlimited travel on Amtrak. The pass is available through many foreign travel agents. Prices in 1994 for a 15-day pass were $208 off-peak, $308 peak; a 30-day pass costs $309 off-peak, $389 peak. (With a foreign passport, you can also buy passes at some Amtrak offices in the United States, including locations in San Francisco, Los Angeles, Chicago, New York, Miami, Boston, and Washington, D.C.) Reservations are generally required and should be made for each part of your trip as early as possible.

Visitors should also be aware of the limitations of long-distance rail travel in the United States. With a few notable exceptions (for instance, the Northeast Corridor line between Boston and Washington, D.C.), service is rarely up to European standards: Delays are common, routes are limited and often infrequently served, and fares are rarely significantly lower than discount airfares. Thus, cross-country train travel should be approached with caution.

The cheapest way to travel the United States is by **bus.** Greyhound, the nation's nationwide bus line, offers an **Ameripass** for unlimited travel for 7 days (for $250), 15 days (for $350), and 30 days (for $450). Bus travel in the United States can be both slow and uncomfortable, so this option is not for everyone.

FAST FOR THE FOREIGN TRAVELER

Automobile Organizations Auto clubs will supply maps, suggested routes, guidebooks, accident and bail-bond insurance, and emergency road service. The major auto club in the United States, with 955 offices nationwide, is the **American Automobile Association (AAA).** Members of some foreign auto clubs have reciprocal arrangements with the AAA and enjoy its services at no charge. If you belong to an auto club, inquire about AAA reciprocity before you leave. The AAA can provide you with an **International Driving Permit** validating your foreign license. You may be able to join the AAA even if you are not a member of a reciprocal club. To inquire, call toll free 800/336-4357. In addition, some automobile-rental agencies now provide these services, so you should inquire about their availability when you rent your car.

Business Hours **Banks** are open weekdays from 9am to 3pm, although there's 24-hour access to the automatic tellers

(ATMs) at most banks and other outlets. Generally, **offices** are open weekdays from 9am to 5pm. **Stores** are open six days a week with many open on Sundays, too; departments stores usually stay open until 9pm one day a week.

Climate   See "When to Go—Climate & Events," Chapter 2.

Currency Exchange   You will find currency-exchange services in major airports with international service. Elsewhere, they may be quite difficult to come by. In New York, a very reliable choice is Thomas Cook Currency Services, Inc., which has been in business since 1841 and offers a wide range of services. They also sell commission-free foreign and U.S. traveler's checks, drafts, and wire transfers; they also do check collections (including Eurochecks). Their rates are competitive and service excellent. They maintain several offices in New York City (tel. for the Fifth Avenue office is 212/757-6915), at the JFK Airport International Arrivals Terminal (tel. 718/656-8444), and at La Guardia Airport in the Delta terminal (tel. 718/533-0784).

In New Orleans, exchange services are also offered at the **First National Bank of Commerce** (210 Baronne St.) and the **Whitney National Bank's** International Department (228 St. Charles Ave.). Many hotels will exchange currency if you are a registered guest.

Drinking Laws   See "Liquor Laws" in "Fast Facts: New Orleans," in Chapter 4.

Electric Current   The United States uses 110–120 volts, 60 cycles, compared to 220–240 volts, 50 cycles, as in most of Europe. Besides a 100-volt converter, small appliances of non-American manufacture, such as hairdryers or shavers, will require a plug adapter with two flat, parallel pins.

Embassies and Consulates   All embassies are located in the national capital, Washington, D.C.; some consulates are located in major cities, and most nations have a mission to the United Nations in New York City.

Listed here are the embassies and East and West Coast consulates of the major English-speaking countries. Travelers from other countries can get telephone numbers for their embassies and consulates by calling "Information" in Washington, D.C. (tel. 202/555-1212).

The **Australian embassy** is at 1601 Massachusetts Ave. NW, Washington, DC 20036 (tel. 202/797-3000). The **consulate** in New York is located at the International Building, 630 Fifth Ave., Suite 420, New York, NY 10111 (tel. 212/245-4000). The consulate in Los Angeles is located at 611 N. Larchmont, Los Angeles, CA 90004 (tel. 213/469-4300).

The **Canadian embassy** is at 501 Pennsylvania Ave. NW, Washington, DC 20001 (tel. 202/682-1740). The **consulate** in New York is located at 1251 Avenue of the Americas, New York, NY 10020 (tel. 212/768-2400). The consulate in Los Angeles is located at 300 Santa Grand Ave., Suite 1000, Los Angeles, CA 90071 (tel. 213/687-7432).

The **Irish embassy** is at 2234 Massachusetts Ave. NW, Washington, DC 20008 (tel. 202/462-3939). The **consulate** in New York is located at 515 Madison Ave., New York, NY 10022 (tel. 212/319-2555). The consulate in San Francisco is located at 655

Montgomery St., Suite 930, San Francisco, CA 94111 (tel. 415/392-4214).

The **New Zealand embassy** is at 37 Observatory Circle NW, Washington, DC 20008 (tel. 202/328-4800). The **consulate** in Los Angeles is located at 10960 Wiltshire Blvd., Los Angeles, CA 90024 (tel. 213/477-8241). There is no consulate in New York.

The **British embassy** is at 3100 Massachusetts Ave. NW, Washington, DC 20008 (tel. 202/462-1340). Great Britain maintains an honorary **consulate** in New Orleans, at 321 St. Charles Ave. (tel. 504/524-4180). The consulate in New York is located at 845 Third Ave., New York, NY 10022 (tel. 212/745-0200). The consulate in Los Angeles is located at 1766 Wilshire Blvd., Suite 400, Los Angeles, CA 90025 (tel. 310/477-3322).

Emergencies Call 911 for fire, police, and ambulance. If you encounter such traveler's problems as sickness, accident, or lost or stolen baggage, call **Traveler's Aid,** an organization that specializes in helping distressed travelers whether American or foreign. Check the local telephone directory for the nearest office.

Holidays On the following national legal holidays, banks, government offices, post offices, and many stores, restaurants, and museums are closed: January 1 (New Year's Day), Third Monday in January (Martin Luther King Day), Third Monday in February (Presidents' Day), Last Monday in May (Memorial Day), July 4 (Independence Day), First Monday in September (Labor Day), Second Monday in October (Columbus Day), November 11 (Veteran's Day/Armistice Day), Last Thursday in November (Thanksgiving Day), and December 25 (Christmas Day).

The Tuesday following the first Monday in November, Election Day, is a legal holiday in presidential-election years.

Information See "Information & Money," in Chapter 2.

Legal Aid If you are stopped for a minor infraction (for example, of the highway code, such as speeding), never attempt to pay the fine directly to a police officer; you may be arrested on the much more serious charge of attempted bribery. Pay fines by mail, or directly into the hands of the clerk of the court. If accused of a more serious offense, it is wise to say and do nothing before consulting a lawyer. Under U.S. law, an arrested person is allowed one telephone call to a party of his or her choice. Call your embassy or consulate.

Mail If you want your mail to follow you on your vacation and you aren't sure of your address, your mail can be sent to you, in your name, c/o General Delivery at the main post office of the city or region where you expect to be. The addressee must pick it up in person and produce proof of identity (driver's license, credit card, passport, etc.).

Generally to be found at intersections, mailboxes are blue with a red-and-white stripe and carry the inscription U.S. MAIL. If your mail is addressed to a U.S. destination, don't forget to add the five-figure postal code, or ZIP (Zone Improvement Plan) Code, after the two-letter abbreviation of the state to which the mail is addressed (CA for California, FL for Florida, NY for New York, and so on).

Newspapers and Magazines The *New York Times,* widely available in large cities, and the magazines *Newsweek* and

Time cover world news. European newspapers and magazines are available in large cities.

Radio and Television   There are dozens of radio stations (both AM and FM), each broadcasting talk shows, continuous news, or a particular kind of music—classical, country, jazz, pop, gospel—punctuated by frequent commercials. Television, with three coast-to-coast networks—ABC, CBS, and NBC—joined in recent years by the Public Broadcasting System (PBS) and a growing network of cable channels, plays a major part in American life.

Safety   See "Safety" in "Preparing for Your Trip," above.

Taxes   In the United States there is no VAT (Value-Added Tax) or other indirect tax on a national level. Every state, and each city in it, is allowed to levy its own local tax on all purchases, including hotel and restaurant checks, airline tickets, and so on. In New Orleans, the **sales tax rate** is 9%.

Telephone, Telegraph, Telex   The telephone system in the United States is run by private corporations, so rates, especially for long-distance service, can vary widely—even on calls made from public telephones. Local calls in the U.S. usually cost 25¢.

Generally, hotel surcharges on long-distance and local calls are astronomical. You are usually better off using a **public pay telephone,** which you will find clearly marked in most public buildings and private establishments as well as on the street. Outside metropolitan areas, public telephones are more difficult to find. Stores and gas stations are your best bet.

Most **long-distance** and **international calls** can be dialed directly from any phone. For calls to Canada and other parts of the United States, dial 1 followed by the area code and the seven-digit number. For international calls, dial 011 followed by the country code, city code, and the telephone number of the person you wish to call.

For **reversed-charge or collect calls,** and for **person-to-person calls,** dial 0 (zero, *not* the letter "O") followed by the area code and number you want; an operator will then come on the line, and you should specify that you are calling collect, or person-to-person, or both. If your operator-assisted call is international, ask for the overseas operator.

For local **directory assistance** ("information"), dial 411; for **long-distance information,** dial 1, then the appropriate area code and 555-1212.

Like the telephone system, **telegraph** and **telex** services are provided by private corporations like ITT, MCI, and above all, Western Union, the most important. You can bring your telegram into the nearest Western Union office (there are hundreds across the country), or dictate it over the phone (a toll-free call, 800/325-6000). You can also telegraph money, or have it telegraphed to you, very quickly over the Western Union system.

Telephone Directory   There are two kind of telephone directories available to you. The general directory is the so-called **White Pages,** in which private and business subscribers are listed in alphabetical order. The inside front cover lists the emergency numbers for police, fire, and ambulance, and other vital numbers (like the Coast Guard, poison-control center, crime-victims hotline, and so on). The first few pages are devoted to community-service numbers, including a guide to long-distance and international calling, complete with country codes and area codes.

The second directory, printed on yellow paper (hence its name, **Yellow Pages)**, lists all local services, businesses, and industries by type of activity, with an index at the back. The listings cover not only such obvious items as automobile repairs by make of car, or drugstores (pharmacies), often by geographical location, but also restaurants by type of cuisine and geographical location, bookstores by special subject and/or language, places of worship by religious denomination, and other information that the tourist might otherwise not readily find. The *Yellow Pages* also include city plans or detailed area maps, often showing postal ZIP Codes and public transportation routes.

Time   The United States is divided into six time zones. From east to west, these are: Eastern Standard Time (EST), Central Standard Time (CST), Mountain Standard Time (MST), Pacific Standard Time (PST), Alaska Standard Time (AST), and Hawaii Standard Time (HST). Always keep the changing time zones in mind if you are traveling (or even telephoning) long distances in the U.S. For example, noon in New York City (EST) is 11am in Chicago (CST), 10am in Denver (MST), 9am in Los Angeles (PST), 8am in Anchorage (AST), and 7am in Honolulu (HST). When it is noon in London (GMT, or Greenwich Mean Time), it is 7am in New York.

Daylight Saving Time is in effect from 1am on the first Sunday in April until 2am on the last Sunday in October, except in Arizona, Hawaii, part of Indiana, and Puerto Rico.

Tipping   See Chapter 4, "Fast Facts: New Orleans."

Toilets   Often euphemistically referred to as rest rooms, public toilets are nonexistent on the streets of New Orleans. They can be found, though, in bars, restaurants, hotel lobbies, museums, department stores, and service stations—and will probably be clean (although ones in the last-mentioned category sometimes leave much to be desired). Note, however, that some restaurants and bars display a notice that "Toilets are for use of patrons only." You can ignore this sign, or better yet, avoid arguments by paying for a cup of coffee or soft drink, which will qualify you as a patron. The cleanliness of toilets at railroad stations and bus depots may be questionable; some public places are equipped with pay toilets that will require you to insert one or two dimes (10¢) or a quarter (25¢) into a slot on the door before it will open. In rest rooms with attendants, leaving at least a 25¢ tip is customary.

THE AMERICAN SYSTEM OF MEASUREMENTS

LENGTH

1 inch (in.)	=	2.54cm				
1 foot (ft.)	=	12 in.	=	30.48cm	=	.305m
1 yard	=	3 ft.	=	.915m		
1 mile (mi.)	=	5,280 ft.	=	1.609km		

To convert miles to kilometers, multiply the number of miles by 1.61 (for example, 50 mi. × 1.61 = 80.5km). Note that this conversion can be used to convert speeds from miles per hour (m.p.h.) to kilometers per hour (km/h).

To convert kilometers to miles, multiply the number of kilometers by .62 (example, 25km × .62 = 15.5 mi.). Note that this same conversion can be used to convert speeds from kilometers per hour to miles per hour.

CAPACITY

1 fluid ounce (fl. oz.)	=	.03 liter		
1 pint	=	16 fl. oz.	=	.47 liter
1 quart	=	2 pints	=	.94 liter
1 gallon (gal.)	=	4 quarts	=	3.79 liter
	=	.83 Imperial gal.		

To convert U.S. gallons to liters, multiply the number of gallons by 3.79 (example, 12 gal. × 3.79 = 45.58 liters).

To convert U.S. gallons to Imperial gallons, multiply the number of U.S. gallons by .83 (example, 12 U.S. gal. × .83 = 9.95 Imperial gal.).

To convert liters to U.S. gallons, multiply the number of liters by .26 (example, 50 liters × .26 = 13 U.S. gal.).

To convert Imperial gallons to U.S. gallons, multiply the number of Imperial gallons by 1.2 (example, 8 Imperial gal. × 1.2 = 9.6 U.S. gal.).

WEIGHT

1 ounce (oz.)			=	28.35 grams		
1 pound (lb.)	=	16 oz.	=	453.6 grams	=	.45 kilogram
1 ton	=	2,000 lb.	=	907 kilograms	=	.91 metric ton

To convert pounds to kilograms, multiply the number of pounds by .45 (example, 90 lb. × .45 = 40.5kg).

To convert kilograms to pounds, multiply the number of kilos by 2.2 (example, 75kg × 2.2 = 165 lb.).

AREA

1 acre			=	.41 hectare	
1 square mile (sq. mi.)	=	640 acres	=	2.59 hectares	= 2.6km

To convert acres to hectares, multiply the number of acres by .41 (example, 40 acres × .41 = 16.4ha).

To convert square miles to square kilometers, multiply the number of square miles by 2.6 (example, 80 sq. mi. × 2.6 = 208km).

To convert hectares to acres, multiply the number of hectares by 2.47 (example, 20ha × 2.47 = 49.4 acres).

To convert square kilometers to square miles, multiply the number of square kilometers by .39 (example, 150km × .39 = 58.5 sq. mi.).

TEMPERATURE

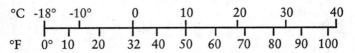

To convert degrees Fahrenheit to degrees Celsius, subtract 32 from °F, multiply by 5, then divide by 9 (example, 85°F − 32 × 5/9 = 29.4°C).

To convert degrees Celsius to degrees Fahrenheit, multiply °C by 9, divide by 5, and add 32 (example, 20°C × 9/5 + 32 = 68°F).

CHAPTER 4

GETTING TO KNOW NEW ORLEANS

1. ORIENTATION
2. GETTING AROUND
• FAST FACTS: NEW ORLEANS
3. NETWORKS & RESOURCES

It can be extremely overwhelming to travel to a city and have no basic information regarding how to get around and where to find what you need. Fortunately, because New Orleans is a small city, you'll come to know it quite well, even if you only have a week, and the people are extraordinarily helpful and friendly. If you still need some help, you'll find listed below just about everything you need to know.

1. ORIENTATION

ARRIVING

Because New Orleans is a gateway city, it has entry transportation of almost every kind available. Once you're there, its layout is fairly simple.

BY PLANE From the airport you can reach the Central Business District by bus for $1.10. The bus leaves the airport and goes to the downtown side of Tulane Avenue between Elks Place and South Saratoga Street just about every 10 minutes from 6 to 9am and from 3 to 6pm, every 23 minutes at other times. The buses are available from 6am to 6:30pm.

You can also get to your hotel by **Airport Shuttle Inc.** The ride will cost $10 per person (one-way), and the van will take you directly to your hotel. There are Airport Shuttle information desks (staffed 24 hours) in the airport. *Note:* If you plan to take the Airport Shuttle back to the airport when you depart, you must call and let them know what time your flight is leaving a day in advance. They will then tell you what time they will be by to pick you up.

A **taxi** from the airport will cost you $21; if there are three or more passengers, the fare will be $8 per person.

If you want to ride in style from the airport to your hotel contact **Olde Quarter Livery, Inc.** (914 N. Rampart St., New Orleans, LA 70116; tel. 504/595-5010). Express transfer service from New Orleans International Airport is available at a rate of $40 for a four-passenger stretch limousine and $60 for a six-passenger limousine. You'll be greeted by a uniformed chauffeur and escorted to the car, which will be waiting just outside the airport's baggage-claim area. Drivers are prompt and efficient—you'll never be left waiting.

BY TRAIN If you arrive by **Amtrak,** you'll be coming into the Union Passenger Terminal at 1001 Loyola Ave. in the Central Business District. There will be plenty of taxis outside the main entrance of the passenger terminal, and it will be a short ride to your hotel if you're staying in the French Quarter or the Central Business District.

BY BUS Arriving by bus will also bring you directly to the Central Business District. The public bus that departs from the airport does so approximately every 10 minutes between 6 and 9am and 3 and 6pm, every 23 minutes at other times. The last bus departs at 6:30pm. I'd recommend taking a cab from the bus terminal to your hotel. There should be taxis out front, but if there aren't, the number for **United Cabs Inc.** is 522-9771.

BY CAR Call before you leave home to ask for directions to your hotel and for the location of the nearest parking garage. Most hotels have parking facilities (for a fee); if they don't, they'll give you the names and addresses of nearby parking lots.

TOURIST INFORMATION

You'll be way ahead if, as far in advance as possible, you contact the **Greater New Orleans Tourist and Convention Commission,** 1520 Sugar Bowl Dr., New Orleans, LA 70112 (tel. 504/566-5011), for their brochures on such subjects as sightseeing, dining, entertainment, and shopping. If you have a special interest, rest assured they'll help you plan your visit around appropriate activities.

Once you've arrived in the city, your first order of business should be to stop by the **Visitor Information Center** at 529 St. Ann St. (tel. 504/566-5031) in the French Quarter. The center is open every day of the week from 9am to 5pm and has excellent walking and driving tour maps and booklets on restaurants, accommodations, sightseeing, special tours, and almost anything else you might want to know about. The staff is multilingual, friendly, and a veritable fount of valuable information not only on New Orleans but also on the entire state of Louisiana.

You can get decent maps almost anywhere in New Orleans. If you'll need them before you leave home, call the Greater New Orleans Tourist and Convention Commission (see above) and they'll send them to you. Otherwise, stop by when you arrive and pick them up. If you rent a car, be sure to ask for maps of the city, because the rental agents have good ones. Major bookstores, like B. Dalton and Waldenbooks, also supply good city maps.

If you're planning excursions outside the city, the places listed above also supply state maps.

CITY LAYOUT

The **French Quarter,** where the city began, is a 13-block-long area between Canal Street and Esplanade Avenue running from the Mississippi River to North Rampart Street. Because of the bend in the river, much of the city is laid out at angles that render useless such mundane directions as north, south, east, and west. New Orleans solved this directional problem long ago by simply substituting *riverside, lakeside, uptown,* and *downtown.* It works, and you'll catch on quickly if you keep in mind that North Rampart Street is the "lakeside" boundary of the Quarter, Canal Street marks the beginning of "uptown," and the Quarter is "downtown." As for building numbers, they begin at 100 on either side of Canal. In the Quarter they begin at 400 at the river (that's because four blocks of numbered buildings were lost to the river before the levee was built). Another reminder of Canal Street's boundary role between new and old New Orleans is the fact that street names change when they cross it (that is, Bourbon Street "downtown" becomes Carondelet "uptown").

Just steps outside the French Quarter, one street behind Esplanade, **Faubourg Marigny** is one of the oldest residential areas of the city.

The **Central Business District** lies directly above Canal Street from the Mississippi River, stretching toward the lake to Loyola Avenue 11 blocks away and over to the elevated expressway 10 blocks from and parallel to Canal.

The beautiful **Garden District** lies between St. Charles Avenue and Magazine Street toward the river and Jackson and Louisiana Avenues. Incidentally the area past Magazine Street near the river is sometimes called the "Irish Channel" because it was home to hundreds of Irish immigrants during the 1800s.

NEIGHBORHOODS IN BRIEF

The French Quarter Made up of about 90 square blocks, this section is also known as the Vieux Carré and is bounded on the north by Canal Street, the east by North Rampart Street, the west by the Mississippi River, and the south by Esplanade Avenue. It is the most historic—and the best preserved—area in the city.

Canal Street and the Central Business District There's no street more central to the life of New Orleans than Canal—the location of *everything* is described in reference to its relation to Canal Street. It took its name from a very shallow ditch that was dug along this border of the French Quarter in its early days. Although the ditch was given the rather grand name of canal, it was never large enough to be used for transport purposes.

The Central Business District (CBD) is roughly bounded by Canal Street and the lake to Loyola Avenue and upriver to the elevated Pontchartrain Expressway—Bus. I-90—and the Mississippi River to the west. There are pleasant plazas, squares, and parks sprinkled among all the commercial high-rise buildings of the CBD, and some of the most elegant of the luxury hotels are located in this area.

The Warehouse District With the revitalization of an area once devoted almost entirely to abandoned warehouses into an upmarket residential neighborhood, the area between Julia and St. Joseph Streets has become a mecca for artists. The area is just loaded with galleries (listed in Chapter 9) that show the works of contemporary artists. The Contemporary Arts Center, 900 Camp St. (see Chapter 7 for a full listing) just beyond St. Joseph toward Howard

Avenue, has facilities for presenting not only art exhibitions but also performances. Also in this area, you will find the Louisiana Children's Museum (see "Cool for Kids," in Chapter 7 for more details). One of my favorite areas in the city, this is a must for contemporary art lovers.

The Garden District   Located uptown and bounded by St. Charles Avenue (lakeside) and Magazine Street (riverside) between Jackson and Louisiana Avenues, it was once (and probably still is) one of the most beautiful areas in the city because of the old Victorian homes that line the streets and the elaborate gardens that used to exist around the outsides of the homes. Unfortunately, most of the gardens no longer exist and some of the houses are in disrepair, but you can still get some idea of what it used to be like.

The Irish Channel   The area between the Garden District (Magazine Street) and the river is known locally as the Irish Channel. No one really knows why—it's true that a good many Irish immigrants settled here, but so did Germans, and for some reason it was never known as the German Channel. Whatever the roots of its name, it is an interesting, although somewhat seedy, section of town these days. It houses many of New Orleans's poor, just as it did in the early days when Irish immigrants struggled to establish themselves in New Orleans and lived along these streets. An illuminating sidelight to the city's history is the fact that between 1820 and 1860 the more than 100,000 Irish newcomers were considered more "expendable" than costly slaves—many were killed while employed doing dangerous construction work and any other manual labor that might endanger health and well-being. In spite of that, there was a toughness and lively spirit that gave the Irish Channel a distinctive neighborhood flavor. Today it is mostly populated by African and Hispanic Americans, and there is still a sort of "street camaraderie" alive here.

Basin Street   You remember Basin Street, of course—the birthplace of jazz. But some people will tell you that Storyville (the red-light district along Basin Street) served only as a place for jazz, which had been around a long time, to come in off the streets. It did that, all right—jazz bands became the house entertainment in the many ornate "sporting palaces" that offered a wide variety of "services," primarily of the sex-for-hire variety. King Oliver, Jelly Roll Morton, and Louis Armstrong were among the jazz greats who got their start on Basin Street in the brothels between Canal Street and Beauregard Square. Storyville operated with wide-open abandon from 1897, when Alderman Sidney Story proposed a plan for the concentration of illegal activities in this area, until an official of the United States Navy had it closed down in 1917.

What you'll find today is a far cry from what was there in those rowdy days. A public housing project for low-income families now sprawls over the site, and by virtue of a series of statues depicting Latin American heroes, it is New Orleans's equivalent of New York's Avenue of the Americas. Simón Bolívar presides over the Canal and Basin Streets intersection; there's also a statue of Mexico's Benito Juarez with the inscription "Peace is based on the respect of the rights of others"; and finally a likeness of Gen. Francisco Morazón, a hero of Central America, given to the city by

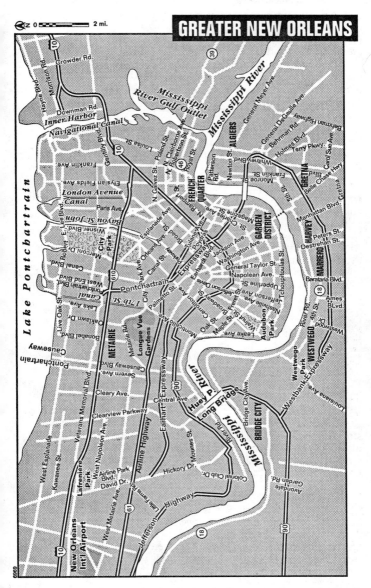

Honduras and San Salvador, is last in line at Basin and St. Louis Streets.

Faubourg Marigny *Faubourg* means suburb, and Marigny is the name of a prominent early New Orleans family. For some years the area (beginning with Frenchmen Street) had been going downhill to a somewhat seedy state; these days, however, small businesses, a good hotel (The Frenchmen, see Chapter 5), several good eateries, and a popular jazz spot are revitalizing Frenchmen Street and its smaller tributaries. Because of Faubourg Marigny's proximity to the Quarter, the restaurants and entertainment there are included with those of the Quarter.

2. GETTING AROUND

DISCOUNT PASSES You can obtain a **VisiTour pass** that will entitle you to an unlimited number of rides on all streetcar and bus lines. It costs $4 for one day, $8 for three days. Ask at your hotel or guesthouse—they'll be able to tell you where you can get the VisiTour pass.

BY BUS New Orleans has an excellent public bus system, and you can get complete information on which buses run where by calling 569-2700 or by picking up an excellent city map at the **Visitor Information Center,** 529 St. Ann St. in the French Quarter. All fares at the moment are $1 (you must have exact change), except for expresses, which are $1.25.

A very special bus ride for your first, farewell, or "tired-feet" tour of the French Quarter is the **Vieux Carré Minibus.** Quaint little vehicles leave Canal and Bourbon Streets at frequent intervals from 5am to 7:23pm. It'll cost you just 60¢ to see all of the French Quarter in comfort, although certainly not in as much detail as is possible on foot.

Along the riverfront, vintage streetcars, affectionately known as the "Ladies in Red," run for 1.9 miles from the Old Mint, across Canal Street, to Riverview. The fare is $1.25, there are convenient stops along the way, and there's ramp access for the disabled—a great stepsaver as you explore this lively area of the city.

BY STREETCAR One treat you really should allow yourself is the 1½-hour ride down St. Charles Avenue on the famous old streetcar line, which has been named a National Historic Landmark. The trolleys run 24 hours a day at frequent intervals, and the fare is $1 each way (you must have exact change). Board at Canal and Carondelet Streets (directly across Canal from Bourbon Street in the French Quarter), sit back, and look for landmarks in this part of town. Lafayette Square is at the 500 block of St. Charles, and across from it is Gallier Hall, built in the 1840s, which was the seat of the city's government for 100 years.

At Lee Circle, a little farther on, you'll see a huge statue of the general (Robert E., that is), which was erected in 1884—take note that he's facing *north* (that's so his back will never be to his enemies). From here on, it's fun to watch the homes that line the avenue as they change from Greek Revival to Victorian to early 1900s. The Garden District begins at Jackson Avenue, and you may want to get off the trolley to explore it fully. Even while riding by, however, you'll see many lovely homes in their garden settings. Loyola and Tulane Universities are at the 6000 block, across from Audubon Park. The park itself is worth a visit—there are huge old live oaks, a zoo, lagoons, a children's amusement park, tennis courts, and a municipal golf course. It extends all the way to the levee at the Mississippi.

The end of the line is at Palmer Park and Playground at Clairborne Avenue, but if you want to mount a shopping expedition at the interesting Riverbend Shopping Area (see Chapter 9), get off at Carrollton. It will cost you another $1 for the ride back to Canal Street, and it's a good idea to sit on the opposite side for the return to watch for things you missed going out. If you would like to transfer from the streetcar to a bus it will cost you 10¢.

BY TAXI   Taxis are plentiful and respond quickly to telephone calls in New Orleans. They can be hailed easily on the street in the French Quarter and some parts of the Central Business District and are usually in place at taxi stands at the larger hotels. Otherwise, telephone and expect a cab to appear in 3 to 5 minutes. In my experience, at least two out of three drivers will get out to open doors for you at both ends of the ride. Rates are $1.70 when you enter the taxi and $1 per mile thereafter. The city's most reliable company is **United Cabs Inc.** (tel. 522-9771).

Touring tip: Most taxis can be hired for an hourly rate for up to five passengers—a hassle-free and economical way for a small group to tour far-flung areas of the city (the lakefront, for example). Out-of-town trips cost double the amount on the meter.

BY CAR   The following is a list of car-rental agencies with their local and toll-free numbers and addresses:

Avis, 2024 Canal St. (tel. 523-4317 or 800/331-1212).
Budget Rent-A-Car, 1317 Canal St. (tel. 524-9031).
Dollar Rent-A-Car, 1910 Airline Hwy. (tel. 467-2285).
Hertz, 901 Convention Center Blvd. #101 (tel. 568-1645 or 800/654-3131).
Swifty Car Rental, 2300 Canal St. (tel. 524-7368).
Value Rent-A-Car, 1701 Airline Hwy., Kenner (tel. 469-2688).

Rental rates vary according to the time of your visit and from company to company, so it's best just to call ahead and see what kind of a rate they can offer you. *Note:* If you're staying for a week or more, be sure to ask about weekly rates—stay away from the daily rates.

Comparatively speaking, driving in New Orleans isn't too difficult and traffic officers are fairly tolerant of moving violations (which isn't to say that you should disregard traffic rules), but they're absolute murder on illegal parking, handing out tickets right and left. For that reason, I strongly suggest that you put the car away for any French Quarter sightseeing (it's more fun, anyway, on foot or by minibus) and use it only for longer jaunts out of congested areas.

French Quarter driving is more difficult than driving in some other areas of the city. All streets there are one-way, and on weekdays during daylight hours, Royal and Bourbon Streets are closed to automobiles between the 300 and 700 blocks. Driving also is trying in the Central Business District, where congested traffic and limited parking make life difficult for the motorist. It is much smarter to park the car and use the public transportation provided in both areas.

ON FOOT   For my money, the *only* way to see the French Quarter and the Garden District is by foot. It's easy to find your way around both of these small areas, and they are crammed with things you won't want to miss. Only by strolling can you really soak up the charm of both these sections. In the Quarter, look through iron gates or down alleyways for glimpses of lovely patios and courtyards and above street level for interesting facades and incredibly delicate lacy iron railings. Along Bourbon Street, intersperse strolls with stops to listen to live jazz groups playing at open-door saloons—there's nonstop music most of the day. In the Garden District, be sure to allow enough time to drink in the beauty of the formal gardens surrounding the fine old mansions.

BY FERRY One of New Orleans's nicest treats is absolutely free. It's the 25-minute (round-trip) ferry ride across the Mississippi from the foot of Canal Street, and it's a joy, whether you go by day for a view of the busy harbor or at night when the lights of the city reflect in the mighty river. If you'd like to do some West Bank driving between trips, the ferry carries both car and foot passengers.

BY BOAT If the horse-drawn carriages represent romance on land, they are matched on the river by several old-time steamboats that leave from the foot of Canal Street or Toulouse Street for river cruises. You'll find details of the cruises in Chapter 7.

BY HORSE & CARRIAGE If you have even one romantic bone in your body, you'll find it hard to resist the authentic old horse-drawn carriages that pick up passengers at Jackson Square. Each horse is decked out with ribbons, flowers, or even a hat, and each driver is apparently in fierce competition with all other drivers to win a "most unique city story" award. No matter which one you choose, you'll get a knowledgeable, nonstop monologue on historic buildings, fascinating events of the past, and a legend or two during the 2¼-mile drive through the French Quarter. They're at the Decatur Street end of Jackson Square from 9am to midnight in good weather; the charge is $8 per adult and $4 for children. *Note:* The carriage ride described here is *not* the one that will take you on your own private tour—those are considerably more expensive.

FAST NEW ORLEANS

American Express The American Express office (tel. 586-8201) is located at 158 Baronne St. in the Central Business District.

Airport See "Orientation," in this chapter.

Area Code The area code for New Orleans is 504.

Babysitters It's best to ask at your hotel about babysitting services—they might even have one of their own. They'll give you all the information you need, including rates. If your hotel doesn't offer any help in finding childcare, try calling American Nursing Service, Inc. (tel. 833-3100, or toll free 800/444-NURS) or Dependable Kid Care (tel. 282-2200).

Business Hours Normally, it's a 9am to 5pm routine, but some stores, particularly in the French Quarter, open late and, as a consequence, stay open later. Just call before you go to be sure.

Car Rentals See "Getting Around," in this chapter.

Climate See "When to Go," Chapter 2.

Driving Rules See "Getting Around," in this chapter.

Emergencies   For fire, ambulance, and police, just dial **911** in an emergency.

Holidays   See "When to Go," Chapter 2.

Hospitals   Should you become ill during your New Orleans visit, most major hotels have in-house staff doctors on call 24 hours a day. If there's not one available in your hotel or guesthouse, call or go to the Emergency Room at **Touro Infirmary**, 1401 Foucher (tel. 897-7011), if you're uptown; or the **Tulane University Medical Center**, 1415 Tulane Ave. (tel. 588-5800), if you're in the Central Business District.

Information   See "Information & Money," Chapter 2.

Laundry and Dry Cleaning   There are many options, but one in the French Quarter is the **Washing Well Laundryteria**, 841 Bourbon St. (tel. 523-9955 or 525-3983); if you get your laundry in by 9am it will be ready by 2pm.

Libraries   The **New Orleans Public Library** (tel. 596-2619) is located at 219 Loyola Ave. It's open Monday to Thursday from 10am to 6pm, Saturday from 10am to 5pm. Consult the phone book for other branch locations throughout the city.

Liquor Laws   Alcoholic beverages are available in New Orleans around the clock, seven days a week. But be warned—although the police may look the other way if they see a pedestrian who's had a few too many (as long as he or she is peaceful and not bothering anyone else), they have no tolerance at all for those who are intoxicated behind the wheel. If you find yourself in that condition far from your hotel, you'd best take a taxi. The legal drinking age in New Orleans is 21 years.

Maps   See "City Layout," in this chapter.

Newspapers and Magazines   To find out what's going on around town, you might want to pick up a copy of the *Times-Picayune* or *New Orleans Magazine*. *Offbeat Publications* is a monthly guide to the city's evening entertainment, art galleries, and special events. It can be found in most hotels. *Where Magazine*, also published monthly, is a good resource for visitors.

Photographic Needs   One of the city's most complete camera shops is the **K&B Camera Center**, 227 Dauphine St. (tel. 524-2266), with a wide selection of cameras and other electronics, as well as film and camera and darkroom supplies. Fast film developing also is featured. It is open Monday through Friday from 8am to 6pm, Saturday from 8am to 2pm.

Post Office   The main post office is located at 701 Loyola Ave. If you're in the Vieux Carré, you'll find a post office at 1022 Iberville St. There's another one at 610 S. Maestri Place.

Religious Services   The following is a list of various religious organizations throughout the city: **St. Patrick's Church,** 724 Camp St. (tel. 525-4413); **St. Mary's Church,** 1116 Chartres St. (tel. 529-3040); **Sixth Baptist Church,** 928 Felicity St. (tel. 525-3408); **First Pilgrim Baptist Church,** 1325 Governor Nicholls St. (tel. 523-1740); **Saint Anna's Episcopal Church,** 1313 Esplanade Ave. (tel. 947-2121); **St. Mark's United Methodist Church,** 1130 N. Rampart St. (tel. 523-0450); **Congregation Anshe Sfard Synagogue,** 2230 Carondelet St. (tel. 522-4714).

Safety   Whenever you're traveling in an unfamiliar city, stay alert. Be aware of your immediate surroundings. Wear a moneybelt.

Don't sling your camera or purse over your shoulder; wear the strap diagonally across your body. This will minimize the possibility of your becoming a victim of a crime. Every society has its criminals, and it's your responsibility to be aware and alert even in the most heavily touristed areas.

In New Orleans in particular, don't walk alone at night, and do not go into the cemeteries alone at any time during the day or night. Ask around locally before you go anywhere—people will tell you if you should take a cab instead of walking or taking public transportation.

Taxis See "Getting Around," in this chapter.

Time and Temperature For information without leaving your room, call 465-9212 for weather and 976-1111 (charges apply) for the time.

Tipping Waiters and taxi drivers are tipped between 15% and 20%. Bellhops should be tipped $1 to carry a few bags to your room; airport porters should be tipped 50¢ for a small bag, $1 for a larger one.

Transit Info Local bus routes and schedules can be obtained from the **RTA Ride Line** (tel. 569-2700).

Useful Telephone Numbers You can reach the **Travelers Aid Society** at 525-8726 and **Union Passenger Terminal,** 1001 Loyola Ave., for bus and train information, at 528-1610.

3. NETWORKS & RESOURCES

If you need more help than what's listed here, call the GNOTCC or the numbers for the organizations listed and ask them for references.

FOR STUDENTS New Orleans has two major colleges, both only a short ride on the streetcar from the French Quarter or the Central Business District. Tulane University has one of the best anthropology departments in the country. The Tulane University Theater puts on some pretty decent productions. Both Tulane and Loyola Universities have student unions that are open to the public, so if you're missing your peers, jump on the streetcar and head for the student unions.

FOR AFRICAN AMERICANS The Greater New Orleans Black Tourism Network (tel. 523-5652) can provide information on tourism that is of interest to Black Americans or to others who are interested in African American culture as it pertains to New Orleans.

FOR GAY MEN & LESBIANS Once you start to find them, you realize that there is an abundance of centers serving gay and lesbian interests, from bars to restaurants to community services to certain businesses. Here are some numbers you might find useful if you need some help finding your way.

Political ACT UP (tel. 522-5105) has a chapter in New Orleans. The Mayor's Advisory Committee on Lesbian & Gay Issues can be reached by calling 826-2955.

Publication *AMbush Magazine,* the Gulf South weekly entertainment/news publication.

Religious Some of the religious organizations that support gays and lesbians are: **Dignity/NO Catholic Church** (tel. 522-6059); **First Unitarian Gay/Lesbian** (tel. 865-7005 or 822-3278 before 10pm); **Grace Fellowship** (tel. 944-9836 or 949-2325); **Jewish Gay & Lesbian Alliance** (tel. 525-8286); and **Vieux Carré Metropolitan Community Church,** 1128 St. Roch (tel. 945-5390).

FOR SENIORS & THE DISABLED "Rollin' by the River," a guide to wheelchair-accessible restaurants and clubs in the French Quarter, is available for a handling fee of $2.25 from the **Advocacy Center for the Elderly and Disabled,** 210 O'Keefe Ave., Suite 700, New Orleans, LA 70112 (tel. 504/522-2337). Seniors are welcome to use this number as well.

CHAPTER 5
NEW ORLEANS ACCOMMODATIONS

1. IN THE FRENCH QUARTER

• **FROMMER'S SMART TRAVELER: HOTELS**

2. OUTSIDE THE FRENCH QUARTER

From the beginning a city that welcomed visitors with open arms and warm hospitality, New Orleans today carries on its tradition of providing travelers with a choice of lodgings in a wide array of styles and prices. And, in spite of the annual influx of hundreds of thousands of visitors needing a place to stay, this spirited city has managed to keep historic districts, such as the French Quarter, free of "progress," that modern disease responsible for those high-rise monstrosities that stick out like sore thumbs and deface many a formerly gracious and historic city. Indeed, it is almost impossible to tell if some of the new French Quarter hotels have been built from scratch or lovingly placed inside the shell of an older building, so faithful has been the dedication to preserving the Quarter's architectural style. Even motor hotels (which have alleviated the ever-present problem of on-street parking) have a look that is distinctly New Orleans.

You'll find those high-rise hotels, of course, but they're more appropriately located uptown, in commercial sections, where they seem to "fit" just fine. In fact, the proliferation of slick new hotels—brought on by the 1984 World's Fair—has done a lot to ease New Orleans's chronic hotel-room shortage.

Hotels are presented in four price classifications here. "Very expensive" hotels, offering plush accommodations and a wide variety of gracious services, will cost upwards of $200 a night for a double room. "Expensive" hotels start in the neighborhood of $160 a night; "moderate" hotels offer double rooms for between $80 and $160. Any hotel in New Orleans where you can get a comfortable room for under $80 is considered "inexpensive." Unless otherwise noted in a particular hotel or guesthouse listing, all accommodations in New Orleans have a private bath.

As for guesthouses, they really *do* make you feel like a guest. Presided over by New Orleanians (or others, charmed by the city, who picked up and moved here), imbued with a special brand of hospitality, many are furnished with antiques and all provide a very homelike atmosphere. After spending time in numerous New Orleans guesthouses, I'd recommend them over hotel-style accommodations. You'll be treated as one of the family, and there's no better way to experience the history of New Orleans, as most guesthouse owners know the background history of their home and are more than willing to share it with you.

A sort of passkey to the lively people who live in New Orleans is **Bed and Breakfast, Inc. Reservation Service,** 1021 Moss St. (P.O. Box 52257), New Orleans, LA 70152 (tel. 504/488-4640, or toll free 800/729-4640). Personable Hazell Boyce can put you up in luxury in 19th-century, turn-of-the-century, or modern residences. Or you can opt for an apartment in the French Quarter or Garden District. Prices range from $35 to $225 single or double occupancy, and she delights in arranging modest lodging for students.

But whatever your preference—be it hotel, motel, guesthouse, or bed-and-breakfast—one thing is certain: You're sure to find much more than a place to lay your head in any of New Orleans's accommodations.

One word of warning, however: In spite of the thousands of rental rooms in New Orleans, there are times when there isn't a bed to be had. Advance reservations (a good idea whatever the season) are a must during spring, fall, and winter months, when the city is crowded. If your trip will coincide with Mardi Gras or Jazz Fest, it isn't an exaggeration to say that you should book as far as a year in advance. Sugar Bowl week and other festival times also flood New Orleans with visitors and require advance planning for accommodations. It's conceivable that you might run across a cancellation and get a last-minute booking, but the chances are remote, to say the least.

If you want to miss the crowds and lodgings squeeze that mark the big festivals, consider coming in the month immediately following Mardi Gras (which begins soon after Christmas with the opening of Carnival season and lasts until "Fat Tuesday," the last day before Lent) or in the summer months (which can be muggy but not unbearable) when the streets are not nearly as thronged.

Since I am personally convinced that the only place to stay is in the French Quarter—the very heart and soul of New Orleans—I'm listing accommodations there first. But if circumstances make another location more desirable for you, you'll find outside-the-Quarter listings in this chapter as well.

Special note: You will almost always be asked to guarantee your reservation by either a deposit or a credit-card charge, no matter what type of accommodation you decide on. Also, rates frequently jump more than a notch or two for Mardi Gras and other festival times, and in some cases there's a four- or five-night minimum requirement.

1. IN THE FRENCH QUARTER

VERY EXPENSIVE

OMNI ROYAL ORLEANS, 621 St. Louis St., New Orleans, **LA 70140. Tel. 504/529-5333,** or toll free 800/THE-OMNI in the U.S. and Canada. Fax 504/529-7089. 351 rms (16 suites). A/C TV TEL

$ Rates: $145 single; $260 double; $320–$1,000 suite. Extra person $30. Children 17 and under free with parents. AE, CB, DC, DISC, MC, V. **Parking:** Valet parking $10.50 per day.

Currently under renovation and considered "the" place to stay (and certainly one of the most beautiful French Quarter hotels) by many veteran visitors, the Omni Royal Orleans is very elegant. That is as it should be, for the present-day hotel opened its doors in 1960 on the site of the 1836 St. Louis Exchange Hotel, one of this country's most splendid hostelries of the mid-19th century. The St. Louis Exchange was a center of New Orleans social life until the final years of the Civil War, when it first became a hospital for wounded soldiers from both the North and the South, then served for a time as the state capitol building and a meeting place of the carpetbagger legislature, and finally was destroyed by a 1915 hurricane. In its heyday of gala soirees and eminent visitors, it was also the innovator of the "free lunch" for noontime drinkers, a tradition of topnotch noontime cuisine that survives even today. The Omni Royal Orleans has proved a worthy successor, with a lobby of marble and brass and crystal chandeliers. Furnishings are truly sumptuous in the guest rooms, and there are extra touches, such as a mint on your pillow every night.

Dining/Entertainment: The classic, gourmet Rib Room is a favorite dining spot for many natives (see Chapter 6), and there's soft music after 8pm in the elegant lobby bar, the Esplanade Lounge (just right for the evening's last drink, no matter where you stay). Touché Bar offers light meals and excellent mint juleps. The rooftop, poolside, palm tree-bordered La Riviera bar and restaurant is a terrific lunch spot, with unobstructed views of the French Quarter.

Services: Concierge, babysitting service, emergency mending and pressing services, complimentary shoe shine, nightly turn-down service, 24-hour room service.

Facilities: Health club, heated pool, beauty and barber shops, florist, sundries shop and newsstand, business center.

WESTIN CANAL PLACE, 100 Iberville St., New Orleans, LA 70130. Tel. 504/566-7006, or toll free 800/228-3000. 438 rms. A/C MINIBAR TV TEL

$ Rates (depending on view): $195–$245 single; $225–$298 double. AE, CB, DISC, DC, MC, V. **Parking:** $12 per night in hotel garage.

The Westin Canal Place has one of the most convenient locations in town—right on the Mississippi River on the Canal Street edge of the French Quarter. Its window-walled 11th-floor lobby is a masterpiece of Carrara marble, fine paintings, and antiques. Each room has a marble foyer and bath. Sweeping river and French Quarter views are among the extras here; however, you may pay extra according to the specific view.

Dining/Entertainment: The lobby makes a lovely setting for afternoon tea. A handsome English-style pub and Le Jardin restaurant are just steps away.

Services: Full concierge service.

Facilities: Heated pool with poolside beverage services, privileges at a nearby 18-hole golf course, special elevator descending directly to Canal Place shops, barbershop, beauty salon.

EXPENSIVE

DAUPHINE ORLEANS HOTEL, 415 Dauphine St., New Orleans, LA 70112. Tel. 504/586-1800, or toll free 800/521-7111. Fax 504/586-1409. 109 rms. A/C MINIBAR TV TEL

$ Rates (including continental breakfast): $130–$180 single; $145–$190 double; $170–$370 suite; $150–$220 patio suite. Extra person $15. Children under 12 free in parents' room. AE, MC, V. **Parking:** Valet parking $9 per night.

There's a sort of casual elegance at the newly renovated Dauphine Orleans Hotel. All rooms have recently been upgraded with a fresh coat of paint, new solid wood headboards and feather pillows on the beds, and new/modern or upgraded period furnishings, making the Dauphine Orleans one of the French Quarter's loveliest properties. There are no fewer than three secluded courtyards at the Dauphine, and history lurks around every corner. The hotel's main building was once the studio of the famous John James Audubon, and the "Patio Suites" across the street from the main building were originally built in 1834 as the home of New Orleans merchant, Samuel Herrmann. In 1991, when the cottages, located adjacent to the main hotel, were renovated, many intriguing aspects of the building were uncovered. The original construction of the cottages was brick between posts and the nails that can now be seen in the wood posts are thought to have come from Lafitte's Blacksmith Shoppe (see Chapter 10 for details). Hidden fireplaces have been uncovered, and in a room that was once the kitchen antique pots and pans were discovered under the floor. While all of the rooms here are nice, I have to admit that I am partial to the cottage rooms.

Dining/Entertainment: The Bagnio Lounge was once a notorious "sporting house" (brothel), and guests are given a copy of the original 1857 license, which still hangs on the wall. Cocktails are served from 3:30pm to midnight on weeknights and 12:30pm to midnight on weekends. The Coffee Lounge is where continental breakfast is served daily from 6:30 to 11am. Afternoon tea is also served daily from 3 to 5pm.

Services: Complimentary French Quarter and downtown transportation, morning paper delivered to your door.

Facilities: Pool, guest library, small fitness room.

HOTEL MAISON DE VILLE, 727 Toulouse St., New Orleans, LA 70130. Tel. 504/561-5858. 23 rms. A/C MINIBAR TV TEL

$ Rates: $140–$245 double; $215–$395 cottage. AE, MC, V. **Parking:** Valet parking $15 per night.

Unique among New Orleans's luxury hotels is the small, European-style Hotel Maison de Ville. Dating back prior to 1742 (it appears on every early map of New Orleans), the Maison was restored several years ago to an old-time elegance marked by marble fireplaces, fine French antiques, gilt-framed mirrors, rich swagged drapes, and matching quilted bedspreads. Guest rooms surround a brick courtyard (one of the loveliest in the Quarter) with a tiered fountain and palm trees. It was here, working at one of the wrought-iron tables, that Tennessee Williams reworked *A Streetcar Named Desire;* his lodgings were in one of the converted slave quarters. Another famous tenant, John Audubon, lived in one of the seven cottages now operated by the hotel while painting the Louisiana portion of his *Birds of America*. The cottages, with brick walls, beamed ceilings, and slate or brick floors, are furnished with antiques and reflect a warm country elegance.

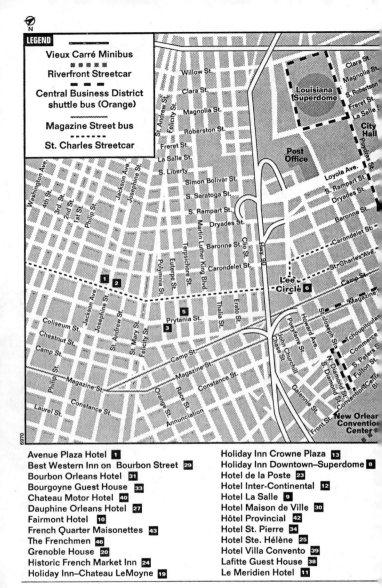

LEGEND

- ▬ ▬ ▬ **Vieux Carré Minibus**
- ✖ ✖ ✖ ✖ ✖ **Riverfront Streetcar**
- ∿∿∿∿ **Central Business District shuttle bus (Orange)**
- ▬▬▬▬ **Magazine Street bus**
- - - - - - - **St. Charles Streetcar**

Avenue Plaza Hotel **1**
Best Western Inn on Bourbon Street **29**
Bourbon Orleans Hotel **31**
Bourgoyne Guest House **33**
Chateau Motor Hotel **40**
Dauphine Orleans Hotel **27**
Fairmont Hotel **10**
French Quarter Maisonettes **43**
The Frenchmen **46**
Grenoble House **20**
Historic French Market Inn **24**
Holiday Inn–Chateau LeMoyne **19**

Holiday Inn Crowne Plaza **13**
Holiday Inn Downtown–Superdome **8**
Hotel de la Poste **23**
Hotel Inter-Continental **12**
Hotel La Salle **9**
Hotel Maison de Ville **30**
Hôtel Provincial **42**
Hotel St. Pierre **34**
Hotel Ste. Hélène **25**
Hotel Villa Convento **39**
Lafitte Guest House **38**
Le Meridien Hotel **11**

Dining/Entertainment: The Maison's very personal service includes a breakfast of fresh orange juice, croissants or brioches, and steaming chicory coffee served on a silver tray in your room, in the parlor, or on the patio. Complimentary sherry and port are served in the afternoon and evening. The Bistro, the hotel's restaurant, is intimate and inviting.

Services: Morning and evening newspapers delivered to your room, shoe-polishing service—rare these days (just leave your shoes outside your door at night and notify the desk).

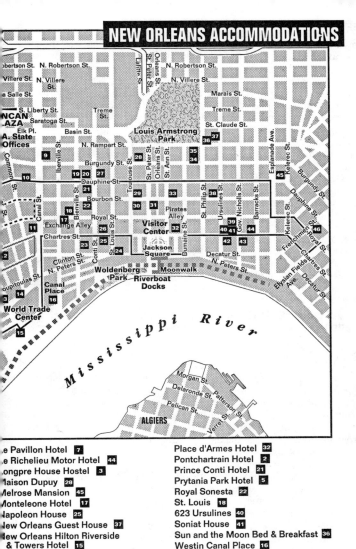

NEW ORLEANS ACCOMMODATIONS

Le Pavillon Hotel **7**
Le Richelieu Motor Hotel **44**
Longpre House Hostel **3**
Maison Dupuy **28**
Melrose Mansion **45**
Monteleone Hotel **17**
Napoleon House **25**
New Orleans Guest House **37**
New Orleans Hilton Riverside
& Towers Hotel **15**
Omni Royal Orleans **26**
P.J. Holbrook's Olde Victorian Inn **35**

Place d'Armes Hotel **32**
Pontchartrain Hotel **2**
Prince Conti Hotel **21**
Prytania Park Hotel **5**
Royal Sonesta **22**
St. Louis **18**
623 Ursulines **40**
Soniat House **41**
Sun and the Moon Bed & Breakfast **36**
Westin Canal Place **16**
Windsor Court **14**
YMCA International Hotel **6**

**MAISON DUPUY, 1001 Toulouse St., New Orleans, LA
70112. Tel. 504/586-8000,** or toll free 800/535-9177. Fax 504/
525-5334. Telex 587418 DUPYHOTEL NLN. 197 rms, 8 suites. A/C
TV TEL
$ Rates: Standard, $140 single; $160 double. Deluxe, $170 single;
$190 double. Superior, $200 single; $220 double, $250–$800 suite.
AE, DC, MC, V. **Parking:** Valet parking $9 per night.
Owned and operated by the Delta Queen Steamboat Company,
Maison Dupuy is a lovely hotel comprising seven French Quarter

town houses. It's also ideally located for French Quarter sightseeing. It's not too large for those who like their privacy but also like to be recognized by the staff.

Rooms are quite large, done in dusty rose and blue-green, and each has a desk, comfortable armchairs, and either two double beds or one king-size bed. All have modern bathrooms with standard amenities, and some have balconies that face either the courtyard or the street.

In the courtyard you can relax at umbrella-covered tables and have a swim, enjoy a cocktail, or just take in the beautiful surroundings.

Dining/Entertainment: The hotel's restaurant, Le Bon Creole, serves breakfast, lunch, and dinner. The lunch and dinner menus feature Cajun and Creole dishes but also serve American favorites. The hotel also does a Sunday "Champagne Jazz Brunch Buffet." The Cabaret Lautrec Lounge has a piano; a large, marble-topped bar; and Lautrec-like murals on the walls—the perfect setting in which to relax for a cocktail before venturing off to dinner. There is also a courtyard patio bar that is open during fair weather.

Services: Room service.

Facilities: Heated outdoor pool; health club with weight station, computerized exercise bikes, and treadmills.

MONTELEONE HOTEL, 214 Royal St., New Orleans, LA 70140. Tel. 504/523-3341, or toll free 800/535-9595. 600 rms. A/C TV TEL

$ Rates: $170 single or double. Extra person $25. Package rates available. AE, DISC, MC, V. **Parking:** $8.

The largest French Quarter hotel, the Monteleone has been family operated by three generations of Monteleones. Covering almost an entire block, it seems to keep growing and expanding over the years without losing a trace of its trademark charm. Recently refurbished, the Monteleone offers accommodations that range in style from luxurious, antique-filled suites to more modern, very comfortable family rooms.

Dining/Entertainment: The trellis-trimmed, green-and-white Le Café restaurant is a favorite with native New Orleanians, and the Carousel Bar, which slowly revolves under its red-and-white-striped canopy, also draws the locals. Up on top, the fabulous Sky Terrace has to be seen to be believed; it houses both the 9-to-5 Bar and the exquisite Sky-Lite Lounge, really a rooftop club that features topnotch live entertainment, such as the famous Dukes of Dixieland.

Services: Room service.

Facilities: Heated swimming pool and fitness center.

ROYAL SONESTA, 300 Bourbon St., New Orleans, LA 70140. Tel. 504/586-0300, or toll free 800/766-3782. 500 rms. A/C MINIBAR TV TEL

$ Rates: $140–$225 single; $160–$260 double. Package rates may be available. AE, CB, DISC, DC, MC, V. **Parking:** $12.75 per night in hotel garage.

The Royal Sonesta is adorned with lacy New Orleans balconies. Its rooms are furnished with period pieces, and many overlook inner patios or the pool—preferable to rooms facing Bourbon Street, which can be noisy. This is an ideal French Quarter location—within walking distance to almost everything. Begue's restaurant

FROMMER'S SMART TRAVELER:
HOTELS

1. Hotel rates skyrocket during the high season and during any major festival, so try to make your trip during the off season.
2. Always ask if the hotel has a special package rate or a weekend discount. You might be pleasantly surprised.
3. Most people want to stay right in the French Quarter, but it is within walking distance from the Central Business District; rates are often cheaper there and at other places outside the Quarter.
4. Always keep the guesthouses in mind. They are small operations, and if they aren't full, the owners will often drop the rates a bit. Because they also include breakfast in the rates, that will save you some money, too.

carries on the tradition of an older New Orleans eating spot of the same name, while Desire offers fresh seafood and an oyster bar. Room service (until 2am), business center, concierge, and a pool and fitness room are available.

ST. LOUIS, 730 Bienville St., New Orleans, LA 70130. Tel. 504/581-7300, or toll free 800/535-9706. 70 rms. A/C TV TEL

$ Rates: $129–$279 single or double. Children under 12 free in parents' room. AE, CB, DC, MC, V. **Parking:** Valet parking $10.50 per night.

Another very special small hotel right in the heart of the Quarter is the St. Louis. Sophisticated elegance after the fashion of a Parisian luxury hotel is the style here—there's even a concierge on hand to render very specialized service. Built around a lovely courtyard that is centered by a marble fountain, the St. Louis is done in true French decor, with antique furniture, crystal chandeliers, and gilt-framed original oil paintings. Some rooms have private balconies overlooking the courtyard, and suites have *private* courtyards.

   Dining/Entertainment: This is the home of an elegant, four-star French restaurant, Louis XVI (see Chapter 6 for a more detailed description).

   Services: Full concierge services, complimentary daily newspaper.

SONIAT HOUSE, 1133 Chartres St., New Orleans, LA 70116. Tel. 504/522-0570, or toll free 800/544-8808. Fax 504/522-7208. 24 rms. A/C TV TEL

$ Rates: $144–$204 single; $152–$222 double; $270 semi-suite; $420–$630 suite. MC, V. **Parking:** Valet parking $10 per day.

Built in 1829 by a wealthy plantation owner, Joseph Soniat Dufossat, the Soniat House is an interesting combination of Creole style and Greek Revival detail. Rodney and Frances Smith purchased the three-story Soniat House in 1982 and have done an excellent job of creating the perfect blend of guesthouse and hotel. Because there is such a small number of rooms, the attention you'll get is more like the kind you'd find in a guesthouse; however, if you'd rather be left on your own, that's possible, too.

   After you ring the bell the doorman will let you in to the

impressive plant-lined carriageway that leads to the fountained courtyard, where you'll find a lily pond (breakfast is served here after 8am upon request). Most of the rooms face this incredibly lush courtyard and have balconies.

All rooms are different in size and decor; furnished with French, English, and Louisianan antiques; and feature polished hardwood floors warmly covered with Oriental rugs. Also, all have phones in the bathrooms, and some hold paintings on loan from the New Orleans Museum of Art. Room 27, which is a large room, has canopied twin beds and exposed brick walls. There is also a small fireplace and a giant antique armoire. One of the suites, which has its own elevator, is located on the third floor. It has exposed wood beams, skylights, and an interesting collection of "found" antique Louisianan and French furniture, as well as more modern furnishings. The space used to be the attic of the Soniat home, and Rodney and Frances decorated it accordingly. Two of the rooms can function as bedrooms, and this suite is ideal for families.

Dining/Entertainment: Brought to your room every morning at 7am is a breakfast of hot biscuits, strawberry preserves (specially made for the Soniat House), fresh orange juice, and coffee; it's $5 extra but worth every penny. There is an honor bar in the parlor next to the reception area.

Services: Same-day cleaning and laundry service; evening turndown; airport transfer on request.

Note: The owners of Soniat House also operate Girod House, which houses two full apartments ($135 and $195) that have been completely renovated and refurnished. Daily maid service is available.

MODERATE

BEST WESTERN INN ON BOURBON STREET, 541 Bourbon St., New Orleans, LA 70130. Tel. 504/524-7611, or toll free 800/535-7891. 186 rms. A/C TV TEL

$ **Rates:** $145 single; $155–$235 double. AE, DISC, DC, MC, V. **Parking:** $8 per night.

This hotel sits on the site of the 1859 French Opera House, the first ever built in the United States; it burned down in 1919. It's hard to tell, however, that the present building hasn't been here for just that many years, so well does its design blend with New Orleans's traditional architecture. All rooms have a Deep South decor and king-size or double beds, and some have balconies overlooking Bourbon Street. Both the Sing-a-Long piano bar and the Reunion Café (a self-service restaurant featuring Creole and Cajun cooking) are popular with guests. Prices hinge on whether your room faces Bourbon Street or has a balcony.

BOURBON ORLEANS HOTEL, 717 Orleans St., New Orleans, LA 70116. Tel. 504/523-2222. Fax 504/525-8166. 211 rms, 50 suites. A/C MINIBAR TV TEL

$ **Rates:** $95–$135 petit queen or twin; $115–$190 deluxe king or double/double; $135–$225 junior suite; $165–$325 town-house suite; $180–$340 town-house with balcony. Extra person $15. AE, DC, DISC, MC, V. **Parking:** $12 per day.

You can't miss the Bourbon Orleans Hotel—its pale salmon and moss green exterior takes up an entire block of the French Quarter. The Orleans Ballroom, located within, dates back to the 1800s and is the oldest part of the hotel. It was constructed in 1815 as a venue for the city's masquerade, carnival, and quadroon balls. In 1881 the building was sold to the Sisters of the Holy Family, who were members of the South's first order of African-American nuns. The Sisters converted the ballroom into a school, and there they remained for 80 years until the building was sold to real-estate developers from Baton Rouge who turned it into an apartment hotel. Today, the hotel occupies three buildings and has recently undergone a $6-million renovation. Public spaces are lavishly decorated with gorgeous chandeliers, Oriental rugs, and marble flooring, and guest rooms have recently been completely redecorated using hunter green and maroon color schemes. A state of the art movie system is available in all guest rooms (it allows you to watch a video of your choosing any time of the day or night). Coffeemakers are supplied in all the rooms, and you can order room service through your TV. A voice-mail system is operational in all guest rooms. There are standard-size rooms, as well as bi-level suites that have a living room with a pull-out queen sofa. The main bedroom is located upstairs. Bathrooms are outfitted with Italian marble, telephones, and hairdryers.

Dining/Entertainment: Café Lafayette is the hotel's restaurant, and there is an elegant lobby bar that features a nightly cocktail hour with free hors d'oeuvres.

Services: Room service, same-day dry cleaning, business service, nightly shoe shine, daily morning newspaper.

Facilities: Pool.

CHATEAU MOTOR HOTEL, 1001 Chartres St., New Orleans, LA 70116. Tel. 504/524-9636. 45 rms. A/C TV TEL

$ Rates: $59 single; $79–$99 double. Seniors receive 10% discount. AE, CB, DC, MC, V. **Parking:** Free

The Château Motor Hotel, with its recently refurbished rooms, is one of the best buys in town. Each room is distinctively decorated. Some have king-size four-poster beds, while others feature painted iron beds, and all have armchairs and/or couches for relaxing after a long day on your feet. There are even a few bed/living-room combinations. Its outdoor swimming pool is surrounded by a flagstone-paved courtyard dotted with chaise longues. Continental breakfast and the morning newspaper are complimentary daily.

THE FRENCHMEN, 417 Frenchmen St., New Orleans, LA 70116. Tel. 504/948-2166, or toll free 800/831-1781. 25 rms. A/C TV TEL

$ Rates (including breakfast): $84–$135 single or double. AE, MC, V. **Parking:** Off-street parking $5 per night.

Situated in two 19th-century buildings, which were once grand New Orleans homes, the Frenchmen is a small inn with an excellent reputation. As you walk in, its elegant lobby sets the tone, and each of the rooms is individually decorated and furnished with beautiful antiques. Standard rooms have one double bed, some rooms have private balconies, and others have a loft bedroom with a sitting area. A pool and Jacuzzi are located in the inn's tropical courtyard. New Orleans's fine restaurants, shops, and nightlife are just steps away from this secluded hotel.

THE HISTORIC FRENCH MARKET INN, 501 Decatur St.,
New Orleans, LA. Tel. 504/561-5621, or toll free 800/827-
5621. Fax 504/566-0160. 76 rms. A/C TV TEL

$ Rates: High season $98–$148 single or double; low season $78–
$138 single or double. AE, MC, V. **Parking:** Available.

Originally built in 1853 for Baron Joseph Xavier de Pontalba, The
Historic French Market Inn has been restored to reflect its original
splendor (some of the original brickwork has been left exposed).
The guest rooms here have a European feel and offer views of the
river. You can get a room with one or two double beds, two
queens, a king, or twin beds. Suites feature full kitchenettes. A continental breakfast of pastries, croissants, fruits, juices, tea, and coffee
is served in the charming, rambling courtyard between 7 and 9am.
A pool and hot tub are available for guests use.

HOLIDAY INN—CHATEAU LEMOYNE, 301 Dauphine St.,
New Orleans, LA 70112. Tel. 504/581-1303, or toll free
800/HOLIDAY. 171 rms. A/C TV TEL

$ Rates: $150–$175 single or double. Extra person $15. AE, CB,
DISC, DC, MC, V. **Parking:** Valet parking $10 per night.

A friend urged me to inspect this Holiday Inn, saying that "It's not
like any Holiday Inn you've ever seen." She was right: Although it
is, in fact, a member of that chain, it is so distinctly French Quarter
that you'd never associate it with any of those highway stopover
hostelries. Housed in buildings over a century old, with arched col-
onnades and winding staircases, the place exudes character and
charm. Patios and converted slave-quarter suites add to the Old
New Orleans flavor, and bedrooms are furnished in a comfortable
traditional style. There's a restaurant on the premises for breakfast
only, otherwise it's room service until 10pm. There's also a bar.
Hotel facilities include a swimming pool. If you plan to do much
sightseeing or business outside the French Quarter, the Château Le
Moyne's location is ideal—only minutes away from the Central
Business District and the streetcar that takes you to the Garden District. And, of course, anything in the Quarter is within easy walking
distance.

HOTEL DE LA POSTE, 316 Chartres St., New Orleans, LA
70130. Tel. 504/581-1200, or toll free 800/448-4927. Fax 504/
523-2910. 100 rms. A/C TV TEL

$ Rates: $105 single; $125 double; $140–$175 junior suite. Children
under 12 free in parents' room. Package rates and senior-citizen discounts available. AE, CB, DC, MC, V. **Parking:** Indoor valet parking $10 per day.

Right in the heart of the Quarter, the Hotel De La Poste has spacious and comfortable rooms, most of which overlook either the
Grande Patio and pool or one of the more interesting French Quarter streets. The courtyard, just remodeled, has a magnificent staircase leading to a second-level outdoor patio. There is an outdoor
pool, and *USA Today* is delivered daily to your room. Services include valet laundry service, concierge tours, room service, a 24-hour
bellman, and babysitting. The hotel has also recently opened
Ristorante Bacco, run by sibling restaurateurs Cindy and Ralph
Brennan. Location, accommodations, and service are all legitimately
deluxe class.

HOTEL STE. HELENE, 508 Chartres St., New Orleans, LA 70130. Tel. 504/522-5014, or toll free 800/348-3888. 26 rms. A/C TV TEL

$ Rates (including continental breakfast): $145–$185 single or double. AE, DC, DISC, MC, V. **Parking:** A lot across the street offers parking for $14 daily.

Located right in the middle of the French Quarter, not far from Jackson Square, Hotel Ste. Hélène is an ideal place to stay during your visit to New Orleans. Here you can be a part of the action, but far enough away from Bourbon Street to escape the noise and mayhem that begins just before dusk.

When you enter the hotel's small but lovely lobby, you'll be greeted by a friendly staff who will direct you through the inner courtyard to your room. With a trickling fountain, greenery, and exposed brick walls, the inner courtyard is the center of the hotel. The rooms vary mainly in size and the type of bed they hold. Room 103, for example, is standard, small in size, with twin beds—ideal for a single traveler. It's also a good bet for families, as it connects to room 104, which is a bit bigger, with a queen-size bed, a couch, and a desk. The superior rooms have king-size beds and balconies. All are clean and comfortable.

The outer courtyard has a flagstone patio with an abundance of lush green plants as well as cast-iron tables and chairs at which you can have your breakfast every morning. There is also a small swimming pool.

HOTEL ST. PIERRE, 911 Burgundy St., New Orleans, LA 70116. Tel. 504/524-4401, or toll free 800/535-7785 or 800/225-4040. Fax 504/524-6800. 74 rms and suites. A/C TV TEL

$ Rates: $120 twin; $135 queen; $160 queen with balcony. Extra person $20. AE, CB, DC, DISC, MC, V. **Parking:** Free.

One of the newest French Quarter hotels, the Hotel St. Pierre is only two blocks from Bourbon Street. Guest rooms here are surrounded by beautiful courtyards, and because of the original floor plan of the old Creole home, room sizes vary greatly throughout the hotel. The Sammy Davis Jr. Suite has two double beds, floral bedspreads, and exposed brick. Some of the rooms are located in the old Creole slave quarters, and most of them have king-size beds. Half of the rooms have fireplaces and all have private bathrooms. A breakfast of pastries, coffee, tea, and juices is served each morning in the breakfast room. There are two pools available for guest use.

LE RICHELIEU MOTOR HOTEL, 1234 Chartres St., New Orleans, LA 70116. Tel. 504/529-2492, or toll free 800/535-9653 in the U.S. and Canada. Fax 504/524-8179. Telex 9102404914. 88 rms, 17 suites. A/C TV TEL

$ Rates: $85–$110 single; $95–$120 double; $150–$450 suite. Extra person or child $15. Ask about their French Quarter Explorer and Honeymoon packages. AE, CB, DISC, DC, JCB, MC, V. **Parking:** Free self-parking on premises.

The restored Le Richelieu Motor Hotel is housed in what was once a row mansion and then a macaroni factory. They're proudest here of their VIP suite, which has three bedrooms, a super kitchen, and even a steamroom, but the "ordinary" guest rooms I saw were all exceptionally nice and much less expensive. Most have brass ceiling fans, many have refrigerators and balconies, and all overlook either the French Quarter or the courtyard. Bathrooms are large and all are outfitted with hairdryers. There's a pool in the large courtyard, with lunch service poolside. The Terrace Café is the hotel's restaurant, and the Terrace Lounge is the bar. Le Richelieu is the only French Quarter motel with free self-parking on the premises—you keep your car keys, so there's no wait for an attendant to bring your car. Local calls also are free, which is a blessing—you won't feel as though your bank balance is dwindling every time you make a dinner reservation.

PLACE D'ARMES HOTEL, 625 St. Ann St., New Orleans, LA 70116. Tel. 504/524-4531, or toll free 800/366-2743. 79 rms. A/C TV TEL

$ Rates (including continental breakfast): $100–$140 single or double. AE, CB, DC, DISC, MC, V. **Parking:** 24-hour parking next door for $9.

The lovely Place d'Armes has one of the most magnificent courtyards in the Quarter, as well as a swimming pool. All rooms are homey and furnished in traditional style; many are wallpapered. Be sure that you ask, however, for a room with a window when you reserve—there are some interior rooms without windows (not all bad, but still, a window is better). The complimentary breakfast is served in a breakfast room, and the location, just off Jackson Square, makes sightseeing a breeze.

PRINCE CONTI HOTEL, 830 Conti St., New Orleans, LA 70112. Tel. 504/529-4172, or toll free 800/366-2743. 49 rms. A/C TV TEL

$ Rates: $120–$135 single or double. AE, DC, DISC, MC, V. **Parking:** Valet parking $9 per night.

The nicest things at the Prince Conti Hotel are the friendly, helpful staff and the comfortable guest rooms, many furnished with antiques and period reproductions. Prince Armand de Conti, the French nobleman who helped back Bienville's expedition to found New Orleans, would be proud of his namesake, with its small lobby beautifully furnished in the French château fashion and the delicate iron grillwork lining the outside of the second-story rooms. A continental breakfast is served in the hotel's breakfast room. The restaurant is open Tuesday through Saturday from 5pm.

INEXPENSIVE

HOTEL PROVINCIAL, 1024 Chartres St., New Orleans, LA 70116. Tel. 504/581-4995, or toll free 800/535-7922. Fax 504/581-1018. 100 rms. A/C TV TEL

$ Rates: $75–$155 double. Summer package rates are available. AE, CB, DC, MC, V. **Parking:** Free.

There are no fewer than five patios—and each is a jewel—at the family-owned Hôtel Provincial. The building dates from the 1830s, and rooms are high-ceilinged, each one decorated distinctively with imported French and authentic Creole antiques. My favorite holds a huge carved mahogany double bed with a high overhanging canopy topped by a carved tiara. Gaslights on the patios and the overall feeling of graciousness make this establishment a real delight, a tranquil refuge from the rigors of sightseeing or nighttime revelry.

The pleasant restaurant serves breakfast, lunch, and dinner at moderate prices.

HOTEL VILLA CONVENTO, 616 Ursulines St., New Orleans, LA 70116. Tel. 504/522-1793. Fax 504/524-1902. 24 rms. A/C TV TEL

$ Rates: $59–$85 single or double; $95 suite. AE, CB, DISC, DC, MC, V. **Parking:** $8 per night.

The Hotel Villa Convento, really a small inn, in many respects resembles a guesthouse because of the personal touch of its owner/operator, the Campo family. The building is a Creole town house with comfortably furnished rooms. Some open to the tropical patio, others open to the street; many have balconies. The lovely "loft" rooms are unique family quarters, each with a queen-size bed on the entry level and twin beds in the loft. A continental breakfast is served in the courtyard, and guests who prefer breakfast in bed may have a tray to take it to their rooms.

GUESTHOUSES

EXPENSIVE

GRENOBLE HOUSE, 329 Dauphine St., New Orleans, LA 70112. Tel. 504/522-1331. 17 suites. A/C TV TEL

$ Rates (including continental breakfast): $185–$265 one-bedroom suite; $235–$355 two-bedroom suite. Weekly rates available. AE, MC, V. **Parking:** There is no on-site parking; however, a convenient lot is around the corner.

The Grenoble House is truly an elegant home away from home. The suites are beautifully and uniquely furnished with a mix of fine antiques and the best of modern fittings—all have fully equipped kitchens. This is an old French Quarter town house built around a courtyard that features a swimming pool with heated whirlpool spa and a barbecue pit. Suites all have king- or queen-size beds (the more expensive have the king-size), and there's a sofa bed in each living room. A very special "extra" here is the personal, attentive service—they'll book theater tickets, restaurant tables, and sightseeing tours and even arrange for a gourmet dinner to be brought to your suite or for a private cocktail party on the patio if you want to entertain friends.

MODERATE

LAFITTE GUEST HOUSE, 1003 Bourbon St., New Orleans, LA 70116. Tel. 504/581-2678, or toll free 800/331-7971. 14 rms. A/C TV TEL

$ Rates (including continental breakfast): $85–$300 single or double. Extra person $22.20. AE, DC, MC, V. **Parking:** $5 per night.

If you think a Bourbon Street address automatically means a noisy, honky-tonk environment, think again. The Lafitte Guest House is located beyond the hullabaloo in a quiet, pleasant residential neighborhood yet is close enough for you to walk anywhere in the Quarter. The three-story brick building, with its typical New Orleans wrought-iron balconies on the second and third floors, was constructed in 1849 and has been completely restored. There are marble fireplaces, exposed brick walls, and 14-foot-high ceilings.

The guest rooms are furnished with a blend of modern reproduction pieces and beautiful Victorian antiques, and each room is individually sized and decorated. Room 5 is described as "New York loft" style apartment, and it overlooks the hotel's lush courtyard. Room 23 has an incredible cypress fireplace; and Room 40 with two queen-size beds and a pull-out couch, can accommodate up to six people and covers the entire top floor of the hotel. There also are a continental breakfast of fresh juice, croissants, jam, butter, and coffee or tea; wine and cheese in the parlor during the "happy hour"; and the daily newspaper—all are included in the room rate.

P. J. HOLBROOK'S OLDE VICTORIAN INN, 914 North Rampart St., New Orleans, LA 70116. Tel. 504/522-2446, or toll free 800/725-2446. 6 rms. A/C

$ Rates (including full breakfast): $100–$170 single or double. Senior-citizen discount. Weekly rates available. AE, MC, V. **Parking:** On-street parking only.

Near the corner of St. Philip Street, next door to the Landmark Hotel, is P. J. Holbrook's place. If you don't opt for P. J. to pick you up at the airport (she'll pick you up *and* drop you off in her white stretch limousine), you'll have to look carefully for the modest, handpainted sign out front, but once you find it, you won't forget it. Upon arrival you'll be treated to freshly baked goodies and a cup of hot tea or lemonade.

Walking into P. J.'s is like walking through time into an old Victorian home. The entire house is done in Victorian style—from the "gathering room" to the dining room. P. J. has gone to the ends of the earth, it seems, to find the perfect pieces, draperies, color schemes, and curios. Even the names of the guest rooms, such as Chantilly, Wedgwood, Chelsea, and Greenbriar, were thoughtfully chosen and each room is decorated just as its name suggests. Most of them have fireplaces, and Chantilly even has a balcony, with a cast-iron table and chairs and hanging plants, that looks out over North Rampart Street. Each room has its own bathroom, although there are a couple with baths across the hall. This doesn't make them any less appealing—it's just more like home.

P. J. herself is a most gracious host who will look after your every need and cook up a breakfast that could probably keep you going for an entire week. A typical breakfast here consists of some kind of bread (banana bread or cinnamon bread), fruit, eggs (all different ways), biscuits, some type of potato, juice, and coffee or hot tea. You can have this feast in the dining area just outside the kitchen; in your room; or in the courtyard, at one of the tables on which there are always white cloths and flowers floating in little bowls. It doesn't matter where you have it, it's going to be incredible, so don't skip it. In the early evening it's nice to sit in the gathering room talking with the other guests, planning your dinner, and perhaps making some new friends, as I did.

The house is nonsmoking, so if you're a smoker be prepared to light up outside; P. J. has a lovely dog, Olivia, who guards the house and charms the guests, so don't plan on bringing any pets. Be sure to sit and chat with P. J. and her staff, Melinda, Gloria, and Andie, because they've got some great New Orleans stories to tell. I could have listened to them all day and night without getting bored. If you ask nicely, they might even tell you about Uncle Leo.

INEXPENSIVE

FRENCH QUARTER MAISONNETTES, 1130 Chartres St., New Orleans, LA 70116. Tel. 504/524-9918. A/C TV

$ Rates: $55–$70 single or double; $65–$90 triple or quad. Extra person $10. No credit cards. Private parking $5 per night. **Closed:** July.

The Maisonnettes are in an 1825 mansion entered through a lovely iron gateway leading to the arched carriage drive and flagstone courtyard in the rear. A wrought-iron balcony rings the second story, overlooking that courtyard and its three-tiered, 17th-century French cast-iron fountain, tropical plants, and vines. Guest units on the ground floor open through wide French doors onto the courtyard or carriage drive, and second-floor rooms overlook the courtyard. All have modern, comfortable furnishings, and Jesse, the butler (who is a delightful part of your stay here), keeps them clean (he's also always on hand to lend cheerful assistance with luggage). Each has a private bath and individually controlled air conditioning and heat, and the morning newspaper is delivered to your door each day.

The hotel is well-located—across the street is the historic Beauregard House; next door is the Ursuline Convent, built in 1734 and said to be the oldest building in the Mississippi Valley; and just a few blocks away from it is the old French Market, where you will likely become accustomed to visiting at the beginning or ending of the day for coffee and beignets. Mrs. Junius Underwood furnishes a privately printed brochure of tips on dining, sightseeing, shopping, and almost anything else to make your visit more entertaining and comfortable, all gleaned from her intimate, longtime association with New Orleans. Children over 12 are welcome, as are "well-behaved" pets.

NEW ORLEANS GUEST HOUSE, 1118 Ursulines St., New Orleans, LA 70116. Tel. 504/566-1177. 14 rms A/C TV

$ Rates (including continental breakfast): $69 single; $79 queen; $89 king. Extra person $15. AE, MC, V. **Parking:** Free in a private off-street lot.

Located just on the fringe of the French Quarter, across North Rampart Street, the New Orleans Guest House is impossible to miss—the exterior is painted hot pink. Ray Cronk and Alvin Payne have been running this renovated Creole cottage, dating from 1848, for 10 years now.

There are rooms in the main house and some in what used to be the old slave quarters. Each is decorated with period furniture and has a unique color scheme. If bright colors scare you, don't worry; the colors inside the guesthouse aren't quite so eye-catching as they are outside. You're sure to find all the guest rooms absolutely restful and tastefully done. Those in the slave quarters are a little smaller than the ones in the main house, but I actually prefer the smaller ones because they all open onto the lush New Orleans–style courtyard. To get to the slave quarter rooms you walk through the covered patio, then out into the sunlight and a veritable tropical garden where you'll find a banana tree, more green plants than I could count, and some intricately carved old fountains that Ray and Alvin have restored to working order. There is a new covered breakfast room with an outdoor patio where you'll be served croissants, fruit, and coffee, tea, or hot chocolate at cozy white-clothed tables. Also located in the courtyard is a beer machine, soda machine, and an ice maker.

You can't beat this place. I think that, until now, it's been one of the best-kept secrets in New Orleans.

623 URSULINES, 623 Ursulines St., New Orleans, LA 70116. Tel. 504/529-5489. 7 suites. A/C TV
$ Rates: $65–$85 single or double. No credit cards. **Parking:** $7 per night.

Owner Don Heil maintains seven suites at 623 Ursulines. Though the four slave-quarter suites are original to the house all are thoroughly modern as far as comfort goes. Each has a living room, bedroom, and private bath and opens onto a courtyard that holds azaleas, towering crape myrtle trees, and magnolias. Three suites of comparable size are in the main house. A decided plus here is the warm hospitality—Don knows New Orleans intimately and is a gold mine of tips on how to make your stay more fun. Don doesn't give his guesthouse a name but simply uses the street number. If you plan to visit New Orleans and are a guesthouse devotee, I heartily recommend that you call in advance for reservations—this is a very popular spot.

SUN AND THE MOON BED AND BREAKFAST, 1037 N. Rampart St., New Orleans, LA 70116. Tel. 504/529-4652. 2 rms A/C TV
$ Rates: $75 single or double. No credit cards. **Parking:** Available.

Kelly and Taina Mechling are the proprietors of this cozy little bed-and-breakfast, whose Spanish name is El Sol y la Luna. They have charmingly furnished and decorated two rooms in Southwest style. Kelly is the son of Keith and Claudine Mechling, who run Mechling's Guest House (see below) not far away on Esplanade Avenue.

Both of the recently renovated rooms have good-sized, comfortable sleeping and sitting areas. The bathrooms are clean and fully equipped. Here you have the added extra of a minirefrigerator in your room, so you can store goodies for midnight snacking. There also are balconies overlooking the courtyard (which features a large fruit-bearing banana tree) between the main house and the guest quarters. Each guest room has a separate entrance, which creates a nice sense of privacy. Continental breakfast can be served in your room or on the deck. Maid service is daily.

Kelly and Taina also run Trade Folk Art Import Export (see Chapter 9 for more details).

GUESTHOUSES JUST OUTSIDE THE FRENCH QUARTER
VERY EXPENSIVE

MELROSE MANSION, 937 Esplanade Ave., New Orleans, LA 70116. Tel. 504/944-2255. Fax 504/945-1794. 8 rms, A/C MINIBAR TV TEL
$ Rates: $215–$275 single or double; $325–$450 suite. AE, MC, V. **Parking:** Free.

✪ If you choose to stay at the Melrose Mansion, you will be met at the airport by a chauffeured stretch limousine, which will whisk you to this guesthouse on the outer limit of the French Quarter—a service that will convince you even before you get there that the Melrose is one of the most splendid guesthouses in the city. Rosemary and Melvin Jones have lovingly restored this three-story 1884 Victorian mansion, with its square turret set at a jaunty angle in one corner, to combine the utmost in luxury with the warm, personal hospitality of a private home. Enormous bath towels, fine soaps, and rooms with names—such as "Miss Kitty's Room"—rather than numbers all contribute to the hospitality. Its architectural style is hard to pin down—in Rosemary's words, it is "a bit of Victorian Gothic, Victorian Italianate, along with a suggestion of the baroque and the classic, as seen in the upper-level Corinthian capitals." The old house has a rich and varied history (ask about Miss Kitty—she was an ex-stripper with a seagoing lover—who lived out her last years here).

Guest rooms are furnished with marvelous antiques, and the crème de la crème has to be the Donecio Suite, with a magnificent four-poster bed, a marble bathroom complete with Jacuzzi and separate dressing room, and a wide balcony on which breakfast often is served. (Lady Bird Johnson was its first tenant and gave it a rave review.) The mansion's elegant drawing room is the focal point for gatherings for afternoon tea or wine-and-cheese trays. Breakfast comes with silver coffee service, beautiful china and crystal, fresh-baked muffins, and fresh fruit and can be served in your room, on the balcony, or at poolside. The Parc Henry Suite, atop the original carriage house and overlooking the pool, sleeps three or four. But the best feature of this place may well be its staff. Rosemary and Melvin are always on hand; there is a wonderfully hospitable butler; and a staff member is always available during the day to make sure that you've got everything you could possibly need. Book as far in advance as possible.

EXPENSIVE

THE HOUSE ON BAYOU ROAD, 2275 Bayou Rd., New Orleans, LA 70119. Tel. 504/949-7711. 4 rms, 2 cottages. A/C

$ Rates: High season $140 single or double; $230 two-bedroom suite with shared bath; $200 cottage suite; $270 private cottage. Low season $105 single or double; $200 two-bedroom suite with shared bath; $170 cottage suite; $220 private cottage. MC, V. **Parking:** Free off-street parking is available.

If you want to stay in a rural plantation setting, but still want to be near the French Quarter, The House on Bayou Road might be just the place for you. Located just off Esplanade Avenue, this intimate Creole plantation home, built in the late 1700s for a colonial Spanish diplomat, has been lovingly restored by owner Cynthia Reeves. As you enter the antique-filled double parlor you'll feel like you're stepping back in time, and every ounce of stress will flow out of your body. Each of the rooms is named for a bayou and is individually decorated. Regardless of their color schemes, all the rooms have a light, airy quality, and Cynthia has paid extraordinary attention to every possible detail. The Bayou St. John Room (the library) holds a queen, four-poster rice bed, has a working fireplace, and is decorated with a masculine color scheme. Bayou Delacroix also has a queen-size four-poster rice bed, but it is decorated with floral prints and has a wonderfully large bath tub. Bayou Cocodrie holds a brass-and-iron half-canopy bed with mosquito netting and can be joined with the Bayou Barataria Room, which has a queen-size pencil-post four-poster bed. The large cottage, which is completely separate from the main house, has three separate rooms, which can be rented separately, or as a whole. It's perfect for a large family. The small Creole cottage, located next door to the large cottage, is a great romantic getaway spot for couples. It has a queen-sized four-poster bed, a queen sofa sleeper, Jacuzzi tub, wet bar, and a porch with a swing and rocking chairs. The grounds are beautifully manicured and you can either sit outside on the patio or in the screened-in porch. At press time plans were underway for a swimming pool. In the morning guests are treated to a full breakfast, and during the day and in the evening there is access to a minirefrigerator filled with beverages. If you choose to stay at The House on Bayou Road you're guaranteed a relaxing, enjoyable vacation that you won't soon forget.

MODERATE

MECHLING'S GUEST HOUSE, 2023 Esplanade Ave., New Orleans, LA 70116. Tel. 504/943-4131. 4 rms. A/C

$ Rates (including full breakfast): $95–$155 single or double. AE, MC, V. **Parking:** Free off-street parking.

Keith and Claudine Mechling (pronounced "Mek-ling") have been carefully restoring this 1860s mansion for a few years now. The guest rooms are on the first floor of the house and retain as many of the original fixtures, windows, and woodwork as could be salvaged. For instance, Claudine and Keith searched through the debris and painstakingly pieced the leaded-glass window in the front door back together. They found that they were missing only one piece and were able to have that piece replicated. They cleaned the original fireplace mantles, some of which are black onyx marble and are quite stunning. They've still got their work cut out for them; the second floor is next on their list, but there's no doubt they'll do a wonderful job and make their guests feel as much at home upstairs as they do downstairs.

The rooms are quite large, and most have fireplaces. The front bedroom, tastefully done in peach, is especially unique because the bathroom is actually part of the room, just as it was in the original house, and it is curtained off. There are a claw-foot bathtub and a tile floor. The rest of the room is carpeted. Another interesting feature of the room is the horsehair mattress that has been in Claudine's family for quite some time. Don't worry about getting poked during the night because Claudine has had the mattress specially wrapped to keep this from happening. If you've never slept on a horsehair mattress before, you should experience it (unless you have a bad back) because it's incredibly soft. The other rooms are equally unique and beautifully decorated. The newest room is the largest and is great for a small family.

Claudine and/or Keith are always on the premises and will give you sightseeing advice as you have your breakfast, or you can sit and talk with them about your day in the evening. You'll feel just as though you were at home. Ask them to point out the old slave quarters in the back and the slave jail next to an enormous old oak tree.

If you choose to stay with the Mechlings you'll be within walking distance of the French Quarter and City Park, but don't walk alone at night—keep the number for United Cab handy. Claudine and Keith are wonderful hosts, and I'd recommend staying with them to just about anyone.

APARTMENTS

BOURGOYNE GUEST HOUSE, 839 Bourbon St., New Orleans, LA 70116. Tel. 504/525-3983 or 504/524-3621. 5 apartments. A/C TEL

$ Rates: Studio, $57 single; $60 double. The Blue Suite, $67 single; $80 double; $95 triple; $110 quad. The Green Suite, $79 single; $90 double; $115 triple; $130 quad. No credit cards. **Parking:** Pay parking nearby.

If you're on a budget, the Bourgoyne is a good place to set up home during your stay in New Orleans.

Behind the front gate and through the stone carriageway is a quaint courtyard. Each studio room has a fully equipped kitchenette, a bathroom, and a double bed. The studios (and bathrooms) are small and a bit outdated, but functional. The larger apartments, or suites, have kitchens, sitting areas, TVs, and room to sleep three or four. If you're staying in the Green Suite, you'll climb the winding staircase to the third floor—pack lightly, or you'll have to make a couple of trips—and enter into the spacious sitting and dining area. The apartment is sparsely furnished with antiques and brass light fixtures, and the hardwood floor is covered with a Persian rug. The focal point of the Green Suite is the bed in the main bedroom. It is covered with a green velvet spread and has an enormous, partially draped mirror hanging on the wall above it. The second bedroom is a bit more modest—"a nook of country charm." Also, a balcony overlooks Bourbon Street. Don't worry about the noise level in the larger apartments as the guesthouse is far enough up Bourbon Street to be unaffected by the sounds of an average day or night. However, if you're planning to stay in the studio rooms and you're a light sleeper you'll do well to find a room elsewhere.

NAPOLEON HOUSE, 500 Chartres St., New Orleans, LA 70130. Tel. 504/524-9752. 1 apartment A/C TV TEL

$ Rates: $125–$250. AE, DISC, MC, V. **Parking:** Not available.

If you'd like to experience French Quarter living as a temporary "local," I can't think of a better place to do it than in the one apartment that Sal Impastato—owner of the historic Napoleon House—has made available. The three-room upstairs flat, with two balconies, was the longtime residence of his uncle, and its furnishings are what might be called "New Orleans homey"—several antique pieces intermingle happily with rather well-worn furnishings of indeterminate age but definite comfort. The apartment is right in the heart of the Quarter, with one of the city's best pubs and light-meal restaurants downstairs. The only danger is that you might find yourself joining the throngs of visitors who have come to New Orleans and never gone back home.

2. OUTSIDE THE FRENCH QUARTER

There are many considerations that could lead you to seek accommodations outside the French Quarter, and you will find a wide price range of hotels and motels in almost any section, whether you wish to be near the universities, in the Central Business District, or on the outskirts of town. There also are several superior guesthouses outside the Quarter.

One thing I should add: With the 1984 Louisiana World Exposition came a flood of new hotels outside the French Quarter. In fact, the bulk of the city's hotel rooms are now outside the French Quarter. To their credit, most of the new establishments have worked to project a distinct New Orleans flavor. Even with all these additional rooms, however, there will be times when booking could be a problem—so the sooner you reserve, the better.

For those of you who prefer the predictability of a chain hotel, you'll be interested to know that there's a Marriott at 555 Canal St. (tel. 504/581-1000, or toll free 800/228-9290) and a Hyatt at 500 Poydras Plaza (tel. 504/561-1234). Also, at press time, plans were underway for the construction of several new hotels, including a Ritz-Carlton (at press time there is no phone number available) and a Comfort Suites Hotel at 346 Baronne St. (tel. 504/523-4401, or toll free 800/221-2222).

VERY EXPENSIVE

FAIRMONT HOTEL, at University Place, 123 Baronne St., New Orleans, LA 70140. Tel. 504/529-7111, or toll free 800/527-4727. 660 rms, 72 suites. A/C TV TEL

$ Rates: $160–$215 single or double. Extra person $25. AE, DISC, DC, MC, V. **Parking:** $10 per day.

New Orleanians still sometimes think of it as the Roosevelt, and today's Fairmont Hotel upholds the tradition of elegance left by its predecessor. There's the feel of luxury from the moment you enter the lobby, with its deep carpeting, dark-red velvet chairs and sofas, magnificent chandeliers, and impressive oil paintings. The rooms are spacious, with marvelous high ceilings and such extras as an electric shoe buffer. Beds are luxuriously outfitted with down pillows and comforters, and bathroom amenities are custom made for the hotel. In short, the Fairmont is a "grand hotel" in the old manner that offers midtown convenience as a bonus.

Dining/Entertainment: For many years, the sophisticated Blue Room presented headliner entertainers—perhaps you remember those old radio broadcasts "from the Blue Room of the Hotel Roosevelt in downtown New Orleans." I'm happy to report that although it was redecorated in recent years, that lovely blue-and-gold decor and French period furnishings have changed very little since the days of my visits years ago. These days, the Blue Room is used for private functions only, except for Sunday, when there's a sumptuous brunch (see Chapter 6). An addition is Bailey's, a casual 24-hour Irish bar that serves a full menu and drinks. For fine dining, there's the romantic Sazerac Restaurant. The rooftop offers a cozy bar that serves beverages and sandwiches.

Services: 24-hour room service, evening maid service.

Facilities: Rooftop health club, pool, tennis courts, beauty shop.

HOTEL INTER-CONTINENTAL, 444 St. Charles Ave., New Orleans, LA 70130. Tel. 504/525-5566, or toll free 800/327-0200. 480 rms, 32 suites. A/C MINIBAR TV TEL

$ Rates: $190–$220 single; $210–$240 double; $350–$1,700 suite. AE, CB, DC, DISC, MC, V. **Parking:** Valet parking $12 per day.

The Hotel Inter-Continental rises in red granite splendor within walking distance of Canal Street shops and the Central Business District. Its luxurious rooms and suites feature writing desks, separate conversation/dressing areas, minirefrigerators and bars, built-in hairdryers, telephones and TVs in the bathrooms, and even safes. The furnishings in both the guest rooms and the public areas are a nice blend of classic and contemporary styling.

The newly renovated Governor's Floor (the 14th) is reminiscent of Louisiana's romantic past, and the rooms feature period antiques, reproductions, artifacts, and decorations that represent the six heads of state for whom the suites are named. All the rooms on this floor are decorated individually, although color schemes are in blues and cream. The floor has a butler service and a VIP lounge, which entitles guests to a complimentary continental breakfast and evening cocktails. The 24-hour lounge is stocked with popular periodicals and magazines.

Dining/Entertainment: The large marble lobby holds a lounge that serves drinks. Gourmet meals are served in the Veranda Restaurant (see Chapter 6 for a full listing), and Pete's Pub has rich paneling and specially commissioned murals of Mardi Gras scenes.

Services: 24-hour room service, laundry and valet service, shoe-shine service.

Facilities: Health club and pool, barber shop and beauty salon, gift shop, business center.

LE MERIDIEN HOTEL, 614 Canal St., New Orleans, LA 70130. Tel. 504/525-6500. 494 rms. A/C MINIBAR TV TEL

$ Rates: $180–$220 single; $200–$240 double. AE, MC, V. **Parking:** Valet parking $12 per night.

The Le Meridien Hotel is one of the city's most dramatic hotels, with lots of marble and a spectacular indoor waterfall. All rooms have multiple-line telephones and a desk and sitting area. Accommodations here are either king- or twin-bedded and are decorated in pleasant coral, peach, and moss green tones.

Dining/Entertainment: La Gauloise is the hotel's Parisian-style bistro. It's open daily from 6:30am to 10pm and serves continuously. The Louis Armstrong Foundation Jazz Club is the hotel's jazz lobby bar and it features entertainment Monday through Saturday.

Services: 24-hour concierge, 24-hour room service, laundry service, babysitting service, complimentary shoe shine, nightly turndown, business center.

Facilities: Health club, sauna, heated outdoor pool, massage and aerobics, beauty salon, gift shop, jewelry store, art gallery.

PONTCHARTRAIN HOTEL, 2031 St. Charles Ave., New Orleans, LA 70140. Tel. 504/524-0581, or toll free 800/777-1700. Fax 504/529-1165. 102 rms. A/C TV TEL

$ Rates: $150–$610 based on single occupancy. Extra person $25. Seasonal packages available. AE, CB, DISC, DC, MC, V. **Parking:** $9 per night.

"Elegant" is the word for the Pontchartrain Hotel, named in honor of Comte de Pontchartrain from the court of Louis XVI and located in the Garden District. The landmark hotel (erected in 1927) is a grand structure built in a Moorish architectural style, and the rooms are beautifully furnished. The service will make you feel like a pampered favorite within minutes of your arrival. The staff of the Pontchartrain is, in fact, accustomed to treating guests well because the hotel is a favorite of dignitaries, celebrities, and even royalty. Everything in this New Orleans institution is in the continental tradition at its finest. Extras include a "Staying with Safety" package for senior citizens (with doorman and elevator operator on duty around the clock).

The hotel and its café are settings for part of New Orleans author Anne Rice's novel *The Witching Hour.*

Dining/Entertainment: The gourmet cuisine of the Caribbean Room (see Chapter 6) is internationally known. Special low-salt, low-cholesterol menus are available on request. Have breakfast in Café Pontchartrain and stop for a drink in the Bayou Bar.

Services: 24-hour room service, complimentary shoe shine, complimentary newspaper, nightly turn-down service.

WINDSOR COURT, 300 Gravier St., New Orleans, LA 70140. Tel. 504/523-6000, or toll free 800/262-2662. Fax 504/596-4513. 324 rms and suites. A/C TV TEL

$ Rates (single or double occupancy): $225–$275 standard guest room; $300–$350 junior suite; $375–$500 full suite; $575–$850 two-bedroom suite. Children under 16 free in parents' room. AE, CB, DC, MC, V. **Parking:** Valet parking $15 per night.

Centrally located, the high-rise Windsor Court is one of the city's loveliest hotels. Two nice touches are the English tea served in a pretty lobby lounge and two corridors that are minigalleries displaying works of art. Italian marble and antique furnishings distinguish the two lobbies.

Each suite features its own individual decor, large bay windows looking out over the river or the city, a private foyer, a large living room, a bedroom entered through French doors, a marble bath, separate his-and-her dressing rooms, and a "petite kitchen." They, as well as the standard guest rooms, are exceptionally spacious and beautifully furnished. This one is truly a standout.

Dining/Entertainment: The Polo Club Lounge is a clubby sort of gathering place; the Grill Room Restaurant serves breakfast, brunch, lunch, and dinner; Le Salon, the lobby lounge, serves light lunch, afternoon tea, cocktails, and sweets and has chamber music and piano music during the day and evening.

Services: 24-hour room service, full concierge service.

Facilities: Among the guest facilities are a health club sporting a resort-size pool, sauna, and steamroom. Numerous conveniences are available for business travelers, who might want to conduct conferences in the privacy of their own suites or in the specially planned meeting spaces.

EXPENSIVE

HOLIDAY INN CROWNE PLAZA, 300 Poydras St., New Orleans, LA 70130. Tel. 504/525-9444. 441 rms. A/C TV TEL

$ Rates: $175 single; $190 double. AE, CB, DC, DISC, MC, V. **Parking:** Valet parking $11 per night; self-parking $7.50.

The Holiday Inn Crowne Plaza has regular guest units, suites, an Executive Floor, and a restaurant and lounge. It's an attractive hotel that includes among its many amenities a pool with poolside beverage service, an exercise room, and free in-room movies. Suites and the 22 rooms on the luxury-level Executive Floor come with a complimentary continental breakfast and refreshments, refrigerators, and a private cocktail lounge.

NEW ORLEANS HILTON RIVERSIDE & TOWERS HOTEL, 2 Poydras St., New Orleans, LA 70140. Tel. 504/561-0500, or toll free 800/445-8667. Fax 504/568-1721. Telex 6821214. 1,602 rms. A/C MINIBAR TV TEL

$ Rates: $175–$295 double; $580–$1,870 suite. Special packages available. AE, CB, DISC, DC, JCB, MC, V. **Parking:** $11 for 24 hours.

The New Orleans Hilton Riverside & Towers Hotel, at the Mississippi River, has perhaps more than any other new hotel integrated itself successfully into the lifestyle of the city. Located in what some are calling the "River Quarter," the Hilton sits right at the riverfront, adjacent to the World Trade Center of New Orleans, the Rivergate Convention Center, and the New Orleans Convention Center, yet it somehow manages to avoid the sterile impersonality projected by so many large hotels. Maybe it has to do with a decor that makes use of warm colors such as tea rose and emerald green; Italian oak and mahogany paneling; travertine marble; and deep-pile, handwoven carpeting. The 90-foot, 9-story, multilevel atrium creates a feeling of space, but it is so well designed that there is none of that rattle-around boxiness that always makes me a little nervous. Guest rooms are, of course, the primary concern of travelers, and those at the New Orleans Hilton are spacious. Most have fabulous views of the river or the city; all are furnished in a country French manner, using muted colors and draperies keyed to the etched toile of the wallcoverings. Light-softening sheer-glass curtains let you take full advantage of those gorgeous views. The epitome of luxury is to be found on the 25th, 26th, and 27th tower floors, which hold 132 guest rooms, including 12 elegant suites. A Towers Concierge is there to help you, and a private lounge and an honor bar with TV and comfortable furniture completes the Towers picture. The third part of the Hilton complex is its 456-room, low-rise Riverside complex perched on the edge of the Mississippi. There are six luxurious suites and eight courtyards with fountains and lush tropical foliage, opening to the river.

Dining/Entertainment: The atrium is broken up into attractive centers, such as the English Bar, Le Café Bromeliad, and the French Garden Bar. There are in fact seven restaurants and lounges within the complex. You will know past doubt that the Hilton has won New Orleans's approval when you learn that Pete Fountain moved his jazz club from the Quarter to a third-floor replica here. On the 29th floor, with spectacular views of river and city, is Horizons, a nightclub where New Orleans jazz reigns supreme.

Services: 24-hour room service, concierge service, laundry/valet/pressing service, airport transportation, shoe-shine service.

Facilities: Guests are eligible for membership in the hotel's Rivercenter Racquet and Health Club, which includes outdoor and indoor tennis courts, squash and racquetball courts, a rooftop jogging track, aerobics classes, tanning beds, massage, a hair salon, and a golf studio.

MODERATE

AVENUE PLAZA HOTEL, 2111 St. Charles Ave., New Orleans, LA 70130. Tel. 504/566-1212. 240 rms. A/C MINIBAR TV TEL

$ Rates: $119–$139 double. AE, CB, DC, MC, V. **Parking:** $9 per day.

The gracious mahogany-paneled drawing room (complete with comfortable sofas and chairs and a large fireplace) of the Avenue Plaza Hotel sets the tone at this small hotel, which was once an apartment building. All rooms are nicely furnished, each with a coffeemaker and refrigerator. There are excellent health-club facilities; a courtyard swimming pool; a rooftop sundeck; and a lovely, window-lined dining room overlooking St. Charles Avenue.

THE COLUMNS, 3811 St. Charles Ave., New Orleans, LA 70115. Tel. 504/899-9308. 19 rms (9 with bath). A/C TEL

$ Rates (including continental breakfast): $70–$165 single or double. AE, MC, V. **Parking:** Available on the street.

The Columns, built in 1883 by Simon Hernsheim, a wealthy tobacco merchant, is one of the greatest examples of a late 19th-century Louisiana residence. You'll be nothing short of impressed by the grand, columned entrance, and once inside you'll feel as though you've stepped back in time. Its architectural style is Italianate, or pre-Queen Anne, and most of the original interior features still exist. The wide mahogany staircase is truly awesome, as is the stained-glass, domed skylight above it.

All the rooms and furnishings are different—some rooms have wood sleigh beds, while others have double beds with intricately carved head- and footboards. Many of the rooms have couches and chairs, while some are much too small to accommodate such furnishings. The rooms with baths have clawfoot tubs, and the rooms without baths come equipped with sinks.

The staff is very friendly; however, it looks as if the furnishings are becoming a bit run down—the hotel's got a lot more charm and character than elegance these days, but it's worth looking into because of the reasonable rates and the clean and comfortable rooms. The Columns, the setting of Louis Malle's film *Pretty Baby,* is listed in the National Register of Historic Places. The hotel's restaurant, Albertine's Tea Room, is open for lunch, dinner, and Sunday brunch. For cocktails, the Victorian lounge is available in the evening.

HOLIDAY INN DOWNTOWN—SUPERDOME, 330 Loyola Ave., New Orleans, LA 70112. Tel. 504/581-1600. Fax 504/586-0833. 297 rms. A/C TV TEL

$ Rates: $90–$205 single or double; $350 suite. Extra person $15. Children 17 and under free in parents' room. AE, CB, DC, DISC, JCB, MC, V. **Parking:** On-site parking $10 per night.

The 17-story Holiday Inn Downtown—Superdome is centrally located, with easy access to New Orleans's business and financial centers, as well as the Louisiana Superdome and the French Quarter. Each recently renovated room has a balcony and city view. Guest rooms, large enough to allow for a "sitting-room" area, are furnished with modern comfortable fittings. The dining room boasts some of the renowned Audubon prints, the hotel lounge is open until 10pm nightly, and there are a rooftop pool and Jacuzzi.

LE PAVILLON HOTEL, 833 Poydras St., New Orleans, LA 70140. Tel. 504/581-3111, or toll free 800/535-9095. Fax 504/522-5543. Telex 161708NLN. 220 rms, 7 suites. A/C TV TEL

$ Rates: $99 single or double; $295–$495 suite. AE. **Parking:** Available.

Established in 1907, the first hotel in New Orleans to have elevators, Le Pavillon truly is, as they bill it, "the belle of New Orleans." The lobby is stunning, with high ceilings, grand columns, plush furnishings, Oriental rugs, detailed woodwork, and 11 crystal chandeliers imported from Czechoslovakia. Each hall features massive Louisiana antiques and has 14 original paintings from the hotel's fine-arts collection.

The standard rooms are similar in terms of furnishings, but the rooms may differ in size just by virtue of the hotel's original floor plan, which for the most part has remained intact. The "Bay Rooms" are standard, with two double beds and bay-window treatments, one of the many special features of the old hotel.

The Pavillon also has some fine suites for very reasonable rates. If you like art deco, you're sure to love the two-bedroom "Art Deco" suite. Another of the two-bedroom suites is the marvelous "Antique Suite." All the furnishings are antiques, and the collection includes pieces by Mallard, C. Lee (who, as a slave, studied under Mallard), Mitchell Rammelsberg, Belter, Badouine, and Marcotte. The beds have feather mattresses and elaborate canopies. If you can afford it and want a real taste of old New Orleans, ask about this one—you won't be disappointed.

The thing that really sold me on Le Pavillon is the fact that every evening in the lobby, guests are treated to complimentary peanut-butter-and-jelly sandwiches and a glass of milk. You really can't beat this place—affordable rates, more than pleasant surroundings, a central location, and PB&J every night!

Dining/Entertainment: The Gold Room, the hotel's large dining room, is open for breakfast, lunch, and dinner every day. A beautiful room, it has a working fireplace, which makes for a cozy atmosphere. The hotel lounge is the Gallery, which serves complimentary hors d'oeuvres Monday to Friday from 4 to 7pm.

Services: 24-hour room service, complimentary shoe shine, full concierge service.

Facilities: Heated rooftop pool.

PRYTANIA PARK HOTEL, 1519 Terpsichore St., New Orleans, LA 70130. Tel. 504/524-0427, or toll free 800/862-1984. Fax 504/522-2977. 62 rms. A/C MINIBAR TV TEL

$ **Rates** (including continental breakfast): $99 single; $109 double; $119 suite. Extra person $10. Children under 12 free. Special packages available. AE, CB, DC, MC, V. **Parking:** Free.

It's hard to know whether to label the Prytania Park Hotel a hotel or a guesthouse. Centrally located in the historic Garden District, owned and enthusiastically operated by Mr. and Mrs. Alvin Halpern, the small hotel has a unique combination of atmospheres. The Victorian Building, which dates from 1834, is beautifully restored and furnished in period hand-carved English pine. The Victorian town-house rooms also have high ceilings and exposed brick walls. The 49 streamlined rooms in the modern addition retain the New Orleans architectural ambience but have more contemporary furnishings than the 13 rooms in the original part of the hotel; they open onto landscaped courtyards and feature the conveniences of microwave ovens and refrigerators. The St. Charles Avenue streetcar line is half a block away, providing quick and easy access to the French Quarter (15 blocks away) and all the major attractions.

Dining out is a pleasure because the hotel is situated in the heart of the uptown restaurant district; cuisine and prices here vary widely enough to fit all kinds of gastronomic yearnings and budgets. You might want to try Gloria's Café, located in the Home Furnishings Store across the street from the hotel. It is also owned by the proprietors of the Prytania Park Hotel. With a choice of contemporary or old-world setting and a friendly, well-trained staff, the Prytania Park is a charming hotel run with the same personal attention as a guesthouse.

INEXPENSIVE

HOTEL LA SALLE, 1113 Canal St., New Orleans, LA 70112. Tel. 504/523-5831, or toll free 800/521-9450 in the U.S. Fax 504/525-2531. Telex 8109516388. 57 rms (42 with bath). A/C TV TEL

$ **Rates:** $39 single without bath, $54 single with bath; $45 double without bath, $64 double with bath. Children under 12 free in parents' room. AE, DC, DISC, JCB, MC, V. **Parking:** Free.

You'll find convenience and comfort at budget prices only half a block outside the French Quarter at the Hotel La Salle. The no-frills rooms are plainly furnished, clean, and comfortable and come with or without private bath. There's an old-fashioned air to the small lobby with its high ceilings, overhead fans, carved Austrian wall clock, and old-time wooden reception desk. Free coffee is always available in the lobby, and a continental breakfast can be served in your room for a small additional charge. Roland and Pat Bahan, who own and operate the La Salle, have been known to arrange such extras as practice rooms for out-of-town musicians who come to audition for the New Orleans Symphony. This is a favorite with European visitors who appreciate bathroom-down-the-hall savings as well as with jazz musicians just arriving in the city.

QUALITY INN MIDTOWN, 3900 Tulane Ave., New Orleans, LA 70119. Tel. 504/486-5541, or toll free 800/827-5541. Fax 504/488-7440. 102 rms. A/C TV TEL

$ Rates: $69–$230 single or double; $180–$230 suite. Extra person $10. Children under 18 free in parents' room. Special packages available. AE, DC, DISC, MC, V. **Parking:** Free.

The Quality Inn Midtown is located only about 5 minutes from the Central Business District. All the rooms have balconies; many face the courtyard and swimming pool, are spacious, and have double beds. Facilities at the Quality Inn include a hot tub, a restaurant, and a lounge.

ST. CHARLES INN, 3636 St. Charles Ave., New Orleans, LA 70115. Tel. 504/899-8888, or toll free 800/489-9908. Fax 504/899-8892. 40 rms. A/C TV TEL

$ Rates (including continental breakfast): $75 single; $85 double. AE, DISC, DC, MC, V. **Parking:** $3 indoor and outdoor.

The St. Charles Inn is only 5 minutes away from Tulane and Loyola Universities and 10 minutes from the French Quarter or Louisiana Superdome via the trolley. Each room has either two double beds or a king-size bed. Facilities here include a lounge and a restaurant, and extras include a continental breakfast served in your room and the morning newspaper.

A GUESTHOUSE

If you're in New Orleans to visit Tulane University, Loyola University, or Newcomb College, you'll want to know about this conveniently located guesthouse.

PARKVIEW GUEST HOUSE, 7004 St. Charles Ave., New Orleans, LA 70118. Tel. 504/861-7564. 23 rms (14 with bath). A/C TEL

$ Rates (including continental breakfast): $60–$65 single without bath, $65–$75 single with bath; $70–$75 double without bath, $75–$85 double with bath. Extra person $10. AE, MC, V. **Parking:** On-street parking.

On the far edge of Audubon Park is the Parkview Guest House, a rambling Victorian structure built in 1884 as a hotel for the Cotton Exposition. It has been in the National Register of Historic Places since 1981. Simply entering the building is like a trip to another era: A front door that sparkles with etched-glass panels admits you to the wide central hall with its gleaming crystal chandeliers. A lovely stained-glass window is the focal point of the large lounge, with its comfortable sofas and chairs, and all the rooms are furnished in antiques. I immediately fell in love with the room on the first floor just to the right of the front door—it has floor-length windows and a carved walnut bed and dresser that strongly appealed to the romantic in my soul. All the rooms, however, reflect an old-fashioned comfort that's hard to resist. Some have balconies. There's a large dining room, with windows overlooking the park, where a continental breakfast is served daily—a pleasant way to start the day. All guests have the use of a refrigerator and ice machine anytime. Three rooms have a bath connecting with another room, and there are individually controlled heat and air conditioning in all.

A YOUTH HOSTEL & A YMCA

The **Longpre House Hostel,** located at 1726 Prytania St., New Orleans, LA 70130 (tel. 504/581-4540), is located in the Garden District within walking distance of the St. Charles streetcar. The rates are $10 per person.

The **YMCA International Hotel** at 920 St. Charles Ave., New Orleans, LA 70130 (tel. 504/568-9622), charges $27 for a single room. Within walking distance of the French Quarter, it has a fitness facility, an indoor pool, a TV, and a restaurant.

CAMPGROUNDS

There are two KOA campgrounds, one on each side of town.

KOA NEW ORLEANS EAST, 56009 Hwy. 433, Slidell, LA 70461. Tel. 504/643-3850.
$ Rates: $17.95 tent for two; $22.95 fullhook site for two; $28.50 "Kamping Kabin." Extra person is $3.50.
The KOA New Orleans East is three-quarters of a mile east of I-10 on La. 433 (exit 263). Full hookups are here, in a country setting that includes two pools, a recreation room, and miniature golf. Riverboat, swamp, and city tours are available.

KOA NEW ORLEANS WEST, 219 S. Starrett Rd. (La. 48), River Ridge, LA 70123. Tel. 504/467-1792.
$ Rates: $20.95 tent for two; $26.95 fullhook site for two. Extra person $3.
This is the campground closest to the west of the city and welcomes tenters as well as vehicles, for which there are full hookups. You can swim in the pool as well as buy provisions in the on-site store. City and boat tours are available; if you want to "do" the French Quarter on your own, there's city transportation as well as rental cars available.

CHAPTER 6

NEW ORLEANS DINING

1. **IN THE FRENCH QUARTER**
   • **FROMMER'S SMART TRAVELER: RESTAURANTS**
2. **DOWNTOWN**
3. **CENTRAL BUSINESS DISTRICT**
4. **UPTOWN [INCLUDING THE GARDEN DISTRICT]**
5. **METAIRIE**
6. **LAKE PONTCHARTRAIN**
7. **NEARBY DINING**
8. **SPECIALTY DINING**
9. **RESTAURANTS BY CUISINE**

A few words about New Orleans restaurants: They number in the hundreds; service will almost always be efficient, friendly, and relaxed; and if your budget keeps you out of the most famous, you'll have no trouble at all finding very good samples of New Orleans specialties in less formal (many times, very inexpensive) places that are just as much fun. I might add that no matter how many restaurants I list in this book, you will surely find on your own at least one that is so great you'll wonder how I missed it.

Because New Orleans has such a great number of really terrific places to eat, because space limitations make it impossible for me to tell you about more than a few, and because I know many of our readers believe the food in this city to be perhaps its greatest attraction, I suggest that you read local publications and ask your concierge or guesthouse host for more dining options.

One of the delights of exploring New Orleans is discovering the many small, inexpensive places to eat, some just as exciting as the better-known restaurants. What you'll find here are some of my favorites—it simply isn't possible to list them all, but do explore on your own—you'll be certain to find others.

Good eating in New Orleans is by no means confined to the French Quarter—you'll find it all over town. To make life easier for you as you move around the city, restaurants in this chapter are listed by area first. Under each geographical breakdown, you'll find the most expensive listed first, then moderate places, and budget places last. Area boundaries for this purpose are rather broad: "downtown" (remember, that's *downriver* from Canal Street) is outside the French Quarter but on the same side of Canal Street; the Central Business district is roughly the area upriver from Canal, extending to the elevated expressway (U.S. 90); "uptown" includes everything upriver from Canal and as far as Carrollton toward the lake, including the Garden District; Metairie is New Orleans's next-door neighbor in Jefferson Parish; "lake," of course, means the area along the shores of Lake Pontchartrain; and "nearby" means across the Mississippi River or Lake Pontchartrain. Turn back to the Greater New Orleans map in Chapter 4 and you'll get the general idea.

1. IN THE FRENCH QUARTER

EXPENSIVE

ANTOINE'S, 713 St. Louis St. Tel. 581-4422.

Cuisine: FRENCH. **Reservations:** Required.

$ Prices: Appetizers $6.25–$24; main courses $15.25–$49. AE, DC, MC, V.

Open: Lunch, Mon–Sat noon–2pm; dinner, Mon–Sat 5:30–9:30pm.

⭐ Who hasn't heard of Antoine's and dreamed of at least one meal in this legendary restaurant, run by the same family for more than 150 years? Once inside the ironwork-adorned building, you're in a world of white tile floors, slowly turning antique ceiling fans, and 15 separate rooms that run the gamut from plainness to grandeur. As for the food, choose from such classics as oysters Rockefeller, alligator soup, chicken Rochambeau, and filet de boeuf marchand de vin; or settle for something simpler from a menu that lists more than 150 selections. To accompany your choice you have at your disposal one of the richest wine cellars in America. Be sure to bone up on your French before you come, for there's not a word of English on the à la carte menu. Even with reservations, be prepared for a wait at peak hours. If you want to dine with locals, try for a table in the Annex.

ARNAUD'S, 813 Bienville St. Tel. 523-5433.

Cuisine: CREOLE. **Reservations:** Recommended.

$ Prices: Appetizers $6.95–$11.50 à la carte, lunch $1.25–$6 table d'hôte; main courses $15.50–$39.95 à la carte, lunch $10.25–$15.50 table d'hôte. AE, DC, MC, V.

Open: Lunch, Mon–Fri 11:30am–2:30pm; dinner, Sun–Thurs 6–10pm, Fri–Sat 6–10:30pm; brunch Sun 10am–2:30pm.

This favorite New Orleans restaurant has a bit of history. Housed in buildings dating back to the 1700s, Arnaud's was opened in 1918 by "Count" Arnaud Cazenave (the fictitious title was bestowed by locals in recognition of his grand manner and great love of life), and after his death in 1948 the old traditions were carried on for many years by his daughter. Then a decline set in that eventually led to the restaurant's desertion by even the most loyal of its wide clientele. But in late 1978 Archie and Jane Casbarian fell in love with the old restaurant, bought it, and began a restoration that would have gladdened the old count's heart. The lovely mosaic-tile floors were patched and polished; the lighting fixtures, dark-wood paneling, original ceiling medallions, and antique ceiling fans were refurbished; Le Richelieu Bar was restored; a delightful Grill Bar was added; and the wood was stripped from interior columns to reveal beautiful fluted iron posts. Flickering gaslights now welcome you into the large dining room where potted palms, beveled-glass windows, and crystal chandeliers re-create a turn-of-the-century air. There also is the upstairs Germaine Wells Mardi Gras Museum, which holds an extensive private collection of Mardi Gras gowns owned by the late Mrs. Wells, the count's daughter and the restaurant's previous owner.

Best of all, of course, is the kitchen and the dining service. The food is once more something to dream of in far-away places. Formally dressed waiters, as knowledgeable, efficient, and friendly as they are stylish, see to your needs at tables laid with classic linen and set with sterling silver, original Arnaud china, fine crystal, and original water decanters. Executive chef Kevin Davis turns out specialties such as shrimp Creole, trout meunière, and a superb crème brûlée, he constantly creates exciting new dishes. At lunch there's an inexpensive table d'hôte selection along with an à la carte menu. The terrific Sunday brunch features eggs Benedict, eggs André, several kinds of omelets, and other specialties, along with the jazz of Sal Alcorn Jr.'s Trio. Prices range from $18.50 to $25.25 for a complete brunch meal. This has been a favored place to eat, especially during Carnival season, with New Orleanians over the years, and I rejoice to report that now it has reclaimed their devotion.

BACCO, 310 Chartres St. Tel. 522-2426.
   Cuisine: ITALIAN/CREOLE. **Reservations:** Recommended.
$ Prices: Appetizers $4.25–$6.50; main courses $12.25–$19.25. AE, DC, MC, V.
   Open: Breakfast Mon–Sat 7–10am, Sun 8:30–10am; lunch Mon–Sat 11:30am–3pm; brunch Sun 10:30am–3pm; dinner daily 5:30–10:30pm.

Located next door to the De la Poste Hotel, Bacco (owned and operated by brother and sister Ralph and Cindy Brennan) is new to the New Orleans restaurant scene. The interior, with pink Italian marble floors, wall and ceiling murals, Venetian chandeliers, and Gothic arches, is as stunning as it is refreshing. At lunch you should try the fried crawfish tails or the melanzane (grilled eggplant filled with ricotta and goat cheese in a fresh tomato sauce) to start. Follow your appetizer with something from the hickory grill—perhaps the hickory-grilled petit filet or the grilled chicken and fettucine Alfredo (grilled chicken breast topped with prosciutto ham, fontina cheese, and served with basil fettucine Alfredo). Begin your dinner with a Creole-Italian specialty, Bacco shrimp (spicy jumbo gulf shrimp roasted in the wood-burning oven, served in a garlic pepper oil) or the steamed mushrooms. One of my favorite dinner entrees is the crawfish ravioli (homemade ravioli filled with crawfish tails, onions, sweet peppers, and Creole seasonings tossed in a sun-dried tomato pesto sauce). The pepper-crusted salmon, which is seared and served with an Italian salsa and garlic spinach, is another good choice. There are daily specials as well. For dessert try the frozen cappuccino (homemade espresso ice served with Grand Marnier double cream and a biscotto), or zuppa anglaise (a chocolate mocha cake soaked with rum and layered with vanilla and chocolate mocha mousse).

BAYONA, 430 Dauphine St. Tel. 525-4455.
   Cuisine: INTERNATIONAL. **Reservations:** Required at dinner; recommended at lunch.
$ Prices: Appetizers $3.50–$6.50; main courses $12–$19. AE, CB, DC, DISC, MC, V.
   Open: Lunch, Mon–Fri 11:30am–3pm; dinner, Mon–Thurs 6–9:30pm, Fri–Sat 6–11pm. **Closed:** Sun.

After bringing success to Le Bistro (see below), chef Susan Spicer decided to put her talents to use in a restaurant of her own. Bayona is her brainchild, and everyone who has had the good fortune of sampling the innovative dishes listed on Bayona's menu agrees—Spicer never misses. The atmosphere in the century-old Creole cottage is convivial and comfortable yet elegant, but if you'd rather have a quiet open-air dining experience there are some tables in the courtyard as well. Begin your meal here with the grilled garlic sausage with fresh goat cheese, roasted peppers, and olives, or the cream of garlic soup (one of Spicer's signature dishes). The grilled shrimp with black-bean cake and coriander sauce is also excellent. As a main course, try the grilled duck breast with a pepper-jelly glaze or the grilled rabbit with lemon, thyme, and garlic sauce. Sweetbreads with a lemon-caper butter is another of Spicer's signature dishes. Desserts change frequently, but I'd advise you to give one or two a try as well. The wine list here is excellent.

BRENNAN'S, 417 Royal St. Tel. 525-9711.

   Cuisine: FRENCH/CREOLE. **Reservations:** Recommended.

$ **Prices:** Appetizers $6.95–$12.50; main courses $28.50–$35. AE, CB, DC, MC, V.

   Open: Daily 8am–2:30pm and 6–10pm. **Closed:** Christmas.

Brennan's, one of the most famous New Orleans restaurants, occupies a 1795 building that was once the home of Paul Morphy, international chess champion. The restaurant has been here since 1946 and from the start has won a place in the hearts of residents and visitors alike. The Brennan family seems dedicated to providing fine food, good service, and exceptional atmosphere. Be prepared, however, for a long wait for breakfast and lunch, even if you have a reservation—if that's a problem, come at dinner, when it's less crowded. The lush tropical patio here has to be seen to be believed, and there's a view of it from any table in the downstairs rooms. *Elegance* is the only word for the interior, but it is warm elegance, not the cold, sterile kind. "Breakfast at Brennan's" has, of course, become internationally famous, and you can breakfast here even in the evening. But if that's what you have in mind, take heed and don't plan another meal that day—you'll want to be able to do justice to the sumptuous dishes listed on a menu that tempts you with items such as eggs Hussarde (poached eggs atop Holland rusks, Canadian bacon, and marchand de vin sauce, served with hollandaise sauce and accompanied by grilled tomato) and trout Nancy (filet of fresh trout sautéed and topped with lump crabmeat, sprinkled with capers and lemon-butter sauce). Even their omelets are spectacular. This is not your typical bacon-and-eggs affair, but breakfast in the tradition of antebellum days in the Quarter, so if you really want to do it right, order one of their complete breakfast suggestions. A typical one begins with eggs Sardou (poached eggs atop creamed spinach and artichoke bottoms, served with hollandaise sauce), followed by grillades and grits, sautéed baby veal (served in a spicy Creole sauce with fines herbes and freshly cracked black pepper), and topped off by crêpes Fitzgerald (served with a sauce of crushed strawberries flamed in maraschino) and hot chicory coffee. A marvelous eye-opener to begin with is an absinthe Suissesse (a legendary Brennan's drink that has the faint flavor of anisette).

BROUSSARD'S, 819 Conti St. Tel. 581-3866.

Cuisine: FRENCH/CREOLE. **Reservations:** Required as far in advance as possible.

$ Prices: Appetizers $8.50–$14.50; main courses $19–$32.75. AE, CB, DISC, DC, MC, V.

Open: Dinner daily 5:30–10pm. Sunday Jubilation Jazz Brunch 10:30am–2pm.

This venerable New Orleans restaurant—it's been here more than 70 years—has three dining rooms. Decor varies from opulent elegance in the largest, the Napoleon Room; to Italian rustic in a smaller room overlooking the courtyard, the Garibaldi Room; to a delightful French country provincial style in the third dining room, the Josephine Room. And you'll find some of the city's best French-Creole cooking in these surroundings. Along with old standbys, you might choose an innovative creation such as the superb shrimp and crabmeat Jean Lafitte (gulf shrimp and lump crabmeat sautéed and delicately flavored with parsley, a hint of garlic, white wine, and shallots). The flaming desserts are simply glorious, with absolutely perfect crêpes and perfectly blended fillings, and the bananas Foster has a marvelous caramelized syrup. There's a strict dress code.

COURT OF TWO SISTERS, 613 Royal St. Tel. 522-7261.

Cuisine: FRENCH/CREOLE. **Reservations:** Required at dinner.

$ Prices: Appetizers $3.75–$12; main courses $15.50–$30; table d'hôte $35. AE, DC, DISC, MC, V.

Open: Daily brunch 9am–3pm; dinner 5:30–11pm.

One of the loveliest and most atmospheric of French Quarter restaurants is the Court of Two Sisters. There are entrances from both Royal and Bourbon Streets into a huge courtyard filled with flowers, fountains, and low-hanging willows, with a wishing well at its center. The building and its grounds were designed by an early French territorial governor of Louisiana to create the atmosphere of his homeland, and the unusual name comes from the Shop of the Two Sisters, operated here in the late 1800s by two sisters, of course. You can dine outside amid all that lush planting or in the Royal Court Room. You'll know you've found a friendly establishment from the very first, because a sign just outside the door lists their hours as "Buffet Brunch 9am to 3pm, Dinner 5:30 to 11pm. Visiting and browsing allowed 3:30 to 5pm. Have a nice day." You can accept that invitation to browse and enjoy a cocktail in the courtyard. An innovation here that is gaining increasing popularity is the daily Jazz Brunch Buffet, which features over 50 dishes (meat, fowl, fish, vegetables, fresh fruits, homemade bread, and pastries) and a jazz band that strolls about, supplying the New Orleans sound. Delicacies such as shrimp Toulouse, Crawfish Louise, and chicken Michelle are good bets at dinner. There is a $15-per-person minimum at dinner.

GALATOIRE'S, 209 Bourbon St. Tel. 525-2021.

Cuisine: FRENCH. **Reservations:** Not accepted.

$ Prices: Appetizers $6.50–$8; main courses $14–$18. AE, MC, V.

Open: Tues–Sat 11:30am–9pm, Sun noon–9pm. **Closed:** Holidays.

This is a restaurant that draws its charm from a comfortable sense of its age; good, unfussy service; and a way with seafood that will leave you beaming. Galatoire's doesn't accept

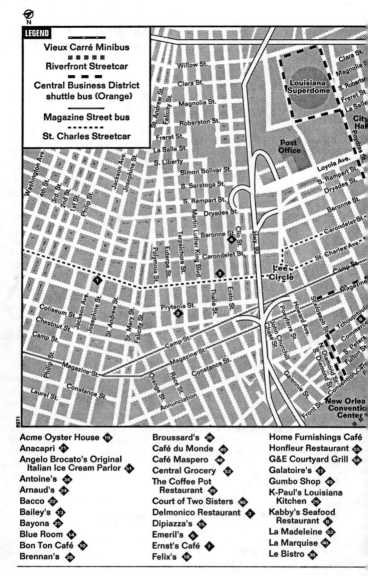

Acme Oyster House ◆19
Anacapri ◆21
Angelo Brocato's Original
  Italian Ice Cream Parlor ◆51
Antoine's ◆34
Arnaud's ◆24
Bacco ◆22
Bailey's ◆13
Bayona ◆25
Blue Room ◆14
Bon Ton Café ◆10
Brennan's ◆28

Broussard's ◆26
Café du Monde ◆48
Café Maspero ◆48
Central Grocery ◆53
The Coffee Pot
  Restaurant ◆39
Court of Two Sisters ◆40
Delmonico Restaurant ◆3
Dipiazza's ◆15
Emeril's ◆6
Ernst's Café ◆7
Felix's ◆18

Home Furnishings Café
Honfleur Restaurant ◆55
G&E Courtyard Grill ◆58
Galatoire's ◆17
Gumbo Shop ◆45
K-Paul's Louisiana
  Kitchen ◆29
Kabby's Seafood
  Restaurant ◆8
La Madeleine ◆42
La Marquise ◆46
Le Bistro ◆38

reservations (even the visiting Duke and Duchess of Windsor had to wait in line), so unless you can take a tip from the natives and go to lunch before noon or dinner before 6pm, you'll line up with everyone else. But, believe me, it's worth the wait. This restaurant has been family-run since 1905, and a critic describes it as one of the most magical eating experiences in town. With its mirrored walls and gleaming brass fixtures, it is certainly one of the loveliest. The seafood dishes simply have no match: Try the trout amandine, the

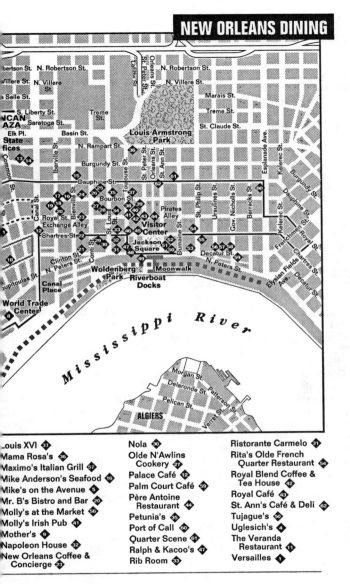

Louis XVI ᪲
Mama Rosa's ᪲
Maximo's Italian Grill ᪲
Mike Anderson's Seafood ᪲
Mike's on the Avenue ᪲
Mr. B's Bistro and Bar ᪲
Molly's at the Market ᪲
Molly's Irish Pub ᪲
Mother's ᪲
Napoleon House ᪲
New Orleans Coffee &
  Concierge ᪲

Nola ᪲
Olde N'Awlins
  Cookery ᪲
Palace Café ᪲
Palm Court Café ᪲
Père Antoine
  Restaurant ᪲
Petunia's ᪲
Port of Call ᪲
Quarter Scene ᪲
Ralph & Kacoo's ᪲
Rib Room ᪲

Ristorante Carmelo ᪲
Rita's Olde French
  Quarter Restaurant ᪲
Royal Blend Coffee &
  Tea House ᪲
Royal Café ᪲
St. Ann's Café & Deli ᪲
Tujague's ᪲
Uglesich's ᪲
The Veranda
  Restaurant ᪲
Versailles ᪲

trout Marguéry, or the perfectly broiled pompano meunière. At lunch, you might opt for the oysters en brochette, the eggs Sardou, or the stuffed eggplant. All come to table in a state of perfection. The à la carte menu is the same at lunch and dinner. (*Tip:* If you go on a Sunday afternoon, you'll find yourself in the company of New Orleans family groups who have made Sunday dinner here a ritual for generations.) Jackets are required after 5pm and all day Sunday.

K-PAUL'S LOUISIANA KITCHEN, 416 Chartres St. Tel. 524-7394.

Cuisine: CAJUN. **Reservations:** Not accepted.

$ Prices: Lunch $6–$16; dinner $23–$32. AE.

Open: Mon–Fri lunch 11:30am–2:30pm, dinner 5:30–10pm.

This is the place that started all the hoopla about Cajun cooking when chef Paul Prudhomme spread its virtues across the entire country. This is also where you'll find the *hottest* interpretation of that cuisine—lots of pepper and other hot seasonings—as well as probably the best. Known for its blackened redfish and Cajun martini (only for the very brave or those with cast-iron innards), K-Paul's also specializes in fiery gumbo, chicken and rabbit from its own farm, and Cajun popcorn (fried crawfish tails). Give the bronzed swordfish with "Crawfish Hot Fanny Sauce" a try if it's on the day's menu—the menu changes daily. You'll have to decide if you really are prepared to wait in line as much as an hour before gaining admittance to the plain, cafélike interior, where harried waitresses will serve you at wooden tables (sans tablecloths) that you'll share with other diners, unless your party numbers four or more. Prices have soared to *very* expensive heights, and service might be a little less attentive than you'd expect, depending on how busy the restaurant is when you go.

LE BISTRO, in the Hotel Maison de Ville, 733 Toulouse St. Tel. 528-9206.

Cuisine: INTERNATIONAL. **Reservations:** Recommended.

$ Prices: Appetizers $3.75–$8; main courses $17–$24. AE, DC, MC, V.

Open: Lunch, Mon–Sat 11:30am–2pm; dinner, daily 6–10:30pm.

Go to Le Bistro for some of the finest and most creative cooking in New Orleans. With white-clothed tables and a banquette running the length of the restaurant, the setting is both intimate and romantic. To start, there's a tasty pork pâté with apple chutney and pistachios or mushroom chimichanga with smoked chipotles and lime creme fraiche. Entrees might run the gamut from pan-seared tuna with black-bean cakes and crawfish salsa to grilled sweetbreads with lemon, oregano, and eggplant caponata. The menu changes seasonally and there's an extensive wine list.

You should make reservations because the restaurant is small—it seats only about 38. It's the perfect place for a romantic dinner.

LOUIS XVI, 829 Toulouse St. Tel. 581-7000.

Cuisine: FRENCH. **Reservations:** Recommended.

$ Prices: Appetizers $5.50–$26.50; main courses $16.50–$29.50. AE, CB, DC, MC, V.

Open: Breakfast, Mon–Fri 7–11am, Sat–Sun 7am–noon; dinner, daily 6–11pm.

Set in the small, stylish St. Louis Hotel, the Louis XVI is a fine restaurant. The elegantly appointed dining room looks onto a lush courtyard complete with a sparkling fountain. Crystal chandeliers and wall sconces bathe diners in a soft, relaxing glow, and everything seems designed to put you in a proper mood for the excellent cuisine.

Rack of lamb and trout Louis XVI are among the stars of the menu, as are beef Wellington, lamb en croûte, and delicious creamed soups. Items on the dessert menu might include crème caramel, bananas Foster, and chocolate profiteroles.

NOLA, 534 St. Louis St. Tel. 522-6652.
   Cuisine: CREOLE. **Reservations:** Recommended.
$ Prices: Appetizers $3–$7; main courses $10–$18. AE, D, DC, MC, V.
   Open: Lunch Mon–Sat 11:30am–2pm; dinner 6pm–10pm Sun–Thurs, 6pm–midnight Fri and Sat.

The brainchild of chef Emeril Lagasse (of Emeril's Restaurant), Nola is one of New Orleans's hottest new restaurants. A two-story establishment, Nola is modern and casual in atmosphere. Sculptures and photographs of food decorate the restaurant, but people don't come to Nola to look at the food, they come here to enjoy Lagasse's culinary creations. At lunch, diners might begin with wood oven baked pocket bread with garlic-infused oil, fresh basil, and parmesan cheese, or a crabcake with roasted red pepper sauce. Entrees at lunch include cedar plank trout with citrus-horseradish crust and lemon-butter sauce served with a spicy slaw and smoked mushroom and tasso pizza with roasted garlic sauce. At dinner you'll find the same pizza on the menu, but as an appetizer. The Lafayette boudin stewed with beer, onions, cane syrup, and Creole mustard served on a sweet potato bread crouton is a great way to begin your dinner here. As a main course at dinner, the wood oven roasted chicken with andouille-eggplant stuffing is excellent, as is the grilled double-cut pork chop with pecan-glazed sweet potatoes and Creole mustard served with a caramelized onion reduction sauce. The piri piri shrimp with homemade chorizo, smoked vegetables, and four-cheese tortellini is another good choice. Desserts run the gamut from Nola Turtle pie with caramel sauce to banana walnut bread pudding with walnut anglaise sauce to Doc's rootbeer float. The wine list is short, but well selected.

RIB ROOM, 621 St. Louis St. Tel. 529-7045.
   Cuisine: RIBS/ROASTS. **Reservations:** Recommended.
$ Prices: Appetizers $6.50–$10.50; main courses $16–$47. AE, MC, V.
   Open: Lunch, daily 11:30am–3pm; dinner, daily 6:30–10:30pm.

Ask almost any New Orleans native for a list of favorite restaurants and chances are that the Omni Royal Orleans Hotel's Rib Room will be at or very near the top. It's a pretty room, with arched windows, high ceilings, natural brick, lots of wood, and open rôtisserie ovens in the back. As you might guess, the specialty is beef, and the Rib Room has raised its cooking to an art. Roasts are exceptional and served piping hot. Prime ribs rank highest in most patrons' esteem, but there are also filets, sirloins, brochettes, tournedos, and steak au poivre. Veal, lamb, and duckling also appear on the menu, as do trout, crab, oysters, and shrimp. At lunch, a variety of egg dishes and salads are offered. At least one meal at the Rib Room is a *must* for any New Orleans visit.

MODERATE

ALBERTO'S, 611 Frenchmen St. Tel. 949-5952.
   Cuisine: ITALIAN. **Reservations:** Not accepted.
$ Prices: Main courses $8–$15. DISC, MC, V.

Open: Lunch Mon–Fri 11am–2:30pm; dinner Mon–Sat 6–11pm.

Alberto's is a small Italian eatery above the Apple Bar with one of the friendliest staffs in the city. Alberto Gonzalez, owner and chef, holds sway in a setting of bare wooden tables, lots of hanging greenery, and a whimsical stuffed parrot. The food here is New Orleans with a touch of Italy—fettucine with shrimp, pasta with clam sauce, cannelloni, and soft-shell crabs with crawfish tails (in season, of course) are a few of the specialties. The prices are amazingly low. Locals flock to this charming little place, so you may have a wait (not such a chore, with the 24-hour bar just downstairs). Frenchmen Street runs parallel to and one block behind Esplanade Avenue.

ANACAPRI, 320 Decatur St. Tel. 522-9056.

Cuisine: ITALIAN. **Reservations:** Recommended.

$ Prices: Appetizers $2–$6.95; main courses $10.25–$18.75. AE, DC, MC, V.

Open: Daily breakfast 7–10am, lunch 11am–5pm, dinner 5–10pm.

Chef Andrea Apuzzo's most recent contribution to the New Orleans restaurant scene is Anacapri. The dining room is attractively arranged and is accented by the works of artist Georgia Haight. On the dinner menu you'll find traditional Italian specialties like fried calamari or melanzana parmigiana regina (layers of eggplant, mozzarella cheese, tomato sauce, and basil) and a couple of unusual surprises, like New Orleans turtle soup, thrown in for good measure. Many pasta dishes are featured on the menu, including lasagnette (pasta layered with paupiette of fish, roasted garlic, and spinach in a light tomato sauce) and raviolo al granchio o langostine (homemade pasta stuffed with crabmeat or crawfish and served in a light cream sauce). The chef also serves up a daily grill featuring fresh fish, veal, beef, and sausage dishes. The anatra alla toscana (roast duckling served crispy with sage, pancetta, and vermouth) is excellent. Several items on the menu have been specially prepared to be low in fat and cholesterol. For dessert go for the tiramisu, a cannoli, or the Anacapri bread pudding (made with hazelnut liqueur).

THE COFFEE POT RESTAURANT, 714 St. Peter St. Tel. 524-3500.

Cuisine: CREOLE. **Reservations:** Not accepted.

$ Prices: Appetizers $5.95–$8.95; main courses $8.50–$17.90; lunch specials $6.75–$9.90. AE, MC, V.

Open: Sun–Fri 8am–1am, Sat 8am–2am.

The exterior of The Coffee Pot, like so many in the Vieux Carré, would never lead you to imagine what you'll find inside. From the outside, it looks like a neighborhood coffee shop, and while it is frequented by many of the inhabitants of the French Quarter, it is not a nondescript place. When you go inside, you'll be walking into a beautiful carriageway loaded with hanging plants and other greenery. There are tables in the carriageway, as well as inside.

The menu features a variety of traditional Creole dishes, such as oysters Rockefeller, blackened redfish, stuffed soft-shell crab, barbecued shrimp, red beans and rice, and bread pudding. There are daily lunch specials, like the white beans and Creole sausage (served Wednesdays); the full breakfast menu of egg dishes, omelets, and pancakes is served from 8:30am to 3pm every day.

G&E COURTYARD GRILL, 1113 Decatur St. Tel. 528-9376.
Cuisine: CONTEMPORARY CREOLE. **Reservations:** Recommended.

$ Prices: Appetizers $4.75–$6.25 at lunch, $5.95–$10 at dinner; main courses $7.75–$10.75 at lunch, $9.75–$20 at dinner. AE, CB, DISC, DC, MC, V.

Open: Lunch Tues–Sun 11:30am–2:30pm; dinner Sun–Thurs 6–10pm, Fri–Sat 6–11pm.

The G&E is another fantastic new arrival on the New Orleans dining scene. The front dining room, with a mural on one wall, is lovely; there's a nice bar as well. However, what really grabbed me is the covered courtyard, where cast-iron chairs and glass-topped tables rest on terra-cotta tile. The best part? There actually *is* an open grill at the back of the courtyard where at least a dozen chickens can be seen slowly rotating on the rotisserie. On your left, as you walk into the courtyard, you'll see some chefs at work.

Nearly three years since its opening people are still raving about the food, and there's frequently a line out the door. Try the smoked salmon wrapped around pickled ginger in a low-salt soy sauce with a spicy wasabi or the beefsteak tomato salad to start. As an entree, the rotisserie chicken in a mint, garlic, tomato, and balsamic vinegar sauce is unsurpassed. Another good choice is the garlic stuffed rainbow trout. There are pasta dishes on the menu as well; pasta jambalaya with chicken, andouille, and cured tasso ham is a good bet. And for dessert I can't think of anything better than the G&E's exceptionally light tiramisu. Go with an open mind and try something new and exciting—you can't really go wrong here.

GABRIELLE, 3201 Esplanade Ave. Tel. 948-6233.
Cuisine: INTERNATIONAL. **Reservations:** Recommended.

$ Prices: Appetizers $3.50–$6.25; main courses $13.50–$22. AE, CB, DC, DISC, MC, V.

Open: Dinner only Tues–Sat 5:30–10pm.

This uniquely shaped little restaurant on Esplanade Avenue, just outside the French Quarter, is gaining a big reputation around town. The white walls, hung with unpretentious pieces of art, and the white-clothed tables topped with fresh flowers create a casual and comfortable atmosphere for diners. The food here is superb (and something of a miracle, I think, considering the size of the kitchen). I started with the warm goat cheese salad with grilled eggplant, marinated sun-dried tomatoes, capers, and green olives and with the first bite I knew I was in for a treat. The crawfish enchilada is also a nice way to start your meal. As a main course I tried the bronzed red snapper with shrimp, garlic, and basil olive oil. The fish was tender and moist, and the flavors blended perfectly. Chef Sonnier (who studied under Paul Prudhomme and Frank Brigsten) also specializes in delectable homemade sausages. Desserts are less sophisticated than they might be, but I might say that I enjoyed my "Peppermint Patty" enormously. It's made of chocolate cake, peppermint ice cream, and chocolate sauce. The lemon pie was also good. There is a small bar, and the wine list is quite nice.

GUMBO SHOP, 630 St. Peter St. Tel. 525-1486.
Cuisine: CREOLE. **Reservations:** Not required.

$ Prices: Appetizers $2.95–$4.95; main courses $4.95–$14.95. AE,

CB, DC, DISC, JCB, MC, V.

Open: Daily 11am–11pm.

In a building dating from 1795, the Gumbo Shop is just one block off Jackson Square. There's a lovely informal atmosphere in both the small patio and the warm indoor dining room. Murals of Old New Orleans, ceiling fans, lots of brass, and a fireplace with an antique mirror hung above the mantel create a charm that seems to make the excellent Creole food taste even better. Their seafood gumbo is a meal in itself, and if you haven't tried jambalaya, this is the place to do so. Featured are red beans and rice, plus a marvelous combination plate with red beans and rice, shrimp Creole, salads, po-boys (ranging from regular ham and cheese to Cajun sausage), and homemade desserts (including just about everybody's favorite, southern pecan pie with ice cream). In addition to the regular menu, fresh fish entrees and dessert specialties are offered daily. There's a full bar and you can also get wines by the bottle or the glass.

MAXIMO'S ITALIAN GRILL, 1117 Decatur St. Tel. 586-8883.

Cuisine: ITALIAN. **Reservations:** Recommended.

$ Prices: Appetizers $4.95–$9.95; main courses $7.50–$24.95. AE, MC, V.

Open: Dinner daily 6pm–midnight.

A friend of mine recommended Maximo's as one of his favorite spots in New Orleans. The restaurant is done in black and gray with a slatted wood ceiling and ceiling fans, and there is an open kitchen at the back of the dining room. You can sit on a stool at the counter surrounding the open kitchen or in a booth.

The menu is interesting and features dishes like Contadina grill (chicken, steak, lamb, and sausage with potatoes and herbs) and veal saltimbocca (with prosciutto, lemon, and parmesan). The penne crawfish diablo and the linguine carbonara are both excellent selections from the pasta menu. All entrees come with a vegetable and fettucine pomodora. This is a very popular spot, and rightly so, so be sure to plan ahead and make reservations.

MIKE ANDERSON'S SEAFOOD, 215 Bourbon St. Tel. 524-3884.

Cuisine: SEAFOOD. **Reservations:** Not accepted.

$ Prices: Appetizers $3.75–$7.95; main courses $8.95–$18.95; daily lunch specials under $7.95. AE, DISC, MC, V.

Open: Sun–Thurs 11:30am–10pm, Fri–Sat 11:30am–11pm.

This is an offshoot of the popular restaurant by the same name in Baton Rouge. As the name implies, seafood is the specialty here, and it comes in all varieties—fried, baked, boiled, or charbroiled. Especially good are the crawfish bisque and the crawfish étouffée. The daily lunch specials, served weekdays, are a bargain, and they change daily. On an average night you should be prepared to wait at least 15 minutes for a table. While you wait, you can go upstairs, have a cocktail, and sit down to some appetizers. It's not the kind of place for a romantic evening—it can get pretty loud and crowded—but it's good food at extremely reasonable prices.

MR. B'S BISTRO AND BAR, 201 Royal St. Tel. 523-2078.

Cuisine: CREOLE. **Reservations:** Recommended.

$ Prices: Appetizers $2.75–$5.75; main courses $14–$26. AE, DC, MC, V.

Open: Lunch, Mon–Fri 11:30am–3pm; dinner, daily 5–10pm; brunch, Sat–Sun 11:30am–3pm.

Mr. B's, owned and operated by Ralph and Cindy Brennan, is one of the most attractive restaurants in town, featuring polished oak floors, warm wood paneling, marble-topped tables, and large bay windows that look out onto Royal Street. In keeping with the bistro spirit, you can drop in for appetizers and a salad or a casual glass of wine or enjoy a full meal. Traditional New Orleans dishes are featured, and two treats here are the wood-roasted duckling (brandy marinated duckling roasted in a wood-burning oven served with a tart, sun-dried cherry sauce and winter cabbage with apples and onions) and the pasta jambalaya (gulf shrimp, andouille sausage, and duck and chicken morsels tossed with spinach fettucine). All prices are lower at lunch than at dinner. Recent items on the dessert menu included strawberry shortcake, tangerine meringue pie, and carrot cake. Besides being a great place for a moderately priced meal, this is a superb "rest-the-feet" break when wandering about the Quarter. There's a jazz brunch on Sunday.

OLDE N'AWLINS COOKERY, 729 Conti St. Tel. 529-3663.

Cuisine: CREOLE/CAJUN/SEAFOOD. **Reservations:** Not accepted.

$ Prices: Appetizers $3.50–$4.25; main courses $4.95–$6.95 at lunch, $12.95–$15.95 at dinner. AE, MC, V.

Open: Daily 11am–11pm.

The Olde N'Awlins Cookery symbolizes several of the city's food traditions. First, it's located in an 1849 building whose history includes having begun as two private residences, a time as a large rooming house that combined the two, a (probable) stint as a brothel, and service as bistro bars and then a disco, before lying idle for nearly two years prior to becoming a restaurant. Since its opening in 1983, the family-operated restaurant has dished up traditional Cajun and Creole favorites and attracted a loyal clientele from the ranks of city residents. Using the freshest of Louisiana seafood and local seasonings, the kitchen turns out specialties such as Cajun jambalaya, blackened redfish, and shrimp Creole, as well as soups, salads, and great desserts. Its blackboard menu changes daily, featuring whatever is freshest. In a rather plain setting that makes use of the original old brick and a delightful courtyard, informality is the keynote. With good prices and a lively, distinctly New Orleans ambience, this is one place where you won't mind a short wait to be seated.

PALM COURT CAFE, 1204 Decatur St. Tel. 525-0200.

Cuisine: FRENCH/CREOLE. **Reservations:** Recommended.

$ Prices: Appetizers $4–$12; main courses $11.95–$14.95. AE, DISC, MC, V.

Open: Wed–Sat 7–11pm, Sun noon–3pm and 6–10pm.

The Palm Court Café is not only a delightful place to enjoy Creole and French culinary specialties but also the repository of a jazz-record collection that will probably contain any classic you might be looking for. Owners Nina and George Buck have a long history in the recording business, as well as a passionate love of good eating, and the Palm Court is a perfect blend of those two loves—your food comes to table accompanied by music from top-line jazz performers. At some point during the evening there's usually a "second-line" march led by the talented dancing waiters, with diners happily jumping up to join in. As for the food—gumbo, shrimp Creole, oysters bordelaise, Creole beef indienne, and jambalaya are just a few of the à la carte menu specials. There's music every night and at Sunday brunch.

PORT OF CALL, 838 Esplanade Ave. Tel. 523-0120.
   Cuisine: BURGERS. **Reservations:** Not accepted.
$ **Prices:** Appetizers $3–$5; main courses $6–$18. AE.
   Open: Sun–Thurs 11am–1am, Fri–Sat 11am–3am. **Closed:** Christmas Day.

After a regular diet of Cajun and Creole food, I got to a point where I couldn't bear to look at another shrimp, oyster, or filet and asked the locals where I could get my hands on a big, fat, juicy hamburger. It didn't take a second of thought for them to tell me to try Port of Call.

Outside you'll see a small sign lit by a red lamp, and perhaps a line. Inside you'll find a cozy wooden interior and an attentive and friendly staff. The mushrooms sautéed in wine sauce are well known around the city, and the hamburgers, which come with a baked potato, are quite a handful. There also are pizzas, excellent filet mignon, rib eye, and New York strip steaks. Because businesspeople come from all over the city to eat here, it's often jammed at regular eating hours—so try it at off hours or before 7pm, when people who work in the Quarter gather here to relax. *Note:* Port of Call also has a take-out service.

RALPH & KACOO'S, 519 Toulouse St. Tel. 522-5226.
   Cuisine: CREOLE/SEAFOOD. **Reservations:** Not required.
$ **Prices:** Appetizers $3.75–$10.95; main courses $8.95–$16.95. AE, DISC, MC, V.
   Open: Mon–Thurs 11am–10:30pm, Fri–Sat 11am–11pm, Sun 11am–9:30pm.
You can't miss Ralph & Kacoo's large, colorful exterior as you walk down Toulouse, and the restaurant may well be crowded no matter when you go. Although your wait for a table here will be at the bar, surrounded by a lively crowd of waitees, it will seldom be for more than 15 to 20 minutes. Once seated at a table, you'll be rewarded by quite good Creole dishes, mostly seafood, at very reasonable prices. Start with the stuffed soft-shell crawfish or the shrimp remoulade. For a main course you might try the trout Ruby, which is trout stuffed with lump crabmeat and topped with a nice hollandaise sauce; or, try the mesquite grilled, blackened, or broiled mahi mahi topped with green onions and served with a Cajun stuffed potato, cole slaw, and hush puppies. Ask about the luncheon specials. Everything is fresh, and the portions are ample.

RISTORANTE CARMELO, 541 Decatur St. Tel. 586-1414.
   Cuisine: ITALIAN. **Reservations:** Not required.
$ **Prices:** Appetizers $2.75–$8.50 at lunch, $4.25–$17.50 at dinner; main courses $5.50–$9.50 at lunch, $9–$28 at dinner. AE, MC, V.

Open: Lunch, daily 11:30am–3pm; dinner, Sun–Thurs 5–11pm, Fri–Sat 5:30–11pm.

Close to the Mississippi River, Jackson Brewery, and Jackson Square, Ristorante Carmelo is conveniently located for a relaxing lunch in the middle of a busy day of sightseeing. The menu says, "At Carmelo you eat and drink Italian," and traditional Italian cuisine is exactly what you get. At dinner you might have the antipasto, fried calamari, linguine al pomodoro (linguine with Italian peeled tomatoes, romano cheeses, and fresh basil), veal picatta, or pollo alla diavola (oven-roasted chicken in tomato sauce with white wine, bell peppers, mushrooms, white onions, capers, red peppers, and olive oil). For dessert you might want to give cannoli a try. Pizza is on the menu, but only as an appetizer—this isn't the kind of place that features pizzas, just good, classic Italian dishes.

RITA'S OLDE FRENCH QUARTER RESTAURANT, 945 Chartres St. Tel. 525-7543.

Cuisine: CREOLE. **Reservations:** Not required.

$ Prices: Appetizers $2.95–$5.95 at lunch, $3.75–$5.95 at dinner; main courses $5.95–$8.95 at lunch, $9.95–$15.95 at dinner. AE, CB, DISC, DC, MC, V.

Open: Daily 11am–10pm.

On the corner of Chartres and St. Philip, Rita's doesn't look like much on the outside, and you're likely to walk right by without even noticing it—*don't*. It's a local place, not yet discovered by tourists. A few friends were going out one night, so I tagged along. I haven't stopped talking about it since.

When you walk in you're given your choice of tables. Most likely you'll feel right at home here—maybe because of the friendly staff, maybe because of the portrait of Rita hanging high above everything in the room, maybe because you're likely to see members of Rita's family having dinner at the back table. There's nothing fancy here—in fact, the pictures often hang a little crooked on the walls. More energy is spent on the food, and the atmosphere is very casual. Personally, that's the way I like it.

One of the nights I went, I had the special, blackened catfish bathed in an incredible Lea & Perrins–and–lemon sauce. While I'd cross mountains and deserts to get shellfish, I'm not crazy about catfish, but I'd have to say that this was some of the best fish I've *ever* had. Unlike average catfish, the variety used at Rita's is farm-raised and corn-fed, which gives it a sweet flavor. Also on the plate were sweet potatoes in a brown-sugar sauce, and they were scrumptious. Another time I tried shrimp Creole, and it was the best I had in New Orleans. The oyster-and-artichoke soup is tasty as well and the gumbo is excellent. You shouldn't miss Rita's bread pudding (and you probably won't because they often bring out a complimentary dish when you're done with your meal)—it's on par with my mother's, and she makes a mean bread pudding.

ROYAL CAFE, 700 Royal St. Tel. 528-9086.

Cuisine: CREOLE. **Reservations:** Not required.

$ Prices: Appetizers $3.50–$8; main courses $4.75–$17.95. AE, MC, V.

Open: Lunch, Mon–Fri 11:30am–4pm; brunch, Sat–Sun 10am–4pm; dinner, daily 5:30–10pm.

The Royal Café is a delightfully casual eatery, with dining rooms on both the ground and the second floors. But it is the upstairs balcony that appeals to most who come here. This balcony find its way into almost every tourist's photos of New Orleans; along with your food, you enjoy a superb view of the French Quarter itself. There's also the Mardi Gras Room for private parties. No matter where you dine, the food will be top-notch. Try New Orleans "lost bread" for breakfast (it's listed as "French Quarter toast" on the menu and it's available on Saturday and Sunday only), a spicy shrimp Creole or a po-boy at lunch, and garlic roasted chicken at dinner. Should you have a bit of difficulty choosing, there's a terrific "Taste of New Orleans" sampler that gives you a cup of gumbo; a green salad; a small bowl of red beans, sausage, and rice; followed by the aforementioned shrimp Creole—served with fresh-baked French bread.

SANTA FE, 801 Frenchmen St. Tel. 944-6854.

Cuisine: MEXICAN/CREOLE. **Reservations:** Recommended.
$ Prices: Appetizers $3–$6; main courses $10–$18. AE, MC, V.
Open: Tues–Sat 5–11pm.

Santa Fe has Mexican cuisine with a huge dash of pure Creole. It has tortillas that come with seafood fillings, a "Mexican gumbo," and seafood burritos. If you hanker for traditional Mexican, order enchiladas or tostados with meat and cheese.

TUJAGUE'S, 823 Decatur St. Tel. 525-8676.

Cuisine: CREOLE. **Reservations:** Recommended.
$ Prices: Five-course lunch $6.50–$12; six-course dinner $22–$25. AE, CB, DC, DISC, MC, V.
Open: Lunch, daily 11am–3pm; dinner, daily 5–11pm.

Tujague's ("Two-jacks") is the second restaurant to occupy this site. The first was run by Madame Bergue, who in 1856 began cooking huge "second breakfasts" for the butchers who worked in the French Market across the way. So well loved were her elaborate, leisurely meals that even today her name lives on in a modern eatery in the Royal Sonesta Hotel. Today Tujague's serves only lunch and dinner but continues the original cook's tradition of simply serving whatever inspiration dictated that day. This is a favorite with New Orleanians, who seem not to mind that there's a very limited menu. At lunch, you have a choice of three entrees (which might include a specialty here, brisket of beef with horseradish sauce; their terrific shrimp remoulade; and the freshest fish available that day), but the five-course meal will consist of soup, salad, entree, vegetable, dessert, and beverage. If something lighter appeals to you, choose gumbo served with a side dish of shrimp salad.

INEXPENSIVE

"Inexpensive" in the French Quarter can often mean "very, very good." That's due, I think, to two things: First, many traditional dishes here are made with low-cost ingredients (red beans and rice, for example); second, there are so many good cooks in this city who can make almost anything taste delicious. So whatever preconceived notions you bring with you about luncheonette-style eateries, be ready to revise them after trying one or two of the following.

FROMMER'S SMART TRAVELER:
RESTAURANTS

1. Don't just go to the city's most famous restaurants. They cost a bundle, and you can probably find food that is just as good for a lot less money at a small, little-known restaurant. (The locals know where these are and in most cases are quite happy to direct you to them.)
2. If you're just dying to eat at one of those world-famous restaurants, go there at lunch—the food is generally the same, and the prices are lower.
3. On a nice day, head for a deli and grab a picnic lunch. Take it to the river and do some people- and boat-watching.
4. New Orleanians love to drink—at all times of the day, but especially at and around dinner time. While drink prices in New Orleans are relatively low compared to other cities, you can add quite a lot to your bill with alcohol alone, so watch it!

ACME OYSTER HOUSE, 724 Iberville St. Tel. 522-5973.
   Cuisine: SEAFOOD. **Reservations:** Not accepted.
$ Prices: Oysters $3.50–$6; New Orleans specialties $5.25–$5.75; seafood $7.75–$9.75; po-boys $4–$5. AE, DC, MC, V.
   Open: Daily 11am–10pm.

If you're an oyster lover, there's nothing quite like standing at the oyster bar in the Acme Oyster House, eating a dozen or so freshly shucked oysters on the half shell. (You can have them at a table, but somehow they taste better at the bar.) If you can't quite stomach them raw, try the oyster loaf. There's also a sandwich menu, with beer, of course, as the perfect accompaniment. This New Orleans institution is a fun place to eat—the shuckers behind the bar are as much a treat as those lovely oysters.

CAFE MASPERO, 601 Decatur St. Tel. 523-6250.
   Cuisine: SEAFOOD/SANDWICHES. **Reservations:** Not required.
$ Prices: Appetizers $2–$4.50; main courses $4–$7.85. No credit cards.
   Open: Sun–Thurs 11am–11pm, Fri–Sat 11am–midnight.

The Café Maspero serves the largest portions I've run into—burgers, deli sandwiches, seafood, grilled marinated chicken, and so on—as well as an impressive list of wines, beers, and cocktails, all at low, low prices. This is a lively spot, especially following a concert, the opera, or the theater, when locals drop by in droves; it's not unusual to see patrons lined up for tables. Be assured, however, that it's worth your time to wait—the quality is as good as the portions are large.

DIPIAZZA'S, 337 Dauphine St. Tel. 525-3335.
   Cuisine: ITALIAN. **Reservations:** Recommended for dinner.
$ Prices: $3.50–$22.95. AE, MC, V.
   Open: Mon–Thurs 11:30am–10:30pm, Fri 11:30am–11pm, Sat 5–11pm.

You won't see this place if you're not looking carefully or if you're on the wrong side of the street. The name is on the front of the awning, which doesn't project too far over the sidewalk. It's a casual, cozy eatery that fills up quickly for dinner, so expect to wait if you're just dropping by. The fairly standard Italian fare is prepared behind the wooden bar in the back, where you can see it. The pasta-and-fagioli soup is good, as are the roasted peppers with mozzarella, anchovies, and capers. You can also get steaks and chicken or veal prepared in the traditional Italian manner. The staff is friendly.

FELIX'S, 739 Iberville St. Tel. 522-4440.
   Cuisine: OYSTERS/CREOLE. **Reservations:** Not required.
$ Prices: Appetizers $4.50–$11; main courses $10–$16.95. AE, MC, V.
   Open: Mon–Thurs 10:30am–midnight, Fri–Sat 10:30am–2am, Sun 10:30am–10pm.

If you get a late-night yen for oysters, try Felix's across the street from the Acme Oyster House. Like its neighbor, Felix's is almost legendary among New Orleanians, and it stays open into the wee hours. In addition to raw oysters, there's a selection of fried or grilled fish, chicken, steaks, spaghetti, and omelets, and the Creole cooking is quite good. Sometimes crowded and noisy, it almost always looks disorganized, but if you pass it by on those grounds you'll be missing a real eating experience.

HONFLEUR RESTAURANT, in the Provincial Hotel, 1024 Chartres St. Tel. 581-4995.
   Cuisine: CREOLE. **Reservations:** Not required.
$ Prices: Appetizers $2–$6; main courses $9–$11. AE, MC, V.
   Open: Daily 7am–9pm.

The bright, charming Honfleur Restaurant serves exceptional food at reasonable cost. Breakfast is especially good here. Lunch specialties include red beans and rice, southern fried chicken, and an open-face roast-beef sandwich that is excellent. At dinner, choose from Creole gumbo, shrimp, trout, and panée veal.

MAMA ROSA'S, 616 N. Rampart St. Tel. 523-5546.
   Cuisine: ITALIAN. **Reservations:** Not required.
$ Prices: Appetizers $1–$3.75; pizzas $7.25–$13.50; specials $5–$7.50. MC, V.
   Open: Tues–Thurs, Sun 10:30am–10:30pm; Fri–Sat 10:30am–11:30pm.

Mama Rosa's Little Slice of Italy serves up a big slice of pizza. While the decor is nothing to brag about—typical red-and-white-checked linen tablecloths, a jukebox, and a bar—the pizzas are. You can get a 10- or 14-inch pizza with a variety of different toppings for very reasonable prices. The crusts are thick, and the more you put on them, the better they are. In fact, the slices are so thick, you could almost compare them to pan pizza. Of course, you can also get pasta, like spaghetti and manicotti, and the salads are big enough to be a full meal. You can even get mini muffalettas as appetizers. One of the big draws is Mama Rosa's homemade bread. The staff can be a bit surly, but most people don't go there looking for a great ambience; they go with one thing in mind—good, fast, inexpensive Italian food—and they get it.

MOLLY'S AT THE MARKET, 1107 Decatur St. Tel. 525-5169.

Cuisine: IRISH PUB. **Reservations:** Not required.

$ Prices: Full breakfast under $10; burgers and sandwiches $3.25–$5.95; entrees $5.95–$9.95. AE, MC, V.

Open: Mon–Thurs 10am–2am, Fri–Sun 8:30am–2pm.

Jim Monaghan, who originated Molly's on Toulouse Street, now devotes full time to his establishment over on Decatur Street across from the French Market. One of the prime movers in the upgrading of what was once a run-down, rather seedy part of the Quarter, Jim has brought his own brand of enthusiasm to this part of town. His warm personality is reflected by staff members who make visitors feel welcome on their first visit and like a valued member of a special club on their return visit. Here you can have breakfast all day and "the best Irish coffee in New Orleans." Try the Molly Burger or the combination platter, which consists of one catfish fillet, half a dozen shrimp, french fries, and a salad. There are a daily special and even a "Pita Sprouter" for vegetarians. For a bit of fun, drop by Molly's on Thursday, when "Media Night" finds a local celebrity behind the bar and a lively crowd of locals in front.

MOLLY'S IRISH PUB, 732 Toulouse St. Tel. 568-1159.

Cuisine: IRISH PUB. **Reservations:** Not required.

$ Prices: Appetizers $3–$5; main courses $4–$8. AE, MC, V.

Open: Daily 24 hrs.

I first found Molly's on a rainy day in the heart of the Quarter when I ducked in for an Irish coffee to ward off the chill and stayed to enjoy a platter of fried oysters, french fries, and salad. And I never had better anywhere else in the city. That says a lot for the kitchen here, especially since there is a very wide variety on the menu. It's a great place to watch all sorts of New Orleans types as well as tourists who find it as I did. Breakfast is served at any hour, making this pub a special favorite of night owls who have a taste for bacon and eggs after a night on the town.

NAPOLEON HOUSE, 500 Chartres St. Tel. 524-9752.

Cuisine: AMERICAN/ITALIAN. **Reservations:** Required for large parties.

$ Prices: Sandwiches and pastries $4.25–$10. AE, MC, V.

Open: Daily 11am–1am.

Giving in a bit to everyday wear and tear on the outside, Napoleon House, at the corner of Chartres and St. Louis Streets, is so named because at the time of the death of the "Little Corporal" there was actually a plot (most likely absinthe induced) hatching in this 1797 National Landmark to snatch him from his island exile and bring him to New Orleans. The third floor was added expressly for the purpose of providing him with a home after the rescue. It wears its history with dignity. There's a limited menu of po-boys, Italian muffuletta sandwiches, and pastries; the jukebox plays only classical music. You can relax inside by the old bar or outside in the courtyard. This is a very popular spot with residents and many visiting celebrities. You can easily picture struggling artists and writers of days long past engaged in conversation at the little café tables or at the bar. If you're looking for some opera and a bit of old New

Orleans, the best time to visit Napoleon House is after dark when the locals gather.

NEW ORLEANS COFFEE & CONCIERGE, 334B Royal St. Tel. 524-5530.

Cuisine: CAFE. **Reservations:** Not necessary.
$ Prices: All items $1.67–$6.95. MC, V (in gallery only).
Open: Sun–Thurs 8am–7pm, Fri–Sat 8am–10pm.

When I first discovered New Orleans Coffee & Concierge in 1992 it was a new addition to the French Quarter scene. I was sure it would be around for quite some time. Three years later it's more popular than ever. It has been transformed from a small café serving pastries and coffee into a full-service, bistro-style café offering breakfast, lunch, and evening appetizers and desserts; and the small art collection the owners had displayed has blossomed into "The Collection," featuring over 30 different artists (including Thomas Mann, Martin LaBorde, Hazel Guggenheim McKinley, and Leslie Kohnke). At breakfast you can get Belgian waffles, breakfast croissant sandwiches, bagels and lox, and French pastries. Items on the lunch menu include soups, gumbo, chicken salad, praline'd ham sandwiches, vegetable sandwiches, and pasta salads. If you're wandering around the Quarter before dinner you might opt to stop in here for hors d'oeuvres that might include baked brie, smoked meats, cheese platters, and dips. There's an exclusive Robert Mondavi Wine Bar available for your tasting pleasure. After dinner you might choose to stop by here and have dessert and a selection from the international coffee bar which features numerous liqueurs that can be mixed with cappuccino or "N'awlins Blend" coffee. For a meal, a treat, or a look through the gallery, New Orleans Coffee & Concierge is one of the best bargains in town.

PERE ANTOINE RESTAURANT, 714 Royal St. Tel. 581-4478.

Cuisine: CAJUN/CREOLE. **Reservations:** Not required.
$ Prices: Appetizers $2.95–$3.50; main courses $3.75–$13. No credit cards.
Open: Daily 9am–midnight.

Père Antoine is an attractive European-style place with huge mirrors in back and flowers out front. Specialties here include Cajun red snapper (cooked in a rich tomato sauce, a nice change from "blackened"), shrimp, and crawfish étouffée. The seafood platter, with catfish, shrimp, scallops, crab, and Cajun popcorn (deep-fried seasoned shrimp), is a real bargain. For lighter meals, there are soups and salads; sandwiches and burgers; omelets; and such New Orleans favorites as red beans and rice, jambalaya, and chicken Creole. Items on the breakfast menu, such as "Belgium" waffles and a "Louisiana Breakfast—The Rajun Cajun" (smoked sausage, green peppers, onion, ham, and a Creole sauce), are available all day.

PETUNIA'S, 817 St. Louis St. Tel. 522-6440.

Cuisine: CAJUN/CREOLE/CREPES. **Reservations:** Not required.
$ Prices: Appetizers $3.95–$6.95; main courses $9.95–$18.95. AE, DISC, MC, V.
Open: Daily 8am–11pm.

Petunia's is settled into an old house between Toulouse and Conti Streets and dishes up enormous portions of New Orleans specialties like shrimp Creole, chicken bordelaise, and Cajun grilled catfish. Breakfast and Sunday brunch are popular here, with a broad selection of crêpes—they are billed as the world's largest (I can't prove it, but they probably are) at 14 inches. Crêpe selections include the "St. Marie," which is a delicious blend of spinach, cheddar, chicken, and hollandaise; and the "St. Francis," filled with shrimp, crab ratatouille, and Swiss cheese. If you have room for dessert, try the dessert crêpes or the peanut butter pie.

PRALINE CONNECTION, 542 Frenchmen St. Tel. 943-3934.
   Cuisine: SOUL FOOD. **Reservations:** Not accepted.
$ Prices: Appetizers $3.50–$6.95 at dinner; main courses $3.95–$6.95 at lunch, $4–$12.95 at dinner. AE, DISC, DC, MC, V.
   Open: Sun–Thurs 11am–10:30pm, Fri–Sat 11am–midnight.

The Praline Connection is fast becoming famous around the city, but visitors probably wouldn't know about it unless it was recommended to them by a friend, as it was in my case. It's a bit out of reach because it's hidden away on Frenchmen Street, which is just behind Esplanade Avenue. If you get back there, you'll find that Frenchmen Street is a veritable treasure trove of restaurants and entertainment.

The interior is bright and airy, with stainless-steel ceiling fans and a black-and-white-tiled floor. It's not the kind of place you'd go for a romantic dinner because the noise level can be quite daunting. The people who go to the Praline Connection go there to eat and have fun; you might even end up talking to the people next to you because sometimes there is not enough room to seat you at a private table.

The food is wonderful, plentiful, and very reasonably priced. The fried chicken is crispy and juicy, and you can get it with almost any kind of beans and rice. There are red beans, white beans, and crowder peas, as well as okra, mustard greens, and collard greens. It's real southern cooking at its best. Praline Connection's newest menu items include fried softshell crawfish and barbecued ribs. At lunch you might try the Hog's Head Cheese with garlic toast to start followed by an oyster or smoked sausage po-boy. A small candy shop is attached (there are a few tables in there, and it's a little quieter than the main dining room) selling pralines as well as other candies. The friendly staff is smartly dressed in black and white. You might have to wait a bit to get a table, but do wait. Praline Connection II (tel. 523-3973) at 901 South Peters Street offers the same menu and a larger dining room.

2. DOWNTOWN

CHRISTIAN'S, 3835 Iberville St. Tel. 482-4924.
   Cuisine: FRENCH/CREOLE. **Reservations:** Recommended.
$ Prices: Appetizers $3–$7.50 at lunch and dinner; main courses

$12.75–$15 at lunch, $12.50–$18.95 at dinner; lunch specials $10–$15. AE, CB, DC, MC, V.

Open: Lunch, Thurs–Fri 11:30am–2pm; dinner, Mon–Sat 5:30–10pm.

Ever eaten in a church? Well, it's a unique experience at Christian's, only about 10 minutes from the French Quarter. Started by a grandson of the Galatoire clan, this lovely restaurant serves lots of seafood specialties, some of which are prepared with the most delicate of French sauces. Try the oysters Roland or saffron shrimp to start; the sweetbreads à la Française or the marvelous bouillabaisse as an entree; and finish it off with café brûlot. If you go for lunch, you might want to try one of their specials. The little church building remains unaltered on the exterior, and inside it's been beautifully restored.

DOOKY CHASE, 2301 Orleans Ave. Tel. 821-2294.

Cuisine: SOUL FOOD. **Reservations:** Recommended at dinner.

$ Prices: Table d'hôte $25; main courses $10–$17.50; Creole feast $37.50. AE, DC, MC, V.

Open: Sun–Thurs 11:30am–midnight, Fri–Sat 11:30am–1am. Lunch buffet daily 11:30am–3pm.

Established in 1941, Dooky Chase has long been a favorite of the locals, but it's only just recently been recognized by critics farther afield as being some of the best soul food in the city. And it's soul food with distinctive New Orleans touches—such as shrimp Dooky with its spicy remoulade sauce, veal panne, and a delicious crawfish étouffée. The fried chicken here is terrific, some of the best I've had in a long time, and steaks also are on the menu. Try the praline pudding for dessert. If you're really in the mood to put on a few pounds, call and reserve a Creole feast for yourself.

While you're there, you might get to see the chef, Leah Chase, who is becoming fast known across the country as one of the great chefs of New Orleans. The decor seems plain, but take a look around, and you'll see that the owners are avid collectors of African American art, a great deal of which is hanging in the restaurant. *Note:* After dark, it is best to go there by cab.

RUTH'S CHRIS STEAK HOUSE, 711 N. Broad St. Tel. 486-0810.

Cuisine: STEAK. **Reservations:** Recommended.

$ Prices: Main courses $8.50–$30. AE, CB, DC, MC, V.

Open: Daily 11:30am–11:30pm.

You won't get an argument locally if you pronounce that the best steak in town is served at Ruth's Chris Steak House. The specialty here is, in fact, prime beef, custom aged, cut by hand, and beautifully prepared. Cuts include filets, strips, rib eyes, porterhouses (for two or more), and more. All the beef prepared at Ruth's Chris Steak House is corn fed. Pork chops and one or two other meats appear on the menu, but this is primarily a steak house—and one that will not disappoint.

There's another Ruth's Chris at 3633 Veterans Blvd. In Metairie (tel. 888-3600). (There are also branches in Baton Rouge and Lafayette—see Chapter 11.)

3. CENTRAL BUSINESS DISTRICT

EXPENSIVE

EMERIL'S, 800 Tchoupitoulas St. Tel. 528-9393.
Cuisine: CONTEMPORARY CREOLE. **Reservations:** Recommended at dinner.
$ Prices: Appetizers $4.50–$6.25 at lunch, $4–$7.50 at dinner; main courses $7.50–$15 at lunch, $14–$25 at dinner. AE, CB, DISC, DC, MC, V.
Open: Lunch, Mon–Fri 11:30am–2pm; dinner, Mon–Sat 6–10pm.

Emeril's was opened in March 1990 by Emeril Lagasse, who used to be head chef at Commander's Palace. He's another of the young, daring, but traditionally schooled chefs who everyone in New Orleans has been talking about as of late.

The restaurant is located in the warehouse district, practically on gallery row. The building was, in fact, once a warehouse, and rather than cover the remaining traces of its history, Lagasse has incorporated exposed pipes in the interior design and created a wonderfully modern establishment.

Lagasse insists on making everything from scratch, including sausage, cheeses, and Worcestershire sauce. To start, try the grilled homemade andouille sausage or the duck-and-wild-mushroom ravioli with a mushroom sauce. As an entree you might have the grilled fresh fish of the day or the roulade of chicken breast with cornbread andouille dressing and baby vegetables. If you don't have time for a full meal at Emeril's, go and have a look at the after-dinner menu, which features some pretty incredible desserts (such as banana cream pie, Emeril's peanut-butter pie, J. K. chocolate soufflé, and Emeril's homemade ice cream) as well as a varied list of wines and liqueurs.

THE VERANDA RESTAURANT, in the Hotel Inter-Continental, 444 St. Charles Ave. Tel. 525-5566.
Cuisine: CONTINENTAL/CREOLE. **Reservations:** Recommended.
$ Prices: Appetizers $5.25–$6.95; main courses $12.50–$22.50. AE, CB, DC, MC, V.
Open: Sun–Thurs 6am–10pm, Fri–Sat 6am–11pm; brunch Sun 11am–3pm.

The Veranda is pretty atypical of what you'd expect a restaurant in a big hotel such as the Inter-Continental to be like. The chef, Willy Coln, is one of the most respected in New Orleans, and that's only the beginning. The atmosphere is both dramatic and comfortable. Its glass-enclosed garden courtyard (with an abundance of greenery) and private dining room make you feel as though you're dining in a stately New Orleans home, and Tuesday through Sunday a harpist makes dining at The Veranda all the more memorable.

The menu is varied, and it is doubtful that you'll find anything to complain about. I started with the Louisiana crabcakes in a light Creole mustard sauce, and for an entree had the red snapper and jumbo lump crabmeat, which was delicious. The rack of lamb glazed with honey, herbs, and Creole mustard is done to perfection. Desserts are incredible—and I know because I tasted every one. You shouldn't pass up this hotel restaurant, it's worth the trip!

MODERATE

BAILEY'S, in the Fairmont Hotel, 123 University Place. Tel. 529-7111.

Cuisine: COFFEE SHOP. **Reservations:** Not required.
$ Prices: All items $3–$12. AE, CB, DC, DISC, MC, V.
Open: Daily 24 hrs.

Bailey's is a cozy spot softly lit by Tiffany-style lamps and decorated with antiques. At any hour of the day you can order breakfast items such as waffles, pancakes, and omelets, or New Orleans specialties such as red beans and rice with hot sausage and a seafood platter. There also are sandwiches and burgers, as well as a nice selection of po-boys. The entrance is at Baronne Street.

BON TON CAFE, 401 Magazine St. Tel. 524-3386.

Cuisine: CAJUN. **Reservations:** Required at dinner.
$ Prices: Appetizers $3.25–$5.25 at lunch, $3.50–$6 at dinner; main courses $8.75–$14.50 at lunch, $18.75–$24.25 at dinner. AE, DC, MC, V.
Open: Lunch, Mon–Fri 11am–2pm; dinner, Mon–Fri 5–9:30pm.

You'll find the Bon Ton Café absolutely mobbed at lunch with New Orleans businesspeople and their guests. Such popularity is largely due to its owner, Al Pierce; his nephew, Wayne; and Wayne's wife, Debbie. Al and Wayne both grew up in the Bayou country, where Al learned Cajun cooking from his mother. He came to New Orleans in 1936; bought the Bon Ton in 1953; and since then has been serving up seafood gumbo, crawfish bisque, jambalaya, crawfish omelet, and other Cajun dishes in a manner that would make his mother proud. Wayne and Debbie are continuing the tradition. This is a small, utterly charming place that's not to be missed if you want to sample true Cajun cooking at its best (more subtle than Creole, making much use of shallots, parsley, bell peppers, and garlic). The lunch menu is semi–à la carte; at dinner the menu is à la carte and table d'hôte.

KABBY'S SEAFOOD RESTAURANT, 2 Poydras St. Tel. 584-3880.

Cuisine: SEAFOOD. **Reservations:** Recommended.
$ Prices: Appetizers $4.75–$7.25; main courses $15.95–$28.95. AE, CB, DC, MC, V.
Open: Lunch, daily 10:30am–2:30pm; dinner, daily 6–11pm.

Dining at Kabby's affords a lookout over the river through a 200-foot-wide, 14-foot-high window. It's a spectacular view, and the decor in earth tones of green, beige, and brown is a charming blend of traditional and art deco styles. You enter through a New Orleans courtyard foyer that features a bubbling fountain, custom-designed lampposts, and tropical plantings. The adjacent bar features a large stained-glass canopy, with live entertainment and dancing in the evening. At lunch, there are salads, sandwiches (oyster loaf, muffuletta, and so on), and other specialties. At night seafood is the thing to order, especially a sumptuous seafood combo, which is a real feast. Beef, chicken, and veal also are on the menu, but remember that this *is* a seafood restaurant.

PALACE CAFE, 605 Canal St. Tel. 523-1661.
Cuisine: CREOLE. **Reservations:** Recommended.
$ Prices: Appetizers $3.50–$5 at lunch, $3.50–$7.75 at dinner; main courses $8.50–$10.50 at lunch, $12–$19.50 at dinner. AE, CB, DC, MC, V.
Open: Daily lunch 11:30am–2:30pm, dinner 5–10pm.

Operated by Brad, Ti, Lauren, and Dick Jr., Brennan family cousins, the Palace Café is a grand café serving contemporary Creole cuisine. Enter through the café's brass-and-glass revolving door and you will be immediately impressed by the spiral staircase in the middle of the restaurant. It's comfortable, the ground floor being almost entirely made up of booths—even for two. Deep green, cream, and brass lend an open, airy feel to the dining room. You can actually see the chefs at work behind a glass wall at the back of the restaurant.

No doubt you'll find something interesting on the menu. The seafood boil features the day's fresh local seafood served on a raised platter (just the way it's done in the grand cafés of Paris). The crabmeat cheesecake is excellent, and the double cut rotisserie pork chop with candied sweet potatoes was delicious and filling—I found it impossible to clean my plate. Fresh, warm bread is served with each course, and you can get wines by the glass. For dessert, you should try the white-chocolate bread pudding or the Mississippi mud pie. The staff is attentive and friendly. If you go for lunch there's likely to be a large business crowd present.

INEXPENSIVE

ERNST'S CAFE, 600 S. Peters St. Tel. 525-8544.
Cuisine: CAJUN/CREOLE. **Reservations:** Not required.
$ Prices: Appetizers $4.50–$6.50; main courses $6.50–$9.95. AE, MC, V.
Open: Lunch, daily 11am–3pm; dinner, Tues–Sat 6–10pm.

There's been a lounge run by the same family in the old brick building that now houses Ernst's Café since 1902. Its brick walls, high ceilings, and heavy timbered bar make it an interesting and attractive setting for excellent sandwiches, salads, red beans and rice, and po-boys at lunch. Dinner appetizers include catfish fingers and Creole gumbo. Main courses range from hamburgers to fried shrimp and catfish plates. If the weather is fine, eat outside.

MOTHER'S, 401 Poydras St. Tel. 523-9656.
Cuisine: CAJUN. **Reservations:** Not accepted.
$ Prices: Menu items $1.75–$15.50. No credit cards.
Open: Mon–Sat 5am–10pm, Sun 7am–10pm

You owe it to yourself to make at least one pilgrimage to Mother's, which is within walking distance of the Louisiana Superdome and a number of major hotels. When you go, be sure to allow time to stand in line—bankers line up with warehouse workers, dockworkers, and just about everybody else from this part of town for *the* best po-boy sandwiches in New Orleans. Made on crisp French bread so fresh that it's just cooled down from the oven, the po-boys here are real creations, many of them served with a rich, thick gravy that may leak out, but the sandwich is so good that you won't mind. Try the roast beef or ham. The ham at Mother's is said to be "the world's best baked ham." The restaurant's most sought-after po-boy is the Ferdi Special which is made of baked ham, roast beef, shredded cabbage, and Creole mustard. There are plate lunches, too, such as the excellent gumbo, red beans, Jerry's award-winning jambalaya, and spaghetti pie. Mother's is always crowded, but don't let that throw you off—by the time you make your way through the line, there'll be room at a table. Mother's serves one of the best breakfasts in the city. The dress is casual.

UGLESICH'S RESTAURANT & BAR, 1238 Barrone St. Tel. 523-8571.

    Cuisine: SANDWICHES. **Reservations:** Not required.

$ **Prices:** Lunch $6–$11. No credit cards.

    Open: Mon–Fri 9:30am–4pm.

Uglesich's, at Erato Street near Lee Circle, is old and more than a little rundown in appearance, but it is well loved locally for its outstanding sandwiches of fried food (leave your jacket behind or you'll carry the fried smell all day). If you're a little homesick and just feel like being part of the neighborhood scene, with the added bonus of eating delicious, freshly prepared, inexpensive food, Uglesich's is the place. You won't regret the trip.

4. UPTOWN (INCLUDING THE GARDEN DISTRICT)

EXPENSIVE

BRIGTSEN'S, 723 Dante St. Tel. 861-7610.

    Cuisine: SEAFOOD/STEAK. **Reservations:** Required a day or two in advance.

$ **Prices:** Appetizers $3.50–$6; main courses $12–$20. AE, DC, MC, V.

    Open: Dinner, Tues–Sat 5:30–10pm.

⭐ In the Riverbend area, Brigtsen's occupies a small house and is presided over by Frank Brigtsen, a former chef at K-Paul's. Frank has a magic touch with seafood. Two of the most popular dishes right now are his roast duck with "dirty" rice and honey-pecan gravy, and the blackened yellowfin tuna with roasted tomato salsa and smoked corn sauce. The menu changes daily.

CARIBBEAN ROOM, in the Pontchartrain Hotel, 2031 St. Charles Ave. Tel. 524-0581.

    Cuisine: FRENCH/CREOLE. **Reservations:** Recommended.

$ **Prices:** Appetizers $3.75–$7.75; main courses $19–$27.50. AE, DISC, MC, V.

    Open: Mon–Sat 6–10pm.

Since it opened in 1948, the Caribbean Room has won a list of culinary awards as long as your arm, and it really epitomizes New Orleans cuisine at its finest. The decor, like that of the rest of the hotel, is infused with a refined (almost understated) luxury. As for service—well, "impeccable" and "solicitous" come to mind. The kitchen turns out appetizer specialties such as oysters and bacon en brochette and bronzed shrimp (jumbo shrimp dusted with Cajun spices, seared in butter and topped with a lobster and garlic demi-glacé). Brilliantly executed main courses like snapper Eugene (filet of snapper sautéed in butter and drizzled with a sauce of shallots, shrimp, lump crabmeat, lemon juice, and Worcestershire sauce) and duckling *vert pres* (slow-roasted half duckling on mixed green with orange-fig gravy and poached pear) are the things that keep diners coming back, and the Mile-High-Pie is what makes them stay for dessert.

COMMANDER'S PALACE, 1403 Washington Ave. Tel. 899-8221.

Cuisine: CREOLE. **Reservations:** Required, sometimes days in advance.

$ Prices: Appetizers $4–$7.50 at lunch, $5–$12.50 at dinner; main courses $13–$19 at lunch, $22–$32 at dinner; full brunch $17–$24; full dinner $29–$39.50. AE, CB, DC, MC, V.

Open: Lunch, Mon–Fri 11:30am–2pm; dinner, daily 6–10pm; brunch, Sat 11:30am–12:30pm, Sun 10am–12:30pm.

The unusual, rather grand blue-and-white Victorian building at the corner of Washington Avenue and Coliseum Street was built as a restaurant in 1880 by Emile Commander and is now owned by members of the Brennan family of French Quarter fame. Commander's Palace is a consistent favorite of locals and visitors alike. The patio, fountains, lush tropical plantings, and soft colors are a perfect backdrop for mouthwatering Creole specialties. Outstanding are such dishes as trout with pecans and a Creole meunière sauce, roasted Louisiana quail with a Creole stuffing of shrimp and crabmeat and a port-wine sauce, and sauté of crawfish. There is also a nice wine list. If you're a jazz buff, don't miss their famous Jazz Brunch, when Joe Simon and his group play Dixieland and the restaurant is decorated with multicolored balloons. Commander's, in addition to serving some of the best food in town, is a fun place and quite a social center.

MIKE'S ON THE AVENUE, Lafayette Hotel, 628 St. Charles Ave. Tel. 523-1709.

Cuisine: NEW ORLEANS/SOUTHWESTERN/ASIAN. **Reservations:** Recommended.

$ Prices: Lunch $12–$17; dinner $20–$40. AE, MC, V.

Open: Lunch, Mon–Fri 11:30am–2pm; dinner, Mon–Sat 6–9:30pm.

Located on the ground floor of the Lafayette Hotel, Mike's on the Avenue has become extremely popular with New Orleanians over the past few years. Chef Mike Fennelly is inspired not only in the creation of culinary delights like his Thai soup made with coconut milk, vegetables, chicken, and shrimp, but in the creation of the canvases that decorate the walls of his restaurant. The cuisine, which Mike and his partner Vicky like to call eclectic, crosses the borders of many different countries. For instance, traditional Louisiana crabcakes are emboldened with the spice of chiles and smoothed by a lobster cream. The sea bass in a Thai curry sauce is excellent. Fennelly is daring with spices, and it pays off. Desserts are equally creative. My favorite is the brioche bread pudding. Before making reservations, you should know that this is not the place to go for a quiet, romantic dinner for two: The high ceilings and the prevalence of glass don't absorb the noise in this lively establishment.

PASCAL'S MANALE, 1838 Napoleon Ave. Tel. 895-4877.
Cuisine: ITALIAN/STEAKS. **Reservations:** Recommended.
$ Prices: Appetizers $4.75–$12.95; main courses $6.95–$10.95 at lunch, $7.95–$19.95 at dinner; specials lunch $5.95–$10, dinner $13.95–$21. AE, DC, DISC, MC, V.
Open: Mon–Fri 11:30am–10pm, Sat 4–10pm, Sun 4–9pm. **Closed:** Sun Memorial Day through Labor Day.

If you have New Orleans friends, chances are they'll take you at least once to Pascal's Manale for barbecued shrimp—if you don't have local friends, by all means go on your own. It's crowded, noisy, and verges on expensive, but you'll leave as much a fan as any native. Don't expect fancy decor or artificial "atmosphere"—the emphasis is on food and conviviality. (Sunday nights feel more like social gatherings than one could reasonably expect at a commercial restaurant.) Pascal's bills itself as an Italian–New Orleans steak house, but for my money, specialties such as veal Marsala, turtle soup, the combination pan roast, tiny buster crabs, and those marvelous barbecued shrimp (a house creation) are the source of its popularity.

UPPERLINE, 1413 Upperline. Tel. 891-9822.
Cuisine: CREOLE. **Reservations:** Required.
$ Prices: Appetizers $4.75–$5.75; main courses $10–$17.50. AE, CB, DC, MC, V.
Open: Dinner, Mon, Wed–Sun 5:30–9:30pm.

Upperline is a small, popular uptown place between St. Charles Avenue and Prytania Street whose chef, Tom Cowman, has put together a varied, creative, Creole-inspired menu. The restaurant's most popular dishes of late include duck roasted with garlic and served with a port sauce; the Upperline shrimp sampler (shrimp with jalapeño cornbread, fried green tomato with shrimp remoulade, and spicy barbecue shrimp with angel hair); or rack of lamb in a spicy merlot sauce. If you can't decide, give the seven-course "Taste of New Orleans" tasting dinner a try. While you eat you'll be surrounded by native New Orleanians, out-of-town visitors, and a wonderful collection of local art—do take time between bites to have a look around. For dessert try the warm raspberry and apple bread pudding, or the double chocolate amaretto mousse. The wine list is excellent.

VERSAILLES, 2100 St. Charles Ave. Tel. 524-2535.
Cuisine: CONTINENTAL. **Reservations:** Required.
$ Prices: Appetizers $4.50–$7; main courses $20.50–$27. AE, MC, V.
Open: Dinner, Mon–Sat 6–10pm.

For dining in the continental manner, you just can't equal the Versailles. The lovely St. Charles Room looks out on tree-shaded St. Charles Avenue through glass walls; the warm, red-walled Marie Antoinette Room is lit with huge cut-glass chandeliers; and the Trianon Room provides elegant seclusion. But what makes the Versailles really special is its food. Chef Dennis Hutley creates specialties such as bouillabaisse marseillaise, almond-sprinkled trout in a beurre blanc sauce, and a delightful weinerschnitzel. They do their own baking (try the hazelnut mousse) and the wine cellar is outstanding. If you're driving, an added plus is free valet parking.

MODERATE

CASAMENTO'S, 4330 Magazine St. Tel. 895-9761.
    Cuisine: SEAFOOD. **Reservations:** Not accepted.
$ **Prices:** Main courses $1.60–$9.10. No credit cards.
    Open: Lunch, Tues–Sun 11:30am–1:30pm; dinner, Tues–Sun 5:30–
    9pm. **Closed:** Mid–June to mid–Sept.

Another of the homey places so loved by people who live in New Orleans is Casamento's. The plain exterior holds a warm, friendly restaurant decorated with Spanish tiles and lots of plants. Almost always crowded (mostly with locals), Casamento's has an excellent oyster bar and some of the best seafood plates in town at unbelievably low prices. Their oyster loaf is especially good, but then so are the fried soft-shell crabs and anything else that you might order here. Incidentally, don't confuse the oyster loaf with the oyster sandwich—the loaf is made with a large loaf of white bread toasted and buttered and filled with fried oysters and large enough for two; the sandwich comes on regular toast. The same goes for the shrimp loaf and the tenderloined trout loaf.

COPELAND'S, 4338 St. Charles Ave. Tel. 897-2325.
    Cuisine: CAJUN/CREOLE. **Reservations:** Recommended.
$ **Prices:** Appetizers $3.25–$6.50; main courses $8–$15. AE, MC, V.
    Open: Sun–Thurs 11am–11pm, Fri–Sat 11am–midnight.

Copeland's, uptown, almost operates on a fast-food basis, yet its dishes are so authentic that it has gained a loyal local following. The setting is attractive, all the ingredients are fresh, and the recipes have been collected from some of New Orleans's leading chefs. Blackened redfish here is excellent; less spicy are redfish Lacombe and redfish Copeland. Veal, steaks, and barbecued lamb ribs are outstanding on the extensive menu.

DELMONICO RESTAURANT, 1300 St. Charles Ave. Tel. 525-4937.
    Cuisine: SEAFOOD/STEAKS. **Reservations:** Not required.
$ **Prices:** Main courses $6.50–$15.50 at lunch, $15.50–$21 at dinner. AE, DC, DISC, MC, V.
    Open: Daily 11:30am–9pm.

A short streetcar ride from the Quarter, the Delmonico Restaurant was founded in 1895 and has been run by the La Franca family since 1911. It is essentially a comfortable, family-style eatery, with just a touch of elegance and one of the most varied menus (many dishes actually come from old family recipes) in New Orleans. As a dedicated seafood lover, I favor the soft-shell crab meunière, but the steaks are very good, and the fresh vegetable salad is a wonder.

FLAGON'S WINE BAR AND BISTRO, 3222 Magazine St. Tel. 895-6471.
    Cuisine: CONTEMPORARY CREOLE. **Reservations:** Not required.
$ **Prices:** Appetizers $3.95–$9.75; main courses $4.95–$10.95 at lunch, $8.95–$15.95 at dinner. AE, MC, V.
    Open: Lunch, Mon–Sat 11:30am–2:30pm, brunch Sun 11:30am–3pm; dinner, Sun–Thurs 6–10pm, Fri–Sat 6–11pm.

Flagon's Wine Bar and Bistro is a pleasant, lighthearted spot for a simple glass of wine, a light repast of sandwiches and/or desserts, or a full meal of such delicacies as grilled swordfish with jalapeño pecan butter and roast duck "Shadows on the Teche." The pastas are delicious (try the pasta with grilled shrimp and Cajun Tasso ham). There are more than 40 fine wines (on a changing wine list) available by the glass, with as many as 350 good vintages to buy by the bottle. The ambience is great. The wine bar is open daily.

GAUTREAU'S, 1728 Soniat St. Tel. 899-7397.
   Cuisine: INTERNATIONAL. **Reservations:** Required.
$ Prices: Appetizers $5.20–$5.95; main courses $12.95–$18.25. MC, V.
   Open: Mon–Sat 6–10pm.

Those of you who knew the old Gautreau's (which, after having closed in November 1989, was reopened by new owners, one of whom is the restaurant's new chef), won't be disappointed to see that the new Gautreau's warm and modest decor has remained the same. The tin ceiling, the old New Orleans photographs, and the famous apothecary cabinet from the original drugstore still holds a varied selection of wines. The menu, however, is quite another thing. The young chef, Larkin Selman, after studying under several chefs in New York, has returned home with some new and exciting ideas in Creole food. Try Selman's famous crabcakes with black bean and cilantro tartare, or for a more down-home taste sensation go for the roasted chicken with garlicky mashed potatoes. The pastry chef does a fine crème brulée and a nice, light tequila lime pie. Try anything and everything—you can't go wrong here!

TAVERN ON THE PARK, 900 City Park Ave. Tel. 486-3333.
   Cuisine: SEAFOOD/STEAKS. **Reservations:** Recommended.
$ Prices: Lunch $10–$12; dinner $15–$20. AE, CB, DC, JCB, MC, V.
   Open: Lunch Tues–Fri 11:30am–2:30pm; dinner Tues–Sat 5pm–10pm or later. **Closed:** Sun and Mon.

Just across from City Park, within sight of the famous "dueling oaks," the Tavern on the Park is a delightful re-creation of art deco eateries of the Prohibition era and it is, in fact, the only remaining building from the Storyville era. The historic building is a marvelous setting for the restaurant's steak and seafood specialties, with broiled cold-water lobster, fresh trout, and superb steaks high on the list of local favorites. Balcony dining is available, weather permitting.

---

5. METAIRIE

BOZO'S, 3117 21st St. Tel. 831-8666.
   Cuisine: CAJUN/SEAFOOD. **Reservations:** Not required.
$ Prices: Lunch $5–$10; dinner $12–$16. MC, V.
   Open: Lunch, Tues–Sat 11am–3pm; dinner, Tues–Thurs 5–10pm, Fri–Sat 5–11pm.

Bozo's has been run by the Vodonovich family for more than 60 years, and you'll find one of the present generation on duty every time the doors open. New Orleanians have much affection for this plain, unpretentious fish house; it's easy to see why when heaping plates of seafood appear cooked to perfection and served by friendly and efficient waitresses. Fried catfish—crisp and utterly delectable—is lightly breaded with cornmeal. Shrimp, oysters, crawfish, crabs, and—well, almost anything that swims or lives in nearby waters—make up the bulk of the menu, which also includes "Mama Bozo's" delectable chicken andouille gumbo; a few steak, chicken, and veal selections; and a good list of sandwiches. The prices are unbelievably low, starting with a bargain gumbo and topping out with the rib-eye steak. Bozo's is worth the trip out to Metairie.

CROZIER'S RESTAURANT FRANCAIS, 3216 W. Esplanade, N. Metairie. Tel. 833-8108.

Cuisine: FRENCH. **Reservations:** Recommended.

$ Prices: Appetizers $2.50–$5.75; main courses $14.75–$19.50. AE, DISC, MC, V.

Open: Lunch, Tues–Fri 11:30am–2pm; dinner, Tues–Sat 6–10pm.

Crozier's, which has moved to Metairie from its lakeside location of many years, has retained its charming European flavor, with fresh flowers and candles on the tables. Authentic French cooking accounts for this restaurant's long-standing popularity, with specialties that include onion soup, duck liver pâté, escargots, coq au vin, escalope de veau, steak au poivre, truite (trout) aux pecans, a fish du jour, and traditional desserts like crème caramel, mousse au chocolate, and various tartlettes. The wine list is limited but good and moderately priced.

---

6. LAKE PONTCHARTRAIN

BRUNING'S SEAFOOD ON THE LAKE, 1924 West End Parkway. Tel. 282-9395.

Cuisine: SEAFOOD. **Reservations:** Not accepted Fri–Sat night.

$ Prices: Appetizers $1.50–$15.95; main courses $1.75–$29.95. AE, DISC, MC, V.

Open: Sun–Thurs 11am–9:30pm, Fri–Sat 11am–10:30pm.

Bruning's has been serving a classic New Orleans seafood menu since 1859 (in fact, the building that houses Bruning's has recently been declared an official Jefferson Parish and New Orleans landmark). You'll dine over the water with a beautiful view of Lake Pontchartrain. The boiled seafood here is especially good, as is the seafood gumbo, and fried dishes show up grease free. A good buy, if you can't make up your mind, is the generous seafood platter. Bruning's fries and broils all seafood to order and will take special dietary needs into consideration during the cooking process. There's a children's menu, and all entrees come with salad, toast, and a potato.

7. NEARBY DINING

LA PROVENCE, 20520 Hwy. 190, Lacombe. Tel. 626-7662.
   Cuisine: FRENCH. **Reservations:** Required, as far in advance as possible.
$ Prices: Appetizers $5–$11; main courses $16.50–$23. AE, MC, V.
   Open: Wed–Sat 5–11pm, Sun 1–9pm.

Across the Lake Pontchartrain causeway in Lacombe (between Slidell and Mandeville) is another French restaurant that rates a rave. It's on U.S. 190 (the Mandeville-Slidell Road) at I-12. La Provence is a jewel of a place that could be bodily transported from the countryside of Louisiana to that of France and be perfectly at home. Founded by a Frenchman with the unlikely name of Chris Kerageorgiou (there's a Greek lurking somewhere in his ancestry, but he was born in Provence), this rustic country inn's atmosphere envelops you the minute you step inside.

There's a great fireplace, waitresses dressed in Provençal costumes (they're local ladies, friendly and efficient), and fragrances from the kitchen that tell you in advance you're in for a great meal. Chris and his Cajun wife, Charlotte, run things, and his creations combine classic French dishes with marvelous Greek, Creole, and south-of-France touches. If I had to pick a favorite, it would probably be poulet au fromage, which enhances chicken with vermouth, shallots, cream, and Swiss and bleu cheeses. The duck à l'orange is positively magnificent, the rack of lamb is superb, and the pompano is unique. I adore this place. The portions are large, and the wine list is extensive (with a nice moderately priced selection as well as rare vintages). Dress is semicasual (jackets optional). This one's a "don't miss" if you have wheels.

MOSCA'S, 4137 U.S. Hwy. 90 West. Tel. 436-9942.
   Cuisine: ITALIAN/CREOLE. **Reservations:** Required weekdays, not accepted weekends.
$ Prices: A la carte $25–$35. No credit cards.
   Open: Dinner, Tues–Sat 5:30–9:30pm. May vary.

About 30 minutes' drive on U.S. 90 west of the city, 4½ miles west of Avondale, there's a plain plywood building with a shell front painted white that holds one of this area's best restaurants. Mosca's is well worth the drive. It was begun in 1946 by Provino and Lisa Mosca, and their son, Johnny, and daughter, Mary, have carried on the unique style of cooking that combines elements of Italian and local Creole cuisine. If an evening out of the city appeals to you, by all means make the trip and sample dishes you won't find anywhere else. I can especially recommend the Italian crab salad (they use vinegar to flavor the crab and pickle the vegetables), and Mosca's Italian oysters are a treat. Other specialties are quail with wild rice; squab and Cornish hen, also with wild rice; and chicken cacciatore (you get the entire chicken). Everything is prepared to order, so you might have to wait as long as 40 minutes. Open hours can vary, so it's safer to call ahead, even on weekends when you can't reserve.

8. SPECIALTY DINING

HOTEL DINING

As I've said earlier, dining in New Orleans is pretty good no matter where you eat—even in hotels, sometimes *especially* in hotels. The best hotel dining can be found at Louis XVI, in the St. Louis Hotel; at the Rib Room in the Omni Royal Hotel; at the Veranda in the Hotel Inter-Continental; and at the Caribbean Room in the Pontchartrain Hotel. For more information, see the listings for these establishments earlier in this chapter.

JAXFEST

For a fun way to sample most of New Orleans's legendary dishes, head for the third level of the Jackson Brewery, St. Peter and Decatur Streets, any day of the week between 10am and 10pm. Given the umbrella name of Jaxfest, the entire level consists of take-out stands for such specialties as red beans and rice, fried chicken, and barbecued ribs; Cajun fried oysters and shrimps, Cajun shrimp salad, and gumbo from **Patout's Cajun** (a branch of one of the western Louisiana Cajun country's leading restaurants); calzone and other Italian treats from **Café Sbarro;** Creole seafood gumbo from **Greco's Fish Market;** and cannoli, spumoni, ice cream, espresso, and so on from **James Brocatto Italian Ice Cream.** "Take-out" here means bringing your food to a pleasant tiled dining area over on the river side or on the wide outside terrace. If you're lucky, you'll do your sampling to the strains of live jazz sporadically performed on the ground level. The prices are unbelievably low at all stands.

LIGHT, CASUAL & FAST FOOD

CAMELLIA GRILL, 626 S. Carrollton Ave. Tel. 866-9573.
   Cuisine: BURGERS/SANDWICHES.
$ Prices: All items under $9. No credit cards.
   Open: Sun–Thurs 9am–1am, Fri–Sat 9am–3am.

S If you're out in the Riverbend area, don't bypass the Camellia Grill. It's right on the trolley line and serves a great variety of sandwiches, omelets, salads, and desserts at low to moderate prices. The hamburgers are really special; the sandwiches are stuffed to overflowing with corned beef, ham, or whatever; and the omelets are enormous. This is one place in which you can count on having a filling meal at low cost, and although it's counter service and you may have a short wait for a seat, surprisingly, you'll be given a real linen napkin. That counter service is actually a bonus feature—it provides a front-row contact with the friendly, entertaining waiters on the other side.

HOME FURNISHINGS CAFE, 1600 Prytania St. Tel. 566-1707.
   Cuisine: CAFETERIA.
$ Prices: All items under $10. No credit cards.
   Open: Lunch, Mon–Sat 11:30am–2pm.

The Home Furnishings Café has a unique uptown setting—it's in a furniture store. Following the example of European shops, the owners of the store have installed an attractive, bright little cafeteria on the second floor. The light-lunch menu varies but always includes salads (chicken, spinach, tuna, and so on), sandwiches, hamburgers, and quiche, with hot dishes such as red bean soup, chicken-curry noodle soup, shrimp Creole, and other local favorites. Everything is freshly made. The desserts are yummy: cheesecake, mousse, and Gloria's chocolate-chip cookies.

BREAKFAST/BRUNCH

In addition to the one listed below, there are some restaurants discussed earlier in this chapter that serve a good brunch, such as the Court of Two Sisters, which is famous for its daily brunch; Arnaud's; Mr. B's Bistro and Bar; and Commander's Palace. You shouldn't overlook Mother's, which, in addition to its famous po-boys, serves a wonderful breakfast.

BLUE ROOM, in the Fairmont Hotel, University Place. Tel. 529-7111.
    Cuisine: SEAFOOD. **Reservations:** Required.
$ Prices: Brunch, $23.50 adults, $12.95 children. AE, CB, DC, MC, V.
    Open: Sun brunch 10am, noon, 2pm.

One of New Orleans's most elegant Sunday brunches is served in the Blue Room of the Fairmont Hotel. There are three seatings. The brunch is buffet style, but the food is much better than the kind you'd find at your regular hotel brunch. You can have oysters, shrimp, salmon, and omelets.

COFFEE, TEA & SWEETS

ANGELO BROCATO'S ORIGINAL ITALIAN ICE CREAM PARLOR, 537 St. Ann St. Tel. 525-9676.
    Cuisine: ITALIAN PASTRY.
$ Prices: All items under $8. No credit cards.
    Open: Mon–Fri 10am–6pm, Sat 10am–11pm, Sun 9am–8pm.

There's been a Brocato's in New Orleans since 1905, and except for a brief interruption, it has been in the French Quarter. It is the Brocato's on whom the city's most demanding hostesses have depended for three generations to cater those occasions for friends and special guests when sweets must reach the heights of sheer perfection. Happily you'll now find them back in new quarters, serving their fabulous ice cream, Italian ices, cannolis, and a whole feast of other pastries. There's another branch of Angelo Brocato's at 214 N. Carrollton Ave. (tel. 486-0078).

CAFE DU MONDE, 813 Decatur, in the French Market. Tel. 581-2914.
    Cuisine: CAFE.
$ Prices: Coffee, milk, hot chocolate, and beignets 90¢. No credit cards.
    Open: Daily 24 hrs. **Closed:** Christmas Day.

This is one of my favorites, an indispensable part of the New Orleans food scene. Across from Jackson Square and absolutely habit-forming, the delightful Café du Monde has been

S a favorite with New Orleanians for years. There are only four main items on the menu—coffee (black or au lait), milk, hot chocolate, and beignets (three to a serving)—and each item costs 90¢. (You can also get a soda served in a big plastic souvenir cup for $1.20.) Beignets (bin-*yeas*), the official doughnuts of Louisiana, are square, doughnutlike confections that come hot, crisp, and covered with confectioner's sugar. One order and a cup of café au lait have served as breakfast, lunch, or light dinner (after one of those "splurge" lunches) for me at one time or another, for the incredible price of $1.80. There's an indoor dining room, but I wouldn't miss sitting outside under the awning to take advantage of the Mississippi River breeze and unexcelled people-watching. Besides your fellow diners, there's all of Jackson Square, with horse carriages lined up across from the café, as well as shoppers headed for the French Market a little farther along Decatur Street. You'll find many a nurse as your neighbor if you show up in the dawn or predawn hours.

LA MADELEINE, 547 St. Ann St. Tel. 568-9950.

Cuisine: FRENCH BAKERY.

$ Prices: Pastries 85¢–$2.25; entrees $3.89–$8.99. AE, MC, V.

Open: Sun–Thurs 7am–8pm, Fri–Sat 7am–9pm.

La Madeleine, at Chartres Street, is one of the French Quarter's most charming casual eateries. One of a chain of French bakeries, it has a wood-burning brick oven that turns out a wide variety of breads, croissants, and brioches. A glass case up front holds marvelous pastries to take out or eat in the cafeteria section, where quiches, salads, soups, sandwiches, and other light entrees are available. This restaurant is delightful for a continental breakfast or light lunch.

LA MARQUISE, 625 Chartres St. Tel. 524-0420.

Cuisine: PASTRY.

$ Prices: 82¢–$2.74. No credit cards.

Open: Daily 7am–5pm.

The tiny La Marquise serves French pastries on the premises, either in a crowded front room that also holds the display counter or outside on a small but delightful patio. Maurice Delechelle is the master baker and guiding hand here, and I promise you, you've never had more delectable goodies. There are galettes bretonnes (butter cookies), pain au chocolat (a rectangle of croissant dough that has been wrapped around a chocolate bar, then baked), cygne swans (éclairs in the shape of swans filled with whipped cream), choux à la crème (cream puffs), and mille-feuilles (napoleons), as well as croissants, brioches, and a wide assortment of strudels and Danish pastries. Prices are minimal (some as low as 50¢), and you can buy coffee in paper cups if you decide to buy your sweet here and take it elsewhere. La Marquise is almost always crowded; if the patio has no seats available, there's always Jackson Square just a few steps away for a dessert picnic.

A larger La Marquise is at 617 Ursulines St., so you can indulge that sweet tooth even when you're not in the Jackson Square vicinity.

P. J.'S COFFEE & TEA COMPANY, 5432 Magazine St. Tel. 895-0273.

Cuisine: COFFEE/PASTRIES.

$ Prices: 80¢–$4. AE, DISC, MC, V.
Open: Mon–Fri 7am–11pm, Sat–Sun 8am–11pm.

P. J.'s is just the place if you're mad about tea or coffee—some 30 different teas and 47 types of coffee are sold here, where they do their own roasting. You can taste as many as 18 teas and 3 or 4 coffees on any given day. Their iced coffee is very special, made by a cold-water process that entails 12 hours of brewing. Assorted pastries are available to go with the brew you choose.

ROYAL BLEND COFFEE & TEA HOUSE, 623 Royal St. Tel. 523-2716.
Cuisine: CAFE.
$ Prices: Pastry 99¢–$2.15; lunch $2.85–$3.25. MC, V.
Open: Daily 7am–8pm.

I'm not sure if I fell in love with this place because it's set back off the street and you walk through a courtyard to get to it or because the sparrows come in and eat crumbs off the floor. Whatever my reason, I think it's a great place. Order your light lunch (sandwiches, quiche, or salad) at the white tile–topped counter and take it out into the courtyard to eat or stay inside at a blue-and-white-tiled table. If you're just in the mood for coffee and pastry, they've got plenty of that, too, and the pastry menu changes daily. If you don't like coffee and tea but like the atmosphere of a café, there's also juice, milk, hot chocolate, and spritzers.

LATE-NIGHT/24-HOUR

The two places listed below are open around the clock. Another great spot for some late-night people-watching and energy boosting so you can continue partying until dawn is Café du Monde, listed above.

THE QUARTER SCENE, 900 Dumaine St. Tel. 522-6533.
Cuisine: CAFE/DINER.
$ Prices: Appetizers $2.50–$5.95; main courses $1.95–$12.95. AE, MC, V.
Open: 24 hrs. **Closed:** Tues 11:30pm–Wed 8:30am.

The Quarter Scene is another one of those places the locals like to frequent, and on entering, you'll see why. There are trellises, replicas of Greek statues (in keeping with the Mardi Gras theme of the city), and lovely floral tablecloths covering café-type tables. You'll feel as if you're out in an elegant courtyard.

The menu runs the gamut from your ordinary grilled-cheese sandwich to pastas and seafood platters. I guess if I found it in New York, I'd call it a diner with a New Orleans twist. You might want to try one of their salads, such as the Rex or the Momus; a sandwich named after your favorite street in New Orleans; or one of their 30 different hamburgers. The breakfast menu is available all day, and on Saturday and Sunday there's a special brunch menu.

ST. ANN'S CAFE & DELI, 800 Dauphine St. Tel. 529-4421.
Cuisine: CAFE/DELI.
$ Prices: $2.25–$12.95. AE, DISC, MC, V.
Open: 24 hrs.

St. Ann's is a cozy little café on the corner of St. Ann and Dauphine Streets. Inside there are a few café tables, giving the feeling that it's more of a local hangout than a tourist attraction. There's nothing fancy about it, and I probably wouldn't even have tried it out if it hadn't been for the raving recommendation of a friend who said that St. Ann's was one of the only things that kept her going when she was first moving into town. Everything here is homemade, and you can get a variety of foods, including sandwiches, pizzas, soups, and salads, as well as breakfast items. Lunch and dinner specials are offered daily, and there's a decent selection of beer and wine.

PICNIC FARE & WHERE TO EAT IT

I have one suggestion for picnic fare, and that's because I don't think anyone should leave New Orleans without first having a muffuletta sandwich from Central Grocery. Go pick one up and then sojourn to a bench in Jackson Square, to the banks of the Mississippi, or to a shade tree in Woldenberg River Park.

9. RESTAURANTS BY CUISINE

CAJUN/CREOLE
Copeland's, Uptown (including Garden District) (M)
Mike's on the Avenue, Uptown (including Garden District) (E)

CAJUN
Bon Ton Café, Central Business District (M)
Bozo's, Metairie (I)
Ernst's Café, Central Business District (I)
K-Paul's Louisiana Kitchen, French Quarter (E)
Mother's, Central Business District (I)
Olde N'Awlin's Cookery, French Quarter (M)
Petunia's, French Quarter (I)

COFFEE SHOP
Bailey's, Central Business District (M)

CONTINENTAL
The Veranda Restaurant, Central Business District (E)

Versailles, Uptown (including Garden District) (E)

CREOLE
Chez Hélène, Downtown (I)
The Coffee Pot Restaurant, French Quarter (M)
Honfleur Restaurant, French Quarter (I)
Mr. B's Bistro and Bar, French Quarter (M)
Nola, French Quarter (E)
Olde N'Awlins Cookery, French Quarter (M)
Palace Café, Central Business District (M)
Père Antoine Restaurant, French Quarter (I)
Petunia's, French Quarter (I)
Ralph & Kacoo's, French Quarter (I)

CREOLE & CONTEMPORARY CREOLE
Emeril's, Central Business District (M)

KEY TO ABBREVIATIONS: E = Expensive; I = Inexpensive; M = Moderately priced; VE = Very Expensive

Flagon's Wine Bar and Bistro, Uptown (including Garden District) (*M*)

G&E Courtyard Grill, French Quarter (*M*)

Gautreau's, Uptown (including Garden District) (*M*)

Gumbo Shop, French Quarter (*M*)

Rita's Olde French Quarter Restaurant, French Quarter (*M*)

Royal Café, French Quarter (*M*)

Tujague's, French Quarter (*M*)

CREPES
Petunia's, French Quarter (*I*)

FRENCH
Christian's, Downtown (*M*)

Crozier's Restaurant Francais, Metairie (*M*)

FRENCH & FRENCH CREOLE
Antoine's, French Quarter (*E*)

Arnaud's, French Quarter (*E*)

Bayona, French Quarter (*E*)

Brennan's, French Quarter (*E*)

Broussard's, French Quarter (*E*)

Caribbean Room, Uptown (including Garden District) (*E*)

Commander's Palace, Uptown (including Garden District) (*E*)

Court of Two Sisters, French Quarter (*E*)

Galatoire's, French Quarter (*E*)

Louis XVI, French Quarter (*E*)

Palm Court Café, French Quarter (*M*)

Upperline, Uptown (including Garden District) (*E*)

HAMBURGERS
Port of Call, French Quarter (*M*)

IRISH PUB
Molly's at the Market, French Quarter (*I*)

Molly's Irish Pub, French Quarter (*I*)

INTERNATIONAL
Bayona, French Quarter (*E*)

Gabrielle, French Quarter (*M*)

Gautreau's, Uptown (including Garden District) (*M*)

Le Bistro, French Quarter (*E*)

ITALIAN
Alberto's, French Quarter (*M*)

Anacapri, French Quarter (*M*)

Bacco, French Quarter (*E*)

Dipiazza's, French Quarter (*I*)

Mama Rosa's, French Quarter (*I*)

Maximo's Italian Grill, French Quarter (*M*)

Napoleon House, French Quarter (*I*)

Pascal's Manale, Uptown (including Garden District) (*E*)

Ristorante Carmelo, French Quarter (*M*)

MEXICAN
Santa Fe, French Quarter (*M*)

RIBS/ROAST
Rib Room, French Quarter (*E*)

SANDWICHES
Café Maspero, French Quarter (*I*)

Sterling Club, French Quarter (*M*)

Uglesich's Restaurant & Bar, Central Business District (*I*)

SEAFOOD
Acme Oyster House, French Quarter (*I*)

Bozo's, Metairie (*I*)

Bruning's Seafood on the Lake, Lake Pontchartrain (*M*)

Café Maspero, French Quarter (*I*)

Casamento's, Uptown (including Garden District) (*M*)

Felix's, French Quarter (*I*)

Kabby's Seafood Restaurant, Central Business District (*M*)

Mike Anderson's Seafood, French Quarter (*M*)

Olde N'Awlins Cookery, French Quarter (M)

Ralph & Kacoo's, French Quarter (M)

SEAFOOD/STEAK

Brigtsen's, Uptown (including Garden District) (E)

Delmonico Restaurant, Uptown (including Garden District) (M)

Tavern on the Park, Uptown (including Garden District) (M)

SOUL FOOD

Dooky Chase, Downtown (M)

Praline Connection, French Quarter (I)

SPECIALTY DINING

Angelo Brocato's Original Italian Ice Cream Parlor, Italian pastry (I)

Blue Room, breakfast/brunch (M)

Café du Monde, café (I)

Camellia Grill, casual food (I)

Home Furnishings Café, cafeteria (I)

La Madeleine, French bakery (I)

La Marquise, pastry (I)

New Orleans Coffee & Concierge, café (I)

P. J.'s Coffee & Tea Company, coffee/pastries (I)

Royal Blend Coffee & Tea House, café (I)

St. Ann's Cafe & Deli, late-night/24-hour (I)

The Quarter Scene, late-night/24-hour (I)

STEAK

Pascal's Manale, Uptown (including Garden District) (E)

Ruth's Chris Steak House, Downtown (M)

NEAR NEW ORLEANS

CREOLE
Mosca's, Hwy. 90 West (E)

FRENCH
La Provence, Lacombe (M)

ITALIAN
Mosca's, Hwy. 90 West (E)

CHAPTER 7

WHAT TO SEE & DO IN NEW ORLEANS

1. **SUGGESTED ITINERARIES**
 • **DID YOU KNOW...?**
2. **THE TOP ATTRACTIONS**
3. **MORE ATTRACTIONS**
 • **FROMMER'S FAVORITE NEW ORLEANS EXPERIENCES**
4. **COOL FOR KIDS**
5. **ORGANIZED TOURS**
6. **MARDI GRAS & OTHER FESTIVALS**
7. **SPORTS & RECREATION**

In many respects the French Quarter is New Orleans, and many visitors never leave its confines. I think that's a mistake, and you will find not only French Quarter sightseeing attractions discussed here, but also attractions located outside the Quarter. The French Quarter is, however, where it all began, and in its 90 or so square blocks, there's more sightseeing excitement than many entire cities—or even states—can boast.

Sightseeing excursions into areas outside the French Quarter will allow you to feel the pulse of the city's commerce, take a look at river activities that keep the pulse beating, stroll through parks more spacious than any that could be accommodated in the Quarter, drive or walk by those impressive "new" homes, get a firsthand view of the bayou/lake connection that explains why New Orleans was settled here in the first place, and run across a few places closely connected to the French Quarter's unique history.

It won't take you long to learn how the streets run, especially if you have armed yourself with the excellent map passed out by the **Tourist Commission,** 529 St. Ann St. (tel. 566-5031). In fact, no one should set out to explore this city—inside or outside the French Quarter—without first stopping at the commission. By combining some of their information with the information in this chapter, you'll find yourself becoming quickly and happily acquainted with the history and charm of New Orleans.

Remember not to allow the quaintness of the city to deaden your safety senses—New Orleans is a major metropolis, with all the crime problems that that entails. Particular areas to steer clear of at night include the outer edges of the French Quarter, the Garden District, and the cemeteries. Try not to walk alone at night, and stay in well-lit, heavily trafficked areas—better yet, take a cab.

Note: During my most recent visit to New Orleans, plans were underway for the building of a brand new Insectarium (which the locals have affectionately renamed The Bug House). The details of the project are sketchy, but something might be happening down by the river by the time you get there.

1. SUGGESTED ITINERARIES

IF YOU HAVE 1 DAY

If you've got only one day in New Orleans, don't despair—the city is small enough for you to be able to get a taste of what it's all about in one day.

I'd suggest that you get there early in the morning and head to Café du Monde for beignets and coffee. Then follow the walking tour of the French Quarter given in Chapter 8 of this book, which shouldn't take too long and will give you a nice sampling of New Orleans architecture, history, and shopping. For lunch, pick one of the restaurants that appeals to you along the way (if you'd like some authentic Creole food, one suggestion would be Rita's Olde French Quarter Restaurant; see Chapter 6 for a more detailed description and other dining options).

After you've had lunch, hop on the St. Charles Avenue streetcar; as you ride, follow along with the streetcar tour given in this book (see Chapter 8). If you're up for another walking tour, try either the tour of the Lower Garden District or the tour of the Garden District, also given in Chapter 8. They average about the same walking time as the French Quarter walking tour, but there aren't any shops, restaurants, or museums to distract you. Whatever you do, be sure to ride the streetcar all the way to the end of the line because you'll see some interesting architecture along the way and you'll get a real feel for the city.

When you get back from the afternoon's activities, you'll probably have a little time to go back to the hotel, rest for a bit, and wash up for dinner. I suggest dining somewhere in the French Quarter. Chapter 6 can help you choose a restaurant if there's not one you've already set your heart on.

After dinner, take a walk over to Bourbon Street—it should be in full swing by the time you finish your meal. If it's jazz you're looking for, it's a little difficult to find these days; however, there are two places right in the French Quarter that you might enjoy—

The Palm Court Café on Decatur Street and Preservation Hall on St. Peter (see Chapter 10 for details on both).

If rock and roll's more your style, you'll have no trouble finding it all along Bourbon Street. Just pop in to any of the clubs along the main drag.

Finally, before you go back to your hotel for a good night's sleep, make a stop at Lafitte's Blacksmith Shop on the corner of Bourbon and St. Philip (see Chapter 10 for details) for a nightcap. This is a place you really shouldn't miss, especially in the fall or winter—it has a working fireplace and is the perfect spot in which to unwind after a long day.

IF YOU HAVE 2 DAYS

A two-day stay in New Orleans will probably be a lot less tiring than trying to see this fabulous city in only one day.

Day 1 I'd suggest that you take your time on the French Quarter walking tour I've worked out for you. Spend some time poking around in the galleries, shops, and museums. If you get up early you can either try to finish before lunch or work your way around to the French Market, where you might grab something on your way through, or maybe stop at Central Grocery for a muffaletta sandwich and either eat it there or, if it's warm enough, take it over to the banks of the Mississippi and watch the barges and steamboats chugging through the muddy waters.

After lunch, I'd suggest a trip over to the Aquarium of the Americas or perhaps a ride on one of the steamboats (most of them leave around 2pm; refer to "Organized Tours," later in this chapter, for exact times and prices). By the time you're finished with that, you'll want to go back to the hotel for a break, then enjoy dinner, and then sample some nightlife (see Chapter 10 for details).

Day 2 If you'd like to get out of the Quarter and explore some of the Garden District, get on the streetcar and head out toward the Riverbend area. Take your time, getting out when you see something that interests you. On the way back to the Vieux Carré, stop in the Garden District and follow the walking tour supplied in Chapter 8 of this book. If you just can't get enough of that wonderful Victorian architecture and your legs can stand it, go ahead and do the walking tour of the Lower Garden District.

If you're not interested in architecture but are interested in art and antiques, I suggest that you head out to Magazine Street and nose around in the antique shops (see Chapter 9 for a listing of shops). On your way back, stop on Julia Street and go gallery hopping (see Chapter 9 for details), then head over to the Contemporary Arts Center (see below).

IMPRESSIONS

"'See Naples and die,' says the proverb. My view of things is that you should see Canal-street, New Orleans, and then try to live as much longer as ever you can."
—G. A. SALA, *AMERICA REVISITED*, 1882.

If you're out in this area late enough to be hungry for dinner, there are plenty of places to eat, so don't think you have to hurry back to the French Quarter, although you might want to do that to take in some nightlife later—after a couple of hurricanes at Pat O'Brien's in the Vieux Carré, you won't be feeling your throbbing feet any longer.

IF YOU HAVE 3 DAYS

Days 1 and 2   Follow "If You Have 2 Days," above.

Day 3   Do some exploring on the other side of the Quarter. Check out Esplanade Avenue with the walking tour listed in Chapter 8. Explore St. Louis III Cemetery and City Park. Head back to the Quarter and check out the shops and sights you missed but wanted to see the last two days. Try a new spot for lunch. Go for a ride around the city in a horse-drawn buggy.

When evening comes, head over to Frenchmen Street to Alberto's (if you're in the mood for Italian cuisine) or the Praline Connection (if you'd rather have soul food) for dinner. There's a great place nearby to go to hear some jazz—Snug Harbor (see Chapter 10).

IF YOU HAVE 5 DAYS OR MORE

If you've got five days or more, you can take it easy.

Days 1–3   Follow the above itineraries, combining or changing them to suit your tastes.

Days 4–5   You can either hang around in the Quarter, or if that's getting a little old for your liking, flip to Chapter 11, "Easy Excursions from New Orleans," and plan a trip to some of the Victorian plantations located nearby and/or to Cajun country, which is home to a truly unique American regional culture.

2. THE TOP ATTRACTIONS

There is so much to see in New Orleans that one thing is certain: No matter how carefully you plan your time, you're bound to get back home and discover that you've missed at least one sightseeing highlight. People who live here will tell you that the only thing to do is move down and settle in to a lifetime of exploration!

THE FRENCH QUARTER

✪ The narrow old streets of the French Quarter are lined with ancient buildings (many a century and a half old) whose fronts are embellished with that distinctive lacy ironwork. Their carriage drives or alleyways are often guarded by more ironwork in the form of massive gates; you can often catch glimpses through these of some of the loveliest courtyards in the world. Secluded from street noises and nosy neighbors, the courtyards provide beauty, relaxation, and privacy—three qualities that have always been important to New

Orleanians—and ventilate the homes. Of course, many of these venerable buildings now serve as entertainment centers that often ring with merriment that is anything but restful; and many more now house shops of every description. But above ground level most also have apartments (many quite luxurious), keeping to the Old World custom of combining commercial ventures with living space. A few are still in the hands of original-owner families. Whatever its present use, almost every building in the Quarter has served as the backdrop for tales of romance and history that would enthrall the dullest soul.

Thanks to the Vieux Carré Commission, not even "progress" is allowed to intrude on a heritage that blends gaiety with graciousness, the rowdiness of Bourbon Street with the quiet residential areas, and the "busyness" of commerce with the sense of leisure and goodwill. Progress is here, all right, with all its attendant benefits, but New Orleans *insists* that it conform to the city's traditional way of life, not the other way around. There's not even a traffic light within the whole of the French Quarter—they're relegated to fringe streets—and street lights are of the old gaslight style. Do not worry about those absent traffic lights—automobiles are banned from Royal and Bourbon Streets during a good part of the day, making these streets pedestrian malls, and the area around Jackson Square is a permanent haven for foot traffic because no vehicles are allowed.

Laid out in an almost perfect rectangle back in 1718 by a French royal engineer named Adrien de Pauger, the French Quarter is easy to get around. And even in these high-crime days, you're relatively safe wandering its streets during daylight hours. After dark, as in most metropolitan areas, it's best to exercise caution when walking alone outside the centers of activity—in New Orleans, that means Bourbon, Royal, and Chartres Streets and the streets that connect them (there's safety as well as fun in the numbers that throng those streets all night long).

Since this area is one of the major attractions in New Orleans, I would suggest that you turn to Chapter 8 and do the walking tour of the French Quarter. It will give you the best overview in terms of historic buildings and the city's history. Many other attractions that aren't covered in the walking tour will be covered in this chapter.

UPTOWN & THE GARDEN DISTRICT

✪ Outside the borders of the French Quarter lies "American" New Orleans. It came into being because of Creole snobbery. You see, those semiaristocratic French Quarter natives had no use for the crass Americans who came flooding into the city after the 1803 Louisiana Purchase, so they presented a united and closed front to keep "their" New Orleans exclusive. Not to be outdone, the newcomers simply bought up land in what had been the old Gravier plantation upriver from Canal Street and set about building *their* New Orleans. Exhibiting the celebrated Yankee flair for enterprise, they very soon dominated the business scene, centered on Canal Street itself, and constructed mansions different from the traditional Quarter residences but surrounded by beautiful gardens. In 1833 what we know now as the Garden District was incorporated as

Lafayette City, and—thanks in large part to the New Orleans-Carrollton Railroad, which covered the route of today's St. Charles Avenue trolley—the Americans kept right on expanding until they reached the tiny resort town of Carrollton. It wasn't until 1852 that the various sections came together officially to become a united New Orleans.

To become better acquainted with another of the city's main areas of interest, turn to Chapter 8 and take one of the walking tours of the Garden District or follow the streetcar tour.

SUPERDOME

✪ The colossal **Louisiana Superdome** is located in the 1500 block of Poydras Street. Tall as a 27-story building, with a seating capacity of 76,000, the windowless structure has a computerized climate-control system that uses over 9,000 *tons* of equipment. It is the largest building in the world in diameter (680 feet), and its grounds cover some 13 acres. Inside, no posts obstruct the view for spectator sports such as football, baseball, and basketball, and movable partitions and seats give it the flexibility to form the best configuration for almost any event. Most people think of the Superdome as a sports center only, but this big flying saucer of a building plays host to conventions, trade shows, and large theatrical and musical productions as well. Entertainment and instant replays are provided via two Diamond Vision screens. Guided tours are run daily at 10am, noon, 2pm, and 4pm (except during Superdome events), and The Dome Café is open Monday through Friday from 11:30am to 2:30pm. For tour information and prices, call 587-3810.

3. MORE ATTRACTIONS

BAYOU ST. JOHN & LAKE PONTCHARTRAIN

Bayou St. John is one of the most important reasons New Orleans is where it is today. When Jean-Baptiste Le Moyne, Sieur de Bienville, was commissioned to establish a settlement that would protect the mouth of the Mississippi River for the French Crown against British expansion, he recognized the strategic importance of the "back-door" access to the Gulf of Mexico provided by the bayou's linkage to Lake Pontchartrain. Boats could enter the lake from the gulf, then follow the bayou to within easy portage distance of the Mississippi mouth. The Native American tribes hereabouts had used this route for years, and Bienville was quick to see its advantages.

The path from city to bayou back in those early days is today's Bayou Road, an extension of Governor Nicholls Street in the French Quarter. The modern-day Gentilly Boulevard, which crosses the bayou, was another Native American trail—it led around the lake and on to settlements in Florida after a relatively short boat trip.

⭐ **FROMMER'S FAVORITE NEW ORLEANS EXPERIENCES**

Beignets and Café au Lait at Café du Monde
A visit to New Orleans just wouldn't be the same without a trip to Café du Monde for a powdered-sugared plateful of those mouthwatering "doughnuts." Grabbing a bag "to go" and sitting along the banks of the Mississippi munching is a real treat.

A Day of Play on Magazine Street Spend the entire day rooting around in the antique shops, galleries, and bookstores on Magazine Street. If you're lucky, you might come across a real find!

A Walk Through the Garden District If you let it, a few hours wandering around the Garden District will take you back in time to the way it was in the Old South—especially on a warm spring day.

An Arts Crawl Along Julia Street There are so many new and wonderful contemporary galleries in what used to be the Warehouse District that you really shouldn't miss ducking in and out from one to the other—it really is worth a trip.

People-watching Along the Fence at Jackson Square It's wonderful to sit on one of the benches at Jackson Square and watch all the people walk by. Strike up a conversation with one of the artists who has "set up shop" along the fence—they have some wonderful stories to tell!

As the new town grew and prospered, planters moved out along the shores of the bayou, and in the early 1800s a canal was dug to connect the waterway with the city. It reached a basin at the edge of Congo Square. The lake itself became a popular recreation area, with fine restaurants and dance halls (as well as meeting places for voodoo practitioners, who held secret ceremonies along its shores). Gradually the city reached out beyond the French Quarter and enveloped the whole area—farmlands, plantation homes, and resorts. So on your exploration of this part of New Orleans, you'll see traces of that development. The canal is gone, filled in long ago, and the bayou itself is no longer navigable (even if it were, bridges were built too low to permit the passage of boats of any size), but residents still prize their waterfront sites, and rowboats and sailboats make use of the bayou's surface.

The simplest way to reach the Bayou St. John from the French Quarter is to drive straight out Esplanade Avenue about 20 blocks. Just before you reach the bayou, you'll pass **St. Louis Cemetery No. 3** (it's just past Leda Street), at which rest many prominent New Orleanians—among them are Thomy Lafon, the black philanthropist who bought the old Orleans Ballroom as an orphanage for African American children and thus put an end to its infamous "quadroon balls," and Father Adrien Rouquette, who lived and worked among the Choctaw. Just past the cemetery, Esplanade reaches Moss Street, and a left turn will put you on that street, which runs along the banks of Bayou St. John.

Drive along Wisner Boulevard, along the bank of Bayou St. John, and you'll pass some of New Orleans's grandest modern homes, which provide a sharp contrast to those over on Moss Street. Stay on Wisner to Robert E. Lee Boulevard, turn right, and drive to Elysian Fields Avenue, then turn left. That's **Louisiana State University's New Orleans campus** on your left (its main campus is in Baton Rouge).

Turn left onto the broad concrete highway that is Lakeshore Drive. It runs for 5½ miles along the lake, and in summer the parkway alongside its seawall is usually swarming with swimmers and picnickers. On the other side are more luxurious, ultramodern residences.

Lake Pontchartrain itself is some 40 miles long and 25 miles wide. Native Americans once lived along its shores on both sides, and it was a major waterway long before white people were seen in this hemisphere. You can drive across it over the **Greater New Orleans Causeway,** the 23¾-mile-long bridge, the longest in the world.

When you cross the mouth of the Bayou St. John, you'll be where the old **Spanish Fort** was built in 1770. Its remains are now nestled amidst elegant modern homes. In the early 1800s there was a lighthouse here, and in the 1820s a railroad brought New Orleanians out to a hotel, a casino, a bandstand, bathing houses, and restaurants that made this a popular resort area.

Look for the **Mardi Gras fountain** on your left. Bronze plaques around its base are inscribed with the names of Mardi Gras krewes, and if you time your lake visit out to coincide with sundown, you'll see the fountain beautifully lit in Mardi Gras colors of purple (for justice), green (for faith), and gold (for power).

Down at the end of Lakeshore Drive, when you come to the old white Coast Guard lighthouse, you'll know you've reached **West End.** This is an interesting little park that's home for several yacht clubs, a marina, and restaurants, many of which have been here for years and look just like lakeside restaurants should (not too fancy—more interested in the view out over the water and good eating than in "decorator-style" interiors). This old fishing community has, over the years, become the main pleasure-boating center of New Orleans, and the Southern Yacht Club here was established in 1840, making it the second oldest in the country. After the railroad began bringing pleasure-seekers here from the city in the 1870s, showboats and floating circuses would often pull up and dock for waterside performances. West End is an excellent place to stop for a bite to eat, if indeed it isn't your destination when you set out for the lakeside with a fresh seafood dinner in mind.

To reach **Buckstown,** which lines the bank of a narrow canal behind the restaurants on the western side of West End park, turn to the left on Lakeshore Drive at the Coast Guard station, then turn right on Lake Avenue (it's the first street you come to).

Buckstown is another small fishing community that still retains its old-time atmosphere. There are also many good seafood restaurants here.

CEMETERIES

In the beginning, burials were made along the banks of the Mississippi, but when the little settlement of New Orleans began to grow, more cemetery space was a necessity. However, there was a big problem: The soggy ground was so damp that graves would fill with water even before the coffins could be lowered. To solve that problem aboveground tombs were constructed. The coffin would be put in place on the ground, walls of brick would be built around it, and then the walls would be plastered and whitewashed. The entrances to the tombs were closed by marble tablets, and many were enclosed with iron fences. Some were even finished off with rounded roofs or topped with eaves—like tiny, windowless houses. It is easy to see why the cemeteries came to be called "Cities of the Dead" because they are arranged along narrow paths, many of which have "street" names. These miniature cities even have their "skyscrapers," since upper floors would be added as members of the same family passed away and were entombed right on top of the existing vault. Along the outer walls of the cemeteries, you'll see rows of wall vaults, or "ovens," which hold the remains of the city's poor. Incidentally, you may be perplexed by the long list of names for just one tomb—that's because, in a miracle of space engineering, New Orleanians use the same tomb over and over, simply removing the old remains after two years have passed and interring a fresh body in the vacated space.

St. Louis Cemetery No. 1, in the 400 block of Basin Street, was the first, established in the 1740s; **St. Louis Cemetery No. 2** is a few blocks away down from Conti Street on Claiborne Avenue (from Iberville to St. Louis Streets), and if you see one of the unmarked "ovens" with red crosses on its concrete slab, that's the other place Marie Laveau may or may not be resting from her voodoo activities. It seems that no matter how many times the slab is painted over, the faithful keep coming back to mark it and ask Marie's favors. **Lafayette No. 1 Cemetery** is in the Garden District bounded by Washington, Prytania, and Coliseum Streets. Perhaps the most beautiful of all is **Metairie Cemetery,** at the intersection of Pontchartrain Boulevard and Metairie Road—and it wouldn't be here at all except for one New Orleanian's pique at being denied admission to the exclusive Metairie Jockey Club at the racetrack that once operated on these grounds. He was an American who, to strike back at those uppity Creoles who wouldn't let him in, bought up the land, turned it into a burial ground, and swore that from then on only the dead would gain admittance.

Before leaving this subject, there is one word of warning that I must add. Because there have been several muggings in St. Louis

---

IMPRESSIONS

"There is no architecture in New Orleans, except in the cemeteries."
—MARK TWAIN, *LIFE ON THE MISSISSIPPI*, 1883.

Cemeteries No. 1 and No. 2 (the oldest), it is best not to walk in them alone. Either go with a party or tour or join the excellent free "City of the Dead" walking tour guided by park rangers of the Jean Lafitte National Park and Preserve. Call 589-2636 for the schedules.

CHURCHES

Sometimes people don't realize that St. Louis Cathedral (discussed at length in Chapter 8's walking tour of the French Quarter) isn't the only church in New Orleans. Below, you'll find a few others that you might want to stop in and have a look at.

ST. ALPHONSUS CHURCH, 2029 Constance St. Tel. 522-6748.

The Irish built St. Alphonsus Church in 1855, and the gallery and columns may vaguely remind you of the St. Louis Cathedral in the French Quarter. A beloved Redemptorist priest, Fr. Francis Xavier Seeles, is buried in the church. He is credited with the working of many miracles; if you visit the church, you're likely to see letters of petition on his tomb.

ST. PATRICK'S CHURCH, 724 Camp St. Tel. 525-4413.

St. Patrick's was founded in a tiny wooden building to serve Irish Catholics in the parish. The present building, begun in 1838, was constructed around the old one, which was then dismantled inside the new building. The distinguished architect James Gallier, Sr., designed much of the interior, including the altar. It opened in 1840, proudly proclaimed as the "American" Catholics' answer to the St. Louis Cathedral in the French Quarter (where, according to the Americans, God spoke only in French).

CHURCH OF ST. JOHN THE BAPTIST, 1139 Dryades St. Tel. 525-1726.

Because you wouldn't be human if you didn't wonder about that gilded dome so prominent against the skyline (especially as you drive on the elevated expressway), I'm including the Church of St. John the Baptist. It was built by the Irish in 1871, and its most noteworthy features (besides the exceptional brickwork of the exterior) are the Stations of the Cross and sacristy murals that were painted during and after World War II by a Belgian artist, Dom Gregory Dewit, as well as the beautiful stained-glass windows crafted by artists in Munich.

OUR LADY OF GUADALUPE INTERNATIONAL SHRINE OF ST. JUDE, 411 N. Rampart St. Tel. 525-1551.

Located on the corner of Rampart and Conti Streets, this building was put up in 1826 as a chapel convenient to the St. Louis Cemetery No. 1—funeral services were held here rather than in St. Louis Cathedral so as not to spread disease within the confines of the Quarter, and it became known as the "Burial Chapel." In the intervening years it has been renovated, and it now houses an International Shrine of St. Jude (the saint of impossible causes, she is often thanked publicly for favors in the "Personals" column of the *Times-Picayune*). Another saint is honored here by a statue next to the main altar. His name is St. Expedite, a name that legend says was given to the statue when it arrived at the church in a packing crate with no identification but stamped "Expedite."

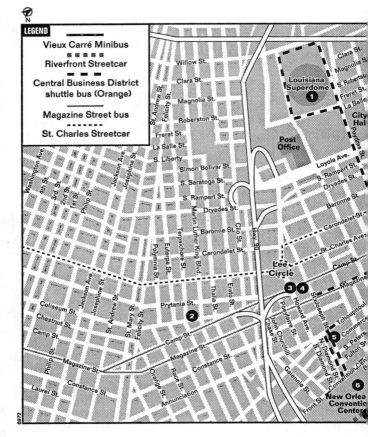

Aquarium of the Americas ⑨
Beauregard-Keyes House ㉕
Cabildo ⑲
Confederate Museum ③
Contemporary Arts Center ④
Gallier House Museum ㉗
Historic New Orleans Collection ⑮
Lafayette No. 1 Cemetery ②

Louisiana Children's Museum ⑤
Louisiana Science Center ⑦
Louisiana Superdome ①
Musée Conti Wax Museum ⑭
New Orleans
  Convention Center ⑥
New Orleans Historic
  Voodoo Museum ㉔

HISTORIC BUILDINGS

One of the historic buildings in New Orleans is the mid-19th-century town house at 826 St. Ann St. It is owned by the New Orleans Spring Fiesta Association. Furnished with lovely antiques of the Victorian era and many outstanding objets d'art from New Orleans's golden age of the 1800s, the house is open to the public by appointment and a $3 donation is requested. It's a lovely peek backward in time. For Spring Fiesta information, contact the

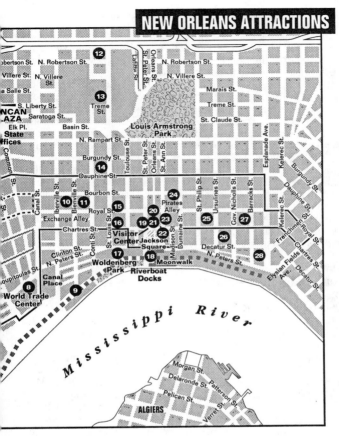

NEW ORLEANS ATTRACTIONS

New Orleans Jazz Museum **11**
New Orleans Pharmacy
  Museum **16**
Old Absinthe House **10**
Old Ursuline Convent **26**
Old U.S. Mint **28**
Pontalba Apartments **22**
Presbytère **23**

Preservation Hall **20**
St. Louis Cathedral **21**
St. Louis Cemetery No. 1 **13**
St. Louis Cemetery No. 2 **12**
Washington Artillery Park **18**
Woldenberg River Park **17**
World Trade Center **8**

association at 826 St. Ann St., New Orleans, LA 70116 (tel. 504/
581-1367).

IN THE FRENCH QUARTER

OLD ABSINTHE HOUSE, 240 Bourbon St. Tel. 523-3181.

Two blocks from Canal Street, the Old Absinthe House was
built in 1806 by two Spaniards and is still owned by their
descendants (although they live in Spain and have nothing to

do with running the place). The drink for which it was named is outlawed in this country now, but with a little imagination you can sip a modern-day libation and visualize Andrew Jackson and the Lafitte brothers plotting the desperate defense of New Orleans in 1815. It's the custom here to put your calling card on the wall, and the hundreds and hundreds of browning cards form a covering not unlike tattered wallpapers. It was a speakeasy during Prohibition, and when federal officers closed it in 1924, the interior was mysteriously stripped of its antique fixtures, including the long marble-topped bar and the old water dripper (used to drip water into absinthe), all of which just as mysteriously reappeared down the street at a corner establishment called, oddly enough, the Old Absinthe House Bar (400 Bourbon). It, too, follows the calling-card custom. If you can't keep all that straight, just remember that if you're in an Old Absinthe House that doesn't have entertainment, you're in the original *house*—if you see that grand brass water dripper on a marble-topped bar, you're in the new home of the original bar and fixtures.

Admission: Free.

Open: Daily 10am–2am.

BEAUREGARD-KEYES HOUSE, 1113 Chartres St. Tel. 523-7257.

This "raised cottage," with its Doric columns and handsome twin staircases, was built by a wealthy New Orleans auctioneer, Joseph Le Carpentier, back in 1826 as a residence. La Carpentier was grandfather to world-famous chess champion Paul Morphy, who was born to his daughter in one of its rooms in 1837. Confederate General PGT Beauregard lived in the house with several members of his family for 18 months between 1865 and 1867. From 1944 until 1970 it was the residence of Frances Parkinson Keyes, who wrote many novels about this region. One of them, *Madame Castel's Lodger,* is directly concerned with the general's stay in the house. *Dinner at Antoine's,* perhaps her most famous novel, also was written here. Mrs. Keyes left the house to a foundation, and the house, rear buildings, and garden are now open to the public. The gift shop has a wide selection of Frances Parkinson Keyes's novels.

Admission: $4 adults, $3 seniors and students, $1.50 children 12 and under.

Open: Mon–Sat 10am–3pm. Tours are offered on the hour.

CABILDO, 701 Chartres St. Tel. 568-6968.

On Jackson Square, the Cabildo is the site of the Louisiana Purchase signing. Exhibits include a Mississippi River collection of steamboat-era artifacts and paintings, Napoleon's death mask, and early Louisiana settlement items. After a devastating fire, the Cabildo has been renovated and completely restored to better than its original condition. In addition to the above-mentioned the museum holds interactive exhibits, china, basketry, woodcarvings, and 19th-century paintings.

Admission: $3 adults, $1.50 students and seniors, children 12 and under free.

Open: Tues–Sun 10am–5pm.

OLD URSULINE CONVENT, 1114 Chartres St. Tel. 529-3040.

Across from the Beauregard-Keyes House is the Archbishop Antoine Blanc Memorial, which includes the Old Ursuline Convent. The Sisters of Ursula were for years the only teachers and nurses in New Orleans—they established the first schools for Catholic girls, for African Americans and for Native Americans, and they set up the first orphanage in Louisiana. The nuns moved out of the convent in 1824 (they're in an uptown location these days), and in 1831 the state legislature met here. It now houses Catholic archives dating back to 1718. Especially noteworthy is the fact that this is the oldest building of record not only in New Orleans but also in the entire Mississippi Valley, and it is the only surviving building from the French colonial effort in what is now the United States. Included in the complex is the beautiful restored old Chapel of the Archbishops, erected in 1845 and still used as a house of worship.

Admission: $4 adults, $2 students and seniors.

Open: Tours Tues–Fri 10 and 11am and 1, 2, and 3pm; Sat–Sun 11:15am, 1 and 2pm.

PONTALBA APARTMENTS, 1850 HOUSE, 523 St. Ann St. Tel. 568-6968.

These historic apartments are located in the Lower Pontalba Buildings, in a restored house of the period. They're authentically furnished from parlor to kitchen to servants' quarters.

Admission: $3 adults, $1.50 seniors and students, children 12 and under free.

Open: Tues–Sun 10am–5pm.

PRESBYTERE, 751 Chartres St. Tel. 568-6968.

Located on Jackson Square, the Presbytère was planned as housing for the clergy but was never used for that purpose. It exhibits the paintings of Louisianan artists as well as displays on local history and culture.

Admission: $3 adults, $1.50 seniors and students, children 12 and under free.

Open: Tues–Sun 10am–5pm.

THE OLD U.S. MINT, 400 Esplanade Ave. Tel. 568-6968.

The Old U.S. Mint houses exhibits on New Orleans jazz and on the city's Carnival celebrations. These displays contain a comprehensive collection of pictures, musical instruments, and other artifacts connected with jazz greats (Louis Armstrong's first trumpet is here), as well as a videocassette theater. Across the hall there's a stunning array of Carnival mementos—from ornate Mardi Gras costumes to a street scene complete with maskers and a parade float. Entrances to the Mint are on both Esplanade Avenue and Barracks Street.

Admission: $3 adults, $1.50 seniors and students, children under 12 free.

Open: Tues–Sun 10am–5pm.

GALLIER HOUSE MUSEUM, 1132 Royal St. Tel. 523-6722.

The Gallier House Museum was built by James Gallier, Jr., as his residence in 1857. The carefully restored town house contains an early working bathroom, a passive ventilation system, and furnishings of the period. The adjoining building houses historical exhibits, as well as films on decorative plasterwork, ornamental ironwork, wood-graining, and marbling. There also are a gift shop, a café, and plenty of free parking at the museum. Special seasonal programs are available.

Admission: $4 adults, $3 seniors and students, $2.25 children 5–11, children under 5 free.

Open: Mon–Sat 10am–4:30pm, Sun noon–4:30pm. Last tour begins at 4pm.

OUTSIDE THE FRENCH QUARTER

PITOT HOUSE, 1440 Moss St. Tel. 482-0312.

The Pitot House is a typical West Indies–style plantation home, restored and furnished with Louisianan and American antiques dating from the early 1800s. Dating from 1799, it originally stood where the nearby modern Catholic school is now. In 1810 it became the home of James Pitot, the first mayor of incorporated New Orleans, and it is now known by his name. It has wide galleries on the sides and large columns supporting the second floor.

Admission: $3 adults, $2 seniors, $1 children under 12.

Open: Wed–Sat 10am–3pm.

JACKSON BARRACKS, 6400 St. Claude Ave. Tel. 271-6262, ext. 242, or 278-6242.

On an extension of Rampart Street downriver from the French Quarter is this series of fine old brick buildings with white columns. They were built in 1834–35 for troops who were stationed at the river forts. Some say Andrew Jackson, who never quite trusted New Orleans Creoles, planned the barracks to be as secure against attack from the city as from outside forces. The Barracks now serve as headquarters for the Louisiana National Guard, and there's a marvelous military museum in the old powder magazine, which has an extensive collection of military items that span the American wars. It's best to call before you go to confirm that the Barracks and museum are open. The museum recently underwent an expansion, and the complex now consists of the original powder magazine and a new annex that holds exhibits from World War II to Operation Desert Storm.

Admission: Free.

Open: Mon–Fri 7:30am–3:30pm.

MUSEUMS & GALLERIES

CONFEDERATE MUSEUM, 929 Camp St. Tel. 523-4522.

Located not far from the French Quarter, the Confederate Museum was established in 1899, close enough to the end of the Civil War for many donations to be in better condition than is sometimes true of museum items. There are battle flags, weapons, personal effects of Confederate President Jefferson Davis (including his evening clothes), part of Robert E. Lee's silver camp service, and many portraits of Confederate military and civilian personalities. A series of detailed pictures traces Louisiana's history from secession through Reconstruction.

Admission: $4 adults, $2 children under 12.

Open: Mon–Sat 10am–4pm.

CONTEMPORARY ARTS CENTER, 900 Camp St. Tel. 523-1216.

⭐ Located outside the French Quarter, in what used to be the warehouse district and is now the Arts District, the Contemporary Arts Center exhibits the artwork of regional, national, and international artists. The CAC also presents theater, performance art, dance, and music concerts. Exhibitions change every six to eight weeks, and performances are weekly. A café and bookshop are open Monday through Saturday.

Admission: $3 general, $2 students and seniors, free to members. Admission is free to all on Thurs. Performance prices range from $3 to $15.

Open: Mon–Sat 10am–5pm, Sun 11am–5pm.

HISTORIC NEW ORLEANS COLLECTION—MUSEUM/RESEARCH CENTER, 533 Royal St. Tel. 523-4662.

⭐ The Historic New Orleans Collection is located within a complex of historic French Quarter buildings. The oldest, constructed in the late 18th century, is one of the few structures to escape the disastrous fire of 1794. Today, the Collection serves the public as a museum and research center for state and local history with history-related gifts in the shop. The Williams Gallery, free to the public, presents changing exhibitions that focus on Louisiana's history and culture. Guided tours are available of both the founders' residence, one of the "hidden" houses of the Vieux Carré, and the Louisiana History Galleries. The History Gallery Tour is a must for all visitors who would like to learn more about Louisiana's colorful and exciting past.

Tours: $2, given Tues–Sat at 10 and 11am and 2 and 3pm. Wheelchair accommodation is available.

Admission: Free.

Open: Tues–Sat 10am–4:45pm.

MUSEE CONTI WAX MUSEUM, 917 Conti St. Tel. 525-2605.

⭐ This museum offers New Orleans history depicted by life-size wax figures with authentic costumes and settings of Louisiana legends (Andrew Jackson, Jean Lafitte, Huey Long, Edwin Edwards, and Pete Fountain), plus an added "Haunted Dungeon" illustrating well-known horror tales. A self-guided Louisiana Legends Walking Tour is provided for $1.50 with your admission to the museum.

Admission: $5 adults, $4.50 seniors over 62, $3 children 4–17, children under 4 are free.

Open: Daily 10am–5pm. **Closed:** Christmas and Mardi Gras Day.

NEW ORLEANS HISTORIC VOODOO MUSEUM, 724 Dumaine St. Tel. 523-7685.

If tales of Marie Laveau have captured your imagination, you'll definitely want to stop by the Voodoo Museum, in the heart of the Vieux Carré. The dark, musty interior seems exactly the right setting for artifacts of the occult from all over the globe and a fitting place in which to learn more of that curious mixture of African and Catholic religions and rituals brought to New Orleans in the late 1700s by former Santo Domingan slaves.

There's a guided voodoo walking tour of the French Quarter that leaves the museum at 1pm daily and visits Congo Square (now Beauregard Square) and a pharmacy displaying voodoo potions. There is another tour that leaves at 1:30pm and takes you on a visit to Marie Laveau's reputed grave. The museum can arrange psychic readings and visits to voodoo rituals if you want to delve deeper into this subject, which has bedeviled New Orleans for centuries.

Admission: $5 adults, $4 students and seniors. French Quarter tour $18 per person, cemetery tour $10 per person.

Open: Daily 10am–dusk.

NEW ORLEANS MUSEUM OF ART, Lelong Ave. Tel. 488-2631.

Located in City Park, this museum is in a neoclassical building housing pre-Columbian, Renaissance, and contemporary art exhibited to show the history of art development. The columned main building is a beauty inside and out. Its first-floor Delgado Great Hall leads to a branched staircase at the back that rises to a mezzanine overlooking the hall. Beautiful! Notice, too, the bronze statue of Hercules as an archer just outside the entrance. The original building, about 80 years old, has been expanded by the addition of three wings, and the art inside does justice to its housing. There's a lovely portrait of Estelle Musson, a relative of the French impressionist painter Edgar Degas, who painted this likeness on one of his visits to the city. The 22 sections of the Kress Renaissance collection, pre-Columbian art, and bronzes by Rodin mix well with 20th-century art. NOMA recently underwent a $23-million expansion project which created more gallery space for portions of the museum's collection (both western and non-western art from the pre-Christian era to the present) that had previously been relegated to storage. In addition, there is now an entire floor devoted to non-western and ethnographic art, including Asian, African, pre-Columbian, Oceanic, and Native American art.

Admission: $6 adults, $3 seniors and children, free to all on Thurs.

Open: Tues–Sun 10am–5pm.

NEW ORLEANS PHARMACY MUSEUM, 514 Chartres St. Tel. 565-8027.

Founded in 1950, the New Orleans Pharmacy Museum is an interesting stop on a tour of the French Quarter. In 1823 the first licensed pharmacist in the United States, Louis J. Dufilho, Jr., opened an apothecary shop here at 514 Chartres St. The Creole-style town house doubled as his home, and in the interior courtyard he cultivated the herbs he would need for fabricating his medicines. Inside the museum you'll find old apothecary bottles, pill tile, and suppository molds as well as the old glass cosmetics counter (pharmacists of the 1800s also manufactured make-up and perfumes). There's even an 1855 black-and-rose Italian marble soda fountain.

Admission: $2 donation per person.

Open: Tues–Sun 10am–5pm.

A MONUMENT

At the corner of Camp and Prytania Streets, you'll see a statue of one Irish immigrant, Margaret Haughery, who toiled in a bakery and dairy and devoted every spare minute to the care of orphans. When she died she left all her hard-won earnings to charity. The **Carrara marble statue,** whose inscription is simply "Margaret," was unveiled in 1884; it was one of the first statues dedicated to a woman anywhere in the country. Appropriately there's a day nursery that dates back to 1850 on the edge of the small park that holds Margaret's monument.

PANORAMAS

WORLD TRADE CENTER OF NEW ORLEANS, 2 Canal St.

Down at the river, the World Trade Center of New Orleans is the center of the city's maritime industry as well as the home of most international consulates. On the 31st floor there's an observation deck that looks out onto the city and a harbor scene that might include naval vessels (from submarines to aircraft carriers), cruise ships (those that simply ply excursions in local waters and those that leave for far-away ports), and freighters flying flags from around the world. For a stunning ride up, use the outside elevator—more timid souls can opt for the one inside. The observation deck, called Viewpoint, is open every day except Christmas and Easter. This is truly an incomparable view. Also included in the admission price are two exciting slide shows about the city, a colorful international flag and map display, and individual audiocassette tours of the observation deck. There are high-power telescopes to zoom in on your favorite site for only 25¢. For more relaxed viewing, go on up to the 33rd-floor revolving cocktail lounge (see Chapter 10).

Admission: $2 adults, $1 children 6–12, children under 6 free.
Open: Daily 10am–4pm.

PARKS & GARDENS

AUDUBON PARK, 6500 Magazine St. Tel. 861-2538.

Across the street from both Loyola and Tulane, Audubon Park sprawls over 340 acres, reaching from St. Charles Avenue all the way to the Mississippi River. This tract of land once belonged to Jean-Baptiste Le Moyne, the founder of New Orleans, and later was part of the Etienne de Bore plantation, where sugar was granulated for the first time in 1794. The city purchased it in 1871; a golf course now lies on the section where the World's Industrial and Cotton Centennial Exposition was held in 1884–85. In spite of having what was then the largest building in the world (33 acres under one roof) as its main exhibition hall, the exposition was such a financial disaster that everything except a Horticultural Hall had to be sold off. (The Horticultural Hall fell victim to a hurricane a little later.) After that, serious work was begun to make this into a park.

The huge trees with black bark you see here are live oaks, and some go back to the days when this was a plantation. They're evergreens and shed only once a year, in early spring. Their spreading limbs turn walkways into covered alleys, and there are winding lagoons, fountains, and statuary, as well as a very nice zoo (see later in this section). Scattered about are gazebos, shelters, and playground areas—and that funny-looking mound over near the river, actually in the zoo, is called "Monkey Hill," constructed so that the children of this flatland city could see what a hill looked like. Especially nice is the pavilion on the riverbank, one of the most pleasant places from which to view the Mighty Mississippi.

As far as I'm concerned, the trees and wandering paths and general atmosphere of peace and quiet are quite enough for any park. But if you're looking for recreation facilities, you'll find those here, too. There's an 18-hole golf course in the front half, picnic facilities, tennis courts, a 1.8-mile jogging track, 18 exercise stations, and horseback riding. The Audubon Zoo is toward the back of the park.

When you reach the end of St. Charles Avenue (where the streetcar turns onto Carrollton Avenue), the green hill over by the river is the levee—if the water happens to be high enough, you'll see the tops of ships as they pass by.

Admission: Free.
Open: 6am–7pm.

CITY PARK, 1 Dreyfous Ave. Tel. 482-4888.

Right at the entrance is a statue of Gen. PGT Beauregard, whose order to fire on Fort Sumter opened the Civil War and whom New Orleanians fondly call the "Great Creole." The park was once part of the Louis Allard plantation; its extensive, beautifully landscaped grounds hold four golf courses, picnic areas, a restaurant, lagoons for boating and fishing, tennis courts, horses for hire for the lovely trails, a bandstand, a miniature train, and Children's Storyland, an amusement area with carnival rides for children (see "Cool for Kids," this chapter, for more details).

The huge old oaks in City Park looked down on a favorite pastime in New Orleans during the 1700s—dueling. To the proud Creoles, nothing—not even death—was to be feared so much as the loss of honor, and when a dispute ended with a heated "under the oaks at sunrise," it was here, under what came to be called the **Dueling Oaks,** that the rendezvous was kept. The practice persisted into the early 1800s (there were, in fact, 10 duels fought on just one Sunday morning in 1837), but duels changed very much in character after Americans arrived on the scene. Creoles observed a very formal and strict dueling etiquette, using the meetings to demonstrate their expertise with rapiers, broadswords, or pistols (fists were never used among gentlemen), and only seldom was either party actually killed. With the Americans, however, came a whole new concept—duels became a fight to the death, with such "rude" weapons as rifles, shotguns, clubs, and even axes. Dueling died out after the Civil War; it had always been forbidden by both church and law (strictures heretofore completely ignored by the proud participants), and after the war there was a stricter enforcement of the laws. One of the mighty oaks became known during the bleak Reconstruction era as the "Suicide Oak" because of its popularity as the setting for that action. Another, McDonogh Oak, is believed to be over 600 years old, and has a 142-foot branch spread.

You'll find the **New Orleans Museum of Art** on Lelong Avenue in City Park in a building that is itself a work of art (see "Museums and Galleries," earlier in this chapter, for more details).

Admission: Free.
Open: 6am–7pm.

CHALMETTE NATIONAL HISTORICAL PARK, St. Bernard Hwy.

To reach the park, continue on St. Claude Avenue until it becomes St. Bernard Highway. The park will be on your right. On these grounds the bloody Battle of New Orleans was waged on January 14, 1815. Ironically the battle should never have been fought at all, since the War of 1812 had by then been concluded by a treaty signed two weeks before in Ghent, Belgium. The treaty was not, however, in effect, and word had simply never reached Congress, the commander of the British forces, or Andrew Jackson, who stood with American forces to defend New Orleans and the mouth of the Mississippi River. The battle did, however, succeed in bringing New Orleanians together more than they had ever been and in making Andrew Jackson a hero forever in this city.

You can visit the battleground and see markers that will let you follow the course of the battle in detail. In the Beauregard plantation house on the grounds, you will find interesting exhibits, and the Visitor Center presents a film and other exhibits on the battle. There also is a National Cemetery here, which was established in 1864; it holds only two American veterans of the Battle of New Orleans, but some 14,000 Union soldiers who fell in the Civil War are buried here. For a really terrific view of the Mississippi River, climb the levee in back of the Beauregard House.

Admission: Free.
Open: Daily 8:30am–5pm.

LONGUE VUE ESTATE & GARDENS, 7 Bamboo Road. Tel. 488-5488.

Just off of Metairie Road, you'll find the lovely, eight-acre Longue Vue Estate, one of the most beautiful garden settings in this area. The mansion is built in the classical tradition. As with the great country houses of England, it was designed to foster a close rapport between indoors and outdoors, with vistas of formal terraces and pastoral woods. Some parts of the enchanting gardens were inspired by those of the Generalife in Granada, Spain; besides the colorful flowering plants, there are formal boxwood arrangement, fountains, and a colonnaded loggia. Highlights are the Canal Garden; Walled Garden; Wild Garden (which features native iris); and Spanish Court (with pebbled walkways, changing horticultural displays, and statuary).

Admission: $6.50 adults, $5.50 seniors, $3.50 children through college age.
Open: Mon–Sat 10am–4:30pm, Sun 1–5pm. **Closed:** Major holidays.

ST. ANTHONY'S GARDEN, Royal and Orleans Streets.

Orleans Street begins at St. Anthony's Garden, in back of the St. Louis Cathedral. Not only was this charming little garden a favorite dueling spot, it is also the site of a marble monument put there by the French government in memory of 30 French marines who died doing volunteer nursing duty during a yellow fever epidemic. The garden is named for a beloved Capuchin priest affectionately called Père Antoine, and the walkway between Chartres and Royal Streets on the downtown side of the cathedral is given the name of Père Antoine's Alley, in his honor.

WASHINGTON ARTILLERY PARK, between Jackson Square and the Mississippi River. Tel. 529-5284.

Just past Jackson Brewery, pretty riverside Washington Artillery Park, with its splashing fountains, has always been a "promenade" for New Orleanians, and now the elevated area has been renamed the Moon Walk (for Mayor "Moon" Landrieu). There are attractive plantings and benches from which to view the city's main industry—its busy port (second only to Amsterdam for tonnage handled each year). To your right you will see the Greater New Orleans Bridge and World Trade Center of New Orleans (formerly the International Trade Mart) skyscraper, as well as the Toulouse Street wharf, departure point for excursion steamboats.

Admission: Free.
Open: Dawn to dusk.

WOLDENBERG RIVER PARK, along the Mississippi River in the French Quarter. Tel. 861-2537.

Some 13 acres of the riverfront, from Canal Street to St. Peter Street, have been converted into the Woldenberg River Park. This oasis of greenery in the heart of the city is centered by a large lawn, with a brick promenade leading to the Mississippi and more than 600 trees—oaks, magnolias, willows, and crape myrtles—and 1,400 shrubs to beautify this tranquil spot. The park is now the setting for the Aquarium of the Americans (see below).

Admission: Free.
Open: Dawn to dusk.

A ZOO & AN AQUARIUM

AUDUBON ZOO, 6500 Magazine St. Tel. 861-5101.

⭐ The Audubon Zoo is one of the top five zoos in the country. Here, in a setting of subtropical plantings, waterfalls, and lagoons, some 1,500 animals live in natural habitats. Don't plan to spend less than two or three hours—more if you have time to spare—in this delightful oasis of animal culture. A terrific way to visit is to arrive on the sternwheeler *Cotton Blossom* (see "Organized Tours," later in this chapter) and depart via the St. Charles streetcar, which is reached by way of a lovely stroll through Audubon Park or on a complimentary shuttle bus. During your visit to the zoo look for the bronze statue of John James Audubon. It's in a grove of trees and the naturalist is shown with a notebook and pencil in hand.

Admission: $7.50 adults, $3.50 children 2–12.
Open: Mon–Fri 9am–4:30pm, Sat–Sun 9am–5:30pm. **Closed:** Holidays.

AQUARIUM OF THE AMERICAS, 1 Canal St. (at the Mississippi River). Tel. 861-2537.

⭐ The one-million-gallon Aquarium of the Americas is located on the banks of the Mississippi River, right on the edge of the French Quarter. Five major exhibit areas and dozens of smaller aquarium displays hold a wonderful collection of fish from North, Central, and South America and are exhibited in environments that mimic their natural ones. You can take a walk through the underwater tunnel in the Caribbean Reef exhibit and feel like you're swimming with the fish. A re-creation of the Gulf of Mexico houses a sampling of fish that you would see if you were swimming around in the Gulf—chances are you'll think twice about that after you've seen the sharks! There's also a wonderful tropical rain forest with piranha and tropical birds. Don't forget to stop by and say hello to the penguins—they're very friendly. The Aquarium is currently undergoing an expansion which will include the addition of a 350-seat IMAX theater (completed by 1995), and a 12,000-square-foot changing exhibit gallery (first exhibit scheduled for 1996).

Admission: $8.75 adults, $6.50 seniors, $4.50 children 2–12.

Open: Memorial Day to Labor Day Sun–Wed 9:30am–7pm, Thurs–Sat 9:30am–9pm; Sept–May Sun–Thurs 9:30am–6pm, Fri–Sat 9:30am–7pm.

4. COOL FOR KIDS

Even though it might not at first appear to be, New Orleans is a great place to bring kids. There's so much for a child to learn in a city so filled with history. Below I've listed some places I think your kids might enjoy (chances are that you will, too).

All kids love the French Market because it's small and there's so much to look at. Take them on a horse-and-buggy ride around the Vieux Carré: You'll learn about the history, and they'll just have a great time imagining themselves in another historical period. Of course, the Riverfront streetcar and a ferry ride on the Mississippi River are fun—you can get them to imagine that they're playing a part in the lives of Huck Finn and Tom Sawyer. Finish it off with a visit to Aquarium of the Americas (see "More Attractions," earlier in this chapter).

Some kids might like a visit to a museum or two, and I'd suggest the Confederate Museum, the New Orleans Historic Voodoo Museum, or the Musée Conti Wax Museum—all listed under "More Attractions," earlier in this chapter.

If you're in the Central Business District for the day, take them over to the Superdome and go on one of the tours that are offered daily (see "Organized Tours," later in this chapter, for details); they'll love seeing where some of their heroes play ball, and they'll be in absolute awe of the enormity of the building.

If they're getting restless being inside so much and the weather is nice, take them to one of the parks listed above and have a picnic lunch.

Below I've listed a couple of things that are absolutely kid-oriented and are worth a visit.

LOUISIANA CHILDREN'S MUSEUM, 428 Julia St. Tel. 523-1357.

This is a marvelous "hands-on" wonderland for the young. They'll delight in fantasies of being a medieval knight or lady-in-waiting, a tugboat captain, or a newscaster. Special projects scheduled on Saturday include puppet workshops, storytelling, and cooking programs. New exhibits include "First Adventures Toddler Playscape," a developmental play area for newborns to 3-year-olds, and "The Shadow Trap," an exhibit that actually allows children to strike a pose and then walk away to see that their shadow has been "trapped" on the wall by a light-sensitive material. The museum is accessible to the handicapped.

Admission: $3.

Open: Tues–Sun 9am–5pm.

CHILDREN'S STORYLAND, in City Park. Tel. 483-9381.

This is an enchanted playground where youngsters can slide down Jack and Jill's hill, climb Little Miss Muffet's spiderweb, or fish in the Little Mermaid's pond. Larger than life fairy-tale figures such as Puss-n-Boots, Rapunzel, and Jack and the Beanstalk will delight children of all ages. It's right across from the tennis courts on Victory Avenue.

Admission: $1.50 children and adults, children under 2 free.

Open: Wed–Sun 10am–4:30pm, except Jan and Feb when it's open only on Sat and Sun.

5. ORGANIZED TOURS

As I've said earlier in this book, the very best way to see the French Quarter is on foot. But once you leave the confines of the French Quarter, sightseeing tours can save a lot of time, to say nothing of wear and tear on the nerves, especially if you're the one behind the wheel. Buses will pick you up at your hotel and deliver you back there, and guides can be depended on for complete, accurate information (as well as occasional entertainment by way of amusing anecdotes and legends about the city). Another marvelous way to view the city is from the riverboats that cruise the harbor and a little stretch of the Mississippi River. Docks are at the foot of Toulouse and Canal Streets, and there's ample parking for the car while you sit back and relax on the water. Reservations are required for all these tours, and I would remind you once more that the prices quoted here are those in effect at press time and are subject to change.

For tours of the plantation houses outside New Orleans, see Chapter 11.

WALKING TOURS

Aside from the walking tours given in Chapter 8, there's an excellent walking tour offered by the nonprofit volunteer group **Friends of the Cabildo** (tel. 523-3939). This tour furnishes guides for a two-hour, on-foot exploration that will provide a good overview of the area. Leaving from in front of the Museum Store, 523 St. Ann St., your guide will "show and tell" you about most of the Quarter's historic buildings' exteriors and the interiors of selected Louisiana State Museum buildings. You're asked to pay a donation of $10 per adult, $5 for seniors over 65 and children from 13 to 20 (those 12 and under are free). Tours leave Tuesday through Sunday at 10am and 1:30pm and Monday at 1:30pm, except holidays. No reservations are necessary—just show up, donations in hand.

Tours by Isabelle, P.O. Box 740972, New Orleans, LA 70174 (tel. 391-3544), conducts small groups on a three-hour city tour in a comfortable, air-conditioned minibus. The tour covers the French Quarter, the cemeteries, Bayou St. John, City Park and the Lakefront, the universities, St. Charles Avenue, the Garden District, and the Superdome. The fare is $25, and departure times are 9am and 1pm. You should call as far in advance as possible to book. For $30 you can join her afternoon Combo Tour, which adds Longue Vue Gardens to all of the above.

Stop by the **Jean Lafitte National Park Service French Quarter Folklife and Visitor Center** at 419 Decatur St. (tel. 589-2636), for details of the excellent free walking tours on a variety of topics conducted by National Park Service rangers. The History of New Orleans tour covers about a mile in the French Quarter and brings to life New Orleans's history and the ethnic roots of the city's unique cultural mix. No reservations are required for this tour or the Tour du Jour (also in the Quarter), which is a "ranger's choice" that varies from day to day. You must book, however, for the two tours outside the Quarter. The Faubourg Promenade Tour takes you on the St. Charles Avenue streetcar and a walk through the Garden District. Both tours are very popular, so book as many as two or three days ahead.

Magic Walking Tours (tel. 593-9693) offers several guided walking tours daily, most of which cost under $10 per person. You might take a tour of St. Louis Cemetery No. 1, the French Quarter, or the Garden District. Or, if you're feeling a little more adventurous, try the Voodoo Tour or the Haunted House, Vampire, and Ghost-Hunt Walking Tour. The tour guides are excellent—not only do they enjoy their jobs, but they are extremely well educated about the city. Reservations are not necessary, but you should call ahead for tour schedules. Meeting places vary according to the tour you choose.

Hidden Treasures Tours (tel. 529-4507) offers guided tours of the Garden District and the Lower Garden District. You'll get to take a tour of one of the cemeteries, view monuments, and enjoy fine examples of southern architecture. Hidden Treasures offers either walking tours or motor tours ($10 and $20 respectively), and advance reservations are required.

Louisiana African American Odyssey, Inc., 10985 N. Harrell's Ferry Rd., Second Floor, Baton Rouge, LA 70816 (tel. 338-6309, or toll free 800/385-6309), offers guided tours to New Orleans and Baton Rouge that are specifically designed to focus on African American history. The New Orleans tours will take visitors to the Amistad Research Center where a large collection of African American culture is preserved; Chalmette Battlefield; Marie Laveau's grave; the Treme area; and the French Quarter.

BUS TOURS

Gray Line, 1300 World Trade Center of New Orleans (tel. 587-0861, or toll free 800/535-7786), has tours of the entire city, including the French Quarter, in comfortable motorcoaches. But take my word for it: The Quarter will demand a more in-depth examination than a view from a bus window. Take one of these excellent (and very informative) tours only after you've explored the Quarter in detail or as a prelude to doing so.

Gray Line's complete city tour begins in the French Quarter, with an informative narration on historic buildings as well as the Creole cottages and elegant mansions along Esplanade Avenue. From Esplanade, you go to City Park, then on to Lake Pontchartrain, the cemeteries, and back to the Garden District for a look at those antebellum mansions. Before delivering you back to your hotel, they'll show you the Superdome, the New Orleans River Bridge, and the Old Custom House. The 45-mile, two-hour trip (departures at 9am, 10am, 11am, noon, and 2:30pm) costs $17 for adults and $8.50 for children. Book ahead.

For $28 per adult and $14.25 per child (and four hours of your time), Gray Line, in addition to the city tour, will throw in a two-hour cruise on the paddlewheeler *Natchez.* You'll have lunch on board (cost *not* included in the tour price) as you take in the sights and sounds of the harbor. This tour has 11:30am and 2:30pm departure times, and you must make an advance reservation. They will pick you up at your hotel.

All tours depart from the ticket office at the corner of Jackson Brewery and Toulouse Street, just one block from Jackson Square. Gray Line also offers plantation tours and a swamp and bayou tour.

BOAT TOURS

The steamboat **Natchez,** 1340 World Trade Center of New Orleans (tel. 586-8777, or toll free 800/233-BOAT), a marvelous three-deck sternwheeler docked at the wharf behind the Jackson Brewery, offers three two-hour cruises daily. The narration is by the professional guides, and there are cocktail bars, an optional Creole buffet, and a gift shop aboard. The fares are $14 for adults ($16.50 in the evening) and $7 for children ($10 in the evening). Those under 3 ride free. Call for sailing schedule. Also, there are jazz dinner cruises. Call for the schedules and the prices.

The sternwheeler **Cotton Blossom,** 1340 World Trade Center of New Orleans (tel. 586-8777), offers a real departure in the cruise world—the exciting Zoo Cruise. Passengers travel the Mississippi by sternwheeler, tour the busy port, and dock to visit the Audubon Zoo, one of the world's finest. There are four round trips daily from the Canal Street dock at Riverwalk, beginning at 9am. The fares are $17.75 round-trip for adults, $9 for children. The *Cotton Blossom* also has an Aquarium cruise that costs $19 for adults (round-trip), $10 for children. If you want to take a combination tour that includes the zoo and the aquarium, it will cost $25.50 for adults, $12.75 for children. Call for exact sailing schedule and to make reservations.

The paddlewheeler **Creole Queen** (tel. 529-4567) departs from the Poydras Street Wharf adjacent to Riverwalk at 10:30am and 2pm for three-hour narrated excursions to the port and to the historic site of the Battle of New Orleans. There is also a 7pm jazz dinner cruise. The ship has a covered promenade deck, and its inner lounges are air-conditioned and heated. Buffet and cocktail services are available on all cruises. The fares are $13 for the daytime cruises and $39 for the nighttime jazz cruise (children $6 daytime, $18 nighttime; children under 3 are free). Call to confirm sailing schedules and current fares.

HORSE-CARRIAGE TOURS

If you don't think your feet are up to walking and you're in the mood for something different, just head for Decatur Street at Jackson Square and hop aboard one of the **horse carriages** at the stand there. For about $8 ($5 for children under 12), you will not only view the Quarter in comfort but also be treated to what is sure to be a highly individualistic narrative on its history from your guide. I've always thought this kind of tour should come under the heading of entertainment in New Orleans because each driver has a personal collection of stories about the landmarks, and if you took several different carriages, you'd get several different versions of New Orleans history. Private horse-carriage tours will cost you significantly more.

SWAMP TOURS

Lil' Cajun Swamp Tours (tel. 689-3213, or toll free 800/725-3213) offers a good tour of New Orleans bayous. Captain Cyrus Blanchard, "a Cajun French-speaking gentleman," knows the bayous like the back of his hand—mostly because it's where he lives. The tour lasts two hours and will run you about $16 for adults, $14 for seniors, and $12 for children if you drive yourself to the boat launch. If you need transportation it will cost you $30 for adults, $15 for children ages 6 to 12. (Note that the boat used on the Lil' Cajun Swamp Tours is much larger than the boat used on many of the other tours.)

Honey Island Swamp Tours, Inc. (tel. 242-5877) will take you to Honey Island Swamp, which covers almost 70,000 acres of protected wildlife area. Small tours are led by experienced and knowledgeable guides and last approximately two hours. Hotel pick-ups in New Orleans are available for a fee, or you can drive to the launch site yourself.

Gator Swamp Tours (tel. 504/484-6100 or toll free 800/875-4287) claims to offer the "longest and most personal swamp tour in the New Orleans area." Gator Swamp Tours takes visitors on a ride through Honey Island Swamp, beyond the bounds of the average swamp tour, into "the wilderness." Like the other tour groups, Gator Swamp Tours offers hotel pick-ups for a fee.

On all of the above tours you're likely to see alligators, bald eagles, waterfowl, egrets, owls, herons, osprey, feral hogs, otter, beaver, frogs, turtles, minks, raccoons, black bear, deer, and nutria.

6. MARDI GRAS & OTHER FESTIVALS

New Orleans means "Festival"—and if you don't believe it, try this simple little "free association" test. What's the first thing that comes to mind when someone says "New Orleans"—Mardi Gras, right? Well, that's the biggie, of course, but it's only *one* of this lively city's celebrations. There's something about the frame of mind here that just won't tolerate inhibitions—whether there's a declared celebration in progress or not! I always feel I'm celebrating something every day that I'm in the "City That Care Forgot."

As for officially designated festival days, a calendar of events issued by the Greater New Orleans Tourist and Convention Commission lists no fewer than 26 spread over the year that are observed either in the city proper or in its neighboring parishes. There's a festival of jazz and food; a celebration of spring when ladies don the costumes of long ago and shepherd an admiring public through gorgeous old mansions; there's a food festival just to celebrate the fine art of eating as it's practiced around there; there's an oyster festival, a catfish festival, and numerous crawfish festivals (which sometimes feature a crawfish race) to celebrate the generous waters of the area; there's a two-week extravaganza built around Bastille Day (the French themselves probably lack the enthusiasm that's shown here for that day); and . . . well, you get the idea. If there's any possible reason to celebrate, New Orleans throws a party.

I can't, of course, cover them all in these pages. I'll tell you about some of the most interesting, and if you take my advice, you'll write or call ahead to the **Greater New Orleans Tourist and Convention Commission,** 1520 Sugar Bowl Dr., New Orleans, LA 70112 (tel. 504/566-5011), for a current calendar of events to see what's going to be happening when you plan your visit. If, however, you don't see anything spectacular listed for the dates of your trip, don't worry—you'll feel festive from the moment you arrive.

MARDI GRAS

Mardi Gras, the biggest of all New Orleans festivals, has been here in one form or another as long as the city itself. Volumes could be written about its history, and almost any native you encounter will have his or her own store of Mardi Gras tales. What follows here is a thumbnail sketch of its background and a quick rundown on present-day krewes, parades, and balls.

To begin with, the name *Mardi Gras* means "Fat Tuesday" in French, and that's a very appropriate name because it is always celebrated on the Tuesday before Ash Wednesday—the idea being that you have a sort of obligation to eat, drink, and be as merry as you possibly can before the Lenten season of fasting and repentance sets in. The name *Carnival* is Latin in origin (from *carnisvale,* meaning "farewell to flesh") and refers to the 40-day stretch from January 6 to Mardi Gras Day (in New Orleans, the Carnival season is officially opened by the Krewe of Twelfth Night Revelers ball, the only one that has a fixed date).

HISTORY Where did the custom start? Nobody knows for certain, but some historians see a relationship to ancient tribal rites connected with the coming of spring. And a glorious, sin-filled, pagan orgy that highlighted mid-February for ancient Romans may have been an early ancestor of today's Mardi Gras. The Christian church did its best to stamp out such wild goings-on, but about all it succeeded in doing was to insist on a strict period of fasting and praying for forgiveness to follow the festive season. The point is that although New Orleans can properly claim Mardi Gras for its own in the United States, its spirit of revelry belongs to the history of the world. So, when the first French settlers arrived at the mouth of the Mississippi, what could be more natural than their bringing Mardi Gras along with them?

When the French explorer Pierre Le Moyne, Sieur d'Iberville, and his group of colonizers camped along the Mississippi in 1699, he didn't bother with keeping records, other than to note that the date was March 3. We don't know for sure, therefore, what that day's activities were in the little camp. What we *do* know is that March 3 was the day before Ash Wednesday in that year, and that he named the spot, some 12 miles north of the river's mouth, "Point du Mardi Gras." It seems likely that with a centuries-long tradition of French Mardi Gras celebration behind him, Iberville celebrated the day in some sort of fashion.

It wasn't long after New Orleans was established in 1718 that the French were at it again, although their Mardi Gras consisted largely of private masked balls and parties, with street dancing limited to the poor (but lighthearted) elements of the population. When the Spanish governors took up residence, they slapped a ban on such doings, and the Americans who began arriving in 1803 continued the ban. It wasn't until 1823 that French Quarter Creoles persuaded the city government to permit the masquerade balls once more, and by 1827 it was legal to wear masks in the streets on the great day. When those street maskers started marching in processions that might—by a *big* stretch of the imagination—be called parades, is uncertain, but in 1837 the *Daily Picayune* published for the first time an account of a Mardi Gras parade.

For the next few years things began to get out of hand, with so much wildness in the streets that it seemed inevitable that the city government would have to do something to quell the disorderliness. The future of Mardi Gras in New Orleans was very much in doubt, as newspapers and citizens aroused by street violence called for a permanent end to the festival. It took six new residents of the city, who had formerly lived in Mobile, Alabama, to turn things around. Determined to save Mardi Gras and restore some semblance of order and dignity to its observance, they met with 13 friends in what was known as "the club room" over the Gem bar at 127 Royal St. What came out of that meeting was a secret society, the Mistick Krewe of Comus, dedicated to preserving the institution of Carnival. They actually coined the "krewe" appellation, and they planned the first formal, torch-lit parade that was the pattern for all that have followed. Still adhered to, as well, is the practice of building each krewe's parade around a central theme, as did the Krewe of Comus in the first parade. It was from the Comus krewe, too, that New Orleanians took the practice of forming secret societies and ending each parade with private fancy balls, always preceded by an elaborate tableau.

The Civil War put a temporary halt to things, but Comus was parading again by 1866. In 1870 a krewe known as the Twelfth Night Revelers was founded and added two new policies that still endure: They began the throwing of trinkets to onlookers (the first thrower was dressed as Santa Claus), and they were the first to have an official "Queen" reign over their ball. A royal visit in 1872 contributed something more to New Orleans's Mardi Gras traditions. The Grand Duke of Russia, Alexis Alexandrovitch Romanov, followed his lady love, a musical-comedy star named Lydia Thompson, from New York when she came to star in *Bluebeard*. The city went all out to welcome him, and when it was learned that his favorite song was Lydia's favorite burlesque tune, "If Ever I Cease to Love You," every band in the Rex parade was asked to play it—that sprightly melody is now the official song of Mardi Gras. Incidentally the prestigious Krewe of Rex was born that year when a group of citizens banded together to raise money for an impressive welcome ceremony for the duke. The royal colors (purple for justice, green for faith, and gold for power) were also adopted as the festival's official colors.

Mardi Gras, despite its avowal of a "pleasure-only" basis, has served a pointed social purpose at least once in New Orleans. During Reconstruction days following the Civil War, public unrest forced the cancellation of the festival in 1875, but in 1877 the Krewe of Momus used as its parade theme "Hades, a Dream of Momus," which held the Grant administration up to such ridicule that the entire country's attention was focused on the deplorable conditions in the South.

Today's traditional ending of Mardi Gras had its beginning in 1882, when Rex and his queen called on the Court of Comus at that krewe's ball. The Krewe of Rex also began throwing medallions instead of trinkets in 1884, and the doubloons that came many years later are an outgrowth of that substitution. The doubloons, usually of aluminum or anodized gold, show the krewe's coat of arms on one side and the parade theme of the year on the other—a marvelous, permanent souvenir of Mardi Gras if you're lucky enough to catch one. You can also purchase them at some stores, but somehow it just isn't the same. They have become highly prized, so hold on to any you may acquire—some serious collector may someday offer a good price. The best way to come by one is to stand in the crowd and yell "Throw me something, mister" along with everyone else as the floats pass by. If your luck holds out, your pleas will be heard, and if your catch is good, you'll get the doubloon before someone else snatches it from the air.

New Orleans's African Americans entered the Mardi Gras scene through a fun-filled backdoor. In 1909 an African American man named William Storey mocked the elaborately garbed Rex by prancing after his float wearing a lard can for a crown. Storey was promptly dubbed "King Zulu." By 1916 his followers had grown so in numbers that they formed the Zulu Social Aid & Pleasure Club, and for years they observed Mardi Gras by wandering all over town, from one barroom to another that would extend hospitality to King Zulu. These days the Zulus get the day off to a start when His Majesty arrives by boat on the river at 7am (at the foot of Canal Street), and they follow a set parade route through the city's streets on proper floats instead of banged-up trucks and wagons they used in their early years. They're worth getting up early to see just for their grass skirts and sometimes outrageous makeup and masks. Besides the monarch in his colorful raiment, there's a "Provident Prince" and a "Big Shot of Africa" to look for, all decked out in the-Good-Lord-only-knows-what. The most notable King Zulu was probably Louis Armstrong in 1949, and in 1980 his good friend Woody Herman realized a longtime dream when he donned blackface and was crowned King of the Zulus.

Other early-morning Mardi Gras groups not to be missed are

the "walking clubs," with names such as Jefferson City Buzzards, the Pete Fountain Half Fast, and Peggy Landry's Silk Stocking Strutters. To quote Arthur Hardy (author of a Mardi Gras guidebook), these clubs are "sometimes mistakenly named 'marching clubs'—actually, they *never* march; some do walk, but more than a few stumble!" You can catch these "marchers," who as much as the krewe parades embody the spirit of the day, anywhere along their St. Charles Avenue route (between Poydras and Washington).

WHAT TO SEE & DO What can you expect to see and take part in if you come to New Orleans for Mardi Gras? First, you must remember that this is, primarily, a party New Orleans throws for itself—those spectacular balls are private, attended only by members and their invited guests. Attendance is by invitation, not by ticket, except, that is, for the Bacchus supper dance (and even those tickets are usually hard to come by). If you should be invited to a krewe ball, there are a few things you should know. You'll be a spectator, not a participant, and unless you're a woman and have been issued a "call-out" card, you'll be seated in a separate section to view the tableau after the previous year's queen and her court have been escorted to seats of honor and masked-and-costumed krewe members have taken their reserved, up-front seats. Members, who guard their secrecy not just during Mardi Gras but year round, are always in costumes and masks—for men it's white tie and tails if the invitation reads *de rigueur*, tuxedos if it reads only *formal*. Women, of course, are always in ballgowns. Those lucky "call-out" women will be seated separately from other guests (even their escorts) until the dancing begins and they've been called out by the krewe member who sent them the card. After a turn around the floor, they'll be given a krewe favor (a souvenir representative of that year's ball theme) and returned to their patiently waiting escorts. As members of the krewe and their ladies continue dancing, the current "royal court" will repair to the queen's supper, where friends and guests will be entertained the rest of the night—and into the morning.

One of the nicest things about New Orleans's private party is that the whole world is invited to come and look, and there are a whole slew of not-so-private entertainments. If you think this town's restaurants and nightclubs and bars and jazz clubs are pretty special most of the time, you should see them during Carnival! You can, in fact, more or less form your own informal "krewe" of friends and have a ball that might be as much fun as those private ones, just by making the rounds in a group.

Whatever else you do or don't do, you surely won't miss seeing a Mardi Gras parade—if, that is, you come during the final 11 days of Carnival. You'll know one's coming when you hear the scream of motorcycle sirens and a herd of motorized police come into view. They'll be followed by men on horseback (sometimes mounted police, sometimes krewe members) who clear the edges of the streets for the approaching floats. The king's float is first in line, with His Majesty enthroned and waving to the mass of cheering humanity with his scepter. Then will come a float with a banner proclaiming the theme of the parade. After that, each float will illustrate some facet of the theme. And it's a grand sight—the papier-mâché lions or elephants or flowers or fanciful creatures or whatever are sometimes enormous (there are people in New Orleans who work all year designing and building Mardi Gras floats), and there's much use of silver and gold tinsel that sparkles in the sunlight or the light of torches. Those torches, or flambeaux, are carried by costumed dancers. Each float has masked krewe members who wave and throw doubloons and souvenirs. In some of the parades, the floats keep coming until you think there's no end to them—in one recent year, Bacchus had 23 and Rex had 25. Each krewe had its designated time and parade route (which makes a current Mardi Gras guidebook invaluable) and most follow some part of St. Charles Avenue, sometimes a portion of Jackson Street as well, and Canal Street, and end up at the Municipal Auditorium, where all parades disband—except the renegade Bacchus with its Rivergate terminus. Because there are more than 50 parading krewes and only 11 days in which to do the parading, the streets are seldom empty, day or night, during this period. And the rollicking, costumed crowd filling the streets is as much something to see as the parades themselves. Every conceivable manner of costumes appears, and maskers made bold by their temporary anonymity carry on in the most outrageous, hilarious manner you can imagine. A great good humor envelops the whole scene, and I absolutely *defy* anyone to look on with disapproval.

On the last day of Carnival, Mardi Gras, the walking clubs are out at the crack of dawn, then King Zulu arrives around 9am, the Rex parade is mid-morning, and Comus closes the day with its evening parade (about 6:30pm). The high point of the final day is probably when Rex, the only Mardi Gras king whose identity is disclosed, arrives on his majestic float. It is a very high honor to be chosen Rex, and the selection always comes from among prominent men in the city, most well past the first blush of youth. Rex's queen, on the other hand, is always one of the current year's pack of debutantes. Although they make for a pretty ill-matched royal couple, there've never been any reports of incompatibility between the rulers-for-a-day. The choosing of Rex and his queen is done in the strictest secrecy, adding to the excitement that attends their first public appearance in the parade.

Another thing that's nice about Carnival in New Orleans is the fact that it doesn't cost the city one red cent, except the cost of extra police for the parades and that of cleaning up the streets after Fat Tuesday. This is truly a private celebration, planned, executed, and paid for by New Orleanians themselves—and I'll wager that if none of us dropped in for the festivities, the celebration would not change one iota.

PLANNING YOUR FESTIVAL Now, for the practicalities—you'd like to be there for Mardi Gras, so the details have to be attended to. First, you can't really just drop in. If you do, you may find yourself sleeping in Jackson Square or on a sidewalk somewhere. Accommodations are booked solid in the city itself and in the nearby suburbs, *so make your plans well ahead and book a room as soon as the plans are finalized.* It is no exaggeration to say that you should plan one year to go to the next and make your reservations right then. Prices are usually a little higher during Mardi Gras, and most hotels and guesthouses impose minimum-stay requirements.

One way to eliminate many of the hassles for space during Mardi Gras is to book a package tour. Amtrak, for example, sometimes offers hotel space and some extras during Carnival, so you should check with your local Amtrak Tour Desk.

You will surely want to join the maskers with your own costumes, and although it's best to plan ahead and come prepared, there are several shops in town that specialize in Mardi Gras costumes and masks (see Chapter 9). One of the most reasonable is the **Mardi Gras Center,** 831 Chartres St. (tel. 524-4384). If you come early enough, they can custom-make a costume to your own design; if not, they are well stocked with new and used costumes, wigs, masks, hats, and makeup.

When you arrive, remember that while the huge crowds add to the general merriment, they also make it more difficult to get in and out of restaurants in a hurry. And your progress from one part of town to another will be slowed down considerably. The point is that you should be sure to come in a relaxed frame of mind, with enough mental flexibility for the delays to be a source of enjoyment (after all, who knows *what* you may see while waiting) and not irritation.

You'll enjoy Mardi Gras more, too, if you've done a little homework before you come. Contact the **Greater New Orleans Tourist and Convention Commission,** 1520 Sugar Bowl Dr., New Orleans, LA 70112 (tel. 504/566-5011), and ask for their current Mardi Gras information.

Just one more thing should be said: You can figure out the future Mardi Gras dates because it always falls exactly 46 days before Easter.

CAJUN MARDI GRAS For a really unique Mardi Gras experience, drive out to "Cajun Country." Lafayette, a booming but charming town in the very heart of French Acadiana, celebrates Carnival in a manner quite different from that of the New Orleans fête—a manner that reflects the heritage and spirit of those hardworking, fun-loving Cajuns. (For their full story, see Chapter 11.) There are three full days of activities leading up to Mardi Gras that are designed to *"laissez les bons temps rouler"* ("let the good times roll," an absolute creed around these parts during Carnival). This is, in fact, second in size only to New Orleans's Mardi Gras, and there's one *big* difference—the Cajuns open their final pageant and ball to the general public. That's right, you can don your formalwear and join right in.

Instead of Rex and his queen, the Lafayette festivities are ruled by King Gabriel and Queen Evangeline. They are the fictional hero and heroine of Longfellow's epic poem *Evangeline,* which was based on real-life lovers who were separated during the British expulsion of Acadians from Nova Scotia just after the French and Indian War, and their story is still very much alive here among descendants of those who shared their wanderings. Things get off to a joyous start with the Children's Krewe and Krewe of Bonaparte parades and ball the Saturday before Mardi Gras, following a full day of celebration at Acadian Village. On Monday night Queen Evangeline is honored at the Queen's Parade. The King's Parade, held the following morning, honors King Gabriel and opens a full day of merriment. Lafayette's African American community stages the Parade of King Toussaint L'Ouverture and Queen Suzanne Simonne about noon, just after the King's Parade. And following *that*, the Krewe of Lafayette invites everyone to get into the act as its parade winds through the streets. Krewe participants trot along on foot or ride in the vehicle of their choice (and some very imaginative modes of transportation turn up every year). If you're still up to it when this parade comes to an end in late afternoon, you can return to the hotel to get ready for the Mardi Gras climax, a brilliantly beautiful, exciting formal ball presided over by the king and queen and their royal court. Everything stops promptly at midnight, of course, as Cajuns and visitors alike depart to observe the solemnity of Lent with the fondly remembered glow of Mardi Gras to take them through to Easter.

Out in the Cajun countryside that surrounds Lafayette, there's yet another form of Mardi Gras celebration, and I'll guarantee you won't find another like it anywhere else in the world. It's very much tied to the rural lifestyle of these displaced people who have created a rich culture out of personal disaster. And since Cajuns firmly believe that nothing is ever quite as much fun alone as it is when shared, you're entirely welcome to come along. The rural celebration goes like this: Bands of masked men dressed in patchwork costumes and peaked hats (*capichons*) set off on Mardi Gras morning on horseback, led by their *capitaine*. They ride from farm to farm, asking at each, "Will you receive the Mardi Gras?" (*"Voulez-vous reçevoir le Mardi Gras?"*) and dismounting as the invariable "Yes" comes in reply. Then each farmyard becomes a miniature festival, as they "make monkeyshines" (*faire le macaque*) with song and dance, much drinking of beer, and other antics loosely labeled as "entertainment." As payment for their show, they demand—and get—"a fat little chicken to make a big gumbo."

When each band has visited its allotted farmyards, all the bands head back to town, where everyone else has already begun the general festivities. There'll be dancing in the streets, rowdy card games, storytelling, and the like until the wee hours, and you may be sure that all those "fat little chickens" go into the "gumbo gros" pot to make a "big gumbo." It's a really "down home" sort of festival, where you can let your hair all the way down. And if you've never heard Cajun music (sort of like American country, but with a difference) or eaten gumbo cooked by real Cajuns, you're in for a treat.

You can write or call ahead for full particulars on both these Mardi Gras celebrations. Contact **Lafayette Parish Convention and Visitors Commission,** P.O. Box 52066, Lafayette, LA 70505 (tel. 318/232-808, or toll free 800/346-1958 in the U.S., 800/543-5340 in Canada).

OTHER FESTIVALS

✪ NEW ORLEANS JAZZ & HERITAGE FESTIVAL By the time mid-April rolls around, Easter has passed, the Mardi Gras is a fond memory of this year and a grand expectation for next, and New Orleanians turn to another festival celebration. Actually the Jazz and Heritage Festival combines two fêtes, as its name implies. From one weekend to another (usually the last weekend in April and the first weekend in May), musicians, mimes, artists, craftspeople, and cooks head out to the Fair Grounds Race Track on the weekends and settle into hotel ballrooms, jazz joints, concert halls, and a special evening concert site to put on a never-ending show of what New Orleans is all about. Over 3,000 performers turn up—and that's not counting the street bands. Famous-name jazz players are drawn to this festival, and they very happily share 11 stages out at the Fair Grounds with lesser-known groups who stomp out rhythm and blues and the voices blended in sweet harmony over at the gospel music tent. You can find your favorite and stand in front of the stage all day long or make the rounds and come back to favorites or to see what new group has taken over. Remember that this is a New Orleans festival—completely unstructured with the emphasis on pure enjoyment. That's out at the Fair Grounds; on weeknights, street bands are everywhere, and if you can't find a performance of *your* kind of music going on somewhere—well, it just must not exist. If traditional jazz happens to be your preference, you'll be in heaven.

As for the "heritage" part of the festival, local craftspeople and imported artisans are there en masse with their wares (you can also see some demonstrations of just how much they work), and that top-priority heritage, good food, is present in such abundance that you'll be tempted to stuff yourself way beyond the limits set by our modern health craze. Red beans and rice, jambalaya, gumbo, crawfish, sweet-potato pie, oysters, fried chicken, andouille, boudin, poboys, crabs, and shrimp—that, believe it or not, is only a partial list of what's available, with plenty of cold beer to wash everything down. There's just nothing quite like munching fried chicken from the Second Mount Triumph Missionary Baptist Church booth in an outdoor setting where the air is filled with strains of traditional jazz, ragtime, reggae, and the blues. There are well over 40 booths, and it's a safe bet that you'll want at least to sample each one, so come hungry.

To find out about the current dates, the artists who will be there and where they'll be performing in concert during the week, and background information, contact the **Jazz and Heritage Festival,** P.O. Box 53407, New Orleans, LA 70153 (tel. 504/522-4786).

SPRING FIESTA One of the best times of the year to visit New Orleans is during the five-day-long Spring Fiesta, which has been going on since 1937. This is the one time you can get to see the inside of some of those lovely old homes. Those ordinarily closed to the public throw open their doors, and hostesses clad in antebellum dress will escort you through the premises, providing about each house or historic building all sorts of information and anecdotes that you might otherwise never know. In the French Quarter, there are balcony concerts by sopranos rendering numbers sung there in the past by Jenny Lind and Adelina Patti. Out on River Road, there are plantation home tours; in the Quarter there are candlelight tours of patios; and as a highlight there is the gala "Night in Old New Orleans" parade, which features carriages bearing passengers dressed as prominent figures in the city's history and some of the best marching bands in town. Spring Fiesta always takes place during one week in April. For full details, reservations, and a schedule of the modest admission fees for some of the homes, you can write to **Spring Fiesta Association,** 826 St. Ann St., New Orleans, LA 70116 (tel. 504/581-1367).

TENNESSEE WILLIAMS FESTIVAL In late March or early April, New Orleans honors perhaps its most illustrious writer. Tennessee Williams, although not born here, once said, "If I can be considered to have a home, it would have to be New Orleans . . . which has provided me with more material than any other city." During the three-day Tennessee Williams–New Orleans Literary Festival, many of his plays are performed, and there are symposiums on his work as well as walking tours of his favorite French Quarter haunts. For dates and details, contact the **Greater New Orleans Tourist and Convention Commission,** 1520 Sugar Bowl Dr., New Orleans, LA 70112 (tel. 504/566-5011).

FRENCH QUARTER FESTIVAL In early April the three-day French Quarter Festival is a spectacular conglomeration of all the ingredients of the unique French Quarter's rich gumbo of life. There are scads of free outdoor concerts, patio tours, a parade, a battle of jazz bands, art shows, children's activities, and talent and bartender competitions. As if that weren't enough, Jackson Square is transformed into the world's largest jazz brunch, when about 40 leading restaurants turn out to serve Cajun/Creole specialties such as jambalaya, gumbo, and crawfish fettucine. For exact dates and other information, write to **French Quarter Festival,** 1008 N. Peters St., New Orleans, LA 70116 (tel. 504/522-5730).

CREOLE CHRISTMAS Trust New Orleans! A few days simply are not enough for this lively city to celebrate Christmas, so the entire month of December is designated as "Creole Christmas." There are all sorts of gala events sprinkled throughout the month's calendar, including tours of 19th-century homes decorated for the holiday, candlelight caroling in Jackson Square, cooking demonstrations, a madrigal dinner, gingerbread house demonstrations, and special Reveillon menus at select French Quarter restaurants. Special "Papa Noël" rates are offered by hotels citywide. For full details, contact **Papa Noël,** 1008 N. Peters St., New Orleans, LA 70116 (tel. 504/522-5730).

FESTIVALS ACADIENS This is a "Cajun Country" celebration—or rather, six celebrations—held during the third week of September in Lafayette. These festivals, lumped under the heading Festivals Acadiens, pay tribute to the culture and heritage of Cajun families who have been here nearly 200 years, since the British expelled them from their Nova Scotia homeland. The festive week includes the Bayou Food Festival, the Festival de Musique Acadienne, the Louisiana Native Crafts Festival, the Acadiana Fair and Trade Show, the RSVP Senior and Craft Show, and Downtown Alive.

At the **Bayou Food Festival,** you'll be able to taste the cuisine of more than 30 top Cajun restaurants. Specialties such as stuffed crabs, crawfish étouffée, oysters Bienville, shrimp Creole, oysters Rockefeller, shrimp de la Teche, catfish en brochette, jambalaya, chicken-and-sausage gumbo, smothered quail, and hot boudin are everyday eating for Cajuns, and this is a rare opportunity to try them all. The Bayou Food Festival is held in Girard Park adjacent to the music festival. Admission is free. And if you're wondering about the quality of Lafayette's restaurant food, let me tell you that it sells more restaurant food per capita than any other American city.

Festival de Musique Acadienne began in 1974, when some Cajun musicians were engaged to play briefly for visiting French newspaper editors. It was a rainy night, but some 12,000 Cajun residents showed up to listen. The walls rang for three solid hours with old French songs, waltzes, two-steps, Cajun rock rhythms, zydeco, and the special music some have dubbed "Cajun Country." Even after all that, nobody wanted to go home. Since then it has become an annual affair, with over 50,000 visitors usually on hand. Because of the crowds, the festival is now held outdoors in Girard Park, where fans can listen in grassy comfort. Performed almost entirely in French, the music includes both traditional and modern Cajun styles (and one form, known as zydeco, combines the blues with more traditional Cajun sounds). The music starts early and ends late, and there's no charge to come to the park and listen. All money from sales of food and beverage stands goes to fund public service projects of the Lafayette Jaycees.

You'll see native Louisiana artisans demonstrating their experience at the **Louisiana Native Crafts Festival.** All crafts must have been practiced prior to or during the early 1900s, and all materials used must be native to Louisiana. Meeting these criteria are such arts as woodcarving of all types (with an emphasis, it seemed to me, on duck decoys), soap making, pirogue (pronounced *pee-rogue*—it's a Cajun canoe, one variety of which is made from a dugout cypress log) making, chair caning, doll making, palmetto weaving, Native American–style basket weaving, quilting, spinning, dyeing, pottery making, jewelry making, alligator skinning, and probably a few more that I've missed.

The **Acadiana Fair and Trade Show** is put on by Lafayette merchants and businesspeople, and there's an indoor display of their good and services, plus an outdoor carnival with rides, a midway, and games. It's sponsored by the Lafayette Jaycees, and free shuttle-bus service for the public from one festival to another is provided by the city.

The elders who have passed crafts down to many of the younger Cajuns you'll see at Native Crafts Festival have their day in the sun at the **RSVP Senior Fair and Craft Show** (the RSVP stands for Retired Senior Volunteer Program). They're all over 60, and it's a rare treat to meet them and see their homemade articles and listen to them talk of the old days.

You can visit the **Acadian Village** any time of the year, but during Festivals Acadiens, special events are often scheduled. If you have any interest at all in Acadiana's history, you'll find this little village a trip back in time. Homes and buildings here are not models or even reconstructions of originals—they're all original old Acadian homes that have been found, restored where needed, and moved to the village to create (or, as the Cajuns say, "reassemble") a typical 1800s village. It's a tranquil, charming spot.

For exact dates and full details on Festivals Acadiens, write or call the **Lafayette Parish Convention and Visitors Commission,** P.O. Box 52066, Lafayette, LA 70505 (tel. 318/232-3808, or toll free 800/346-1958 in the U.S.; 800/543-5340 in Canada).

FOR FROG FANCIERS To prove my point that just about anything is cause for celebration in New Orleans and its environs, let me tell you about the **Rayne Frog Festival.** It's held in Cajun Country, just a few miles west of Lafayette. The Cajuns can hold their own when it comes to drumming up festivals—a harvest, a new season, a special tradition, a special talent, or just the job of being alive—and in this case they simply turn to the lowly frog as an excuse for a *fais-dodo* (dance) and a waltz contest. Not to forget the reason for it all, things get underway with frog races and frog-jumping contests—and if you arrive without *your* frog, there's a "Rent-a-Frog" service. To wind things up, there's a lively frog-eating contest. The Rayne Frog Festival is held in September. For dates and full details, contact **Lafayette Parish Convention and Visitors Commission,** P.O. Box 52066, Lafayette, LA 70505 (tel. 318/232-3808, or toll free 800/346-1958 in the U.S.; 800/543-5340 in Canada). If this festival is not exactly your cup of tea, just glance over the list of other festivals scheduled. This is festival country!

7. SPORTS & RECREATION

For those who prefer spectator sports on their vacations, the National Football League (NFL) team, the **New Orleans Saints,** plays in the **Superdome** every year from August to September.

Tulane University has football, basketball, and baseball teams. The **University of New Orleans** also has outstanding baseball and basketball teams. Every year, two college football teams participate in the **Sugar Bowl,** which is played in the Superdome.

Just call, or stop by, the Superdome and ask for schedules and prices (tel. 587-3810).

GOLF Rental clubs and instructions are available at each of these golf courses: **Bayou Oaks Golf Course,** 1040 Filmore St. (tel. 483-9396); **Audubon Golf Course,** in Audubon Park between Magazine Street and St. Charles Avenue (tel. 865-8260); **Eastover Country Club,** 5690 Eastover Dr. (tel. 241-4400).

HORSEBACK RIDING Here are a couple of places where you can get private and group riding lessons (be sure to call for rates): **Cascade Stables,** in Audubon Park (tel. 891-2246); **City Park Riding Stables,** Marconi Drive and Filmore Street at City Park (tel. 483-9398).

TENNIS The following places offer tennis for a small fee (you should call ahead for information): **Audubon Park Tennis Center,** Audubon Park, enter on Magazine Street (tel. 895-1042); **City Park Tennis Center,** Wisner Tennis Courts in City Park (tel. 483-9383); **N.O.R.D. Tennis Center,** 4025 S. Saratoga St. (tel. 896-4747); **Pontchartrain Park Tennis Center,** 5001 Haynes Blvd. (tel. 283-9734).

CHAPTER 8

STROLLING AROUND NEW ORLEANS

1. **THE FRENCH QUARTER**
2. **THE GARDEN DISTRICT**
3. **THE LOWER GARDEN DISTRICT**
4. **ESPLANADE RIDGE**
5. **A STREETCAR TOUR**

New Orleans really lends itself to walking, and it's absolutely the best way to get to see and do as much as you can during a short period of time. If you try these walking tours, you're sure to leave New Orleans feeling like you know something about the city's layout.

WALKING TOUR 1 — The French Quarter

Start: The intersection of Royal and Bienville Streets.

Finish: Jackson Square.

Time: Allow approximately 1½ hours, not including time spent in shops or historic homes.

Best Times: Any day of the week after 10am because New Orleans takes a little while to awaken in the mornings.

Worst Time: The only bad time to do this walk is at night, because some attractions won't be open and you won't be able to get a good look at the architecture.

Taking a stroll through the French Quarter is an absolute must during any visit to New Orleans—this is the most colorful part of what is arguably the most interesting city in the United States. This tour will take you along a number of the streets, to old buildings and other landmarks and will give you a taste of the mixture of history and legend that is so much a part of the French Quarter's fame.

From your starting point at the corner of Royal and Bienville Streets, head into the Quarter to:

1. **339 Royal Street,** the old Bank of the United States, which was built in 1800—notice its fine hand-forged ironwork. On the right-hand corner of Royal and Conti Streets you'll see:
2. **The Bank of Louisiana,** 334 Royal Street. The old Bank was erected in 1826 by Philip Hamblet, Tobias Bickle, and Benjamin Fox. Since the bank's liquidation in 1867, the

building has suffered a number of fires (in 1840, 1861, and 1931) and has served the community as the Louisiana State Capitol, an auction exchange, a criminal and then a juvenile court, and a social hall for the American Legion. At the present time it houses the police station for the Vieux Carré. Stay on Royal Street and you'll come to:

3. **The Rillieux-Waldhorn House,** 343 Royal Street. Now the home of Waldhorn Antiques (est. 1881), it was built between 1795 and 1800 for Vincent Rillieux, the great-grandfather of the French Impressionist artist Edgar Degas. Note the wrought-iron balconies—they are a lovely example of Spanish colonial workmanship. Cross Conti Street and head onto the next block of Royal Street and you'll see:

4. **403 Royal Street.** Designed by Benjamin H. Latrobe, one of the architects of the Capitol in Washington, this structure opened in 1821 as home of the Louisiana State Bank. Just ahead you'll see the famous:

5. **✪ Brennan's Restaurant,** 417 Royal Street. Brennan's has been housed in this building, also built by Vincent Rillieux, since 1955 (see Chapter 6 for full listing). This was one of many buildings erected after the fire of 1794 destroyed over 200 of the original architectual beauties along this street. From 1805 to 1841 it was home to the Banque de la Louisiane. Next, take a look at:

6. **437 Royal Street.** Masonic Lodge meetings were held regularly in a drugstore here back in the early 1800s. But something more important to American culture also happened here, when the druggist, Antoine A. Peyehard, served after-meeting drinks to lodge members in small egg cups, whose French name (*coquetier*) was Americanized to "cocktail." Cross St. Louis Street and on the right, about mid-block, you'll see:

7. **The Brulatour Court,** at 520 Royal Street. It is a splendid home built in 1896 for wine merchant François Seignouret. WSDU-TV now maintains offices here, but you're welcome to walk into the courtyard, one of the few four-walled courtyards in the French Quarter. Notice the elaborate, fan-shaped ironwork on the right end of the third-floor balcony. Incidentally, the wine merchant is virtually revered today for the fine furniture he produced (with a graceful "S" worked into the ornamentation of every piece). On the other side of the street is:

8. **The Merieult House,** at 533 Royal Street. Built in 1792, this was the only building in the area left standing after the fire of 1794. The first owner's wife very nearly became the mistress of a French castle when Napoleon offered one in exchange for her hair, which was flaming red (he wanted it for a wig to present to a Turkish sultan). This dignified and beautiful New Orleans residence must have been quite enough for Madame Merieult, however, for she flatly refused the emperor. Nowadays this is home to the Historic New Orleans Collection–Museum/Research Center (see Chapter 7 for tour times and information). If you continue along Royal Street across Toulouse Street, you will soon come to one of the best-known landmarks in the Quarter:

9. **The Court of Two Sisters,** 613 Royal Street. It was built in 1832 for a local bank president, on the site of the 18th-century home of an earlier French governor. The two sisters were

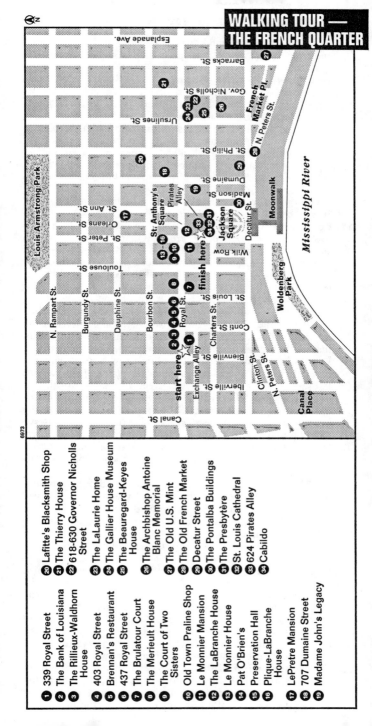

WALKING TOUR — THE FRENCH QUARTER

N

Esplanade Ave.

Barracks St.

Gov. Nicholls St.

Ursulines St.

French Market Pl.

N. Peters St.

St. Philip St.

Dumaine St.

Madison St.

Pirates Alley

St. Anthony's Square

St. Ann St.

Orleans St.

Jackson Square

St. Peter St.

Wilk Row

Toulouse St.

Decatur St.

Moonwalk

Mississippi River

St. Louis St.

Bourbon St.

Dauphine St.

Burgundy St.

N. Rampart St.

Louis Armstrong Park

Charters St.

Conti St.

Royal St.

finish here

Woldenberg Park

Bienville St.

Exchange Alley

start here

Iberville St.

Clinton St.

N. Peters St.

Canal St.

Canal Place

6973

1 339 Royal Street
2 The Bank of Louisiana
3 The Rillieux-Waldhorn House
4 403 Royal Street
5 Brennan's Restaurant
6 437 Royal Street
7 The Brulatour Court
8 The Merieult House
9 The Court of Two Sisters
10 Old Town Praline Shop
11 Le Monnier Mansion
12 The LaBranche House
13 Le Monnier House
14 Pat O'Brien's
15 Preservation Hall
16 Plique-LaBranche House
17 LePretre Mansion
18 707 Dumaine Street
19 Madame John's Legacy

20 Lafitte's Blacksmith Shop
21 The Thierry House
22 618-630 Governor Nicholls Street
23 The LaLaurie Home
24 The Gallier House Museum
25 The Beauregard-Keyes House
26 The Archbishop Antoine Blanc Memorial
27 The Old U.S. Mint
28 The Old French Market
29 Decatur Street
30 The Pontalba Buildings
31 The Presbytère
32 St. Louis Cathedral
33 624 Pirates Alley
34 Cabildo

Emma and Bertha Camors (whose father owned the building), and from 1886 to 1906 they ran a curio store here. When you spot the:

10. **Old Town Praline Shop**, at 627 Royal Street, walk through the shop entrance to the back of the store to see another of New Orleans's beautiful courtyards. This 1777 building is where Adelina Patti, the noted opera singer, came for a visit and stayed to become something of a local heroine in 1860. Only 17 at the time, Adelina saved the local opera company from financial ruin when she stepped in as a last-minute replacement for an ailing lead soprano in "Lucia de Lammermoor"—she was a tremendous hit, and the season was an assured success.

On the right side at the corner of Royal and St. Peter Streets (before crossing St. Peter) is:

11. **Le Monnier Mansion**, at 640 Royal Street, which once towered above every other French Quarter building as the city's first "skyscraper," all of three stories high when it was built in 1811. A fourth story was added in 1876. At this same intersection, also on the right, but on the other side of St. Peter is:

12. **The LaBranche House** (now the home of the Royal Café), 700 Royal Street, probably the most photographed building in the Quarter—and no wonder. Take a look at the lacy iron grillwork, with its delicate oak-leaf-and-acorn design, that fairly drips from all three floors. Actually, there are 11 LaBranche buildings, three-story brick row houses built between 1835 and 1840 by wealthy sugar planter Jean Baptiste LaBranche. Eight face St. Peter Street, one faces Royal, and two face Pirates Alley; it was only when wrought-iron balconies came into vogue about 1850 that they were added to the St. Peter and Royal Street facades. If you plan to preserve them on film, the best vantage point is diagonally across Royal Street so that both street exposures will show in your picture.

After getting a good look at the LaBranche House, go left down St. Peter Street to:

13. **Le Monneir House** at no. 714. Built in 1829 by a prominent physician who carried this name, it was the home for several years during the 1860s of Antoine Alciatoire, who ran a boarding house here. His cooking became so popular with locals that he later gave up catering to open the famous Antoine's restaurant, which is run, even today, by his descendants. A few doors down is:

14. **Pat O'Brien's**, 718 St. Peter Street, a swinging, fun-filled nightspot (see Chapter 10). The building was known as the Maison de Flechier when it was built in 1790 for a wealthy planter. Later Louis Tabary put on popular plays here, and it is said that the first grand opera in America was performed within its walls. Sightseeing in New Orleans just wouldn't be complete without a look at the gorgeous courtyard, even if you don't want to indulge in a hurricane or two.

15. ✪ **Preservation Hall**, at 726 St. Peter Street. Scores of people come to hear some of the best jazz in the country after 8pm, but a daytime stop will give you a glimpse through the big, ornate iron gate of a lush tropical courtyard in back.

Continue walking to the:

16. **Plique-LaBranche House** at no. 730. This house, which was built in 1825 and sold to Giraud M. Plique, was bought by Jean Baptiste LaBranche in 1829. Originally, it was the site of New Orleans's first theater, the St. Peter Street Theatre. Unfortunately, the theater burned down in the fire of 1816.

Turn right off of St. Peter Street to begin your walk up Dauphine (pronounced "*daw*-feen") Street. The first stop is:

17. **LePretre Mansion,** 716 Dauphine Street. No one has ever reported the presence of ghosts in this house, but they may well be there. As in the LaLaurie house over on Royal Street, the walls here could tell a tale of horror. Back in 1792 there arrived in New Orleans a wealthy Turk, the brother of a sultan. That he was enormously wealthy was immediately apparent, and his entourage included many servants, as well as a "family" of five beautiful young girls. They all landed in the Crescent City in the *Youseff Bey,* a Turkish freighter that evidently had been hired for their exclusive passage. Rumors quickly spread that this Turk's riches, as well as the girls, were actually the stolen property of the sultan. Be that as it may, the Turk rented the LePretre house for the summer when its owner left to spend the season on his downriver plantation, and the palatial home very quickly became the scene of lavish entertainments with guest lists that included the cream of society. On one fateful night, however, shrieks were heard by neighbors, followed by complete silence the next morning, with no signs of activity. Eventually neighbors entered the house and found the summer tenant's body lying in a pool of blood surrounded by the bodies of the five young beauties. There was no sign of his servants. To this day no one knows if they were responsible for the murders or if the freighter crew, with late-founded loyalty to the sultan, decided to return the ruler's stolen goods to win his favor (or, as seems more likely, they may have stolen the gold and embarked on a career of piracy at sea). Another explanation put forth was that members of the sultan's court followed his brother to avenge the sultan and return the gold. In 1968 this tale of terror was the Mardi Gras theme of the Krewe of Niobe.

Continue along Dauphine, crossing Orleans and St. Ann Streets. Go right at the corner of Dauphine and Dumaine Streets and you'll find that there's an interesting little cottage at:

18. **707 Dumaine Street.** Focus your attention on this building's roof—after the 1794 fire, all houses in the French Quarter were required by law to have flat tile roofs, and although most have since covered them with conventional roofs, this one is still in compliance with that long-ago ruling.

Down the street is a house known as:

19. **Madame John's Legacy,** 632 Dumaine Street. There are those who say this is the oldest building on the Mississippi River. Others dispute that claim, saying that only a few parts of the original building survived the 1788 fire and were used in its reconstruction. Be that as it may, the house was erected in 1726, just eight years after the founding of New Orleans, and the reconstruction follows the original design meticulously. Its

original owner was a ship captain who died in the 1729 Natchez Massacre; upon his death the house passed to the captain of a smuggling ship. It has had no fewer than 21 owners since. The present structure is a fine example of a French "raised cottage." The above-ground basement is built of brick-between-posts construction (that simply means that bricks were used only to fill in a wooden frame because locally made bricks were too soft to be the primary building material), covered with boards laid horizontally. The hipped, dormered roof extends out over the veranda. Its name, incidentally, comes from a fictional quadroon who was bequeathed the house in "Tite Poulette," a Creole short story written by George Cable. Now a part of the Louisiana State Museum complex, it is open to the public on a regular basis.

Go left at the corner of Dumaine and Chartres Streets and follow Chartres to the next corner; make a left onto St. Philip Street and walk until you get to the corner of St. Philip and Bourbon Streets. Opposite, you will see:

20. ✪ Lafitte's Blacksmith Shop, at no. 941. For many years now, it has been a bar (for the full story, see Chapter 10), but the legend is that Jean Lafitte and his pirates posed as blacksmiths here while using it as headquarters for selling goods they'd plundered on the high seas. It has survived (thanks to the loving care of its owners in recent years) in its original condition, and you can still see the brick-between-posts construction. Step inside and the dusky interior will kindle your imagination—it's a tribute to its modern-day owners that they haven't let the age of chrome and plastic come anywhere near this old place.

Go right on Bourbon Street and make a right turn onto Governor Nicholls Street. You will then see:

21. The Thierry House, 721 Governor Nicholls Street, which was built in 1814 and started an architectural trend that spread throughout the entire state. Designed by architect Benjamin Henry Latrobe when he was just 19 years old, the house is in the Greek Revival style and features a classic portico.

On the next block of this street is:

22. 618–630 Governor Nicholls Street. Henry Clay's brother, John, built a house for his wife here in 1828, and in 1871 this two-story building was added at the rear of its garden. It was in this later building that Frances Xavier Cabrini (later sainted by the Catholic church) conducted a school.

Backtrack to the corner of Royal and Governor Nicholls Streets. Take a left onto Royal and look for:

23. The LaLaurie Home, at 1140 Royal Street. You may want to be sure you walk by this house in broad daylight—after dark you might be disturbed by ghostly moans or the savage hissing of a whip; you might even catch a glimpse of a small African American child walking on the balcony. This is the Quarter's haunted house. Its story is a New Orleans tale of horror: It seems the very beautiful and socially prominent Delphine LaLaurie lived here and entertained lavishly, until one night in 1834 when a fire broke out and neighbors crashed through a locked door to find seven starving slaves chained in painful positions, unable to move. The rescuers were appalled and highly incensed. When the next day's newspapers suggested that the dazzling hostess might have set the fire herself, a mob assembled outside the house. Madame LaLaurie and her family escaped their neighbors' wrath. However, they still fled the city, and the heartless woman did not return to New Orleans until several years later, after she died on the Continent—and even then her body had to be buried in secrecy.

A few doors down is:

24. **The Gallier House Museum,** at 1132 Royal Street. This was built by James Gallier, Jr., as his residence in 1857 (see Chapter 7 for more details).

At the corner of Royal and Ursulines Streets, take a left and continue down to Chartres until you get to:

25. **The Beauregard-Keyes House,** 1113 Chartres Street. This place has more than one claim to fame (see Chapter 7 for the details).

Across the street is:

26. **The Archbishop Antoine Blanc Memorial,** 1114 Chartres Street, which includes the Old Ursuline Convent and the Archiepiscopal Residence and was completed in 1752 (see Chapter 7 for more information).

Continue walking along Chartres Street until you get to Esplanade (pronounced "Es-pla-*nade*") Avenue. Esplanade served as the parade ground for troops quartered on Barracks Street. It is a lovely, wide avenue lined by some of the grandest town houses built in the late 1800s. (If you're interested in viewing some of the aforementioned town houses, one of the walking tours following this one concentrates on the architecture of the Esplanade Ridge. See below.) The entire 400 block of Esplanade is occupied by:

27. **The Old U.S. Mint.** This was once the site of Fort St. Charles, one of the forts built to protect New Orleans in 1792. (Its troops also used Esplanade as a parade ground.) It was here that Andrew Jackson reviewed the assortment of "troops" (comprised of pirates, volunteers, and a nucleus of trained soldiers) he would lead in the Battle of New Orleans (more information on this museum can be found in Chapter 7).

Follow Esplanade and turn right at the corner of North Peters Street. Follow North Peters until it intersects with Decatur Street—at this point you will have reached the back end of:

28. **The Old French Market.** This European-style market has been here for well over 150 years, and today it has a farmer's market, innumerable shops, restaurants, coffee stands, and some nonpareil people-watching. Take your time and shop; you'll probably find some things you can take back as souvenirs for family and friends.

Across from the Old French Market is:

29. **Decatur Street.** A large section of this street—from Jackson Square all the way over to Esplanade—was not too long ago a seedy, run-down area of wild bars and cheap rooming houses. No more. An exciting renaissance resulted in all sorts of interesting shops and oldtime eateries, such as Tujague's (823 Decatur). Decatur Street is far from "finished"—it's already drawing a local clientele with a slightly bohemian flavor, and as more casual/smart bars open and nightlife assumes

a relaxed "respectability," it will no doubt attract even larger crowds. At any rate, as you walk toward St. Ann Street, follow Decatur Street and allow some time to stroll and browse. And as you pass 923 and 919 Decatur Street, let your imagination conjure up the Café de Refugies and Hôtel de la Marine that were here in the 1700s and early 1800s and were gathering places for pirates, smugglers, and European refugees (some of them outlaws); it was a far cry from today's scene.

REFUELING STOP If you're walking in the area of 923 Decatur around lunchtime, pop into the **Central Grocery** and pick up a muffaletta sandwich. You can get them at many restaurants and delis around the city, but the ones at Central are far and away the best! There are little tables at which to eat inside Central Grocery, or you can take your food and sit outside.

If you had something else in mind, there are actually a number of restaurants along this stretch that can ease any number of gastronomic cravings. See Chapter 6 for details on the restaurants you see along the way.

Decatur Street will take you to Jackson Square. Turn right onto St. Ann Street; those twin, four-story, red-brick buildings here as well as on the St. Peter Street side of the square are:

30. The Pontalba Buildings, with some of the most beautiful cast-iron balcony railings in the Quarter and a history that reflects the determination of a plucky New Orleans woman to compete with those upstart American "uptowners" and keep business concerns in the Quarter by providing elite-address shops and living quarters on the square. Indeed, these are said to be the first apartment buildings in the country—they were designed by Baroness Micaela Almonester Pontalba (she was the daughter of the Don Almonester responsible for rebuilding the cathedral; see below). They were begun in 1849 and built under her direct supervision; you can see her mark today in the entwined initials "A-P" in the lovely ironwork. The row houses on St. Ann Street, now owned by the State of Louisiana, were completed in 1851.

At the corner of St. Ann and Chartres Streets, turn left and continue around Jackson Square; you will see:

31. The Presbytère, at 751 Chartres Street, originally designed to be the rectory of the cathedral. The Baroness's father financed the building's beginnings, but he died in 1798, leaving only the first floor done. In 1813, building was completed. It was never used as the rectory but instead it was first rented and sold to the city in 1853 only to be used as a courthouse.

Next you'll come to:

32. ✪ The St. Louis Cathedral. The building standing here today is the third erected on this spot. A hurricane destroyed the first in 1722. Then, on Good Friday of 1788, the bells of its replacement were kept silent for religious reasons rather than ringing out the alarm for a fire that eventually went out of control and burned down over 850 buildings, and the cathedral was once again destroyed. Rebuilt in 1794, largely through the generosity of Don Almonester (who is buried in front of St. Joseph's shrine on the right as you face the altar), it is of Spanish design, with a tower at each end and a higher central tower, and its construction is of brick covered with stucco to protect the mortar from dampness. Inside, look for the six stained-glass windows depicting St. Louis (French King Louis IX) at various stages of his life and canonization. There's also a spectacular painting on the wall above and behind the main altar, showing St. Louis (the cathedral's patron saint) proclaiming the Seventh Crusade from the steps of Notre Dame. You're welcome to poke around inside on Monday through Saturday from 9am to 5pm and on Sunday from 1:30 to 5pm. On the other side of the cathedral you'll come to Pirates Alley. Go right down Pirates Alley to:

33.624 Pirates Alley, In 1925, the literary great William Faulkner lived here and worked on his first novel, *Soldier's Pay*. While here he contributed to the *Times-Picayune* and to a literary magazine, the *Double Dealer*.

If you continue this way along Pirates Alley, you'll reach Royal Street. Turn left and at the corner of Royal and St. Peter Streets, turn left again and follow St. Peter back to Chartres. On the right side of the cathedral (as you face the Mississippi River), also facing Jackson Square, is the:

34.Cabildo, on the corner of Chartres and St. Peter Streets. It has been, in turn, a French police station and guardhouse, the statehouse of the Spanish governing body (the Very Illustrious Cabildo), New Orleans's City Hall, and the Louisiana State Supreme Court. Since 1911 it has been the permanent home of the Louisiana State Museum.

One further note: If you think those old Civil War cannons out front look pitifully small and ineffective by modern standards, you might like to know that in 1921, in a not-so-funny prank, one was loaded with powder, an iron ball was rammed down its muzzle, and it was fired in the dead of night. That lethal missile traveled from the Cabildo's portico across the wide expanse of the Mississippi and some six blocks inland before landing in a house in Algiers, narrowly missing its occupants!

REFUELING STOP You've finished! Now, go back across Decatur Street to ✪ **Café du Monde**—you shouldn't miss a stop here for the beignets and coffee; no trip to New Orleans is complete without them. If you've still got a little bit of energy left after you've indulged yourself, take a walk over to the river and relax on a bench for a while.

WALKING TOUR 2 — The Garden District

Start: Jackson and St. Charles Avenues.

Finish: First and Prytania Streets.

Time: 45 minutes to 1½ hours, depending on your pace.

Best Times: Anytime during the day.

Behind the impressive exteriors of the mansions along St. Charles Avenue and its side streets are such ornate fixtures as mahogany banisters, mantels of rosewood or Italian marble, winding staircases, crystal chandeliers, and priceless antiques. The large colonnaded and balconied homes of the Garden District—many with lavish formal gardens—are well worth a look.

To reach the Garden District, catch the St. Charles streetcar at Canal and Carondelet Streets and get off at Jackson Avenue.

From the corner of Jackson and St. Charles, walk up St. Charles to:

1. **2220 St. Charles Avenue,** the House of Broel. Today it's a bridal shop, but this stately home dates from 1850. Inside you can view a gasolier that is original to the house (it has since been converted to electric) and you'll be able to see an enormous mirror that was bought for the home after it was purchased by the Liberty Shop in 1920. The owner of the House of Broel also has a private collection of art from around the world. The admission fee for the tour is $5 (it's a short tour), and the house is open Monday through Saturday from 10am to 4pm.

   After exiting the House of Broel (if you decided to take the tour), follow St. Charles Avenue to First Street, and make a left. As you walk along First Street you'll cross Prytania and Coliseum Streets (notice the exceptional wrought iron on 1315 First Street), as well as Chestnut Street before you get to:

2. **1239 First Street.** Can you believe that this house was built for only $13,000? Of course, that was in 1857. The interior woodwork is especially notable. The hexagonal wing off to one side was an afterthought, added in 1869. Notice the beautiful ironwork embellished with a rose pattern.

   On the other side of the street is:

3. **1236 First Street.** This house was constructed in 1847 by one John Gayle for his young bride. Its interior features elaborate plaster ceiling medallions and black marble mantelpieces.

   On the next block across Camp, at the right-hand corner of Camp and First Streets, look for:

4. **1134 First Street.** Dating from 1850, this building is noted as the place where Confederate President Jefferson Davis died while a guest in 1889. Note the Tower of the Winds capitals on the second-floor columns.

   Turn left on Camp Street to Philip Street onto which you'll make another left. Walk along Philip Street and you will soon see:

5. **1220 Philip Street.** This all-wood residence was built in the 1850s. A subsequent owner was a wealthy sugarcane and molasses dealer whose nephew, Isaac Delgado, donated his art collection to start the Museum of Art. Isaac spent most of his growing-up years in this house.

   Down the street is:

6. **1238 Philip Street.** The beautiful gardens here brought citywide fame to the owner, John Rodenberg. The building, constructed in 1853, has the two-story columned gallery typical of houses in this district.

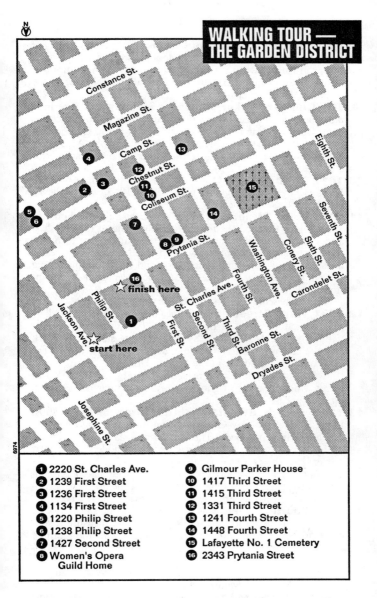

N

Constance St.

Magazine St.

Camp St.

Chestnut St.

Coliseum St.

Prytania St.

finish here

Philip St.

St. Charles Ave.

Jackson Ave.

start here

First St.

Second St.

Third St.

Baronne St.

Dryades St.

Josephine St.

Eighth St.

Seventh St.

Sixth St.

Coney St.

Carondelet St.

Washington Ave.

Fourth St.

① 2220 St. Charles Ave.
② 1239 First Street
③ 1236 First Street
④ 1134 First Street
⑤ 1220 Philip Street
⑥ 1238 Philip Street
⑦ 1427 Second Street
⑧ Women's Opera Guild Home
⑨ Gilmour Parker House
⑩ 1417 Third Street
⑪ 1415 Third Street
⑫ 1331 Third Street
⑬ 1241 Fourth Street
⑭ 1448 Fourth Street
⑮ Lafayette No. 1 Cemetery
⑯ 2343 Prytania Street

As you stroll along Philip Street you'll come to Chestnut Street. On Chestnut, turn left and walk to Second Street. Turn right here, cross Coliseum Street, and look on the right side for:

7. 1427 Second Street. This is not the original site of this 1845 house. It was moved to the city location from Mrs. Jane Fawcett's nearby plantation, and it didn't gain the decorative ironwork until the 1930s.

Turn left at Prytania Street where you'll see:

8. **The Women's Opera Guild Home,** at 2504 Prytania. For a small donation you can take a look inside (Mondays only, except in August when it's closed) at the early 19th-century and Victorian furnishings. As you continue along Prytania, at the corner of Third Street is:

9. **The Gilmour Parker House,** at 2520 Prytania. The light pink home with palladian windows and wrought-iron balconies dates from 1853 and was built for Thomas Corse Gilmour, an English cotton merchant. It was later sold to John M. Parker whose son later became Governor of Louisiana. Also at this corner is:

10. **1417 Third Street.** Originally the carriage house of 2520 Prytania Street, this structure was built in 1853, with walls 13 inches thick. Next door is:

11. **1415 Third Street.** A tobacco merchant built this house in 1865, and it featured the first indoor plumbing in the city. It is also one of the largest mansions in the area. Be sure to notice the beautiful double gallery with rounded ends. The interior boasts a marvelous winding staircase, and there's an interesting carved wooden eagle, fished from the river after a violent storm, adorning the dining-room chimneypiece.

    Cross Coliseum and on the corner you'll see:

12. **1331 Third Street.** James Gallier designed this Italian villa–style home for in-laws of Edgar Degas, the French impressionist painter, in the 1850s. In 1884 its elaborate stables out back and the cast-iron galleries were added, to make it one of the most outstanding houses in the Garden District.

    When you get to Camp Street, turn right to reach Fourth Street, where you turn right again. At the corner of Chestnut, on the right is:

13. **1241 Fourth Street,** which dates from the mid-1800s. Louis Herman, a New Orleans cotton broker, started building this house from the back. The kitchen and slave quarters went up in 1844, then when the "big house" was added up front at a later date, the two were connected.

    Continue along Fourth, crossing Chestnut and Coliseum Streets. If your French Quarter sightseeing included the Corn-stalk Hotel on Royal Street, you'll see a twin to that fence at:

14. **1448 Fourth Street.** This house was built in 1859 for Col. Robert Short of Kentucky. Its double parlors measure a spacious 43 by 26 feet, and the cast-iron fence with the motif of cornstalks entwined with morning glories was cast in Philadelphia.

    At Prytania Street, turn left. If you need a breather, go into The Rink Shopping Mall on the other side of Prytania. There are a few benches and a great bookstore, but as of this printing, no refreshments. Turn left again onto Washington Avenue and soon you'll see:

15. **Lafayette No. 1 Cemetery,** with its aboveground tombs, on your right. This particular cemetery was laid out in 1833, and yellow fever victims had it almost completely filled by 1852. The little wooden mortuary first served as a Catholic church at another location—it dates from 1844 (see Chapter 7

for more information). *Note:* For safety reasons I would advise that you stay outside the cemetery.

REFUELING STOP At the corner of Washington Avenue and Coliseum Street, you'll find **Commander's Palace,** which was built as a restaurant in 1880 by Emile Commander and has from the start been a favorite with New Orleanians (see Chapter 6 for a full discussion). You could stop here for lunch, but proper dress and reservations are required.

When you're finished at Commander's Palace, head back to Prytania and go right. Follow Prytania to:

16. 2343 Prytania (now the Louise S. McGehee School for girls). Wealthy sugar planter Bradish Johnson built this elegant town house, and it cost him $100,000 even back in 1872. It was probably designed by Paris-trained architect James Freret, and before a deadly hurricane in 1815, the magnolias out front were said to be the largest in the country.

Keep walking and when you get to Josephine Street, turn left to reach St. Charles Avenue and the streetcar; or, if your feet aren't hurting too much, pick up where you left off on the next walking tour, which is a tour of the Lower Garden District. It will also take you back to St. Charles Avenue and to the streetcar.

WALKING TOUR 3 — The Lower Garden District

Start: First and Prytania Streets.

Finish: St. Charles Avenue and Melpomene.

Time: 1½ hours.

Best Times: Anytime during the day.

The Lower Garden District is a particularly interesting area because it is in this neighborhood that you will find a wonderful collection of 19th-century Greek Revival architecture. Unfortunately, the neighborhood has become run down and some of the most incredible beauties have been demolished. Still, I hope that with this walk you'll get a good feel for what the Lower Garden District used to be like. Try to imagine the gardens, which no longer exist, as you walk. *Note:* Because the Lower Garden District has seen better days you should be alert to any and all activity around you. Remember, you're in a major city and you must keep your physical safety in mind as you explore.

FROM THE FRENCH QUARTER TO FIRST STREET Walk from your hotel (even if you're not in the French Quarter) to St. Charles Avenue. Get on the streetcar (fare $1) and ride it all the way to First Street.

When you leave the streetcar, walk one block on First Street to your left (if you're facing the direction in which the streetcar was running when it dropped you off) to Prytania Street and your first stop will be at:

1. **2343 Prytania Street,** the Louise McGehee School. Originally built as a private home in 1872, it was made an all-girl school in 1929. (See the last entry of the walking tour of the Garden District for more details.)

   Continue along Prytania Street to:

2. **2221 Prytania,** which is a beautiful residence. In particular, note the Corinthian columns.

   Continue on Prytania, crossing Jackson. If you stop at:

3. **2127 Prytania,** you'll get to see a typical Greek Revival raised villa. There are some wonderful features on this house, most notably the cast-iron fence and gallery, as well as the carved lintel. This house also has wonderful Corinthian columns.

   On the corner of Josephine and Prytania you'll see:

4. **The Gospel Temple Church** (now the Fellowship Missionary Baptist Church), at 2101 Prytania Street. It was built in 1901, originally as a Presbyterian church, and is a wonderful stone church—perhaps Renaissance revival would best describe this heavy but beautiful piece of architecture.

   Continue walking on Prytania Street. Look for a three-story masonry building at:

5. **1823 Prytania Street.** Now a home for the elderly, this building was once known as St. Anna's Asylum, a home for "destitute" women and their children. The asylum cared not about religious preference but about the women and their children—and apparently it advertised itself as such. It was officially recognized by the state as an organization in 1853 and was built on land donated by William Newton Mercer. Note the Doric portico raised on scored piers, as well as the cupola on the roof.

   On the next block is:

6. **Eagle Hall,** at 1780 Prytania Street, a commercial building that was built for Philip Meyer, who in 1851 bought the triangular site created by the intersecting streets. It was built to be a commercial building, and that is evidenced by the wide facia, which was meant for holding a large sign advertising the store. The structure was occupied for a time by the Eagle Hall, a civic organization. Lafayette Volkstheater opened there in August 1862, and German political meetings were held there during and after the Civil War.

   Turn right when you get to Felicity Street. At the corner of Felicity and Coliseum, on the right, is:

7. **1805 Coliseum Street.** Built in the mid-1850s, this classic raised villa with Greek and Italianate features was built for Edward Nave, a native Virginian and a prominent New Orleans commission merchant. If you can, take a close look at the doors, which hold the type of etched glass that came into vogue after 1870.

   Continue on Felicity. On the right is an Italianate villa at:

8. **1328 Felicity Street.** It was built in 1869 for John Augustus Braffer and was recently restored (1977–79). A few doors down is:

9. **1322 Felicity Street.** This Italianate masonry house was built in 1870 for John McGinty. The unique cast-iron gallery and Corinthian columns are extraordinary in their detail.

   Another Victorian Italianate house on the left is the:

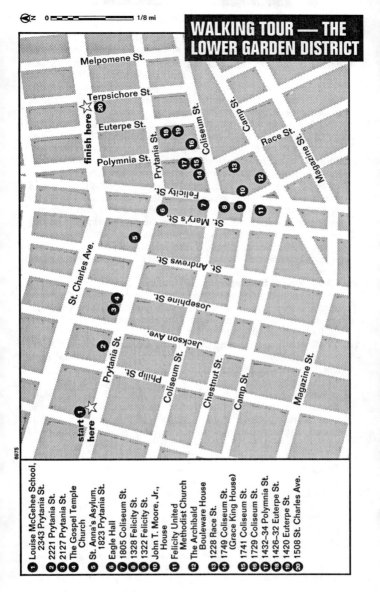

0 |====|====| 1/8 mi

Melpomene St.

Terpsichore St.

finish here ☆ 20

Euterpe St.

18 19

Prytania St.

16

Coliseum St.

Camp St.

Race St.

Magazine St.

Polymnia St.

17 15

14

13

12

Felicity St.

10

St. Mary's St.

6

7

8 9

11

5

St. Andrews St.

St. Charles Ave.

Josephine St.

3 4

Jackson Ave.

Coliseum St.

Chestnut St.

Camp St.

Magazine St.

2

Prytania St.

Philip St.

start here ☆ 1

6975

1. Louise McGehee School, 2343 Prytania St.
2. 2221 Prytania St.
3. 2127 Prytania St.
4. The Gospel Temple Church
5. St. Anna's Asylum, 1823 Prytania St.
6. Eagle Hall
7. 1805 Coliseum St.
8. 1328 Felicity St.
9. 1322 Felicity St.
10. John T. Moore, Jr., House
11. Felicity United Methodist Church
12. The Archibald Boulware House
13. 1228 Race St.
14. 1749 Coliseum St. (Grace King House)
15. 1741 Coliseum St.
16. 1729 Coliseum St.
17. 1432–34 Polymnia St.
18. 1426–32 Euterpe St.
19. 1420 Euterpe St.
20. 1508 St. Charles Ave.

10. John T. Moore, Jr., House, at 1309 Felicity Street.
Erected in 1880, it is a great study for the admirer of architecture. It has a wonderful overhanging roof and what is known as a scalloped verge board. The iron cresting on top is particularly interesting to look at because it forms a belvedere. You could probably stand and look at this house for hours and not notice every detail.

Continue along Felicity and you can't help but notice the:

11. **Felicity United Methodist Church,** at 1226 Felicity, a late Gothic Revival–style church that was built in 1888 after an earlier church on the same site burned down in 1887. Originally there stood two steeples atop the towers on the present building—unfortunately, a hurricane blew them down in 1915. The building at 1217 Felicity, across the street from the church, is worth noticing—I think its triangular shape is interesting, although it is not recognized as a historical landmark.

When you reach the corner of Felicity and Camp, take a left onto Camp Street. The next stop is:

12. **The Archibald Bouleware House,** at 1531 Camp Street. Built in 1854, it's a two-story gallery with Corinthian columns on both levels, which is quite uncommon—usually, these houses might have Corinthian columns on one level, but not the other. Another interesting feature of this house is the arched iron trellis out front—it is one of a very few surviving examples of this once-common decorative piece for the garden.

As you continue down Camp Street, you'll run into Race Street—take a left at the corner. Look for the three-story house at:

13. **1228 Race Street,** dating from 1867. Because the gallery on the second floor is wooden, you would assume that it is much older than it is. It is actually the replacement for the original simple cast-iron balcony and was built there after 1900.

Follow Race Street to Coliseum Street. Go right to:

14. **1749 Coliseum Street.** This was the house of Grace King, noted Louisiana historian, fiction writer, scholar, and essayist. King, born in New Orleans in 1852, is noted for having written *Memories of a Southern Woman of Letters* (1932). The fluted columns out front often welcomed such friends as Mark Twain and Sherwood Anderson. King never married, and she lived in this house for many years with her two sisters. For about 30 years the house was a meeting place for the artists and writers who lived in New Orleans at the time. Nearby is:

15. **1741 Coliseum Street,** known as the Hugh-Wilson House. This building was originally owned by a commission merchant. Note the front gallery with Ionic columns above and Doric columns on the ground floor.

On the corner of Polymnia, notice the house at:

16. **1729 Coliseum Street,** This particular house was originally built in the 1830s and stood at a different location (904 Orange Street). In 1981 it was moved to its present location and was restored. When you see it you'll know it, because it is one of very few restored homes in the area.

In 1858 the house was purchased by Henry Hope Stanley, born in Britain, who came here and became a cotton merchant. At some point, he met and took into his home a Welsh cabin boy who had jumped ship. Stanley and his wife decided to make the boy a part of their family and named him Henry Morton Stanley. When the Civil War began young Henry left New Orleans and became a member of the Confederate Army. After having been a prisoner of war he was released and then found himself in New York, where he became a journalist. His newspaper sent him to Africa, at which point he searched for and found Dr. David Livingston—it was he who asked, "Dr. Livingston, I presume?" He eventually earned a knighthood due to his other African adventures.

After taking a left from Coliseum onto Polymnia, look for a Greek Revival house at:

17. 1432–34 Polymnia Street (between Coliseum and Prytania Streets). Notice the full-length pillars that support the gallery. This house is a good example of what the whole neighborhood looked like before the use of cast iron became so widespread after 1850. Before the use of cast iron, wood cisterns, gazebos, picket fences, and galleries gave the neighborhood a feeling entirely different from that of the later Garden District, when homes began to drip with cast-iron balconies, fences, and the like. Be sure to look at the unique side carriage entrance to 1434.

At the corner of Polymnia and Prytania Streets, take a right and walk down to Euterpe. Go right again. As you walk along Euterpe Street, have a look at the Greek Revival row houses at:

18. 1426–32 Euterpe Street. They are a good example of the row houses typical of the Lower Garden District. Also note the shotgun double houses at 1423–25 and 1427–29 Euterpe. They are called "shotgun" because the rooms fall one directly behind the other.

As you walk along, look at the house that occupies the site of:

19. 1420 Euterpe Street (on the right between Coliseum and Prytania Streets). This house dates from the early 1850s and was the residence of John Thornhill, a prominent commission merchant and cotton factor.

When you get to Coliseum Street, go left. Follow Coliseum to Terpsichore. Turn left on Terpsichore and follow it across Prytania to St. Charles Avenue. Turn right at the corner of St. Charles Avenue and at:

20. 1508 St. Charles Avenue, you'll see what once was probably a stunning three-story Victorian. Note the dormer and semioctagonal bay. It has some great detail work. This particular house was built in the late 1800s or early 1900s and it is currently home to a doll museum.

Here you can wait for the steetcar—there's a stop right across St. Charles from the doll museum.

WALKING TOUR 4 — Esplanade Ridge

Start: 2023 Esplanade Avenue, in front of Mechling's Guest House.

Finish: City Park.

Time: Allow approximately 1½ hours, not including museum, cemetery, and shopping stops.

Best Times: Monday through Saturday early or late morning.

Worst Times: Sunday when attractions are closed. Also, don't walk in this area after dark—be sure to start the walk early enough.

A stroll down Esplanade Avenue to City Park offers a look at a sampling of New Orleans architecture in an area that is not often explored. Many of the proud homes on Esplanade no longer house just one family, but have become boarding houses, apartments, and restaurants. Recent improvements to the Esplanade area indicate that it is experiencing a much-needed revitalization.

From the French Quarter, stroll up Esplanade Avenue to your first stop:

1. **2023 Esplanade Avenue.** Once a plantation home, this building is now under the owership of Keith and Claudine Mechling (pronounced "*Mek*-ling"). Keith and Claudine are in the process of renovating the home, which they are running as a guesthouse (see Chapter 5 for a full listing). Claudine may be serving a full English tea or ice-cold lemonade in the afternoon, but you should call ahead to let her know you're coming. Down the street a bit is the:

2. **Widow Castanedo's House,** at 2033–35 Esplanade Avenue. Widow Castanedo lived in this home, on land purchased by her grandfather, Juan Rodriguez, in the 1780s, until her death in 1861. She is famous for having battled the city against the extension of the Esplanade. (It is believed that her house was moved to its present location when the Esplanade was finally extended.)

   The house has a late Italianate appearance, similar to the nearby no. 2023, and is split down the middle and inhabited today by two sisters. This splitting of a house was very common at one time, and a pair of siblings often lived one on each side.

   At the corner of Miro and Esplanade is:

3. **2139 Esplanade Avenue.** This building is a great example of typical "Esplanade Ridge Style." The home was built for William Chambers, most likely a short time after the Civil War. Note the Ionic columns on the upper level. On the opposite side of the same corner is:

4. **2176 Esplanade Avenue,** a simple, classic-style town house. It was the second Bayou Road home built by Hubert Gerard, the man who built the Mechling Guest House at 2023.

   Veer left at the fork at Miro Road to stay on Esplanade and look for the statue of the:

5. **"Goddess of History—Genius of Peace,"** which is on the triangular piece of land at the crossover of Bayou Road, Esplanade Avenue, and Miro Street. In 1886 the piece of land was given to the city by Charles Gayarre, and George H. Dunbar donated the original statue to be placed there. Purchased from the Audubon Park Cotton Centennial Commission, the statue was destroyed in 1938, and the present one is a replacement.

   No one knows why, but only half of the house at:

6. **2306 Esplanade Avenue** has survived. At present, the house is most notably known as the Musson-Degas House because the home was originally purchased by the uncle of Edgar and René Degas. Edgar Degas, French impressionist painter, is said to have painted the portrait of René's wife, Estelle Musson

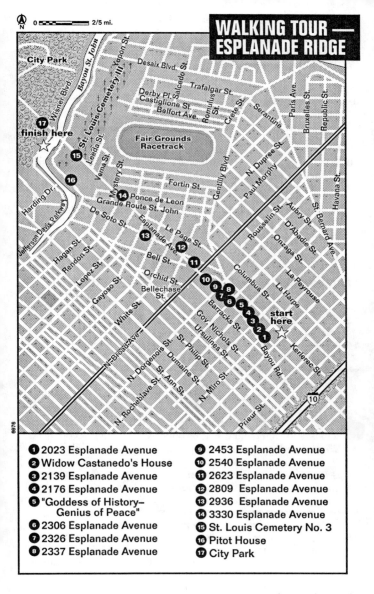

WALKING TOUR — ESPLANADE RIDGE

0 ━━━━━ 2/5 mi.

City Park
Bayou St. John
Wisner Blvd.
Desaix Blvd.
Vienon St.
Salcedo St.
Trafalgar St.
Derby Pl.
Castiglione St.
Belfort Ave.
Romulus
Crete St.
Serantine
Paris Ave.
Bruxelles St.
Republic St.

17 finish here

St. Louis Cemetery No. 3

15

Leeda St.
Vena St.

Fair Grounds Racetrack

Fortin St.
Gentilly Blvd.
N. Dupree St.
Paul Morphy
Havana St.

16

Harding Dr.
Mystery St.

14 Ponce de Leon
Grande Route St. John

De Soto St.
Esplanade Ave.
Le Page St.
Rousselin St.
Aubry St.
St. Bernard Ave.
D'Abadie St.
Onzaga St.
La Peyrouse

13

Jefferson Davis Parkway

Hagan St.
Rendon St.
Lopez St.

12

Bell St.

11

Orchid St.
Bellechase St.
Gayoso St.
White St.
Columbus St.
La Harpe

10
9 8
7
6 5
4
3

Barracks St.
Gov. Nichols St.
Ursulines St.

2
1

start here

N. Broad Ave.
St. Philip St.
Dumaine St.
N. Dorgenois St.
St. Ann St.
N. Miro St.
N. Rocheblave St.
Prieur St.
Bayou Rd.
Kerlerec St.

10

6976

- **1** 2023 Esplanade Avenue
- **2** Widow Castanedo's House
- **3** 2139 Esplanade Avenue
- **4** 2176 Esplanade Avenue
- **5** "Goddess of History–Genius of Peace"
- **6** 2306 Esplanade Avenue
- **7** 2326 Esplanade Avenue
- **8** 2337 Esplanade Avenue
- **9** 2453 Esplanade Avenue
- **10** 2540 Esplanade Avenue
- **11** 2623 Esplanade Avenue
- **12** 2809 Esplanade Avenue
- **13** 2936 Esplanade Avenue
- **14** 3330 Esplanade Avenue
- **15** St. Louis Cemetery No. 3
- **16** Pitot House
- **17** City Park

(which is now in the New Orleans Museum of Art), during the time he spent living at 2306.

Next door to the Musson-Degas House is:

7. 2326 Esplanade Avenue, the home of a well-known local artist. You'll know the house by the collection of small metal houses, cinderblock sculptures, and a beautiful metal-crafted marlin on the front porch. The house, known as the Reuther House, was owned by Joseph Reuther, a baker, in 1913.

In passing, take a look at 2325, 2329, and 2331—all are interesting examples of Creole cottages. Nearby is:

8. **2337 Esplanade Avenue,** showing a style of New Orleans architecture that was dominant during the late 19th century— the shotgun house. Take a close look at:

9. **2453 Esplanade Avenue.** Although this house at the corner of Dorquenois Street (which used to be one of a pair until the other house was demolished) has been changed extensively architecturally, it's one of the few remaining mansard-roofed homes on Esplanade Ridge. The lovely home at:

10. **2540 Esplanade Avenue** was built in the 1850s and is an example of simple classic style. On the next block is:

11. **2623 Esplanade Avenue,** a classical revival Victorian that was built in 1896 by Louis A. Jung. Note the Corinthian columns. The Jungs donated the triangular piece of land at the crossover of Esplanade Avenue, Broad Street, and Crete Street to the city on the condition that it would remain a public piece of land. It is officially known as DeSoto Park.

Continuing along in a lakeside direction along Esplanade, take notice of these three houses:

12. **2809 Esplanade Avenue,** one of the more decorative Victorian Queen Anne center-hall houses on Esplanade Ridge.

13. **2936 Esplanade Avenue,** a little less than a block away and a nice example of what's known as a Gothic villa.

14. **3330 Esplanade Avenue,** built in the Creole cottage style and a lovely galleried, frame home.

REFUELING STOP At the intersection of Mystery Street and Esplanade you'll find a little grouping of shops and restaurants. If you're in the area at lunchtime you might want to stop at **Café Degas** for a leisurely meal. If you're more health conscious and don't mind eating outside, I'd highly recommend **Wholefoods**—stop in and get a quick sandwich or salad.

If you're not ready for lunch, stop in at **Brew Time,** which is located behind **Café Degas,** for a cup of coffee and some pastry. When you're done exploring and have gathered enough energy to continue, continue walking along Esplanade.

In a few minutes you'll see the:

15. **St. Louis Cemetery No. 3** on your right. If you've been putting off going into the cemeteries because of the crime associated with them, this is one you can explore in relative safety. You can pick up brochures in the office there.

After you've spent some time in the cemetery, head back out to Esplanade and continue walking toward City Park. When you get to the bridge, you can go left, following the signs, to see:

16. **Pitot House,** which is open for public viewing (see Chapter 7 for a description), or you can continue walking straight into:

17. **City Park,** where you can explore the amphitheater, museum, and gardens (see Chapter 7 for more details).

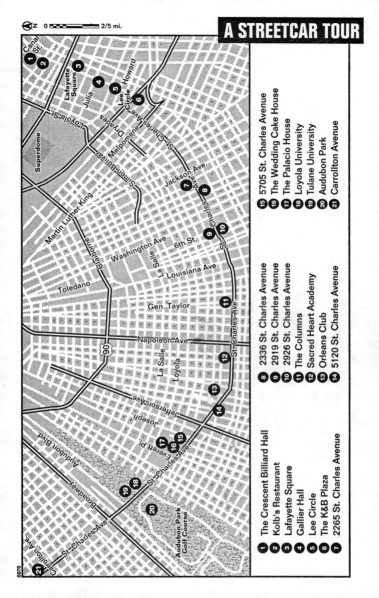

0 — 2/5 mi.

Map legend:

1. The Crescent Billiard Hall
2. Kolb's Restaurant
3. Lafayette Square
4. Gallier Hall
5. Lee Circle
6. The K&B Plaza
7. 2265 St. Charles Avenue

8. 2336 St. Charles Avenue
9. 2919 St. Charles Avenue
10. 2926 St. Charles Avenue
11. The Columns
12. Sacred Heart Academy
13. Orleans Club
14. 5120 St. Charles Avenue

15. 5705 St. Charles Avenue
16. The Wedding Cake House
17. The Palacio House
18. Loyola University
19. Tulane University
20. Audubon Park
21. Carrollton Avenue

A STREETCAR TOUR

Start: St. Charles Avenue and Canal Street.

Finish: The town of Carrollton.

Time: 45 minutes to 1½ hours, providing you either don't descend the streetcar or you spend only about 45 minutes grabbing a quick bite to eat. This does not include time spent wandering at any of the stops.

Best Times: Around 11am, since this will allow for a leisurely morning and afternoon spent wandering and exploring, enabling you to return back to the Central Business District or the Vieux Carré in time to get dressed for dinner.

One of the best ways to see the most historic and architecturally interesting neighborhoods of New Orleans is to ride the famous streetcar that runs along St. Charles Avenue. It will take you through the Garden District, past the universities and Audubon Park to Riverbend and Carrollton.

On the corner of Canal and St. Charles, while you wait for the streetcar, have a look at:

1. **The Crescent Billiard Hall,** 115 St. Charles Avenue. It was built in 1826, and in 1865 the whole thing was remodeled so that the inside was turned into an enormous billiard hall. The Pickwick Club, founded in 1857 (incidentally, the members of the Pickwick Club had a hand in founding the Krewe of Comus in the same year), took over the building in 1950.

    Once on the streetcar, notice:

2. **Kolb's Restaurant,** at 121–123, 125–127 St. Charles. The building at 125–127 St. Charles was originally a museum (ca. 1844); however, it closed shortly after opening. Kolb's Restaurant (presently housed in both buildings—121–123 was built in 1853) began as a saloon and has been in operation since 1898.

    From your perch in the car take note of:

3. **Lafayette Square,** located on your left between stops 3 and 4 and next door to the Federal Court of Appeals.

4. **Gallier Hall,** 545 St. Charles Avenue, also between stops 3 and 4, but on the right side, is an impressive Greek Revival building that was the inspiration of James Gallier, Sr. Erected between 1845 and 1853, it served as City Hall for just over a century. Several important figures in Louisiana history are entombed in Gallier Hall, including Jefferson Davis and General Beauregard.

    Soon after Gallier Hall (between stops 6 and 7), the streetcar will go screeching around:

5. **Lee Circle,** at St. Charles and Howard Avenues. If you look out the window to the left, you will be able to see the statue of Robert E. Lee atop an impressive pedestal and column. It was officially raised and dedicated in 1884. Also between stops 6 and 7, you'll notice on your right side:

6. **The K&B Plaza,** at St. Charles Avenue and Lee Circle, because of the collection of sculpture outside the K&B headquarters building. There is an equally impressive collection inside the lobby, which is open to the public from 9am to 5pm during the week. If you're an art lover, this is one place you should hop off the streetcar and have a look. Inside you will find works by many noted sculptors, including Henry Moore. Some say that it is one of the finest collections in the country.

    Continuing your ride, you will see these four houses:

7. **2265 St. Charles Avenue,** on your right. The famed James Gallier, Jr., was one of the architects of this house, built in 1856; the wide wing was added later.

8. 2336 St. Charles Avenue, on your left. When this cottage was built in the 1840s, the avenue was a dirt road known as Nyades, nothing like the broad street you see today.

9. 2919 St. Charles Avenue. Here you'll see the Christ Church Cathedral on your right. It is one of the oldest Protestant churches in the Mississippi Valley. This is the fourth building on the site, and it suffered the loss of a steeple in a 1915 hurricane.

10.2926 St. Charles Avenue. This house was built in 1882, with a gallery for every room and an early air-conditioning system—a 12-inch space between inner and outer walls. Don't be confused by the number 710 above the front door—it's left over from an outdated numbering system.

On your right between stops 21 and 22, you'll see:

11.The Columns, at 3811 St. Charles; this is the spot where *Pretty Baby* was filmed (accommodations are offered here; see Chapter 5). You'll know it by the enormous columns and the sprawling front porch.

Soon afterward, you'll look out the right side of the streetcar and wonder what that huge brick building with the cupola is; it's the:

12.Sacred Heart Academy, 4521 St. Charles, between stops 24 and 25. This is a prestigious all-girl Catholic school that was built in 1899.

For a look at one of the oldest buildings on St. Charles, look out on the right between stops 27 and 28 and you'll see the:

13.Orleans Club, at 5005 St. Charles. It is a private social and cultural women's club, but it was built in 1868 by a Colonel Lewis as a wedding gift for his daughter. It is sometimes used for debut teas and wedding receptions.

The interesting Neo-Italianate mansion on your left at:

14.5120 St. Charles Avenue was built in 1907 by the owners of one of the largest department stores in New Orleans. It changed hands a number of times (one owner was the silent-screen star Marguerite Clark) before it was finally donated to the New Orleans Public Library as a memorial to the son of Mr. and Mrs. Harry Latter, who was killed during World War II. If you'd like to get a good look at the inside of one of these places, get off at stop 27 or 28 and poke around inside the library—it's worth it just to see the painted ceiling and the paneling.

If you were swept away by *Gone with the Wind,* you may want to stop at:

15.5705 St. Charles. A replication of Tara is located between stops 30 and 31 on the right side. It was constructed in 1941.

On your right between stops 31 and 32 is:

16.The Wedding Cake House, 5809 St. Charles, one of the most talked about houses in the city. It's a beautiful Victorian mansion that you couldn't miss if you tried. Nearby on your left you will see:

17.The Palacio House, at 5824 St. Charles, between stops 31 and 32. It is a nice example of Italianate architecture. A few stops down is:

18. Loyola University, 6363 St. Charles Avenue. The university occupies the 6000 block of St. Charles Avenue on the site of a preparatory school, Loyola Academy, that stood there from 1904 to 1911, when the university was established. The campus covers some 14 acres and its brick-front main buildings form three sides of a square facing the avenue. Behind these buildings the modern Dana Center student union is a popular gathering spot, and its café and snack bar are open to visitors. Loyola, incidentally, is the largest Catholic university in the South.

Right next door is prestigious:

19. Tulane University, at 6823 St. Charles, between stops 36 and 37. It is the older university of the two, dating as far back as 1834, when the Medical College of Louisiana was founded. The University of Louisiana, begun in 1847, was merged with the Medical School, and when Paul Tulane left a bequest of $1 million to the combined schools, the name was changed in gratitude to the benefactor. That generous gift financed what is now one of the country's leading medical and law schools. (The medical school has since moved to a downtown campus on Tulane Avenue.) An interesting facet of the education offered here is its emphasis on the Code Napoleon, a rather peculiar system of law practiced in this country only in Louisiana. Also on campus is the Harriet Sophie Newcomb Memorial College for Women, which was founded in 1886 and was located in the Garden District until it moved here in 1918. Nowadays it's an undergraduate college of Tulane University.

As you pass by Tulane and Loyola the entrance to:

20. Audubon Park can be seen on your left (it is also between stops 36 and 37). For more information about the park, see Chapter 7.

A REFUELING STOP The Riverbend (stops 43 and 44) area is a wonderful little spot for a rest, a bit of shopping, or a bite to eat. I would definitely recommend getting off the streetcar at this point, just to do some exploring. You might want to get a burger at the **Camellia Grill** or coffee and pastries at **La Madeleine** (a branch of the one located in the French Quarter).

If you feel like it, ride the streetcar to the end of the line. It's interesting just to have a look at:

21. Carrollton Avenue. For instance, at 719 S. Carrollton, that antebellum building is now the Benjamin Franklin Public High School, but it was originally built as Carrollton's courthouse.

Along this section of Carrollton Avenue, you'll see yet another architectural style much used in New Orleans, the "shotgun house." Only one room wide, the little house would permit a bullet fired through the front door to go right out the back, passing through every room in the house.

CHAPTER 9

SAVVY SHOPPING

**1. THE SHOPPING
     SCENE**
2. SHOPPING A TO Z

Like everything else in New Orleans, shopping is fun. I say that as a dedicated nonshopper, the type that helps to keep the mail-order houses in business. Still, the shops in this city are so different, so intriguing, that I'm in and out of them all along the streets. Almost anything you could want is on sale in New Orleans—you can even have one of those marvelous old-time ceiling fans shipped back home. If you can't find something, you can find someone to make it for you: The place is loaded with craftspeople and artisans who use such disparate materials as cast iron, wood, leather, fabric, brass, plastic, and precious metals.

Antique shops are really special here, many with patios and gardens that actually seem to enhance their goods. Some are located in old French Quarter homes, giving another dimension to browsing. And the emphasis that was always placed on fine home furnishings in New Orleans has left a residue of some of the loveliest antiques I've ever viewed. Many came from Europe in the early days; others were crafted right in the city by cabinetmakers, internationally known for their exquisite pieces. And for the nautically minded, there are shops that specialize in marine antiques, wonderful mementos of long-ago voyages and the ships that made them.

Because New Orleans is an international port city, its shops are filled with a rich variety of imported items from countries around the world. Home furnishings, kitchen utensils, pottery, designer clothes, whatever else you can name—the world's best is on sale here. Art galleries, too, display the works of leading artists as well as those from the area. The creation of fine jewelry is a much-practiced art; some of the jewelry shops will seem more like art galleries.

You'll notice an abundance of gift shops—the postcards, sunglasses, and T-shirts displayed outside won't let you miss them. Don't dismiss them all as cheap souvenir places. Some of my most blissful browsing has come as a surprise when I entered such a place to buy postcards and found an interior stocked with imaginative imported gift items. (This is not true of all these little shops, but it pays to look.)

The following list is far from complete; if you don't see a particular category that is of special interest to you, be assured that you'll more than likely find it when you arrive in New Orleans. For convenience, I'll describe first the major shopping centers, followed by shops grouped by category.

The hours for most shops are Monday through Saturday from 10am to 5pm. Many, however, are open later on Saturday night and Sunday afternoon, especially in the French Quarter, where souvenir shops are likely to remain open until 11pm every day of the week.

1. THE SHOPPING SCENE

CANAL PLACE At the foot of Canal Street (365 Canal St.) where it reaches the Mississippi River, this stunning shopping center holds over 50 shops, many of which are branches of some of this country's most elegant retailers. The three-tiered mall has polished marble floors, a landscaped atrium, fountains, and pools. Stores in this sophisticated setting include Brooks Brothers, Jaeger, Bally of Switzerland, Saks Fifth Avenue, and Laura Ashley. Open: Mon–Wed, Fri–Sat 10am–6pm; Thurs 10am–8pm; Sun noon–6pm.

THE ESPLANADE People are raving about The Esplanade (1401 West Esplanade), a mall which houses over 150 stores and specialty shops. Big name stores that are represented include Macy's, Dillard's, Mervyn's, Yvonne LaFleur, and The Limited. There is also a large food court. Open: Mon–Sat 10am–9pm, Sun noon–6pm.

THE FRENCH MARKET Shops within the Market begin on Decatur Street across from Jackson Square, and include candy, cookware, fashions, crafts, toys, New Orleans memorabilia, and candles. Open: 10am–6pm (Farmer's Market & Café du Monde open 24 hours).

JACKSON BREWERY Just across from Jackson Square, the old brewery building has been transformed into a joyful jumble of shops, cafés, delicatessens, restaurants, and entertainment. The 125 shops and eateries within its walls include fashions, gourmet and Cajun-Creole foodstuffs, toys, hats, crafts, pipes, posters, and souvenirs. Keep in mind that many shops in the Brewery close at 5:30 or 6pm, before the Brewery itself closes. Open: Sun–Thurs 10am–10pm, Fri–Sat 10am–9pm.

JULIA STREET From Camp Street over toward the river on Julia Street, you'll find great contemporary art galleries lining the street. Of course, some of the works are a bit pricey, but there's a lot that's absolutely affordable if you're interested in collecting. You'll find many of them listed below.

MAGAZINE STREET This major uptown street runs from Canal Street to Audubon Park, with some six miles of more than 140 shops (some of which are listed below), some in 19th-century brick storefronts, others in quaint cottagelike buildings. Among the offerings are antiques, art galleries, boutiques, crafts, and dolls.

RIVERBEND The Riverbend district is in the Carrollton area. To reach it, ride the St. Charles Avenue streetcar to stop 44, then walk down Maple Street one block to Dublin Park, the site of an old public market once lined with open stalls. Nowadays, renovated shops inhabit the old general store, a produce warehouse made of bargeboard, and the town surveyor's raised-cottage home. Among the outstanding shops are Yvonne LaFleur, whose romantic fashions have appeared on TV and movie screens; and the Cache Pot, with a concentration of unusual, high-quality gifts.

RIVERWALK This popular shopping development is an exciting covered mall that runs right along the river from Poydras Street to the Convention Center. Among the specialty shops at this location, you'll find Eddie Bauer, The Limited, and Banana Republic, plus several eateries and periodic free entertainment. Open: Mon–Thurs 10am–9pm, Fri–Sat 10am–10pm, Sun 11am–7pm.

UPTOWN SQUARE At 200 Broadway, this unique shopping center consists of a maze of one- and two-story buildings interspersed with pleasant plazas and fountains. It's a central place to find fine fashions (Holmes Department Store has a large branch here), family clothing, housewares, distinctive gifts, toys, plants, books, and wines. There's also a cafeteria-style restaurant upstairs, with balcony seating if you wish. Open: Mon–Sat 10am–6pm, some shops open Sun.

---

2. SHOPPING A TO Z

ANTIQUES

ACQUISITIONS ANTIQUES, 2025 Magazine St. Tel. 522-7974.
On its two floors, this shop houses the antiques of six different dealers. You'll find a great variety of items, from furniture to picture frames and mirrors. Open: Mon–Sat 10am–5pm, Sun noon–5pm.

AUDUBON ANTIQUES, 2023 Magazine St. Tel. 581-5704.
Audubon has everything from collectible curios to authentic antique treasures at reasonable prices. Open: Mon–Sat 10am–5pm, Sun noon–5pm.

AURAT ANTIQUES, 3009 Magazine St. Tel. 897-3210, or toll free 800/676-8640.
Owners Robert and Martha Lady collect and import incredibly beautiful Indo-Portuguese and Anglo-Indian colonial furnishings as well as Oriental rugs, dhurries, kilims, and other collectibles. Open: Mon–Sat 10am–5pm.

BOYER ANTIQUES—DOLLS & BUTTONS, 241 and 328 Chartres St. Tel. 522-4513.
In addition to an assortment of antiques, you'll find an enchanting collection of old dolls and doll furniture. Open: Daily 9:30am–5pm.

LUCULLUS INC., 610 Chartres St. Tel. 528-9620.
An unusual shop, Lucullus Inc. has a wonderful collection of culinary antiques as well as 17th-, 18th-, and 19th-century furnishings to "compliment the grand pursuits of cooking, dining, and imbibing." Open: Mon–Sat 9am–5pm.

MAGAZINE ARCADE ANTIQUES, 3017 Magazine St. Tel. 895-5451.
This large and fascinating shop once housed the Garden District's classiest mercantile. Today it holds an exceptional collection of European, Asian, and American furnishings; old medical equipment; porcelain; turn-of-the-century steam and gasoline engines; music boxes; doll houses; toys and games; and antique jewelry. Try to plan plenty of time to browse through it all. Open: Mon–Sat 10am–5pm.

MISS EDNA'S ANTIQUES, 2029 Magazine St. Tel. 524-1897.

Miss Edna's has a wonderful selection of furniture, specialty items, and curios. Call for hours.

ART GALLERIES

In addition to those listed below, there are a great number of galleries in what used to be the warehouse district and is now a center for the arts. You can pick up a brochure called "Arts in the Warehouse District" that lists a fairly large number of galleries on Julia Street and some of the surrounding streets. Though there are many wonderful galleries on Royal Street, don't forget the old warehouse district, especially if you're interested in contemporary art.

A GALLERY, 322 Royal St. Tel. 568-1313.

A Gallery specializes in 19th- and 20th-century rare photographs and books and has most recently shown the works of Jock Sturges, Sandy Skoglund, and E. J. Bellocq. Open: Daily 10am–6pm.

ARIODANTE, 535 Julia St. Tel. 524-3233.

A contemporary craft gallery, Ariodante features, among other things, beautiful glasswork and ceramics by today's artists. A recent show featured lighting designs, including hand-blown glass lamps, by various artists. Open: Daily 10am–9pm.

LA BELLE GALERIE, 738 Royal St. Tel. 529-3080.

La Belle Galerie has a great collection of African American art. There aren't too many galleries in New Orleans specializing in African American art, so this one stands out. I saw some terrific pieces in the gallery on my last visit.

BERGEN GALLERIES, INC., 730 Royal St. Tel. 523-7882, or toll free 800/621-6179.

Bergen Galleries has the city's largest selection of posters and limited-edition graphics—including New Orleans works; Mardi Gras; jazz; and artists such as Erté, Nagel, Maimon, Tarkay, and a large collection of works by sought-after African American artists. The service from Margarita and her staff is friendly and extremely personable. Open: Daily 9am–9pm.

THE DAVIS GALLERIES, 3964 Magazine St. Tel. 897-0780.

The Davis Galleries features West and Central African traditional art. Works on display might include costuming, basketry, textiles, weapons, and jewelry. Open: Tues–Sat 10am–6pm.

DIXON & DIXON OF ROYAL, 237 Royal St. Tel. 524-0282.

Dixon & Dixon features 18th- and 19th-century primitive and oil paintings, as well as decorator-quality Oriental rugs. Open: Mon–Sat 9am–5pm, Sun 10am–5pm.

ENDANGERED SPECIES, 619 Royal St. Tel. 568-9855.

The owners of Endangered Species have traveled the world (35 countries) collecting art objects and artifacts. Here you'll find tribal masks, unusual jewelry, carved ivories, and hand-woven textiles. Open: Mon–Sat 10am–6pm, Sun 11am–4pm.

GALERIE SIMONNE STERN, 518 Julia St. Tel. 529-1118.

Galerie Simonne Stern features paintings, drawings, and sculptures by contemporary artists. Recent shows included the works of

Doyle Gertjejansen, Simon Gunning, Andy Nasisse, and Frank Fleming. Open: Daily 10am–8pm.

HANSON GALLERIES, 229 Royal St. Tel. 566-0816, or toll free 800/388-1331.

Hanson Galleries has a special showing of new originals and graphics by Peter Max and also works by Neiman, Kostobi, Thysell, Deckbar, Zjawinska, and Hart. Open: Mon–Sat 10am–7pm, Sun 11am–5pm.

HILDERBRAND GALLERIES, 4524 Magazine St. Tel. 895-3312.

For contemporary works of fine art, including the works of perhaps Arcadio Cancio, Mark Messersmith, or Ray Burggraf, try Hilderbrand Galleries. Open: Daily 10am–9pm.

IMPORTICOS, 736 Royal St. Tel. 523-0306.

If you're interested in handcrafted imports from Central America and Indonesia, stop by Importicos where you'll find a selection of jewelry, pottery, textiles, and leather items. Open: Daily 10am–6pm.

INDIGO NIGHTS GALLERY, 434 Julia St. Tel. 524-2892.

Indigo Nights holds a wonderful collection of New Orleans antiques and home furnishings as well as paintings and other exquisite objets d'art. New Orleans artists Susan Brechtel (art silks), Judy Faget (textiles), Tony Green (paintings in various media), Porche-West (photography), Edward David Surla (paintings in egg tempera), Julia Thigpen (paintings in oils), and Guy Wilson (lighting designs) are all represented at Indigo Nights. Open: Tues–Sat 11am–6pm.

NAHAN GALLERIES, 540 Royal St. Tel. 524-8696.

Nahan Galleries specializes in works of major artists and original graphics. It is also the publisher for Theo Tobiasse, Max Papart, and others. Open: Mon–Sat 9:30am–6pm, Sun 11am–6pm.

NEW ORLEANS SCHOOL OF GLASSWORKS, 727 Magazine St. Tel. 529-7277.

This place is difficult to categorize, simply because it serves multiple purposes—allowing artists and blossoming artists in the area of glasswork to take classes, work, show, and sell their pieces. Absolutely unique to the area, it is worth a visit during gallery hours. Daily glassblowing, fusing, and slumping demonstrations are offered. A new printmaking, papermaking, and bookbinding studio has recently been added. Book and paper art classes are also available. Open: Mon–Sat 11am–5pm.

TRADE FOLK ART IMPORT EXPORT, 828 Chartres St. Tel. 596-6827.

Taina and Kelly travel to Mexico frequently and bring back some wonderful pieces of folk art. If you know nothing about Mexican folk art, you should really stop by and look around. Trade Folk Art also features Southern folk artists. They'll also give you an education if you ask. Open: Daily 10am–5pm.

BOOKS

For literary enthusiasts there are the **Maple Street Bookstore,** 7523 Maple St. (tel. 866-4916), which has three locations throughout the city including The Maple Street Children's Book Shop at

7529 Maple St. (tel. 861-2105); **De Ville Books and Prints,** 1 Shell Square (tel. 525-1846); and **Beaucoup Books,** 5415 Magazine St. (tel. 895-2663). **Little Professor Book Center of New Orleans,** 1000 S. Carrollton Ave. (tel. 866-7646), stocks one of the best general collections.

The nationwide chain stores are also well-represented: **B. Dalton** has stores at 714 Canal St. (tel. 529-2705) and in the New Orleans Center on the second level, next to the Hyatt Hotel at 1400 Poydras (tel. 525-1016).

BECKHAM'S BOOKSHOP, 228 Decatur St. Tel. 522-9875.

Beckham's has two entire floors of old editions and some rare, secondhand books that will tie up your whole afternoon or morning if you don't tear yourself away. The owners also operate **Librairie Bookshop,** at 823 Chartres St., which you'll surely have found if you're a book lover. Open: Daily 10am–6pm.

BOOKSTAR, 414 N. Peters St. Tel. 523-6411.

Bookstar is a large, attractive bookshop in the Jackson Brewery complex. Without doubt, it stocks one of the largest selections of books and magazines in the city, and its enthusiastic and knowledgeable staff can help you find the printed word on virtually any subject you can name. Open: Daily 10am–midnight.

FAULKNER HOUSE BOOKS, 624 Pirates Alley. Tel. 524-2940.

This is a small bookstore with a big history. It was here that Southern fiction writer and Nobel Prize winner William Faulkner lived while he was writing *Soldier's Pay.* Today the shop holds a large collection of first-edition Faulkners, including copies of *The Sound and the Fury,* as well as rare and first-edition classics by many other authors. For book lovers, this shop is a must stop on a trip to New Orleans. Open: Daily 10am–6pm.

GEORGE HERGET BOOKS, 3109 Magazine St. Tel. 891-5595.

George Herget Books is another of New Orleans's great bookstores. Over 20,000 rare and used books covering absolutely every subject imaginable are available for your browsing and collecting pleasure. If you find yourself on Magazine Street, stop in and visit George Herget. Open: Mon–Sat 10am–5:30pm.

OLIVE TREE BOOK STORE, 927 Royal St. Tel. 523-8041.

I love this bookstore because it is absolutely piled high, wall to wall, with books—there's hardly room to walk around. They carry old and rare books, as well as records and magazines. Open: Daily 10am–10pm.

CANDIES & PRALINES

AUNT SALLY'S PRALINE SHOPS, INC., 810 Decatur St. Tel. 524-5107.

At Aunt Sally's, in the French Market, you can watch skilled workers perform the 150-year-old process of cooking the original Creole pecan pralines right before your eyes. You'll know they're fresh. The large store also has a broad selection of regional cookbooks, books on the history of New Orleans and its environs, Creole and Cajun foods, folk and souvenir dolls, and local memorabilia. They'll ship any of your purchases, which can considerably lighten the load going home. Open: Daily 8am–8pm.

LAURA'S ORIGINAL PRALINE AND FUDGE SHOPPE, 115 Royal St. Tel. 525-3886.

Laura's is said to be New Orleans's oldest candy store, established in 1913. There are seven varieties of pralines on sale here, plus hand-dipped chocolates, rum-flavored pecans, Vieux Carré Foods, and their great praline sauce. Open: Daily 9am–9pm.

LEAH'S CANDY KITCHEN, 714 St. Louis St. Tel. 523-5662.

While the other candy stores listed above are all good, Leah's, in my opinion (you might prefer one of the others—I suggest you torture yourself and try them all), has the best pralines in the city. Everything, including the candy fillings (as they make many different types of candy, including chocolate-covered pecan brittle, which is incredible), is made from scratch. Open: Mon–Sat 10am–10pm.

CANDLES

FRENCH MARKET GIFT SHOP, 824 Decatur St. Tel. 522-6004.

Here you'll find a delightful collection of handcrafted beeswax candles in beautiful, artistic shapes and sizes. Brass candlesticks and other candle-related items, as well as a large array of gift items and collectibles (clowns, masks, music boxes, and so on), make this much more than just a candle shop. Open: Daily 9am–9pm.

COSTUMES

There are a number of shops specializing in Mardi Gras finery. One tip to remember is that New Orleanians often sell their costumes after Ash Wednesday, and you can sometimes pick up a one-time-worn outfit at a small fraction of its cost new.

LITTLE SHOP OF FANTASY, 523 Dumaine St. Tel. 529-4243.

Mike Stark, Laura Guccione, and Jill Kelly make all the pieces in their shop. Mike creates the feathered masks, and Jill does the velvet hats, cloaks, and leather masks. Some of them are just fun and fanciful, but there are some extraordinary and beautiful ones as well.

MARDI GRAS CENTER, 831 Chartres St. Tel. 524-4384.

Mardi Gras Center carries sizes 2 to 50 and has a wide selection of new, ready-made costumes as well as used outfits. It also does custom costumes and carries all accessories such as wigs, masks, hats, makeup, and jewelry. Open: Mon–Sat 10am–5pm.

FASHION

A legacy of New Orleans's elegant past is the locals' love of fashion; shops around the city accommodate them by providing everything from high-fashion designer clothes to the latest "funky" styles.

SAKS FIFTH AVENUE, 301 Canal St. Tel. 524-2200.

In addition to the high-quality fashion and accessories for men and women for which they are nationally known, Saks also offers a personalized shopping service, the Fifth Avenue Club. This branch is in Canal Place. Open: Mon–Wed and Fri–Sat 10am–7pm, Thurs until 8pm.

TOWN AND COUNTRY, 1432 St. Charles Ave. Tel. 523-7027.

Opened almost half a century ago, this shop has a warm, friendly atmosphere that encourages leisurely examination of the fine fashions. There are designer collections, distinctive dresses and jewelry, and some truly smashing accessories. Open: Mon–Fri 9:30am–5:30pm, Sat until 5pm.

YVONNE LEFLEUR/NEW ORLEANS, 8131 Hampson St. Tel. 866-9666.

Yvonne LeFleur, a confessed incurable romantic, is the creator of original designs so beautifully feminine that they'll invite fantasies of past golden ages. Her custom millinery, silk dresses, evening gowns, lingerie, and sportswear are surprisingly affordable, and all are enhanced by her own perfume. Her store is located in the Riverbend district. Open: Mon–Tues and Fri–Sat 9:45am–6pm, Wed–Thurs until 8pm.

FOOD

CAFE DU MONDE COFFEE SHOP, 800 Decatur St. Tel. 581-2914.

If you want to try your hand at making those scrumptious beignets, you can buy the mix at the Café du Monde, in the French Market. To make it complete, pick up a tin of their famous coffee (a special blend of coffee and chicory). The shop also has a very good mail-order service. Open: Daily 24 hrs.

GIFTS

There are literally hundreds of gift shops in New Orleans, with merchandise ranging from very expensive to junky. The following are the ones I found most attractive.

ANGEL WINGS, 710 St. Louis St. Tel. 524-6880.

If you're looking for something unusual, that's not necessarily your typical New Orleans tourist souvenir, you should stop by Angel Wings. They have a wonderful collection of jewelry, accessories, and curios. Open: Mon–Sat 10am–10pm, Sun 10am–6pm.

KRUZ, 432 Barracks St. Tel. 524-7370.

Kruz has a collection of international pieces, including books, incense, musical recordings from various countries, as well as handbags, musical instruments, and clothing. It's a great little store that's worth a stop. Open: Mon–Fri 11am–6pm, Sat and Sun 11am–6:30pm.

LITTLE MEX, 1017–21 Decatur St. Tel. 529-3397.

I don't really know how to tell you about this amazing store. From a rather unimposing entrance, you walk into an interior that goes on and on. And it's filled with just about everything under the sun. There are imports from all over the world—a huge selection from Mexico; leather goods; straw, wheat, and bamboo products; baskets (I bought a great one to carry an accumulation of purchases already made); metal sculpture; dolls; brass and copper items; and more. All I can say is to be sure to allow some extra time for some of the best browsing in the French Quarter. Open: Daily 9am–5pm.

PONTALBA HISTORICAL PUPPETORIUM, 514 St. Peter St. Tel. 522-0344 or 944-8144.

There's an excellent puppet presentation of New Orleans history here in Jackson Square, but you can also purchase puppets. In fact, the puppetorium has the largest collection in the United States. Open: Daily 9:30am–5:30pm.

SANTA'S QUARTERS, 1025 Decatur St. Tel. 581-5820.

If you're walking down Decatur Street in July and suddenly hear "Jingle Bells," you'll know you've found this year-round Christmas store. It's an enchanting place, with ornaments from around the world, all kinds of decorations, and so many Christmas ideas that you may finish up all your holiday shopping months in advance. Open: Daily 9:30am–5:30pm.

HATS

In addition to the shop listed below, you can also get hats—fun costume hats—at Little Shop of Fantasy, listed above.

MEYER THE HATTER, 120 St. Charles Ave. Tel. 525-1048, or toll free 800/882-4287.

Men will find distinguished headwear—one of the largest selections of fine hats and caps in the South—with labels such as Stetson, Dobbs, and Borsalino in this fine shop, which opened in 1894 and is now run by third-generation members of the same family. Open: Mon–Sat 9:45am–5:45pm.

JEWELRY

BEDAZZLE, 635 St. Peter St. Tel. 529-3248.

If you like contemporary jewelry, head for Bedazzle, where they have "jewelry as art." They've got everything you'd find in a traditional jewelry store, only it's a lot more interesting. It's worth a stop, and the staff is extremely helpful and friendly. Open: Daily 10:30am–6pm.

JOAN GOOD, 809 Royal St. Tel. 525-1705.

I love Joan Good for its wonderful collection of antique jewelry. While they do have some fairly typical pieces, like their competitors on Royal Steet, they also have some very unusual pieces. I saw some cameos in there that were exquisite, as well as some uniquely designed rings. It's worth stopping just to see what they have when you're in town. Open: Daily 10am–6pm.

MIGNON FAGET LTD., Canal Place, Level One. Tel. 524-2973.

The striking originals of New Orleans's own Mignon Faget have won national fame, and a visit to her studio display room, at Level One, Canal Place, is a real treat. Handcrafted designs in gold, silver, and bronze d'oré include pendants, bracelets, rings, earrings, shirt studs, and cufflinks. Open: Mon–Wed and Fri–Sat 10am–6pm; Thurs 10am–8pm; Sun noon–6pm.

NEW ORLEANS SILVERSMITHS, 600 Chartres St. Tel. 522-8333.

Here you'll find jewelry, both old and new, in gold and silver, as well as a variety of reproductions of antiques. Open: Mon–Sat 9:30am–5pm.

QUARTER MOON, 918 Royal St. Tel. 524-3208.

All the jewelry in the shop is handmade by the owners, Michael and Ellis Shallbetter. The pieces are interesting and entirely unique—since they're handmade, you won't find anything like them anywhere else.

RUMORS, 513 Royal St. Tel. 525-0292.

Chances are, you won't miss Rumors. They've got an incredible selection of earrings—they call it "art for ears." I'm still amazed at their stock. If you're crazy about earrings, you should stop in—no doubt something will strike your fancy. Open: Sun–Thurs 9:30am–6pm, Fri–Sat 9:30am until closing.

LEATHER GOODS

RAPP'S LUGGAGE AND LEATHER, 604 Canal St. Tel. 568-1953.

Rapp's carries an extensive selection of leather goods, from the most expensive designer luggage to duffle bags, wallets to attaché cases, and many unique gifts that you'd never expect to find in a leather-goods store. Gift wrapping and monogramming are free. The quality is high, and the prices are reasonable. This store can also repair luggage. There are branches at Uptown Square, 200 Broadway (tel. 861-1453); Esplanade Mall, Kenner (tel. 467-8283); 3250 Severn at 17th Street, Metairie (tel. 885-6536); and New Orleans Center (tel. 566-0700). Open: Daily 10am–5:30pm (call to confirm hours of other branches).

THE OCCULT

THE BOTTOM OF THE CUP TEAROOM, 732 Royal St. Tel. 523-1204.

At the Bottom of the Cup Tearoom, psychics and clairvoyants specialize in palm reading, crystal gazing, tea-leaf reading, and tarot. You can also get your astrological chart done. It's been open since 1929 and bills itself as the "oldest tearoom in the United States." In addition to having a psychic consultation you can also purchase books, jewelry, crystal balls, tarot cards, crystals, and healing wands here. Open: Mon–Sat 9am–9pm, Sun 11–7.

PERFUME

BOURBON FRENCH PERFUME COMPANY, INC., 525 St. Ann St. Tel. 522-4480.

Located right off Jackson Square, the Bourbon French Perfume Company is where you should go if you're looking for your own personal, custom, hand-blended fragrance. Of course, you may also choose from their ready-made line of perfumes and colognes as well. They've been creating perfumes from natural oils for over 150 years. On a recent visit I noticed some beautiful handblown Egyptian glass perfume bottles. Open: Daily; hours vary so call ahead.

HOVE PARFUMEUR, LTD., 824 Royal St. Tel. 525-7827.

Hove is another excellent place to go for unusual fragrances.

They've been in business for over 60 years, and in the creation of their perfumes, powders, potpourri, and soaps they utilize scents that are commonly found in New Orleans. Open: Mon–Sat 10am–5pm.

PIPES & TOBACCO

YE OLDE PIPE SHOPPE, 306 Chartres St. Tel. 522-1484.

Mr. Edwin Jansen's shop won my heart in about two seconds flat (or maybe it was Mr. Jansen himself). His grandfather, August, founded this place way back in 1868 and at one time repaired Jefferson Davis's pipes. Nowadays, *my* Mr. Jansen hand-makes beautiful briar pipes, repairs broken pipes, and sells pipe accessories and enough tobacco blends to keep you puffing all year long. This is not a fancy shop but a warm, comfortable stopping-off place for pipe lovers. While you're there, take a look at the marvelous collection of antique pipes put together by his father and grandfather. In keeping with the character of this special place, the pipes aren't shown off in some sort of velvet-lined display, but are just heaped in a glass case, making it sort of an adventure to run your eyes over one after the other, trying to imagine each in the fond hand of its original owner. Over the years Mr. Jansen has developed a firm philosophy about pipes and their smokers and has written an excellent book (free for the asking) about them. If pipes are your thing, don't fail to search this place out and spend some time with a kindred spirit. Open: Mon–Sat 10am–5pm.

TOYS

THE LITTLE TOY SHOPPE, 900 Decatur St. Tel. 522-6588.

The dolls here are some of the most beautiful I've ever seen, especially the Madame Alexander and Effanbee ones—and the New Orleans–made bisque and rag dolls. In addition to "heros" wood toys from Germany and "All God's Children" collectibles, there are cuddly stuffed animals, dollhouses and furniture, toy soldiers, and miniature cars and trucks. Open: Mon–Thurs 9:30am–5:30pm, Fri–Sat 9:30am–9pm, Sun 10am–9pm.

UMBRELLAS

1107 DECATUR STREET. Tel. 523-7791.

They call her "the Umbrella Lady," but her real name is Anne B. Lane. You'll find her in her upstairs studio. A Quarter fixture, she's the creator of wonderful Secondline umbrellas as well as fanciful "southern belle" parasols. Look for the umbrellas displayed on her balcony. Open: Hours vary so call ahead.

WOODCRAFTS

IDEA FACTORY, 838 Chartres St. Tel. 524-5195.

One of my favorite shops in the French Quarter, the Idea Factory features all sorts of handcrafted wood items, including toys, kinetic sculptures, door harps, signs, boxes, and office supplies (business-card holders, in/out trays, etc.). Many of the items are made right on the premises so if you're lucky you might get to see one of the craftspeople at work. Also featured is the jewelry of Thomas Mann. Open: Mon–Sat 10am–6pm, Sun noon–5pm.

CHAPTER 10

NEW ORLEANS NIGHTS

1. **THE PERFORMING ARTS**
   - **THE MAJOR CONCERT/ PERFORMANCE HALLS**
2. **THE CLUB & MUSIC SCENE**
3. **THE BAR SCENE**
4. **MORE ENTERTAINMENT**

In New Orleans, entertainment has long started with jazz. It used to be everywhere—on the streets of the French Quarter, in jazz clubs all over the city, and in the heart and soul of everyone who lived here. Jazz and blues now share the music marquee with rock and roll and other popular music, but whatever the sound, it's still no trouble to find a raucous, all-night party in this city. But there's more to New Orleans than just its heady nightlife. Its rich French heritage, strongly spiced by the Italians who've become such a part of its life, has left a real love of classical music and opera. Theater, too, plays a part in New Orleans entertainment.

1. THE PERFORMING ARTS

In spite of the fact that it's a little off the regular routes for touring Broadway shows, New Orleans attracts some very good national companies, and there's surprisingly good local theater. The city has a long-standing love affair with footlight entertainment—Le Petit Théâtre du Vieux Carré is one of the oldest playhouses in this country, light opera appeared as early as 1810, and grand opera was first sung here in 1837. Opera enjoyed its peak years during the Gay Nineties and the early part of this century and thrived until a fire destroyed the famous old French Opera House in 1919. It wasn't until 1943 that the New Orleans Opera House Association was formed to present several operas a season, with stars from New York's Metropolitan Opera Company in leading roles, supported by talented local voices. Occasionally the Met's touring company will also book performances here. If you're an opera buff and in town during one of the local offerings, don't pass it up—there's nothing amateurish about these productions. You'll likely find them (as well as concerts by top performers and symphony orchestras, ballets, and recitals by local and imported talent) in one of two buildings: the New Orleans Theatre of the Performing Arts or the New Orleans Municipal Auditorium (which also accommodates such general-audience shows as circuses, prize fights, ice shows, and the popular summer pops symphony concerts).

The New Orleans Philharmonic Symphony Orchestra plays a subscription series of concerts during the fall-to-spring season, and the pops concerts on June and July weekends. Live theater got a big boost in early 1980 when the grand old Saenger Theatre was reopened after being rescued from demolition by a determined group of New Orleanians. There's also a good dinner theater going strong, and sometimes good cabaret can be found in bar or lounge settings. In short, you're unlikely to hit town when there *isn't* something worthwhile going on in the performing arts.

Note: Because ticket prices vary widely according to performance, your best bet is just to call the numbers listed below before you go.

MAJOR CONCERT HALLS & ALL-PURPOSE AUDITORIUMS

THE MUNICIPAL AUDITORIUM, 1201 St. Peter St. Tel. 565-7470.

The Municipal Auditorium, just across a flowered walkway from the Theatre of Performing Arts in the Cultural Center complex in Louis Armstrong Park, is used for just about every kind of entertainment—from the circus to touring theatrical companies to ballets and concerts. This is where most of the marvelous, elaborate Mardi Gras balls are held.

THEATRE OF THE PERFORMING ARTS, 801 N. Rampart St. Tel. 529-2278.

This theater, opened in early 1973, has become the favored venue for lavish touring musical shows as well as concerts. Opera and ballet also appear here in season. It's a part of the 32-acre New Orleans Cultural Center complex in Louis Armstrong Park, adjacent to the French Quarter.

THEATERS

In addition to the listings below, possibilities for theatrical performances (check when you're here, because none of these is open on a regular basis) include **N.O.R.D. Theatre** (tel. 483-2536), for productions sponsored by the New Orleans Recreation Department; **Tulane Univeristy Theatre** (tel. 865-5361), which puts on student plays of very high caliber; and the **Louisiana Superdome** (tel.

THE MAJOR CONCERT/PERFORMANCE HALLS

Albert Lupin Theatre, Tulane University. Tel. 865-5361.
Contemporary Arts Center, 900 Camp St. Tel. 523-1216.
La Maison des Beaux Arts, 1140 St. Charles Ave. Tel. 524-4ART.
Le Petit Théâtre du Vieux Carré, 616 St. Peter St. Tel. 522-2081.
Municipal Auditorium, 1201 St. Peter St. Tel. 565-7470.
Theatre of the Performing Arts, 801 N. Rampart St. Tel. 529-2278.
Orpheum Theatre, 212 Loyola St. Tel. 522-0500.
Saenger Theatre, 143 N. Rampart St. Tel. 524-2490.

587-3810)—yes, that's right, the Superdome—which frequently hosts entertainment not even remotely connected with sports.

LA MAISON DES BEAUX ARTS, St. Charles Ave. Tel. 524-4ART.

If you're interested in contemporary theater, the place to call is La Maison des Beaux Arts. Since its opening in 1992, it has slowly earned a reputation as one of New Orleans's premiere theaters, and has proven that theater is alive and well in the city that care forgot. Recently La Masion des Beaux Arts began a season made up completely of the works of up-and-coming playwrights. Call ahead for schedules and ticket prices.

LE PETIT THEATRE DU VIEUX CARRE, 616 St. Peter St. Tel. 522-2081.

⭐ If you hear people talking about "The Little Theater" right in the heart of the French Quarter, this is it. It's one of the oldest nonprofessional theater troupes in the country and periodically puts on plays that rival the professionals in excellence. Check when you're here to see if the footlights are up.

SAENGER THEATRE, 143 N. Rampart St. Tel. 525-1052.

The Saenger Theatre is *the* theater news in New Orleans. First opened in 1927, it was regarded as one of the finest in the world, and it has now been completely restored in all its finery. The decor is Renaissance Florence, with Greek and Roman sculpture, fine marble statues, and glittering cut-glass chandeliers. The ceiling is alive with twinkling stars, with realistic-looking clouds drifting by. It's a setting the likes of which are fast disappearing from the American theater scene, and New Orleans is to be congratulated for preserving such opulence. First-rate Broadway productions such as *Cats, Les Misérables, Fiddler on the Roof,* and *Can Can* (with Chita Rivera) play here regularly. Check to see what's on when you're in town.

2. THE CLUB & MUSIC SCENE

When the sun goes down, New Orleans lights up. In the French Quarter, Bourbon Street turns into a 10-block-long street party, posh downtown hotel supper clubs start to swing, and uptown hideaways come to life with music. Jazz, that uniquely American contribution to the world's music, was born here and still permeates the city; performers both black and white, both newcomers and old-timers, join together to keep the traditional sound alive at all hours in the French Quarter and after dark outside the Quarter. You'll still find uninhibited dancers performing in the streets outside jazz spots (sometimes passing the hat to lookers-on); jazz funerals for departed musicians (the trip to that final resting place accompanied by sorrowful dirges and "second liners" who shuffle and clap hands to a mournful beat); the return (a joyful, swinging celebration of the deceased's "liberation"); and occasionally a street parade (even when it isn't Carnival), complete with brass band.

The bars and clubs listed below are some of the hot spots at the time I researched this edition of the book; however, the notoriously fickle fortunes of the nightclub business make your best bet to walk up and down Bourbon Street and follow the sounds of your favorite type of music and the loudest (or quietest) crowd to a spot you might like to try. *Note:* Most places open for happy hour and stay open until the wee hours.

JAZZ & BLUES
IN THE FRENCH QUARTER

I once heard a horse-and-carriage driver state unequivocally that the corner of St. Peter and Bourbon Streets was "the world's heaviest jazz corner." He may well be right, for jazz pours out of just about every door (and most are wide open) in this area. Not just any jazz, mind you, but *great* jazz, and it begins early in the day and doesn't stop until there's no one left to tap a toe. Almost anyplace along here will be a good spot to spend an evening, but if you're like most, you'll pop into several.

FRITZEL'S EUROPEAN BAR AND CUISINE, 733 Bourbon St. Tel. 561-0432.

You might walk right past this small establishment, but that would be a big mistake, for since 1974 this 1836 building has attracted some of the city's best musicians, who perform on the tiny stage in back. There are frequent jam sessions here in the wee hours, when musicians end their stints elsewhere and gather to play just for themselves. The bar stocks a variety of German liqueurs, as well as imported beers, and there's a menu of German sandwiches (knockwurst, bratwurst, and so on, on Black Forest bread), hamburgers, po-boys, and red beans and rice—all at budget prices. But go along late at night if you want to catch "musicans' music." Open Sunday through Thursday from 11am to 2am, Friday and Saturday from 11am to 5am.

Admission: No cover charge (one drink per set minimum).

HOUSE OF BLUES, 225 Decatur St. Tel. 529-1421.

Live blues performances are staged here in Dan Ackroyd's second House of Blues (the first was opened in Boston), which is one of the largest and most advanced music performance venues of its genre. Recent musical performers included James Belushi, Aerosmith, Tab Benoit, and the Latin Jazz All-Stars. There's a gospel brunch offered every Sunday at noon (reservations are strongly recommended). Open Monday through Thursday and Sunday from 8pm to 2am, Friday and Saturday from 8pm to 4am.

Admission: Cover charge $5–$15.

JELLY ROLL'S, 501 Bourbon St. Tel. 568-0501.

Every Monday and Saturday night you can hear the sounds of trumpeter Al Hirt who plays upstairs in the Jumbo Room beginning around 9:30pm. Other live performers are featured as well, including The New Red Hot Peppers (Friday through Sunday 4 to 8pm), and occasionally, Billy Fayard & The New Orleans Levee Board and Bobby Lonero and the New Orleans Express. Open daily from 8pm until . . . .

Admission: One-drink minimum.

JIMMY BUFFETT'S MARGARITAVILLE CAFE, 1104 Decatur St. Tel. 592-2565.

Live entertainment is featured nightly at Jimmy Buffett's. Performers have recently included Walter "Wolfman" Washington, Wayne Toups, George Porter and the Runnin Pardners, Wanda Rouzan and a Taste of New Orleans, Sunpie Barnes and the Louisiana Sunspots, and the Burton Anderson Blues Band; Jimmy Buffett himself is known to show up and play a set from time to time. Call ahead for ticket and schedule information. Show times are 9pm Sunday through Thursday, 9:30pm on Friday and Saturday.

Admission: Charges vary according to performers.

JOHN WEHNER'S FAMOUS DOOR, 339 Bourbon St. Tel. 522-7626.

Extant since 1934, the Famous Door is the oldest music club on Bourbon Street. There's jazz in the afternoon, and in the evening Dixieland jazz begins at 9pm. Karaoke is available between sets.

Admission: One-drink minimum per set.

KALDI'S COFFEEHOUSE/COFFEE MUSEUM, 941 Decatur St. Tel. 586-8989.

By day Kaldi's is a popular coffeehouse, but at night on the weekends (beginning at 8pm) you can listen to live jazz while sipping a cup of java and munching on pastries. Open Sunday through Thursday from 7am to midnight, Friday and Saturday from 7am to 2am.

Admission: Free.

MAISON BOURBON, 641 Bourbon St. Tel. 522-8818.

You might start your evening at Maison Bourbon, which keeps its doors open to the sidewalk and employs three bands every day to play from 2:15 or 3:15pm to midnight or 2am.

Admission: One-drink minimum.

NEW STORYVILLE JAZZ HALL, 1104 Decatur St. Tel. 522-2500.

Here there's a one-drink-per-set minimum and a cover charge determined by who's playing at the moment. Traditional Dixieland played by top bands gets things started, and on some nights the beat takes on a contemporary note as the evening progresses. Children are welcome here, and there's limited food service.

Admission: Call ahead for cover charge.

OLD ABSINTHE HOUSE BAR, 400 Bourbon St. Tel. 525-8108.

Don't confuse this place with the Old Absinthe House at 240 Bourbon. That's right, they both have the same name, and what's more, they're both entitled to it. The one on the corner of Bourbon and Bienville Streets (that's no. 240) can claim the original *site*, while all the original fixtures are now to be found at no. 400, on the corner of Bourbon and Conti. That situation came about when federal agents padlocked the original (it was operating as a speakeasy) during the 1920s, and some enterprising soul broke in, removed the bar, the register, 19th-century prints, ceiling fans, an antique French clock, and a handsome set of marble-based fountains once used to drip water into absinthe (which has been banned in the United States since 1918 because it's a narcotic). They all turned up soon afterward in the establishment on the corner a block away, and New Orleans was blessed with two "original" Old Absinthe Houses. Anyway, it's the one at 400 Bourbon where you'll find rhythm and blues and progressive jazz—and you'll find drinks only at the other. Beginning at 9pm nightly, the music is continuous, sometimes with as many as three groups alternating, until all hours—there's no legal shutdown time in New Orleans, and it isn't unusual to find things still going strong here as dawn breaks. On weekends there's also daytime music. Blues dominate on the bandstand. Drinks cost from $2.

Admission: No cover charge.

PALM COURT CAFE, 1204 Decatur St. Tel. 525-0200.

This is one of the most stylish jazz haunts in the Quarter. Nina and George Buck have created an oasis of civilized dining (linen on the table, lace curtains at the street windows, and international cuisine—see Chapter 6 for details) in which to present top-notch jazz groups Wednesday through Saturday and on Sunday for a jazz brunch. One very special feature is the collection of jazz records for sale in a back alcove, many of them real finds for the collector. Open Wednesday through Saturday from 7am to 11pm, Sunday brunch from 11am to 3pm, dinner from 5 to 10pm.

Admission: Call ahead for cover charge.

PRESERVATION HALL, 726 St. Peter St. Tel. 523-8939.

Dear to the hearts of all jazz devotees (and I count myself among them) is Preservation Hall, where jazz is found in its purest form, uncluttered by such refinements as air conditioning, drinks, or even (unless you arrive very early) a place to sit. The shabby old building offers only hot, foot-tapping, body-swaying music, played by a solid core of old-time greats who never left New Orleans. Nobody seems to mind the lack of those other refinements—indeed, not only is the place itself always packed, but its windows are frequently lined by the faces of those who stand on the sidewalk for hours just to listen.

Admission is unbelievably low, and if you want to sit on one of the much-sought-after pillows right up front or a couple of rows of benches just behind them, be sure to get there a good 45 minutes before the doors open. Otherwise, you must stand. The music goes on until 12:30am, with long sets interrupted by 10-minute breaks and the crowd continually changing as parents take children home at bedtime (the kids *love* the hall) and sidewalk listeners move in to take vacant places. There's a marvelous collection of jazz records on sale, some of them hard-to-find oldies. Open nightly from 8pm to 11pm.

Admission: $3.

THE SECOND LINE, 216 Bourbon St. Tel. 523-2020.

For Dixieland, blues, rhythm and blues, and big band swing, visit the Second Line, one of Bourbon Street's newest music clubs. Inside you'll find three bars and a big dance floor. Every night you can hear New Orleans–style jazz, and blues, and in the afternoon on Sunday, stop by for a Dixieland jam session. Be sure to pick up their calendar of events when you're in town.

Admission: No cover charge.

SNUG HARBOR, 626 Frenchmen St. Tel. 949-0696.

On the fringes of the French Quarter (one street beyond Esplanade), Snug Harbor has earned top popularity from residents and visitors alike for its nightly presentation of contemporary jazz and blues. Seating is on two levels to provide good viewing of the bandstand, and there's full dinner service (local Cajun and Creole specialties and steak) as well as a light menu of sandwiches. The acts change every night. Open Monday through Saturday from 5pm.

Admission: $8–$15 depending on performer.

OUTSIDE THE FRENCH QUARTER

PETE FOUNTAIN'S, in the New Orleans Hilton, 2 Poydras St. Tel. 523-4374 or 561-0500.

Pete Fountain is one of those loyal native sons who has never been able to sever hometown ties. For more than 20 years he held forth in his own Bourbon Street club, but these days you'll find him here, in a re-creation of his former Quarter premises, which seats more than twice the number that could be accommodated in the old club. The plush interior—gold chairs and banquettes, red velvet bar chairs, lacy white iron-railinged gallery—sets the mood for the popular nightspot, located at the Mississippi River. Pete is featured in one show a night, Tuesday through Saturday at 10pm. The club is on the hotel's third floor. You'll need reservations.

Admission: Varies; call for rates and to confirm show times.

TIPITINA'S, 501 Napoleon Ave. Tel. 895-8477.

Here there's jazz, rhythm and blues, and almost every other form of music. At Tip's, it all depends on the artist playing, and that covers a *lot* of territory. Past performers in this New Orleans staple have included the Neville Brothers and Bo Diddley. Back in its 1977 beginnings this was home for the revered Professor Longhair up until his death in 1980, and you'll be greeted by a bronze bust of the beloved musician as you enter. Open daily from 5pm (6pm on Saturday).

Admission: Cover charge varies according to performer.

CAJUN MUSIC

MAPLE LEAF BAR, 8316 Oak St. Tel. 866-9359.

Uptown in the Carrollton area, the Maple Leaf Bar may be the best place outside the bayous to hear Cajun music (mostly on Thursday and weekends) played by top musicians of that genre. Other nights it might be rhythm and blues, rock and roll, or reggae. Dancing is "encouraged," so you may find yourself out on the floor two-stepping to that Cajun beat. There's a jukebox offering an eclectic mix of musical styles, from classical to jazz to ragtime to Cajun, and there's a strong tradition of good conversation ranging from literary subjects (poetry readings every Sunday afternoon feature local and visiting poets and writers) to music, to sports, and to almost any topic you choose. Come 10pm, however, the jukebox gives way to live music. Thursday nights and some weekends celebrate the lively music and dancing from southwest Louisiana's Cajun country, with standouts such as the Filé Cajun Band and the black Cajun zydeco renditions of Dopsie and his Cajun Twisters. Open daily.

Admission: $3–$8, depending on day of week and performer.

MICHAUL'S LIFE CAJUN MUSIC RESTAURANT, 701 Magazine St. Tel. 522-5517, or toll free 800/299-2333.

You'll find good Cajun music here in the Warehouse District. If your feet begin tapping to the catchy rhythms but you're uncertain of the steps, Michaul's will give you free dance lessons. The cuisine is as Cajun as the music. Dinner is daily from 6pm to midnight. Reservations are recommended.

Admission: Free.

MULATE'S, 201 Julia St. Tel. 522-1492.

This Cajun restaurant, which has been popular in other parts of Louisiana, has recently opened in New Orleans. There's a huge, central bar, and a stage for live Cajun music performances. Cajun dancing takes place nightly. Open daily from 11am to 11pm.

Admission: Free.

PATOUT'S CAJUN CABIN, 501 Bourbon St. Tel. 529-4256.

Located right on Bourbon Street, Patout's Cajun Cabin features the music of Cajun country as performed by The Can't Hardly Play Boys and Mudbug Deluxe. Open daily from 11am to midnight (music begins at about 7pm).

Admission: One-drink minimum.

CABARET

No doubt I am taking great liberties with the word *cabaret,* but this seems as good a place as any to mention the legendary skin shows of Bourbon Street. There are a number of establishments offering this sort of entertainment in the 300 and 400 blocks of Bourbon; you'll be able to tell what you're getting into before you go in—club owners frequently open their doors to try to lure in the paying public with music and a more or less unobstructed view of the dancers inside. There are also a couple of traditional cabaret theaters in New Orleans; see below.

BAYOU CABARET THEATRE, 4040 Tulane Ave., corner of S. Carrollton Ave. Tel. 486-4545.

Conveniently located in the Central Business District, the Bayou Cabaret Theatre is small, and the performances are done "in the round," so that you can see everything at all times. Table service is offered before curtain, during intermission, and after the performance. There is an adequate beer and wine list. You must reserve your table in advance. Open at 1:30pm for 2pm matinee, and at 7:30pm for 8pm performance.

Admission: $16 adults, $14 seniors.

CHRIS OWENS CLUB, 735 St. Louis St., corner of Bourbon St. Tel. 523-6400.

✪ If you like your entertainment on the sexy side but aren't quite game for Bourbon Street's strippers, this is the place to go. This talented and very beautiful woman puts on a solo show of fun-filled jazz, popular, country and western, and blues while (according to one devoted fan) revealing enough of her physical endowments to make strong men bay at the moon. Between shows, there's dancing on the elevated dance floor. Audience participation is encouraged—join in the conga line, which is popular with visitors and locals alike. Call for show times and to make reservations.

Admission: $11 includes show and one cocktail ($15 on New Year's Eve).

ROCK

CAT'S MEOW, Bourbon St. Tel. 523-1157.

Cat's Meow is always full, and it's no wonder—they play popular rock songs all night long. The interior is bright and colorful, and the crowd the club attracts is young and loud.

Admission: Free.

MID-CITY LANES ROCK AND BOWL, 4133 S. Carrollton Ave. Tel. 482-3133.

Another popular spot for some good ol' rock and roll is Mid-City Lanes Rock and Bowl. Yes, you guessed it, it's a rock club and a bowling alley—you literally rock *and* bowl. It's great fun—give it a try! Open daily from noon until everyone gets too tired to lift the ball.

Admission: Day rates daily $1.75 per game or $8 per hour; evening rates Sun–Thurs $8 per hour, Fri–Sat $10 per hour.

WORLD MUSIC

CAFE BRASIL, 2100 Chartres St. Tel. 947-9386.

Live music ranging from jazz to rock and blues is featured here nightly. The crowd is eclectic, and the atmosphere is friendly and welcoming of all lifestyles and varieties of people. Open nightly; shows begin between 10 and 10:30pm.

Admission: Varies according to performer.

CAFE ISTANBUL, 534 Frenchmen St. Tel. 944-4180.

If your choices in music are varied, Cafe Istanbul (a Turkish restaurant by day) is just the place. You'll be able to hear anything from hip-hop to reggae to Latin music. Entertainment is live. Call ahead for the current schedule of events. The club is open from 10:30pm until . . . .

Admission: Varies according to performer.

LUCKY PIERRE'S WORLD BEAT, 735 Bourbon St. Tel. 523-5842.

At this dance club there are nine giant-screen TVs where music videos play constantly. In addition, there's a beautiful marble bar, a piano bar (featuring a pink baby grand piano), and a pool/gameroom. World Music is featured, but Top 40 is also on the playlist. Open daily from 5pm to 5am.

Admission: Free.

3. THE BAR SCENE

LAFITTE'S BLACKSMITH SHOP, 941 Bourbon St. Tel. 523-0066.

Lafitte's dates back to 1772. Legend has it that the privateer brothers Pierre and Jean Lafitte used the smithy as a "blind" for their lucrative trade in contraband (and, some say, slaves they'd captured on the high seas). It had pretty much deteriorated by 1944, when a honeymooning visitor fell in love with and devoted most of the rest of his life to making it a social center for artists, writers, entertainers, and journalists. He did this all without changing one iota of the musty old interior—even today you can see the original construction and "feel" what it must have been like when it was a privateers' hangout. Unfortunately Tom Caplinger's penchant for treating good friends such as Tennessee Williams and Lucius Beebe to refreshments "on the house" was stronger than his business acumen, and he eventually lost the building. All this is history, but I think it helps explain the comfortable, neighborhood air that still pervades Lafitte's. The interior is all exposed brick, wooden tables, and an air of authenticity. It's a good drop-in spot any time of day, but I especially enjoy relaxing in the dim, candlelit bar at the end of a festive night when "Miss Lily" Hood holds forth at the piano.

PIANO BARS

ESPLANADE LOUNGE, in the Royal Orleans, 621 St. Louis St. Tel. 529-5333.

For a nightcap to the strains of top-notch piano music in one of the city's loveliest settings, stop by the Esplanade.

PAT O'BRIEN'S, 718 St. Peter St. Tel. 525-4823.

Pat O'Brien's has been famous for as long as I can remember for its gigantic, rum-based Hurricane drink, served in 29-ounce hurricane lamp-style glasses. In addition, its let-your-hair-down conviviality has earned it a special place among so many residents that it sometimes has a neighborhood air usually associated with much smaller places. There are three bars here—the main bar at the entrance and one of the loveliest patio bars in existence have no entertainment—but it's the large lounge just off the entrance that is the center of a Pat O'Brien's fun night. The fun comes from several teams of pianists alternating at twin pianos and an emcee who tells jokes. The entertainers seem to know every song ever written, and when they ask a patron "Where're you from?" quick as a wink they'll break into a number associated with the visitor's home state. Requests are quickly honored, and sing-alongs develop all night long, sometimes led by a patron who's been invited up to the bandstand. There's no minimum and no cover, but you should know that if you buy a drink and it comes in a *glass* you'll be paying for the glass until you turn it in at the register for a $2 refund.

A BAR WITH A VIEW

TOP OF THE MART, World Trade Center of New Orleans, 2 Canal St. Tel. 522-9795.

The view is breathtaking any time of day, but especially so after dark, from the Top of the Mart, at the river. The large lounge located on the 33rd floor makes a complete circle every 90 minutes. From up there you'll see the bend in the Mississippi that gives New Orleans its "Crescent City" title, and the reflected lights of ships in the harbor remind you that this is not only a fun town, but also a very busy and important port. As you revolve, the layout of the city unfolds all the way to Lake Pontchartrain. There's no admission charge and no cover. Since no meals are served (only drinks), children aren't permitted. One tip: Don't lay your belongings on the windowsill when you're seated—*it* doesn't revolve, and you'll wind up either chasing them around the room or waiting in the hope they'll come back around to you.

GAY BARS

Below you'll find listings of New Orleans's most popular gay nightspots. For more information you might want to check in *This Week Guide,* which is a great source for the gay community in New Orleans and for those visiting. You'll find them stashed all over town, and they're free.

BOURBON PUB, 801 Bourbon St. Tel. 529-2107.

The Bourbon Pub attracts a young male crowd, offering dancing and a video screen. It's open 24 hours and every time I've ever been in or been by, the place is packed.

CAFE LAFITTE IN EXILE, 901 Bourbon St. Tel. 522-8397.

When Tom Caplinger lost Lafitte's Blacksmith Shop, friends say that it broke his heart. But he rallied and a little later opened a new place down the block toward Canal Street called the Café Lafitte in Exile (the exile is his own, from that beloved blacksmith shop). The new digs flourish even after his death as an elite gay bar.

CHARLENE'S, 940 Elysian Fields. Tel. 945-9328.

Charlene's is known as the only lesbian bar in town. It's a little out of the way if you're staying in the Quarter, but there's dancing and live entertainment, so you might think it worth the trip.

THE MINT, 504 Esplanade Ave. Tel. 525-2000.

⭐ A popular spot within the gay community in New Orleans, The Mint is always full. There's live entertainment all the time (including impersonation), so you should ask around or look in *This Week Guide* to find out what's happening during your visit. Happy hour is nightly from 5 to 9pm, and the club itself is open Monday through Friday from noon until the wee hours, Saturday and Sunday from 10am on.

THE STERLING CLUB, 700 Burgundy. Tel. 522-1962.

This is a wonderful neighborhood spot with its dark-wood paneling and leather armchairs. There is a piano for anyone who wants to bang out a tune and also a TV. You can get meals all day and all night because it's open 24 hours. The crowd here is very mixed—gay and straight frequent the place; however, it is gay-owned and -operated.

4. MORE ENTERTAINMENT

AN EVENING CRUISE

One of the loveliest evenings out in New Orleans is to be found out on the water. The *Creole Queen* (tel. 524-0814, or toll free 800/445-4109) is a paddlewheeler built in the tradition of its forebears, which made its debut at the 1984 World's Fair and now offers superb Creole dinners and jazz cruises nightly. Departures are at 8pm (boarding at 7pm) from the Canal Street Wharf. The fare is $39 per person (which includes a sumptuous Creole buffet), and there's continuous bar service, as well as live jazz and dancing against a backdrop of the city's sparkling skyline. Schedules are subject to change, so call ahead to confirm days and times.

CASINOS

In addition to the riverboat gambling listed below, as this book goes to press New Orleans is beginning plans for a temporary land-based casino to be located in the New Orleans Municipal Auditorium in Armstrong Park. Harrah's plans to build a permanent casino that will be open sometime in 1995.

STAR CASINO, No. 1 Star Casino Blvd. Tel. 243-0400, or toll free 800/504-STAR for reservations.

Docked at South Shore Harbor on Lake Pontchartrain, Star Casino was the first to grace the waters of New Orleans when city gambling was legalized. At the paddlewheeler's dock you'll find an information and reservations booth, credit office, restaurant, gift shop, and cocktail lounge. The neon-trimmed interior holds 760 slot machines, 39 gaming tables, and video poker. Each cruise lasts two hours.

Admission: Free.

Open: Departure times are 1:45 and 10:45am, 1:45, 4:45, 7:45, and 10:45pm.

QUEEN OF NEW ORLEANS AT THE HILTON RIVERBOAT CASINO, New Orleans Hilton Riverside. Tel. 587-7777.

The _Queen of New Orleans_ is an authentic re-creation of a turn-of-the-century riverboat casino that features over 700 slot machines and scores of gaming tables. The boat actually cruises the Mississippi—it's not permanently docked. Don't worry, however, about getting motion sickness—you'll be so intent on your game that you'll hardly be aware of the fact that the boat is moving. There are six cruise times daily (seven on Friday and Saturday), and boarding begins 45 minutes before the scheduled cruise. I would strongly advise buying your tickets in advance, especially for the evening cruises, so you won't have to wait in line (lines can be enormously long), and getting there as soon as the doors open for boarding so you can stake out your machine before the masses beat you to it. Slot machines are the most popular form of gambling on the boat, and they range from 25¢ to $100 slots. At the time of my last visit, a small food court was planned for the boat—Lucky Dogs, Mother's, and the Italian restaurant Andrea's were the three food vendors represented. Drinks are free during your cruise. Children are not allowed in the gaming rooms.

Admission: At press time, admission was $12 for adults, but there has been talk about dropping the admission fee altogether, so call ahead to check prices.

Open: Cruise times at press time were 8:45am, 11:45am, 2:45pm, 5:45pm, 8:45pm, 11:45pm, and 2:45am (Friday and Saturday only), but the schedule seemed to be in a constant state of change, so confirm these times before you make plans.

CHAPTER 11

EASY EXCURSIONS FROM NEW ORLEANS

1. THE PLANTATIONS ALONG THE GREAT RIVER ROAD

2. CAJUN COUNTRY

New Orleans can serve as the hub for two interesting side trips. The first centers on the great plantation homes that line the banks of the Mississippi; the second will take you a little over 100 miles west of New Orleans to the heart of Acadiana, where the unique, delightful culture of the Cajuns lives on. Although a day trip is enough to see some of the plantation houses that are open to the public, the other trip will probably require an overnight stop; both will very likely lure you to stay for more than just one night. I must warn you, too, that should you become hooked on the romanticism of the plantations, it is quite possible to keep rambling north of the River Road to visit those in the St. Francisville area, an exploration that also calls for an overnight stay—and I'll tell you about old homes in which you can actually spend the night if you plan far enough ahead.

1. THE PLANTATIONS ALONG THE GREAT RIVER ROAD

BACKGROUND

In the beginning, the planters of Louisiana were little more than rugged frontierspeople as they spread out along the Mississippi from New Orleans. Swamplands had to be cleared, with a mighty expenditure of sweat and muscle. And the indigo—the area's first cash crop—had to be transported downriver to New Orleans before there was any return on all that work, no mean feat in itself. Even today, as you drive on the modern highways that course through some of the bayous, it's not hard to imagine what it must have been like for those early settlers.

Fields were cleared, swamps were drained, and crops were planted, however, in spite of all the obstacles. And rough flatboats and keelboats (with crews even rougher than their vessels) could get the produce to market in New Orleans—sometimes. Once the boats were on the river, if they weren't capsized by rapids, snags, sand-bars, and floating debris, there was the danger that their cargos would be captured by murdering bands of river pirates. It was the crudeness of these men (and a few amazing women) who poled the boats to New Orleans; collected their pay for the journey; and then went on wild sprees of drinking, gambling, and brawling that first gave the Creoles of the French Quarter their lasting impression of all Americans as barbarians, a conviction that was later to influence the growth and development of the city.

By the 1800s Louisiana planters had introduced farming on a large scale, thanks to their use of (and dependence on) slave labor—a fact that would ultimately bring about their downfall. With large numbers of African Americans performing the back-breaking work in the fields, more and more acres went under cultivation, and King Cotton arrived on the scene to prove the most profitable of all crops. Sugarcane, too, brought huge monetary returns, especially after one Etienne de Bore discovered the secret of successful granulation. Rice became a secondary crop. Always there were natural dangers that could spell disaster for planters—a hurricane could wipe out a whole year's work, and the capricious river could, and did, make swift changes in its course to inundate entire plantations. Nevertheless the planters persevered, and for the most part they prospered.

THE RIVERBOATS After 1812, the planters turned to the new-fangled steamboat for speedier and safer transportation of their crops to the market. When the first of these (the *New Orleans*, built in Pittsburgh) chugged downriver belching sooty smoke, it was so dirty, dangerous, and potentially explosive that it was called by some a "floating volcano." Before long, however, vast improvements were made, and over a 30-year period the image of the steamboats changed to that of veritable floating pleasure palaces. Utilitarian purposes (moving goods to market and the planters and their families to town) were always primary, but the lavish staterooms and ornate "grand salons" put a whole new face on river travel and made a profound change in plantation life. A planter could now travel in comfort with his wife, children, and slaves, which induced many to spend the winters in elegant town houses in New Orleans. After months of isolation in the country, where visitors were few, the sociability of the city—with its grand balls, theatrical performances, elaborate banquets, and other entertainments—was a welcome relief. Also, it became possible to ship fine furnishings back upriver to plantation homes, and thus the planters could enjoy a more comfortable and elegant lifestyle along the banks of the river.

Those wonderful floating pleasure palaces did, alas, add another element of danger to the lives of some planters. For along with the prosperous plantation families, Northern merchants, carpetbag-carrying peddlers, European visitors, and poor immigrant families who made up passenger lists, came the most colorful and dramatic passenger of all—the riverboat gambler. Perhaps because they were natural-born gamblers (didn't they gamble on Nature itself every year?), plantation owners were drawn like magnets to the sharp-witted, silver-tongued professionals. Huge fortunes were won and lost on Ole Man River, and more than once when cash, luggage, and jewelry were depleted, the deed to a plantation went on the table, to be raked in by a well-dressed, cigar-smoking pro. During one famous game, which went on for three days without interruption, it was said that over $37,000 in gold was on the table at one point. Thus a planter might leave his plantation home a wealthy man and arrive at journey's end a pauper. And if the gamblers didn't get him, the steamboat captains might. As the vessels became grander and grander and more and more efficient, the captains and pilots took to racing one another—a hazardous practice that caused the loss of many boats and even more lives and fortunes.

THE PLANTATION HOUSES It was during this period of prosperity, from the 1820s until the beginning of the Civil War, that most of the impressive plantation homes were built. Each was usually built as the focal point of a self-sustaining community and almost always was located near the riverfront, with a wide, oak-lined avenue leading from its entrance to a wharf. On either side of the avenue would be *garçonnières* (much smaller houses, sometimes used to give adolescent sons and their friends privacy; others were guesthouses for travelers who stopped for a night's lodging). Behind the main house, the kitchen was built separately because of the danger of fire, and the overseer's office was close enough for convenience. Some plantations had, behind these two structures, pigeon houses, or dovecotes—and all had the inevitable slave quarters, usually in twin lines bordering a lane leading to cotton or sugarcane fields. When cotton gins and sugar mills came along, they were generally built across the fields, out of sight of the main house.

In the beginning, the main houses were much like the simple "raised cottage" known as Madame John's Legacy, on New Orleans's Dumaine Street—with long, sloping roofs; cement-covered brick walls on the ground floor; and wood and brick (brick between posts) used in the living quarters on the second floor. They suited the sultry Louisiana climate and swampy building sites and made use of native materials. There's a distinct West Indies architectural influence seen in houses of the colonial period, very unlike the grander styles that were to follow in the 1800s.

In the 1820s homes were built that combined traces of the West Indian style with some Greek Revival and Georgian influences—a style that has been dubbed Louisiana Classic. Large rounded columns usually surrounded the main body of the house, wide galleries reaching from the columns to the walls encircled upper floors, and the roof was dormered. The upper and lower floors consisted of four large rooms centered by a wide hall. They were constructed with native materials, with a few imported interior details, such as fireplace mantels. Remember that there were no stone quarries in Louisiana, and if stone was used (which wasn't very often), it had to be shipped from New England and transported up the Mississippi from New Orleans. But the river flowed through banks of clay, and with so many slaves, bricks could be made right on the spot. Cypress, too, was plentiful, and such a water-loving wood was perfect for the hot, humid climate, which could quickly deteriorate less impervious woods. Thus the cypress was used for house beams and even for railings on the galleries (unlike the fancy cast iron so much used in New Orleans). To protect the homemade bricks from dampness, they were plastered or cement covered, and sometimes the outer coating was tinted, although more often it was left to mellow into a soft, off-white color. The columns were almost always of plastered brick, but very occasionally of cypress wood. Even their capitals were of these materials, except for a rare instance when cast iron was used. These houses, then, took some features from European architecture and some from the West Indian styles that so well suited the location and adapted them to local building materials.

By the 1850s planters were more prosperous, and their homes became more grandiose. The extravagance of Victorian architecture was embraced and given a unique Louisiana flavor, the features of Northern Italian villas crept in, and some plantation homes followed Gothic lines (notably the fantastic San Francisco Plantation, sometimes called "steamboat Gothic"). As planters and their families traveled to Europe more frequently, they brought home ornate furnishings for their houses, which had begun to grow in size as well as elegance. European masters were imported for fine woodworking, until Louisiana artisans such as Mallard and Seignouret developed skills that rivaled or surpassed those from abroad. Ceilings were adorned by elaborate "medallions" from which glittering crystal chandeliers hung, and on wooden mantels and wainscoting the art of *faux marbre* ("false marble") began to appear. In short, plantation owners seemed determined to make their country homes every bit as elegant as their New Orleans town houses. They were developing a way of life dedicated to graciousness and hospitality unlike any other in American history.

As they grew in opulence, the plantation houses expanded in size—some had as many as 30 or 40 rooms. They were so large partly because families were quite large in those days. But even more important, any social life in the country had to come from neighbors or friends visiting for several days or weeks. After all, travel was difficult, and there just was no such thing as "popping in for a call." But there were other reasons, too, and they had to do with that well-known Southern pride. Madewood, for example, over on Bayou Lafourche, was built for no other reason than to outshine Woodlawn, the beautiful home of the builder's brother. In another case, two suitors of one young woman put up rival, massive houses in an attempt to win her affections. It was a simple case of antebellum "keeping up with the Joneses."

Underneath the planters' enormous wealth and power lay an economy built on the backs of slaves. It was, as world history has many times shown, an unhealthy foundation, and inevitably it crumbled with the beginning of the Civil War. Farming on a scale as large as was practiced on the plantations was impossible without that large, cheap labor base. And when plantation owners went away to war, the management of the plantations deteriorated even where slaves stayed on. During Reconstruction, lands were often confiscated and turned over intact to those unable for financial or other reasons to run the large-scale operations; many were broken up into smaller, more manageable farms. Increasing international competition began to erode the cotton and sugar markets that had built such large fortunes. And as industrialism moved south, there was no place for life as it had been lived in the golden plantation years.

It is hard to remember when you walk through the grand old homes left in the wake of the plantation era that the culture they embody began, reached a lofty pinnacle, and then died away in the span of less than 100 years. As almost its only—and certainly its most eloquent—relic, this culture left houses the like of which will undoubtedly never again be seen.

THE PLANTATION HOUSES TODAY   Since the beginning of this century, several of these houses have been the victims of fires or floods. Some have been torn down to make way for other things, such as industrial plants. Others, too costly to be maintained in modern times, have been left to the ravages of dampness and decay. But for a few, fate has been more kind—wealthy families have bought the houses and restored them with love and affection, retaining their feeling for "the good life" and filling them with family heirlooms or treasured antiques. The encroachment of modernity has been restricted primarily to the installation of plumbing and electricity. Some are used only as private residences, but you can visit others for a small admission fee (which, in some instances, supplements the owner's own resources to keep up the old house). No home open to the public is owned by descendants of the original owners. Today's visitors are, then, truly indebted to those "outsiders" who have gone to such lengths to preserve one part of our heritage that might otherwise have disappeared completely.

PLANNING YOUR TRIP

All the plantation homes shown on the map are within easy driving distance of New Orleans. How many you take in on any one day will depend, I suspect, on your endurance behind the wheel, your walking stamina (you'll cover a lot of ground touring the houses), and how early you set out. You'll be driving through "country" Louisiana, and I might as well warn you that some of what you'll see is really quite tacky—the modern, industrial economy that prevails through most of the area just isn't pretty to look at. Also, don't expect to enjoy broad river views as you drive along the Great River Road (the name given to the roadway on *both* sides of the Mississippi)—you'll have to drive up on the levee for that. You will, however, pass through little towns that date back to plantation days, and in your own car you'll have the luxury of turning off to inspect interesting old churches or aboveground cemeteries that from a tour bus window can only be glimpsed. I think it's a good idea to make your first plantation inspection via one of the excellent tours listed below, then take the car exploring after you've gained some familiarity with the territory. Another advantage of the tours is the detailed background information furnished by the guides—your own ramblings will be the better for it.

One word about this particular group of homes: If you should happen to be in New Orleans on Christmas Eve and drive along River Road, your way will be lit by huge bonfires on the levees—they're to light the way for the Christ Child (an old Latin custom), and residents along here spend weeks collecting wood, trash, and anything that's flammable to make the fires blaze brightly.

Because not all Louisiana plantations actually bordered the Mississippi River (many were on bayous that also provided water transportation), some of the grand old homes have survived at locations too far away from New Orleans to be visited in a single day. I'm listing those separately, with the recommendation that you try to stay overnight at one of those that offers guest accommodations. I'll also include accommodations in Baton Rouge and St. Francisville, either of which can serve as a convenient tour base.

TOURS As I said in the beginning, it's an excellent idea to take a plantation-house bus tour from New Orleans before setting out on your own. Most of the tours visit only one or two of the houses I have described, leaving plenty for your private exploration. My experience has been that tour guides are exceptionally well informed, and the buses are an easy, comfortable way to get around in unfamiliar territory. Almost every tour company operates a River Road plantation tour.

One tour I especially like is the 7-hour River Road plantations tour offered by **Gray Line,** 2345 New Orleans World Trade Center (tel. 504/587-0861). The two plantations visited are San Francisco and Houmas House. All admissions are included in the $33 charge. Tours, departing at 9am, pick you up at and deliver you to your hotel. The cost of lunch at a country restaurant, however, is not included and generally runs $6 to $8, sometimes more.

If you prefer a smaller tour group, **Tours by Isabelle,** P.O. Box 740972, New Orleans, LA 70174 (tel. 504/391-3544), takes no more than 14 people in a comfortable minibus on a 6½-hour expedition to visit Oak Alley Plantation and Nottaway Plantation (with a stop in front of Houmas House and Tezcuco Plantation). The tour departs only when six or more people request it, so you might have to wait a day or two until they can get a large enough group together. Other tours offered by Tours by Isabelle include a 4½ hour Cajun Bayou Tour (the boat tour is 1½ hours); the 5-hour Eastbank Plantation Tour (which includes guided tours of San Francisco Plantation and Houmas House, with stops in front of Tezcuco, Bocage, and Hermitage Plantations); and the Grand Tour (a visit to Oak Alley Plantation, lunch, a Cajun Bayou Tour, and a stop in front of Destrehan Plantation).

PLANTATIONS WITHIN THE NEW ORLEANS AREA

WHAT TO SEE & DO

I'll start with the plantations nearest New Orleans and describe them in the order in which they appear on the map, although that is not necessarily the order in which you will view them.

A mile and a half above Destrehan, look for **Ormond** plantation house, a two-story structure with columns and gallery and a wing on each end (it's not shown on our map because it isn't open to the public). The house has in recent years been bought and beautifully restored as a private residence, but its early history is one of tragedy. Built sometime before 1790 by one Pierre de Trepagnier on land granted him by the Spanish government, it witnessed the mysterious disappearance of Pierre, when he went off with a complete stranger and was never seen or heard from again; the wiping out of almost an entire family by yellow fever; and the murder of its owner during Reconstruction, when his body was found riddled with bullets and hanging from a live oak tree. From all appearances the house is now seeing happier days and its future looks bright. You can't go inside, but it is certainly worth a slow-down and long look as you pass by.

DESTREHAN MANOR, La. 48 (P.O. Box 5), Destrehan, LA 70047. Tel. 764-9315.

A free person of color named Charles built this house, located 22 miles from New Orleans along the River Road, in 1787. The wings on either side were added in 1805, and between 1830 and 1840 it was renovated from French Colonial to Greek Revival. Some of the largest live oaks in the state are on the grounds. Its double galleries are surrounded by Doric columns that support the central structure's hipped roof. Inside, you can see the original woodwork and some interesting antiques. There's also a gift shop, and you can purchase light refreshments. The American Oil Company, which had bought the property, presented the house (in a state of deterioration) to the River Road Historical Society, and during its restoration some of the earliest methods of construction were uncovered. The society has left some glimpses of the construction open for visitors to see. Destrehan is the oldest plantation home remaining intact in the Lower Mississippi Valley that is open to the public. There are guided tours.

Admission: $6 adults, $5 teenagers and seniors, $3 children 6 and over, children 5 and under free.

Open: Daily 9:30am–4pm.

SAN FRANCISCO, La. 44 (P.O. Drawer AX), Reserve, LA 70084. Tel. 535-2341.

This fantastic mansion, located two miles north of Reserve, was built between 1853 and 1856 by Edmond B. Marmillion. Unfortunately, Mr. Marmillion died shortly after its completion and was never able to occupy the home, which was willed to his two sons, Valsin and Charles. In 1855, while on a grand tour of Europe, Valsin had met and married Louise Seybold. They returned to Louisiana on March 5, 1856 and remained in the United States for two years before they again traveled to Europe. Upon their return to Louisiana in late 1859 Valsin and Louise undertook to redecorate their home. When they were finished, Valsin jokingly declared to his friends that he was *"sans fruscin,"* or "without a cent" to his name. This is how the plantation home gained its first name, St. Frusquin. When the estate was sold to Achille Bougere, the name was changed to San Francisco.

Though its name has changed over the years, the legacy of Edward Marmillion is a fantasy come true, even after all these years. The Gothic three-story house has broad galleries that look for all the world like a ships' double decks, and twin stairs lead to a broad main portal much like one that leads to a steamboat's grand salon. (Novelist Frances Parkinson Keyes visited the house and used it as the setting for her novel, *Steamboat Gothic*.) Galleries are trimmed with lacy tailings between the fluted columns. Inside, the owner created beauty in every room through the use of carved woodwork and paintings alive with flowers, birds, nymphs, and cherubs on walls and ceilings of cypress tongue-and-groove boards. The dazzling restoration includes English and French 18th-century furniture and paintings. There's also a small gift shop.

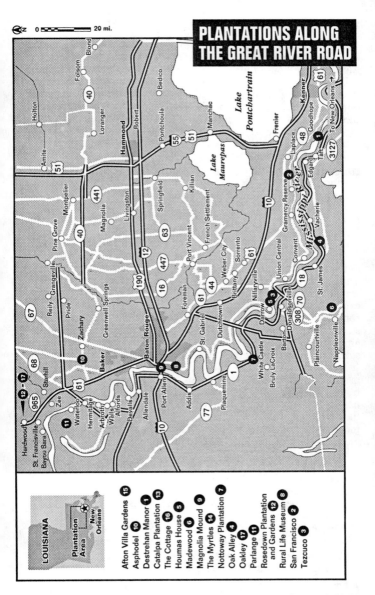

PLANTATIONS ALONG THE GREAT RIVER ROAD

0 ——— 20 mi.

Afton Villa Gardens **15**
Asphodel **10**
Destrehan Manor **1**
Catalpa Plantation **13**
The Cottage **16**
Houmas House **5**
Madewood **6**
Magnolia Mound **9**
The Myrtles **14**
Nottoway Plantation **7**
Oak Alley **4**
Oakley **17**
Parlange **11**
Rosedown Plantation and Gardens **12**
Rural Life Museum **2**
San Francisco **2**
Tezcuco **3**

LOUISIANA
Plantation Area
New Orleans

Admission: $6.50 adults, $3.75 children 12–17, $2.50 children 6–11, children under 6 free.

Open: Daily 10am–4pm. **Closed:** Holidays (including Mardi Gras Day).

TEZCUCO, 3138 La. 44, Darrow, LA 70725. Tel. 562-3929.
Just upriver from the Sunshine Bridge (55 miles from New Orleans), Tezcuco ("Resting Place") was one of the last plantation houses built before the Civil War. Although small, the raised

cottage was some five years in the building, using slave labor, wood from surrounding swamps, and bricks from kilns on the plantation. Although the house follows the traditional floor plan of a central hall flanked by two rooms on either side, an unusual feature is the staircase leading to the gallery at each end, as well as the expected central stair. Outbuildings include gazebos, the Civil War Museum, shops, a commissary, a chapel, and a life-size dollhouse.

Admission: $6 adults, $5 children 13–17 and seniors, $3 children 4–12, children 4 and under free.

Open: Daily 9am–5pm.

OAK ALLEY, 3645 La. 18, Vacherie, LA 70090. Tel. 504/ 265-2151.

On La. 18 between St. James and Vacherie, Oak Alley is 60 miles from downtown New Orleans and is probably the most famous plantation house in Louisiana. It was built in 1839 by Jacques Telesphore Roman III and named Bon Séjour—but if you'll walk out to the levee and look back at the quarter-mile avenue of 300-year-old live oaks, you'll see why steamboat passengers quickly dubbed it "Oak Alley," a name that soon replaced the original. Those trees were planted, it is thought, by an early settler; Roman was so enamored of them that he planned his house to have exactly as many columns—28 in all. The fluted Doric columns completely surround the Greek Revival house and support a broad second-story gallery. Inside, the floor plan is traditional, even to the attic, with a wide central hall flanked by two large rooms on each side. Oak Alley lay disintegrating until 1914, when Mr. and Mrs. Jefferson Hardin, of New Orleans, bought it and moved in. Then in 1925 it passed to a Mr. and Mrs. Andrew Stewart, whose loving restoration is responsible for its National Historic Landmark designation. Both the Stewarts have passed on now, but two members of their staff, who have been here for years, stay on to guide visitors through the home. It is furnished just as it was during the Stewarts' lifetime—with a comfortably elegant mix of antiques and more modern pieces.

Overnight accommodations are available in several cottages at rates of $85 to $115. Also, there's a restaurant open for breakfast and lunch daily from 9am to 3pm.

Admission: $6.50 adults, $3.50 students, $2 children 6–12, children 5 and under free.

Open: Mar–Oct, daily 9am–5:30pm; Nov–Feb, daily 9am–5pm. **Closed:** Thanksgiving, Christmas, and New Year's.

HOUMAS HOUSE, 40136 La. 942 Burnside, Darrow, LA 70725. Tel. 473-7841.

Fifty-eight miles from New Orleans, this lovely old house had very humble beginnings in a four-room cabin built in the 1700s on land originally owned by members of the Houmas tribe. When the massive Greek Revival main house was built out front, the original house was retained and survives today. The impressive main house is 2½ stories tall, with 14 columns on three sides supporting the wide gallery. At either side are hexagonal *garçonnières* (small cottages intended for the young male family members or to put up travelers for the night), and a carriageway is formed where the original house is connected to the main house.

The late Dr. George Crozat, of New Orleans, purchased the house some years ago and went about restoring it as a comfortable home for himself and his mother, bringing in authentic furnishings of the period in which it was built.

Magnificent live oaks, magnolias, and formal gardens frame Houmas House in a way that is precisely what comes to mind when most of us think "plantation house." It so closely fits that image that it's been used in the movies—you may, in fact, already have seen its exterior if you saw *Hush, Hush, Sweet Charlotte*. There's an interesting gift shop out back. To get to Houmas House, take I-10 from New Orleans or Baton Rouge. Exit on La. 44 to Burnside, turn right on La. 942.

Admission (including guided tour): $7 adults, $5 children 13–17, $3.50 children 6–12, children under 6 free.

Open: Feb–Oct, daily 10am–5pm; Nov–Jan, daily 10am–4pm. **Closed:** Holidays.

MADEWOOD, 4250 La. 308, Napoleonville, LA 70390. Tel. 504/369-7151.

You won't want to miss this magnificent house on Bayou Lafourche, just below Napoleonville, one of the best preserved of the plantation mansions. It was built by the son of a wealthy planter who had originally come from North Carolina in 1818. Madewood, the creation of the youngest of three brothers, was built for the sole purpose of outdoing his older brother's elegant mansion, Woodlawn. Four years were spent cutting lumber and making bricks, and another four were spent in actual construction. It was finally completed in 1848, but the owner never got to gloat over his brother, because he died of yellow fever just before it was finished.

The large, two-story Greek Revival house of stucco-covered brick is set on a low terrace, and on either side connecting wings duplicate its design. Inside, the ceilings are 25 feet high; the central hallways are huge, as are the bedrooms; and there's a winding carved walnut staircase. Madewood has more than 20 rooms, including a tremendous ballroom. Outside there are a carriage house and the family cemetery. Truly, it's more than worth the drive.

The overnight accommodations offered here are really rather special. If you elect to stay in one of the main-house guest rooms, you'll have the run of the place, much more like a guest in a private home than a paying member of the public. For example, you'll be greeted with wine and cheese in the library, dine by candlelight in the dining room, and have brandy and coffee in the parlor. There's no telephone or TV in your room, only antique furnishings, wonderful old canopied beds, and coffee in bed the next morning. The rate ($165 for two including meals) covers a sumptuous multicourse dinner of regional specialties (shrimp gumbo, fresh seafood and/or poultry, bread pudding, and so forth) and a plantation breakfast, as well as the cheese, wine, and brandy. Choose one of the three suites in an elegant 1820s raised cottage and your rooms will be a little more informal in furnishings and more secluded. Call to reserve.

Admission: $5 adults, $3 children and students.

Open: Daily 10am–5pm. **Closed:** Holidays.

WHERE TO DINE

In Donaldsonville

LAFITTE'S LANDING RESTAURANT, at the foot of Sunshine Bridge on La. 70 Access Rd. (P.O. Box 1128), Donaldsonville, LA 70346. Tel. 473-1232.

Cuisine: CAJUN. **Reservations:** Recommended.

$ Prices: Main courses $16.95–$24.95. DISC, MC, V.

Open: Tues–Sat 11am–3pm and 6–10pm, Sun 11am–8pm.

This huge raised cottage, built in 1797, was said to be one of Jean Lafitte's hangouts. Today there's a good restaurant and lounge in the building, a good stopping point for lunch. You might want to try the hurricane broiled shrimp with fresh herbs and honey butter to start, and as a main course, try the trout Lafitte. The desserts change daily. Since the hours can change, you might want to call ahead to check or make reservations.

In Burnside

THE CABIN, La. 44 at La. 22. Tel. 473-3007.

Cuisine: CAJUN. **Reservations:** Recommended.

$ Prices: All items $4.25–$12.50. AE, MC, V.

Open: Mon–Wed 8am–3pm, Thurs 8am–9pm, Fri–Sat 8am–10pm, Sun 8am–6pm.

The Cabin is another good eating place appropriate to a day of plantation viewing. It is a slave cabin from the Monroe plantation, built about 1830. Nowadays it holds interesting antiques and good Cajun cooking. Seafood lunches include blackened redfish, fried catfish, fried stuffed shrimp, and fried stuffed crab. There is also a po-boy menu. Specialties of The Cabin include crabmeat au gratin, broiled red snapper, and crawfish étouffée. Try the buttermilk pie or the homemade bread pudding for dessert.

PLANTATIONS FARTHER AFIELD

Most of the plantations described below are clustered in the area around St. Francisville, north of Baton Rouge. An overnight stay is a virtual necessity if you want to see any number of these houses, and you'll really get into the spirit of things if you plan your overnight at any of the accommodations offered by the plantations described below. You may, however, wish to stay in St. Francisville itself or even in Baton Rouge. At the end of this section, I'll tell you about accommodations in both places. If you plan to make Baton Rouge your base, the St. Francisville tour will cover approximately 100 miles, and you will want to set aside at least one full day, probably two. In Baton Rouge itself, there is one plantation home, and about 30 miles northwest is another, both of which you may want to include in your sightseeing.

The very first thing you should do is contact the **Baton Rouge Area Information Center,** 730 North Blvd., Baton Rouge, LA 70802 (tel. 504/383-1825), to ask for their useful "Baton Rouge Visitors Guide," which contains maps of attractions in the city and surrounding area.

WHAT TO SEE & DO

MAGNOLIA MOUND, 2161 Nicholson Dr., Baton Rouge, LA 70802. Tel. 343-4955.

This home was built in the late 1700s as a small settler's house. As prosperity came to the lower Mississippi Valley, the house was enlarged and renovated, eventually becoming the center of a 900-acre plantation. Its single story is nearly 5 feet off the ground and has a front porch 80 feet across. The hand-carved woodwork and the ceiling in the parlor are authentically restored. Magnolia Mound takes its name from the grove of trees on a bluff overlooking the Mississippi, which is its setting. One of the oldest wooden structures in the state, it is typical French Creole in architecture and furnished in Louisiana and early Federal style. Costumed guides take you through.

Admission: $3.50 adults, $2.50 seniors, $1.50 students, 75¢ children.

Open: Tues–Sat 10am–4pm, Sun 1–4pm.

RURAL LIFE MUSEUM, 6200 Burden Lane, Baton Rouge, LA 70808. Tel. 765-2437.

Louisiana State University's Rural Life Museum is a marvelous open-air museum on Burden Research Plantation at Essen and I-10. Authentically restored buildings include an overseer's house, slave cabins, a one-room school, a country church, and a barn that holds artifacts dealing with rural life from the 18th century to the early 20th century.

Admission: $3 adults and children 12 and up, $2 children under 12.

Open: Mon–Fri 8:30am–4pm (weekends seasonally).

NOTTOWAY PLANTATION, Mississippi River Road (P.O. Box 160), White Castle, LA 70788. Tel. 504/545-2730.

This magnificent house—located 69 miles from New Orleans and about 25 miles from Baton Rouge—has been likened to a castle, and you're likely to agree when you see its 22 enormous columns supporting the original slate roof. Built in 1859, a blend of Greek Revival and Italianate architecture, the house has 64 rooms and a total area of over 53,000 square feet. It was saved from Civil War destruction by the kindness of a Northern gunboat officer who had once been a guest there, and kindness still blesses it, for the present owners have lovingly restored its rooms to their former glory. The white ballroom, with its hand-carved cypress Corinthian columns, archways, delicate plaster friezework, and original crystal chandeliers, is especially lovely.

Randolph Hall restaurant serves lunch from 11am to 3pm and dinner from 6 to 9pm; you may stay overnight in one of the restored bedrooms with private bath for $125 to $250 double occupancy, which includes a wake-up tray of hot sweet-potato muffins, a full plantation breakfast served on the garden veranda, and a tour of the house.

To get here from Baton Rouge, take I-10 West to the Plaquemine exit, then La. 1 south for 18 miles. (From New Orleans, follow I-10 West to the La. 22 exit, then turn left on La. 70

across the Sunshine Bridge; exit onto La. 1 and drive 14 miles north through Donaldsonville.)

Admission: $8 adults, $3 children 12 and under.

Open: Daily 9am–5pm. **Closed:** Christmas.

PARLANGE, HC62, New Roads, LA 70760. Tel. 638-8410.

Located 29 miles northwest of Baton Rouge on Louisiana Highway 1, this plantation is one of the few that still functions as a working farm. Built in 1750 by Marquis Vincent de Ternant, the house is one of the oldest in the state, and its two stories rise above a raised brick basement. Galleries encircle the house, which is flanked by two brick *pigeonniers*. Indigo was planted here at first, then in the 1800s sugarcane became the plantation's main crop. Today, sugarcane, corn, and soybeans are grown, and the plantation also supports its own cattle. During the Civil War this house was host to generals from both sides (Gen. Nathaniel Banks of the Union and Gen. Dick Taylor of the Confederacy)—not, of course, at the same time. To get to Parlange, drive 19 miles west on U.S. 190, then 10 miles north on La. 1

Admission: $7 adults, $4 children 6–12.

Open: Daily 9am–5pm (last tour is at 4pm). It's best to call ahead to confirm tour times and open hours.

ASPHODEL, La. 68 (mailing address: Rt. 2, Box 89), Jackson, LA 70748. Tel. 654-6868.

Located on La. 68 north of Baton Rouge and east of St. Francisville, Asphodel is a charming example of the Greek Revival style popular in the 1800s. Built about 1833, it consists of a raised central section with two identical wings of brick covered with a smooth plaster made with sand from a nearby creek. Doric columns line the gallery of the central section and support its gabled roof. Each wing has its own small porch. Asphodel has been seen in films, such as *The Long Hot Summer*. On the grounds, the old Levy house (built in the 1840s) was moved here in recent years and is now used as an inn and a very fine restaurant. In addition to the mansion itself (now the private home of its current owners), there are leafy forest trails open to visitors.

Admission: $5.

Open: Mon and Fri by appointment only.

OAKLEY, La. 965 (P.O. Box 546), St. Francisville, LA 70775. Tel. 635-3739.

Oakley Plantation, three miles east of U.S. 61, features the lovely old house where John James Audubon came to study and paint the wildlife of this part of Louisiana. Built in 1799, it is a three-story frame house with the raised basement so typical of that era. The two galleries are joined by a curved stairway, and the whole house has a simplicity that bespeaks its age. When Audubon was here, he tutored a daughter of the family and painted some 32 of his *Birds of America* series. When you visit the house today, you will see some original prints from Audubon's *Elephant Folio* and many fine antiques. A walk through the gardens and nature trails will explain why this location had such appeal for Audubon. Oakley is, as a matter of fact, now a part of the 100-acre Audubon State Commemorative Area, a wildlife sanctuary that would have gladdened the naturalist's heart. In the kitchen building there is now a gift shop, but you can still see the huge old kitchen fireplace where the family's meals were once cooked.

Admission: $2; those under 12 or over 61 free.

Open: Mon–Sat 9am–5pm, Sun 1–5pm. **Closed:** Thanksgiving and Christmas Day.

ROSEDOWN PLANTATION AND GARDENS, I-10 and U.S. 61 (P.O. Box 1816), St. Francisville, LA 70775-1816. Tel. 635-3332.

Just east of St. Francisville on I-10 and U.S. 61, you'll find Rosedown. This truly magnificent home was built in 1835 by a descendant of George Washington on land granted by the Spanish in 1789 to a founder of the Port of Bayou Sara on the Mississippi River. The two-story house, flanked by one-story wings, combines classic and indigenous Louisiana styles. There are the typical columns and wide galleries across the front; the house is made of cement-covered brick. A wide avenue of ancient oaks, their branches meeting overhead, leads up to the house, and the formal gardens are as impressive as the house itself. As is fitting in such a garden, marble statues of gods and goddesses dot the winding pathways. Inside, the house still holds the massive furniture of its original owner, as well as a winding stairway and many beautiful murals and paintings. Rosedown is one of the most beautiful examples of antebellum plantation homes, and whether you're a lover of architecture, antiques, or horticulture—or simply of beauty—you'll find this an interesting stop.

Admission: Adults, $10 house and gardens; children under 12, $4.

Open: Mar–Oct, daily 9am–5pm; Oct–Mar, daily 10am–4pm. **Closed:** Dec 24–25.

CATALPA PLANTATION, off U.S. 61 (P.O. Box 131), St. Francisville, LA 70775. Tel. 635-3372.

This lovely old plantation is five miles north of St. Francisville off U.S. 61. The great oaks that line the unusual elliptical drive leading up to the house were planted from acorns by Mamie Thompson's great-great-grandfather. This charming woman, Catalpa's present owner, leads guests through her home, regaling them with stories about the many family heirlooms and priceless antiques within its walls (the slightly dented silver tea service, for example, lay buried in a pond during the Civil War, and the lovely hand-painted china was done by none other than John James Audubon). Mrs. Thompson often greets guests with sherry and homemade cheese biscuits, then invites them to linger on the front porch for coffee at the tour's end.

Admission: $5 adults, $2 children 6-12, children under 6 free.

Open: Daily 10am–4pm by appointment only.

THE MYRTLES, U.S. 61 (P.O. Box 1100), St. Francisville, LA 70775. Tel. 504/635-6277.

A little over one mile north of the intersection with Louisiana Highway 10 along U.S. Highway 61 is this beautiful house, built in 1795. Its gallery measures 110 feet in length, and the elaborate iron grillwork is reminiscent of French Quarter houses in New Orleans. The Myrtles is in an astonishingly good state of preservation, especially inside, where the intricate plaster moldings are still intact in each room and the silver doorknobs (glass-coated) and even colonial wallpaper in the entry hall are just as they were when the house was built. The 1½-story house is set in a grove of great old live oaks, as is only fitting for a place that is locally believed to have at least one ghost. When this old home was restored in recent years, much attention was given to filling it with furnishings authentic to the period in which it was built. Overnight accommodations are available, with private or shared baths, at rates of $82.50 to $143 double, which includes plantation breakfast and tour. There are also "Mysteries" on Friday and Saturday evenings that are great fun—call for details and prices.

Admission: $6 adults; $3 children.

Open: Daily 9am–5pm. **Closed:** Christmas.

AFTON VILLA GARDENS, U.S. 61 (P.O. Box 99), St. Francisville, LA 70775. Tel. 635-6773.

There's no longer a great plantation home on this site (a little over three miles north of St. Francisville), but Afton Villa was one of the finest until it burned in 1963. Its alley of great oak trees (one of the longest known) is still there, as are the beautiful formal gardens with their boxwood maze and statuary. The Gothic gatehouse also remains. The gardens are a real delight, with something flowering almost every season. It is perhaps at its best, however, in March and April.

Admission: $4 adults, children under 12 free.

Open: Mar–June and Oct–Nov, Wed–Sun 9am–4:30pm. **Closed:** July–Sept and Dec–Feb.

THE COTTAGE, 10528 Cottage Ln., at U.S. 61, St. Francisville, LA 70775. Tel. 504/635-3674.

⭐ This rambling country home five miles north of St. Francisville is really a series of buildings constructed between 1795 and 1859. For my money, this is *the* place to make your Great River Road sightseeing headquarters (see "Where to Stay," below). The low, two-story house has a long gallery out front, a perfect place to sit and relax for an evening. The first house was built entirely of virgin cypress taken from the grounds. Many of the outbuildings date from 1811, when Judge Thomas Butler (of "the Fighting Butlers," prominent in American history) acquired the property. The judge carried on the family tradition of involvement in national affairs, as did his children. In fact, after his victory at the Battle of New Orleans, Gen. Andrew Jackson, along with a troop of officers (including no fewer than *eight* Butlers), stopped off here for a three-week stay on his way from New Orleans to Natchez. Among the historic treasures on the grounds is a shiny, custom-designed carriage made for the judge in 1820.

There are several outbuildings still intact, one of them a miniature cottage that was Judge Butler's office until his death, after which it became the plantation schoolhouse. Only two of the original 25 slave cabins remain. The interior of The Cottage looks very much as it did when the Butlers lived here, with hand-screened wallpaper, a 19th-century love seat (with space for a chaperone), and needlepoint fire screens made by the ladies of the Butler family. This is a working plantation of some 360 acres. It takes little or no imagination when staying at The Cottage to feel that you've managed to step through a time warp back to the days when plantation homes were not "open to the public" but were the center of a gracious, now-vanished way of life. Even if you don't stay as a guest, do visit.

Admission: $5 per person.

Open: Daily 9am–5pm.

WHERE TO STAY

In addition to the establishments listed below, you might consider the accommodations at Madewood, Nottoway Plantation, and The Myrtles, all described earlier in this chapter. All should be booked well in advance.

For help in finding bed-and-breakfast facilities throughout Louisiana, contact the **Southern Comfort Bed & Breakfast Reservation Service,** P.O. Box 13294, New Orleans, LA 70118 (tel. 504/861-0082, or toll free 800/729-1928. Fax 504/861-3087).

In St. Francisville

BARROW HOUSE INN, 524/9779 Royal St. (P.O. Box 1461), St. Francisville, LA 70775. Tel. 504/635-4791. 5 rms, 3 suites. A/C, TV

$ Rates: $75–$85 double, $95–$110 suite. Extra person $15. MC, V.

The Barrow House Inn is two guesthouses, the Barrow House and the Printer's House. Both are listed on the National Register of Historic Places and located in the heart of St. Francisville's charming historic district. The Printer's House, dating from the 1780s, is the oldest in town and was built by the monks for whom St. Francisville is named. Just across the street is the New England saltbox style Barrow House (ca. 1809). Owned by an enterprising couple from Houston, the houses have been lovingly restored and furnished in 1840s to 1880s antiques. Lyle and Shirley Dittloff, the personable owners/innkeepers, offer a choice of continental or full breakfast, and their acclaimed gourmet dinner (guests only) is by candlelight in the historic dining room. Both meals are served on fine china and sterling silver. The best rooms, the Victorian and Empire suites each have a bedroom and formal parlor and allow access to the full-service kitchen and Audubon sun room. Guests also have access to an original edition Audubon collection and a small space museum dedicated to Shirley's father, one of the pioneers in America's space exploration.

THE COTTAGE, 10528 Cottage Ln., at U.S. 61, St. Francisville, LA 70775. Tel. 504/635-3674. 5 rms. A/C TV

$ Rates (including breakfast and tour of house and grounds): $80–$85 single; $95–$99 double. MC, V. **Parking:** Available.

To really get into the spirit of a plantation homes tour, you can't do better than to stay at The Cottage. A full description of the house has already been given above, but I probably should add that the owners have, rather whimsically, planted a few rows of cotton between the camellias and azaleas in the garden, so if you've never seen King Cotton in its native habitat, this is your chance. On steamy hot days you can cool off in the swimming pool. There are two rooms in the main house and three in the wing added in 1850, all furnished with lovely antiques (even some canopied four-poster beds). A highlight of any stay here is the early-morning (8am) serving of steaming chicory coffee, with fresh cream and sugar, on a silver tray with bone china cups—and it comes, in old plantation style, right to your bedroom door. Half an hour later you sit down to a full plantation breakfast in the formal dining room: a splended repast of hickory-smoked bacon, eggs, grits (naturally), coffee, and homemade biscuits—an absolutely perfect way to begin the day. There's also Mattie's House Restaurant on the grounds for dinner. This place is popular with weekenders from New Orleans and other neighboring towns, as well as with tourists, which makes it essential to book as far ahead as you possibly can.

ST. FRANCIS HOTEL ON THE LAKE, P.O. Box 440, St. Francisville, LA 70775. Tel. 504/635-3821, or toll free 800/826-9931 in LA, 800/523-6118 in all other states. Fax 504/635-4749. 101 rms. A/C TV TEL

$ Rates: $65.95 single; $70.95 double. AE, DC, DISC, MC, V. **Parking:** Free.

In St. Francisville, this is your best bet. It's on Highway 61 Bypass, with attractive guest rooms (some have TVs and facilities for the disabled), a restaurant, a coffee shop, a lounge, an outdoor pool, and dog kennels.

In Baton Rouge

HILTON BATON ROUGE, 5500 Hilton Ave., Baton Rouge, LA 70808. Tel. 504/924-5000. Fax 504/925-1330. 297 rms. A/C TV TEL

$ Rates: $75–$85 single; $80–$95 double. Discounted family rates available. AE, DC, DISC, MC, V. **Parking:** Free.

All rooms here are Hilton quality. There are an indoor pool, health spa, a lounge, and a dining room.

QUALITY INN, 10920 Mead Rd., Baton Rouge, LA 70816. Tel. 504/293-9370, or toll free 800/395-8847. 150 rms. A/C TV TEL **Directions:** Sherwood Forest Boulevard Exit at I-12.

$ Rates: $42–$59 single or double. Extra person $3. AE, CB, DC, DISC, MC, V. **Parking:** Free.

If a motel suits you better than a hotel, try the Quality Inn here. The nicely furnished rooms have oversize beds, in-room safes, and in-room complimentary coffee. There are a pool, dining room, and a lounge with entertainment and dancing six nights a week from 5pm to 2am. All the rooms have cable TVs (with in-room movies available). A game room and a co-op laundry are accessible to all guests.

SHERATON BATON ROUGE, 4728 Constitution Ave., Baton Rouge, LA 70808. Tel. 504/925-2244. Fax 504/927-6925. 280 rms, 10 suites. A/C TV TEL **Directions:** From New Orleans, take I-10 to the College Drive exit.

$ Rates: $63–$93 single, $73–$103 double. Extra person $10. AE, CB, DC, DISC, MC, V. **Parking:** Free.

This hotel is a good stop after you've spent the day driving from plantation to plantation on the way to Lafayette because it offers all the conveniences you would expect at a Sheraton. You'll have cable TV in your room so you can relax after that hard day of driving, and each of the rooms has two double beds as well as a desk. If you want even more pampering, ask for a room on the Concierge floor and you'll have access to the private lounge, complimentary cocktails, and complimentary breakfast.

Dining/Entertainment: Legends Sports Bar allows you to relax in a country-club atmosphere and take in some sports. Café Azalea offers a traditional Cajun menu.

Services: Room service.

Facilities: Pool.

WHERE TO DINE

In Baton Rouge

MIKE ANDERSON'S SEAFOOD, 1031 W. Lee Dr. Tel. 766-7823.

Cuisine: SEAFOOD. **Reservations:** Not accepted.

$ Prices: Main courses $10.95–$24.95. AE, DC, DISC, MC, V.

Open: Mon–Thurs 11:30am–2pm and 5–9:30pm, Fri–Sat 11:30am–10:30pm, Sun 11:30am–9pm.

Mike Anderson's is one of Baton Rouge's better seafood eateries, yet it's surprisingly inexpensive. The menu holds a multitude of finny and shelly choices, prepared in every manner you can imagine. Freshness is everything here; the portions are quite large, and the prices are low.

MULATE'S CAJUN RESTAURANT, 8322 Bluebonnet. Tel. 767-4794.

Cuisine: CAJUN. **Reservations:** Not required.

$ Prices: Main courses $5.95–$14.95. AE, MC, V.

Open: Daily 7am–10:30pm.

If you haven't yet gotten to the Mulate's in New Orleans, there's also a branch of the famous Mulate's Cajun Restaurant (from Breaux Bridge) near I-10, with the same Cajun friendliness, great food, and live Cajun music every night of the week.

RUTH'S CHRIS STEAK HOUSE, 4836 Constitution. Tel. 925-0163.

Cuisine: STEAK. **Reservations:** Not required.

$ Prices: Appetizers $2–$6.95; main courses $8.95–$21.50. AE, MC, V.

Open: Daily 11:30am–11:30pm.

Steak lovers who became addicted to Ruth's Chris Steak House in New Orleans will be happy to know there's a branch here, with the same high-quality meats and the same moderate price range.

2. CAJUN COUNTRY

Just what *is* Cajun Country? Its official name is Acadiana, and it consists of a rough triangle of Louisiana made up of 22 parishes (counties), from St. Landry Parish at the top of the triangle to the Gulf of Mexico at its base. Lafayette is its "capital," and it's dotted with towns such as St. Martinville and New Iberia and Abbeville and Jeanerette. You won't find its boundaries marked on any map with the name "Acadiana" stamped across it. But within those 22 parishes, there lives a people whose history and culture and way of life is so distinctive that crossing into this area is akin to stepping through the portals of another country. Even their language differs from any other in the world.

BACKGROUND

THE PEOPLE   And just *who* are these Acadians, or "Cajuns"? If you've gone through the standard American schooling, you probably already know something about them. Think of Henry Wadsworth Longfellow's epic poem *Evangeline*—the story of two lovers who spent their lives wandering the face of this land searching for each other after being wrenched from their homeland. Evangeline and her Gabriel were Acadians, part of a tragic band of French Canadians who became the forefathers of today's Cajuns.

Their story began in the early 1600s, when colonists from France began settling the southeastern coast of Canada. There, in a region they named Acadia, they developed a peaceful agricultural culture based on the simple values of a strong religious faith (Catholic), a deep love of family, and an abiding respect for their relatively small land holdings. Isolated from the mainstream of European culture for nearly 150 years, their lives were filled with hard work lightened by pleasant gatherings of families and friends punctuated by their unwavering devotion to their church. This satisfying pastoral existence was maintained until 1713, when Acadia became the property of the British under the Treaty of Utrecht. Even then, the Acadians were determined to keep to their peaceful existence under the new rulers, but that became impossible. For more than 40 years they were continually harassed by representatives of the British king who tried to force them to pledge allegiance to that monarch and to renounce Catholicism and embrace the king's Protestant religion. That course was so abhorrent to Acadians and they were so steadfast in their refusals that in 1755 the British governor of the region sent troops to seize their farms and ships to deport them. Villages were burned; husbands and wives and children were separated as ships were loaded; and a 10-year odyssey began for these sturdy, gentle people.

Some were returned to France, some went to England, many were put ashore in the English colonies along America's east coast, and some wound up in the West Indies. The deportation voyages, made on poorly equipped, overcrowded ships—none had enough food, clothing, or other provisions for their large human cargoes— took a huge toll, and hundreds of lives were lost in the process. As for the survivors, their Acadian culture was so strongly ingrained that many who were sent to France and England returned to America as much as 20 years later. Those who went ashore in Massachusetts, Connecticut, New York, and Pennsylvania went varied ways—some went into indentured service for a few years to labor-hungry colonial merchants and farmers, some immediately took to the long overland walk back to Canadian territory, but *all* held foremost in their aims a reunion with families from whom they'd been so rudely torn. Those taken to Maryland were met with a somewhat warmer welcome by colonists there and were given greater latitude in work and living quarters until they, too, could take up the search for loved ones.

Louisiana, with its strong French background, was a natural destination for Acadians hoping to reestablish a permanent home, and those who were transported to the West Indies were probably the first who headed there. By 1763 there was a fairly large contingent in the New Orleans area. The territory was under Spanish domination at the time, but the shared Catholic religion and the industriousness of the newcomers made them welcome, and many Acadians were given land grants in outlying areas. In 1765 a man named Bernard Andry brought a band of 231 men, women, and children to the region now known as Acadiana. Joseph Broussard, one of the Acadian leaders, was instrumental in making an agreement with one of the largest landowners to give each immigrant family the use of one bull and five cows with calves for six consecutive years. They agreed, at the end of that time, to return the same amount of livestock, plus one-half the increase or the money realized from the sale of one-half the increase.

The land on which they settled differed greatly from that which they had left in Nova Scotia. The swampy land was low-lying and boggy, interlaced with bayous and lakes. No one has ever come up with an exact description of the bayous (called "bayuk" by the Choctaw). Longfellow's poem comes close when he describes what the Acadians found when they arrived:

> Soon [they] were lost in a maze of sluggish and
>   devious waters,
> Which, like a network of steel, extended in every
>   direction.
> Over their heads, the towering and tenebrous boughs
>   of the cypress
> Met in a dusky arch, and trailing mosses in mid-air,
> Waved like banners that hang on the walls of ancient
>   cathedrals.

Suffice it to say that a bayou is something less than a river but more than a creek; it is sluggish, with little or no current. But the swamps were forested with live oak, willow, ash, and gum, and they teemed with wildlife. Given land that mostly bounded the bayous, the Acadians went to work with a will, building small levees, or dikes, along the banks, draining fields for small farms and pastures, and taking to the swamps to hunt and trap the plentiful game for food and furs. The isolation of their new home did not bother them a bit—it was perhaps the only thing this location had in common with the land they had left.

Always attuned to family closeness, children would build homes close to parents, and thus small settlements developed. The homes they constructed were marvelously adapted to the locale. From the swamps they took cypress for their houses. To provide insulation between inner and outer walls, they again turned to natural materials, filling spaces with a mixture of mud and Spanish moss (*bousillage*). They pitched roofs high so that frequent rains would drain off, and they utilized the attic space thus created as sleeping quarters for the family's young men (this was called a *garçonnière*).

And in order to get maximum use from every inch of interior space on the ground floor, stairways up to the *garçonnières* were placed outside on the front porch. The stairs did double duty as seating space when families gathered at one house (for that matter, so did the porch itself, which was many times used for extra sleeping space).

Incidentally, as far as Longfellow's poem goes, two things remain to be straightened out: The real Evangeline was Emmeline Labiche, and her sweetheart was Louis Pierre Arceneaux. And her story has a different ending from the one the poet assigned to his two lovers. Emmeline found her Louis Pierre, after many years of searching, right in Cajun Country in the town of St. Martinville. The real-life tragedy was that by then Louis had given up hope of ever finding her and was pledged to another. She died of a broken heart in Louisiana, *not* in Philadelphia as in the poem.

CUISINE From their surroundings, too, came much of what has come to be known as Cajun cooking. Using ingredients that could be locally grown, the Acadians prepared foods as their own French culinary heritage dictated, threw in some Spanish treatment, added a bit of Native American methods (they'd always gotten on well with local Native Americans, in both Nova Scotia and Louisiana), picked up African secrets, and came up with a unique cuisine that is now justly famous. The dishes that evolved are based on a *roux,* made by combining oil and flour, which is slowly browned in a heavy pot. Into the roux go seasonings and native meat or seafood (sometimes both), and the mixture is left to simmer until (as one Cajun told me) it is "good." As a variation, okra is sometimes used to make gumbo instead of the roux. In that case, one final step is omitted—filé (ground sassafras leaves), which is added to all roux-based gumbo when it is served into the bowl (*never* during cooking), does not appear in the okra-based dishes. Served over rice, either version is delicious. Combining various meats and seafoods with rice and seasonings, the Acadians created jambalaya. And from the plentiful crawfish, they came up with crawfish étouffée, a rich blending of the small fresh-water cousin of the lobster with those delectable seasonings, again serving the result on a bed of rice. What all this adds up to is some of the best, and most unique, eating in the world—the food alone is sufficient justification for an expedition into Cajun country. One final word about this wonderful feast: The Cajuns will invariably doctor any or all of these specialties with a dash of hot sauce (usually that produced on the large hot-pepper plantation near New Iberia, known to us as "Tabasco"). If you follow their lead, do so with caution—when they say "hot," they mean *hot!*

MUSIC Cooking is an important ingredient of any large family gathering, whatever the occasion, whether it be to help one another with harvests or slaughtering, celebrate the end of such tasks, or just to enjoy a sociable hour or two together. Another ingredient, equally important, is the music, which any Cajun will tell you makes the food taste better. With roots probably found in medieval France, it is almost wholly an orally transmitted art form (few Cajun melodies have ever been committed to paper). The simple lyrics and strains are either very sad or very happy, and I defy you to listen to one of the numbers and keep your feet still. From the time when they used only a fiddle and triangle, Cajun musicians have expanded and now play guitars, harmonicas, accordions, and drums, but always with the distinctive sound of their special music. The best possible place to hear the music is at a *fais-dodo* (a term once used to tell the babies to "go to sleep" when they were stashed in a room apart from the one in which there would be dancing in someone's home). Nowadays a *fais-dodo* usually takes place in a dance hall, in a village square, or even in the streets, and if you're lucky enough to run across one, stop the car and join in— the Cajuns *love* company, and in no time at all you'll be dancing with the best of them. And if you don't just happen on a dance, feel free to drop in at any dance hall you pass, no matter its outer appearance. (If you can hear live music, don't hesitate to go in, for you won't be a stranger long.)

Special note: If you become completely beguiled by this special music and the special people who play it—and if you're hardy enough for an early Saturday-morning drive—there's a unique happening you won't want to miss in the little town of Mamou, some 53 miles northwest of Lafayette. (To get there, take I-10 West to the Crowley/Eunice exit, and turn right on La. 13; Mamou is about 32 miles north of Crowley, 11 miles north of Eunice.) Every Saturday at about 8am, Cajuns from miles around congregate in **Fred's Lounge,** 420 6th St. (tel. 318/468-5411), for a live broadcast of music, local news, and commercials the likes of which you won't hear anywhere else. Broadcast times are 9:15 to 11am (on station KVPI, 1050 AM on the dial), but the music swings right on to 1pm. In spite of the early hour, the ambience is that of a nighttime get-together, with conviviality running high and the bar doing a brisk business. This is no slick broadcast—the "studio" is a roped-off section of the dance floor, the men behind the mikes and instruments are rugged Cajuns who work hard in the outdoors all week, and the audience crowds the floor dancing with friends and neighbors. It's a memorable experience! *Note:* Fred's Lounge is *only* open on Saturday.

PLANNING YOUR TRIP

The Cajun Country map on page 227 shows a circular drive that could allow you to take in one or two of the plantation homes en route to Baton Rouge (if you take River Road instead of I-10 as shown here) before turning west on I-10 to reach Lafayette. The Interstate highway runs along the edge of Acadiana, but the little town of Breaux Bridge, just off it on La. 31, is real Cajun Country, and of course Lafayette is its heart. A return to New Orleans via U.S. 90 will take you right through the history, legend, and romance of this region. It's too long a drive for one day, so you'll want to book accommodations in Lafayette for at least a one-night stay. If you take I-10, the distance from New Orleans to Lafayette is 134 miles; from Lafayete to New Orleans via U.S. 90 is 167 miles. You should know in advance, however, that this is true "wandering country," which explains why I wouldn't *dare* set out by a step-by-step itinerary. I'll list some of the things to be sure not to miss, confident that you will find scores of other Cajun Country attractions on your own. Along the way I'll mention some of the outstanding Cajun restaurants (but rest assured, it's almost impossible to get bad food out here), and tell you about places to stay overnight.

The best tip I can give you, however, is that you write or call ahead to the **Lafayette Parish Convention and Visitors Commission Center,** P.O. Box 52066, Lafayette, LA 70505 (tel. 318/ 232-3808, or toll free 800/346-1958 in the U.S. outside Louisiana, 800/543-5340 in Montreal and Quebec)—it'll send you tons of detailed information to make your trip even more fun. The center is open daily from 9am to 5pm, if you want to stop in while you're there (the driving directions are in the section on Lafayette, below).

You might also contact the **Southern Comfort Bed & Breakfast Reservation Service,** P.O. Box 13294, New Orleans, LA 70118 (tel. 504/861-0082, or toll free 800/729-1928. Fax 504/861-3087), which can help you locate carefully screened bed-and-breakfast accommodations throughout Louisiana.

If there is just no way you can find time to get out to Cajun Country for an extended visit, I suggest that you take one of the excellent day tours listed below. It's a good introduction to the area, and maybe on your next New Orleans visit (rest assured, there will be another) you'll be able to drive out for an in-depth exploration of this fascinating region.

If, on the other hand, you can get here during festival time (see Chapter 7), you'll have a terrific time, right along with native Cajuns, who enjoy their festivals with real gusto.

TOURS   And what if you simply cannot spare the time to wander around Cajun Country? Well, you can still go home with at least a taste of this totally different region. If you can set aside a day for activities outside of New Orleans, one of these tours will give you a glimpse of how and where the Cajuns live.

Tours by Isabelle, P.O. Box 740972, New Orleans, LA 70174 (tel. 504/367-3963), specializes in small-group tours via a comfortable, air-conditioned minivan. You are driven across the Mississippi to visit Cajun Country and then provided with a 1½-hour narrated swamp tour. The Cajun Bayou Tour fare is $40 and leaves New Orleans at 1pm, returning around 6pm.

The *Bayou Jean Lafitte,* 1340 New Orleans World Trade Center (tel. 586-8777), a modern passenger ship, departs daily at 11am from the Toulouse Street wharf across Jackson Square for a 5½-hour Bayou Cruise. The 45-mile route takes you back into the intrigue and charm of Bayou Barataria, where Jean Lafitte and his notorious buccaneers once thrived. A professional guide fills you in on the history of the region. There are a snack bar, a cocktail bar, and a gift shop on board. Adults pay $15 and children over 3 pay $8; children under 3 sail free.

BREAUX BRIDGE

WHAT TO SEE & DO

Just off I-10 on La. 31, this little town, founded in 1859, prides itself on being the "Crawfish Capital of the World." Its famous Crawfish Festival and Fair has drawn as many as 100,000 to the town of 4,500 permanent residents, and it's the most Cajun affair you can imagine—with music, a unique "bayou" parade, crawfish races, crawfish-eating contests, and lots more. It's such a

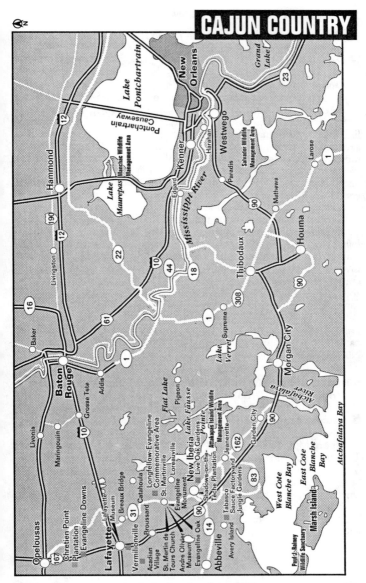

splendiferous party, in fact, that it takes a full year to recover. It's always held the first week in May, so you're in luck if that's when you plan to come. Otherwise, you'll have to be content with stopping by for some of the best Cajun eating to be found.

WHERE TO DINE

CRAWFISH TOWN U.S.A., 2815 Grand Point Hwy., Breaux Bridge.
Cuisine: SEAFOOD/CAJUN. **Reservations:** Recommended.

Directions: From Lafayette, take I-10 to Henderson (exit 115). Follow the signs, you can't miss it.

$ Prices: Appetizers $3.95–$5.95; main courses $7.95–$18.95. AE, DC, MC, V.

Open: Daily 11am–11pm.

This restaurant is a must for anyone who wants to experience real Cajun cooking in a Cajun-style environment. The restaurant is housed in an early 1950s barn and was established in 1986 by natives Deanna and Jerry Guidry. Because it's in a barn, the dining room is large, open, airy, and informal. The tables are great for family-style dining, as they are large, of light wood, and have a picnic-table feel to them. You could spend hours just looking at the Cajun memorabilia and Louisiana political posters on the walls. There's a TV in the back, and the ceilings are covered with baseball caps, T-shirts, and old license plates.

The food is as pleasant as the dining room, and they'll do it to your taste—mild, strong, or extra hot. They say that they serve the biggest crawfish in the world, and I don't doubt it—the steaming platters of boiled crawfish that come out of the kitchen by the hundreds look almost like small lobsters, rather than your average crawfish. The crawfish étouffée and the gumbo are delicious. Of course, you shouldn't miss the bread pudding here. And, if you just can't decide what you want, go for the "Seafood Festival Platter," which consists of a cup of gumbo, jambalaya, crawfish étouffée, grilled catfish, shrimp, seafood pie, froglegs, crawfish, a crawfish pattie—all served with grilled potatoes, vegetables, and garlic bread. No matter what you try here, you'll go away trying to figure out when you can come back.

MULATE'S CAJUN RESTAURANT, 325 Mills Ave., Breaux Bridge. Tel. 318/332-4648.

Cuisine: CAJUN. **Reservations:** Recommended.

$ Prices: Appetizers $3.50–$5.95; main courses $5.95–$15.95. AE, MC, V.

Open: Mon–Sat 7am–10:30pm, Sun 11am–11pm.

This is a roadside cafe with cypress-board walls, where Cajun owner Goldie Comeant takes great care to make every dish authentic to her heritage. Stuffed crab is a specialty. There's also an excellent Cajun breakfast Monday through Saturday. Seven nights a week and at noon on Saturday and Sunday there's live Cajun music. Mulate's is a good introduction to the Cajun world of friendliness, unique food, and music. The prices are quite reasonable.

LAFAYETTE

If you haven't written to it in advance, make your first stop at the office of the **Lafayette Parish Convention and Visitors Commission Center,** where the helpful staff will tell you everything you could possibly want to know about their region and send you out loaded with material to enlighten your stay. Turn off I-10 onto U.S. 167 South (it's the first exit), and you'll find the office in the center of the median at 1400 NW Evangeline Thruway (tel. 318/232-3808, or toll free 800/346-1958 in the U.S., 800/543-5340 in Montreal and Quebec); it's open Monday to Friday 8:30am to 5pm, and from 9am to 5pm on Saturday and Sunday. Located near the intersection of Willow Street and the Thruway, the attractive offices are housed in Cajun-style homes set in landscaped grounds that include a pond and benches. It is a restful spot to sit and plan your Cajun Country excursion.

WHAT TO SEE & DO

Once you've met the engaging Cajuns who live in this region, you really shouldn't leave without exploring the bayous and swamps that have helped shape their hardy character. Gliding through misty bayous dotted with gnarled cypress trees dripping Spanish moss, seeing native water creatures and birds in their natural habitat, and learning just how Cajuns harvest their beloved crawfish—it's an experience not to be missed. To arrange just such a voyage, contact Terry Angelle at **Angelle's Atchafalaya Basin Swamp Tours,** Whiskey River Landing, P.O. Box 111, Cecilla, LA 70521 (tel. 318/228-8567). His tour gives you nearly two hours in the third-largest swamp in the United States, with Cajun guides who have spent their lives thereabouts and who travel the mysterious waterways as easily as you and I walk city streets. There's a glass-enclosed boat for large groups and a small, open boat for up to four. The fares are $8.50 for adults, $7.50 for seniors, and $4 for those under 12. Departure times are 10am and 1, 3, and 5pm (the last only during the summer).

To reach Whiskey River Landing from I-10, take Exit 115 to Henderson, go through Henderson to the levee, and turn right. The Landing is the third exit on the left.

If you're in Cajun Country between the first week in April and Labor Day and happen to be a devotee of the "sport of kings," you can enjoy an evening of racing at **Evangeline Downs,** three miles north of town on U.S. 167. Post time and racing days change periodically, so be sure to check. Don't bring the kids, though—no minors are allowed. For current schedules and clubhouse reservations, call 318/896-RACE.

In the very heart of Lafayette, on the grounds of the University of Southwestern Louisiana, there's a lovely **natural swamp** environment. Although small, it gives the effect of being in the wild, and during warm months you'll actually see alligators. Water birds of several varieties, as well as turtles, are almost always on hand, and during April the swamp is abloom with Louisiana irises. If you want to know more about the lake and how it is used as a teaching tool, contact the **University News Service,** University of Southwestern Louisiana, Lafayette, LA 70504 (tel. 318/231-6475). If you just want to get closer to the sort of swampland seen most often from highways, you'll find Cypress Lake next to the Student Union on the USL campus, between St. Mary Boulevard and University Avenue, Hebrard Boulevard and McKinley Street.

ACADIAN VILLAGE, 200 Greenleaf Dr., Lafayette. Tel. 318/981-2364, or toll free 800/962-9133.

⭐ Just south of La. 342, you'll find a reconstructed (actually, reassembled) Cajun bayou community at Acadian Village. Houses have been moved from original locations to this site beside a sleepy bayou, and a footpath on its banks takes you past these historic structures. The buildings hold a representative collection of Cajun furnishings. There's a gift shop, too, where you can buy Cajun handcrafts and an interesting selection of books on this unique culture. To get here, take I-10 to Exit 97. Go south on La. 93 to Ridge Road, then take a right, followed by a left on W. Broussard.

Admission: $5.50 adults, $4.50 seniors, $2.50 children 6–14, under 6 free.

Open: Daily 10am–5pm. **Closed:** Holidays.

VERMILIONVILLE, 1600 Surry St., Lafayette. Tel. 318/233-4077, or toll free 800/99-BAYOU.

✪ A recent addition to the Lafayette scene is this marvelous reconstruction of a Cajun/Creole bayou village from the 1765–1890 era. Vermilionville sits on the banks of the brooding Bayou Vermilion, directly adjacent to the airport on U.S. 90. Hundreds of skilled artisans labored to restore original Cajun homes and to reconstruct others that were typical of such a village but unavailable. Homes of every level in society are represented, from the most humble to one of a well-to-do farmer. The costumed staff in each give a vivid demonstration of daily life back then; craftspeople ply their crafts in traditional ways; and, in the performance center, authentic music, plays, dancing, and storytelling hold sway. There are a restaurant serving Cajun/Creole cuisine and a gift shop. It's a great introduction to the Cajun way of life and a pleasant way to spend an afternoon. To reach Vermilionville, take I-10 to Exit 103A. Get on the Evangeline Thruway going south and keep going until you get to Surrey Street, then follow the signs.

Admission: $8 adults, $6.50 seniors, $5 students, children under 6 free.

Open: Daily 10am–5pm. **Closed:** Thanksgiving and Christmas Day.

LAFAYETTE MUSEUM, 1122 Lafayette St., Lafayette. Tel. 318/234-2208.

Louisiana's first Democratic governor, Alexandre Mouton, once lived in the antebellum town house (built in the early 1800s) with square columns and two galleries that now houses the Lafayette Museum. Its cupola, attic, and entire second floor, incidentally, were added in 1849. Inside, in addition to the antiques, paintings, and historic documents you might expect to find, there's a colorful collection of Mardi Gras costumes that were worn by Lafayette's krewe kings and queens.

Admission: $3 adults, $2 seniors and students of all ages.

Open: Tues–Sat 9am–5pm, Sun 3–5pm. **Closed:** Holidays.

CHRETIEN POINT PLANTATION, Chretien Point Rd., Sunset. Tel. 318/233-7050 or 318/662-5876.

One of Cajun Country's most intriguing plantation mansions is only a short drive (about 15 miles) north of Lafayette. Allow yourself at least an hour to explore this columned home, built in 1831 on a 1776 Spanish land grant. The house itself is fascinating, but even more so are the tales of past owners. Its history includes links to privateer Jean Lafitte, a flamboyant gambler, his equally flamboyant widow, a ghost or two, a buried treasure (never recovered), and a Civil War batttle fought right out front. And if you remember the scene in *Gone with the Wind* in which Scarlett O'Hara shoots a marauding Union soldier on the staircase at Tara, the staircase here was the one that was copied for the movie. To get here, take I-10 West to Exit 97, then go north about eight miles through Ossun, Vatican, and Cankton. A little over two miles north of Cankton, turn left onto Parish Road 356 (toward Bristol), then turn right on Chretien Point Road; the plantation is about a mile farther on your left.

Admission: $5.50 adults, $2.50 children 4–12, under 4 free.
Open: Daily 10am–5pm. Last tour 4pm. **Closed:** Holidays.

WHERE TO STAY

BOIS DES CHENES INN, 338 N. Sterling, Lafayette, LA 70501. Tel. 318/233-7816. 3 suites. A/C TV
$ Rates (including breakfast): $75–$95 single; $85–$105 double. AE, MC, V. **Parking:** Free.

In Lafayette, the three suites at the Bois Des Chenes Inn are in the carriage house of an 1820s Acadian-style plantation home, the Charles Mouton House. Now listed on the National Register of Historical Houses, Bois Des Chenes was once the center of a 3,000-acre cattle-and-sugar plantation. Its restoration has been a labor of love that is reflected in the careful selection of antique furnishings, most of Louisiana French design. All guest accommodations are tastefully furnished with antiques of different periods, and each has a small refrigerator and down pillows. The rates include a Louisiana-style breakfast, a bottle of wine, and a tour of the house. The owner, a retired geologist, conducts nature and birding trips into the Atchafalaya Swamp as well as guided fishing and hunting trips. Smoking is not permitted. Booking as far in advance as possible is recommended.

DAYS INN, 1620 N. University, at I-10, Lafayette, LA 70506. Tel. 318/237-8880, or toll free 800/325-2525. 103 rms. A/C TV TEL
$ Rates: $44.20 single or double. AE, DC, DISC, MC, V. **Parking:** Free.

Guest rooms at the Days Inn are above average, which is typical for this reliable chain. There are facilities for the disabled in some rooms, a coffee shop, a restaurant, and an outdoor pool.

HOLIDAY INN CENTRAL—HOLIDOME, 2032 NE Evangeline Thruway, Lafayette, LA 70509. Tel. 318/233-6815, or toll free 800/942-4868. 250 rms. A/C TV TEL
$ Rates: $58–$74 single or double. AE, CB, DC, DISC, JCB, MC, V. **Parking:** Free.

The Holiday Inn has superior guest rooms, some of which are equipped for the disabled. There are a lounge, a coffee shop, a good restaurant, an indoor pool, a whirlpool, a sauna, a game room, lighted tennis courts, a jogging track, a playground, a picnic area, and a gift shop.

HOTEL ACADIANA, 1801 W. Pinhook Rd., Lafayette, LA 70508. Tel. 318/233-8120, or toll free 800/826-8386. 290 rms, 5 suites. A/C TV TEL **Directions:** From New Orleans take I-10 West to exit 103A. Follow the Evangeline Thruway to Pinhook Road. Go right onto Pinhook, follow Pinhook across the bridge, and you'll see the hotel on your left.

$ Rates: $70–$155 single or double. AE, DC, DISC, MC, V. **Parking:** Free.

Hotel Acadiana is a great value. The rates are low, but you have all the modern conveniences you'd expect to find in a large chain hotel: Two double beds in each room, a minirefrigerator, a fully equipped bathroom, cable TV, and a warm, friendly staff. You'll also be in a location central to any sightseeing you might want to do. If you really want to be in the lap of luxury, ask for a room on the Executive floor, where you'll have access to a private lounge.

Dining/Entertainment: Café Raintree offers great Cajun cuisine in a New Orleans environment.

Services: Room service, laundry service, concierge service, complimentary airport shuttle.

Facilities: Outdoor pool, health club.

LAFAYETTE HILTON AND TOWERS, 1521 Pinhook Rd., Lafayette, LA 70508. Tel. 318/235-6111, or toll free 800/33-CAJUN. 327 rms. A/C TV TEL

$ Rates: $80–$85 single or double; $175–$250 suite. Discounted rates available on weekends and for senior citizens, students, faculty members, and military. AE, DC, MC, V. **Parking:** Free.

The centrally located Lafayette Hilton and Towers has nicely appointed guest rooms and suites. Some have private patios. There is a good restaurant overlooking the bayou; a lounge with live music and dancing Monday through Saturday; and a heated pool.

WHERE TO DINE IN & AROUND LAFAYETTE

ANGELLE'S, on U.S. 167 North, across from Evangeline Downs Racetrack. Tel. 318/896-8416.

Cuisine: CAJUN. **Reservations:** Recommended.

$ Prices: Main courses $8.25–$20.95. AE, CB, DC, DISC, MC, V.

Open: Daily 10am–10pm.

Angelle's is in a Cajun-style building with a high-pitched roof, three fireplaces, and surrounding porch. It's a relaxed, friendly establishment known for its Cajun seafood dishes and steaks.

CAFE VERMILIONVILLE, 1304 Pinhook Rd. Tel. 318/237-0100.

Cuisine: INTERNATIONAL/CAJUN. **Reservations:** Recommended.

$ Prices: Appetizers $4.50–$8.95; main courses $12.95–$20.95. AE, DISC, DC, MC, V.

Open: Lunch, Sun–Fri 11am–2pm; dinner, Mon–Sat 6–10pm.

Closed: Holidays.

In a beautifully restored historic Acadian building of cypress and handmade brick that dates from 1799, Café Vermilionville seats you in a glassed-in dining room overlooking the courtyard and herb garden. The superb menu represents the best of Louisiana French and Cajun cuisines, with lots of fresh seafood features.

MCGEE'S ATCHAFALAYA CAFE, McGee's Landing, near Henderson. Tel. 318/228-7555.

Cuisine: CAJUN. **Reservations:** Recommended. **Directions:** Take Exit 115 off I-10 to Highway 352 and follow signs to McGee's Landing.

$ Prices: Main courses $5–$14. AE, CB, DISC, DC, MC, V.

Open: Summer, daily 11am–10pm; winter, Mon–Thurs 11am–5pm, Fri–Sun 11am–10pm.

Built right out over bayou waters, this large, bright, family-run restaurant is both a visual and a culinary delight. Wide windows line the walls, with views of the bayou, houseboats anchored in the Atchafalaya Basin, fishing boats puttering about, and the occasional tour boat heading for the inner depths of the bayou. As for the food, it is delicious. Home cooking is the style here, using the freshest of seafood and other local products and a deft touch of Cajun seasoning. I instantly fell head over heels for their shrimp étouffée, then made an absolute glutton of myself with their spicy hushpuppies. The prices are extremely moderate for the quality. There's music on Friday and Saturday nights. They can also book you on one of those bayou tours to round out your Cajun Country experience.

PREJEAN'S, 3480 U.S. 167 North. Tel. 318/896-3247.

Cuisine: CAJUN. **Reservations:** Not required. **Directions:** Take I-10 to Exit 103B, at which point you will get on I-49 to U.S. 167 North. Follow the signs—it's next to the Evangeline Downs Racetrack.

$ Prices: $12–$16; children's menu $2–$6. AE, CB, DC, DISC, MC, V.

Open: Daily 11am–11pm.

Prejean's is a place to enjoy both superb traditional and award-winning nouvelle Cajun cooking. You'll almost always find a large gathering of locals here. You can choose to be seated either in the big dining room with its marvelous stained-glass mural depicting a cypress shrimp boat on bayou waters or in the lounge with its oyster bar. The rustic setting is enhanced by an impressive collection of fish trophies from the Gulf of Mexico, waterfowl from inland, and reptiles from the swamp. Their 14-foot Louisiana alligator is prominently displayed near the front door. In season, heaping platters of boiled crawfish come out of the kitchen in a continuous stream, along with shrimp, oysters, gumbo, alligator, steaks, and all sorts of local dishes. Every night beginning at 7pm there's live Cajun music, which transforms all those happy diners into happy party-goers at a Cajun *fais-dodo*.

PRUDHOMME'S CAJUN CAFE, 4676 NE Evangeline Thruway, near Carencro. Tel. 318/896-7964.

Cuisine: CAJUN. **Reservations:** Not accepted. **Directions:** Take Exit 103B off I-10. Go north on I-49 to Exit 7 (three miles past racetrack). The restaurant is located on the right side of Frontage Road.

$ Prices: Main courses $6.95–$14.95. AE, DISC, MC, V.

Open: Tues–Sat 11am–10pm, Sun 11am–2:30pm.

Set in an Acadian country home built of cypress, this restaurant is run by Enola Prudhomme, who is easily the equal of her famous brother, Paul, in the kitchen. Assisted by her son and two sons-in-law, she dishes up wonderful dishes from a menu that changes daily, according to what fresh ingredients are available at the time. Blackened tuna and eggplant pirogue (eggplant skiff filled with seafood in a luscious cream sauce) are just two of her specialties. There's ramp access for the disabled.

RANDOL'S SEAFOOD RESTAURANT CAJUN DANCE HALL, 2320 Kaliste Saloom Rd. Tel. 318/981-7080, or toll free 800/962-2586.

Cuisine: CAJUN. **Reservations:** Recommended. **Directions:** Take I-10 from New Orleans to the Evangeline Thruway (Exit 103A), then follow the Thruway to Pinhook Road. Turn right onto Pinhook and follow Pinhook to Kaliste Saloom Road (right). Randol's will be on your right.

$ Prices: Appetizers $3.95–$6.95; main courses $4.50–$16.95. MC, V.

Open: Lunch, Mon–Fri 11am–2pm; dinner, Mon–Fri 5:30–10pm, Sat–Sun 5:30–10:30pm. **Closed:** Holidays.

Randol's is a happy combination of good Cajun food and Cajun music that is sure to have you up two-stepping on the dance floor between courses. Your fellow dancers are likely to be locals enjoying their own *fais-dodo* at this popular place. In fact, so imbued are they with the lively Cajun spirit that they eagerly volunteer when owner Frank Randol is in need of dancers for his traveling Cajun food and dance show, which has been booked as far north as New England. Back home, seafood is the star of the menu, all of it fresh from bayou or gulf waters, and Randol's will serve it fried, steamed, or grilled, as you prefer. The prices are moderate.

ST. MARTINVILLE

This historic old town goes all the way back to 1765, when it was a military station known as the **Poste des Attakapas.** It is also the last home of Emmeline Labiche, Longfellow's Evangeline. There was a time, too, when it was known as "la Petite Paris"—many French aristocrats fled their homeland during the French Revolution and settled here, bringing with them such traditions as fancy balls, lavish banquets, and other forms of high living.

WHAT TO SEE & DO

ST. MARTIN DE TOURS CHURCH, Main Street, St. Martinville. Tel. 318/394-6021 or 394-7334.

This is the Mother Church of the Acadians, and the building you see was constructed in 1836, on the site of the original. It is also the fourth-oldest Roman Catholic church in Louisiana. Father George Murphy, an Irish priest, was the first to associate it with its patron saint, St. Martin, back in the 1790s, and there's a noteworthy portrait of the saint behind the main altar. You'll also see the original box pews, a replica of the grotto of Lourdes, an ornate baptismal font (which some say was a gift from King Louis XVI of France), and the lovely old altar itself.

EVANGELINE MONUMENT, Main Street, St. Martinville.

Longfellow's heroine is commemorated by a statue to the side and slightly to the rear of St. Martin's Church. It was donated to the town in 1929 by a movie company that came here to film the epic. The star of that movie, Delores del Rio, is supposed to have posed for the statue. Legend says that the real-life Evangeline, Emmeline Labiche, lies buried here.

EVANGELINE OAK, Port Street and Bayou Teche, St. Martinville.

This ancient old oak is where her descendants say Emmeline's boat landed at the end of her long travels from Nova Scotia. Legend has it that it was here, too, that she learned of her lover's betrothal to another.

LONGFELLOW-EVANGELINE COMMEMORATIVE AREA, La. 31, St. Martinville.

Situated on the banks of Bayou Teche, just north of town, 157 acres hold a park on land that once belonged to Louis Pierre Arceneaux, Emmeline's real-life Gabriel. The Acadian House Museum on the grounds (tel. 394-7334), dating from about 1765, is typical of the larger Acadian homes, with bricks that were handmade and baked in the sun, a cypress frame and pegs (instead of nails), and bousillage construction on the upper floor. You can also see the *cuisine* (outdoor kitchen) and *magazin* (storehouse) out back. Admission to the Acadian House Museum is $2, and it is open daily 9:30am to 4:30pm.

WHERE TO STAY

OLD HOTEL CASTILLO INN [LA PLACE D'EVANGELINE], 220 Evangeline Blvd., St. Martinville, LA 70582. Tel. 318/394-4010. 5 rms. A/C

$ Rates (including breakfast): $65–$90 single or double. AE, MC, V. **Parking:** Free.

The Old Hotel Castillo Inn in St. Martinville appears on the National Register of Historical Places. Set on the banks of the Bayou Teche, virtually under the branches of the Evangeline Oak, the Greek Revival building began life in the early 1800s as a residence and inn and for many years served as a high school for girls. It blossomed into its present incarnation under the loving direction of Peggy and Gerald Hulin.

The very spacious rooms at the inn are comfortably furnished with some antiques and four-poster beds that are either double- or queen-size. Daybeds can be furnished at no extra charge. One room is so gigantic that it quite easily accommodates two queen-size beds.

WHERE TO DINE

LA PLACE D'EVANGELINE, 220 Evangeline Blvd. Tel. 318/394-4010.

Cuisine: CAJUN. **Reservations:** Recommended.

$ Prices: All items under $25. AE, MC, V.

Open: Sun–Thurs 8am–9pm, Fri–Sat 8am–10pm.

Located in the historic Old Hotel Castillo Inn (see above), La Place d'Evangeline is a warm, homey room where "friendly" certainly defines the service. All three meals are served. Breakfast features regional favorites of beignets, pain perdu, and café au lait. Seafood and steaks share the à la carte menu with soup-and-salad combinations, po-boys, and such traditional homemade desserts as peach cobbler and fudge pecan pie.

THIBODEAUX CAFE AND BARBER SHOP, 116 Main St., St. Martinville. Tel. 318/394-9268.
    Cuisine: CAJUN. **Reservations:** Not required.
$ Prices: 90¢–$6.50. No credit cards.
    Open: Mon–Fri 7am–3pm.

⭐ The menu is not extensive and the Thibodeaux Café and Barber Shop is definitely not for everyone—but for mingling with locals on a one-to-one basis in a "down-home" setting, it is not to be missed. It's just across from St. Martin de Tours Church, and you'll find the tiny eating space a warm, homey, friendly place to relax from all that sightseeing. Best of all, you'll find good, home-cooked dishes—from gumbo or soup to complete dinners of local origin—at incredibly low prices. It's open for all three meals (and I heartily recommend breakfast here) on weekdays, breakfast and lunch on weekends.

Special note: When you're in the Thibodeaux Café and Barber Shop, ask about Max Greig; if he's available, strike a deal to have him take you on one of his very special Cajun Country tours. Max is a true Cajun raconteur who grew up in the Acadian House in Longfellow-Evangeline State Park. Although he claims to speak only "Cajun French, Creole French, Parisian French, and a little bit of English," he's actually quite fluent in English (with a beautiful French accent, of course), and he probably knows more tall tales of the Cajun variety than anyone else going. You'll find this fascinating charmer in the café nearly every afternoon—if not, the people there will know how to get in touch with him, and it's worth the effort.

NEW IBERIA

This interesting town had its beginnings in 1779 when a large group of immigrants from the Spanish province of Màlaga, 300 in all, came up Bayou Teche and settled here. Incorporated in 1813, its history changed drastically after the arrival of the steamboat *Plowboy* in 1836. New Iberia became the terminal for steamboats traveling up the bayou from New Orleans, and it promptly developed the rambunctious character of a frontier town. In 1839, however, yellow fever traveled up the bayou with the steamboats and killed over a quarter of the population—many more were saved through the heroic nursing of an African American woman called Tante Félicité who had come here from Santo Domingo and went tirelessly from family to family carrying food and medicine. (She had had the fever many years before and was immune.) During the Civil War, New Iberia was a Confederate training center that was attacked again and again by Union troops. Confederate and Union soldiers alike plundered the land to such an extent it is said that local Acadians threatened to declare war on *both* sides if any more of their chickens, cattle, and farm produce were appropriated. The steamboats continued coming up the bayou until 1947 (I'll bet you didn't know the steamboat era lasted that long anywhere in the United States). New Iberia has continued its growth and is known as the "Queen City of the Teche."

WHAT TO SEE & DO

Take one of Annie Miller's **Swamp and Marsh Tours** for a unique, close-up look at the bayou and its wildlife. In a comfortable boat, you'll visit a rookery of nesting egrets and herons and say hello to "Smilin' Sam," the alligator who has come to look for his daily feeding from the friendly operators of this very personal and delightful cruise. Call 504/879-3934 for current schedules and rates, and to find out which location (there are several) is nearest you. *Note:* This is also worth a drive out from New Orleans. Take U.S. 90 West through Houma (about 57 miles), exit right at the tourist office on St. Charles Street, then turn left at the stoplight onto Southdown/Mandalay Road and proceed to Miller's Landing on Big Bayou Black.

SHADOWS-ON-THE-TECHE PLANTATION, 317 E. Main St., New Iberia. Tel. 318/369-6446.

This splendid home was built in 1834 for David Weeks, a wealthy planter, and it is beautifully preserved. It reflects the prevailing classical taste of the times, as seen in its Greek Revival facade. The two-story house is built of rose-colored brick and sits amid oak trees, camellias, and azaleas. One of the most authentically restored and furnished homes in the state, this is now the property of the National Trust for Historic Preservation. From New Orleans it is approximately a three-hour drive. Follow U.S. 90 to La. 14—Shadows-on-the-Teche is at the intersection of Routes 14 and 182.

Admission: $5 adults, $4 seniors, $3 children 6–11, under 6 free.

Open: Daily 9am–4:30pm.

TABASCO SAUCE FACTORY AND JUNGLE GARDENS, Avery Island. Tel. 318/365-8173.

Avery Island, on La. 329, south of New Iberia, is underlaid by a gigantic salt dome and the oldest salt-rock mine in the Western Hemisphere. But it is the fiery-hot peppers that grow especially well here that have brought Avery Island its greatest claim to fame. Tabasco brand pepper sauce, so loved not only in Cajun country but also all over the world, is made by a closely knit family and equally close workers who cultivate and harvest the peppers, then nurse them through a fermentation process first developed by Edmund McIlhenny, founder of McIlhenny Company. You can tour the Tabasco factory and visitor's center, which includes an old-fashioned Tabasco Country Store. You may want to take a driving or walking tour (for a fee) of the Jungle Gardens afterward. The gardens cover more than 200 acres, with something in bloom continuously from November through June. There are a Buddha from A.D. 1000 in the Chinese Garden, sunken gardens, a bird sanctuary (with great numbers of egrets and herons), and tropical plants.

Admission: Free.

Open: Factory, Mon–Fri 9am–4pm, Sat 9am–noon; garden, daily 9am–5pm.

LIVE OAK GARDENS, 284 Rip Van Winkle Rd., New Iberia. Tel. 318/367-3485.

If time permits, plan to spend a morning or an afternoon at Live Oak Gardens. Its location is known as Jefferson Island, although it isn't a proper island at all but a piece of land held up higher than its surroundings by one of the five massive salt domes in coastal Louisiana. Set on the shores of Lake Peigneur, it's a place of huge oak trees, some 350 years old or more, that are draped with Spanish moss and colorful blooming plants. So beguiled by its beauty was actor Joseph Jefferson, who gained national fame for his portrayal of Rip Van Winkle, that in 1869 he purchased land there and erected an extravagant three-story home, much of which he designed himself, with elements of French, English, Moorish, and Victorian Steamboat architecture. The result is a surprisingly gracious home with ingenious practical touches—such as the natural air conditioning afforded by a "well" in the center of the house.

Although Jefferson did more than a little landscaping and gardening on the grounds, it was the Bayless family—who bought the estate from Jefferson's heirs in 1917—who are responsible for the colorful panorama you see today. The gardens were well developed when disaster struck in 1980—the lake disappeared after an oil company drilled into the salt mine, creating a gigantic whirlpool so powerful that it sucked in all the waters of the lake and huge portions of the gardens adjacent to it. Today all has been repaired; the gardens have been rebuilt; and you'll see only the glory of camellias, azaleas, crape myrtles, tulips, and even a Japanese garden. Tour the home, which is filled with antiques and landscapes painted by the talented Jefferson, then take time to stroll among the blossoms and beneath the live oaks. An old legend of buried Jean Lafitte treasure gained some credence in 1923, when three boxes of ancient gold and silver coins were unearthed beneath the trees.

Admission: $7.50 adults, $6.50 seniors, $4 children.

Open: Daily 9am–5pm (winter, daily 9am–4pm). **Closed:** Holidays.

INDEX

Acadiana, 221–38
Acadian House Museum (St. Martinville), 235
Acadians, 5, 8, 17, 151, 222–23. *See also* Cajuns
  Festivals Acadiens, 154–55
Acadian Village (Lafayette), 155, 229–30
Accommodations, 52–80. *See also* list of *individual establishments at end of Index*
  in Baton Rouge, 220–21
  in the French Quarter, 53–72
  outside the French Quarter, 72–80
  in Lafayette, 231–32
  money-saving tips, 59
  reservations, 53, 150
  in St. Francisville, 219–20
  in St. Martinville, 235
African Americans
  Black Heritage Festival, 25
  Mardi Gras and, 148
  networks and resources for, 50
  tour focusing on African-American history, 143
Airport, 41
Air travel, 28, 33–34, 41
American Express, 48
Amtrak, 28, 34, 42
Annual events, festivals and fairs, 25–27, 145–56. *See also specific events*
Antiques, shopping for, 183–84
Aquarium of the Americas, 140–41
Archbishop Antoine Blanc Memorial, 163
Architecture. *See* Esplanade Ridge, walking tour; Garden District, walking tour; Historic buildings; Plantation houses
  books about, 21
Armstrong, Louis, 10, 13, 22
Arriving in New Orleans, 41–42
Art galleries, 126, 184–85
Art museums
  Contemporary Arts Center, 135
  New Orleans Museum of Art, 136, 138
Asphodel (Jackson), 216
Audubon, John James, 55, 216, 217
Audubon Park, 137–38, 180
Audubon Zoo, 140
Avery Island, 237

Babysitters, 48
Balls, 61, 147, 149
Bars, 200–202
Basin Street, 44
Baton Rouge
  accommodations in, 220–21
  plantation houses, 215–16
  restaurants in, 221
  tourist information, 214
Bayous, 223, 236
  tours of, 145, 229, 237
Bayou St. John, 125–28
Beauregard-Keyes House, 132

Bechet, Sidney, 10, 13
Bed-and-breakfast reservation services, 53, 219, 226
Bellocq, Ernest J., 13–14
Bienville, Sieur de (Jean-Baptiste Le Moyne), 3–4, 125, 137, 147
Black Heritage Festival, 25
Boat tours. *See* Cruises
Books about New Orleans, 19–21
Bookstores, 185–86, 190
Breaux Bridge, 226–28
Broussard, Joseph, 223
Buckstown, 127–28
Burnside, 214
Buses, 46
  tours, 143–44, 209
Business hours, 34–35, 48, 181
Bus travel, 28–29, 34, 42
Butler, Thomas, 218

Cabaret, 199–200
Cabildo, 132, 165
Cable, George Washington, 14, 19
Café du Monde, 114–15, 126, 165
Cafes, 114–16, 126
Cajun Country, 221–38
Cajuns, 5, 8, 222–24
  Acadian Village (Lafayette), 155, 229–30
  cuisine of, 17, 224
  Festivals Acadiens, 154–55
  Mardi Gras, 151–52
  music, 198–99, 224–25
  Rayne Frog Festival, 156
  tours, 226, 236
  Vermilionville (Lafayette), 230
Calendar of events. *See* Annual events, festivals and fairs
Cameras and film, 49
Campgrounds, 80
Canal Street, 43, 124
Candy stores, 186–87
Capote, Truman, 14
Carnival. *See* Mardi Gras
Cars and driving
  automobile organizations, 34
  to Cajun Country, 225
  to New Orleans, 29, 42
  rentals, 47
  safety tips, 32–33
Casinos, 203
Catalpa Plantation (St. Francisville), 217
Cemeteries
  history of, 128
  Lafayette No. 1 Cemetery, 128, 168–69
  Metairie Cemetery, 128
  National Cemetery, 139
  safety in, 128–29, 169
  St. Louis Cemetery No. 1, 128
  St. Louis Cemetery No. 2, 128
  St. Louis Cemetery No. 3, 126–27, 176
Centers, shopping, 182–83
Chalmette National Historical Park, 139

Children
  books for, 21
  sightseeing for, 141–42
Children's Museum, Louisiana, 141–42
Children's Storyland, 142
Chretien Point Plantation (Lafayette), 230–31
Churches and cathedrals
  Church of St. John the Baptist, 129
  Felicity United Methodist Church, 172
  Gospel Temple Church, 170
  Our Lady of Guadalupe International
      Shrine of St. Jude, 129
  St. Alphonsus Church, 129
  St. Louis Cathedral, 164–65
  St. Martin de Tours Church (St.
      Martinville), 234
  St. Patrick's Church, 129
Church of St. John the Baptist, 129
City Park, 138
Civil War, 6–7, 134, 138, 139, 147, 165,
  207, 215, 216, 217, 236
Climate, 24–25
Clothes
  packing for your trip, 27
  shopping for, 187–88
Clubs, 194–200
Coffee, 18
Concert halls, 193
Confederate Museum, 134
Congo Square (now Beauregard Square), 11,
  136
Consulates, 35–36
Contemporary Arts Center, 135
Cooking lessons, 19
Costumes, shopping for, 187
Cottage, The (St. Francisville), 218–20
Cotton Blossom, 140, 144
Crafts festival, 155
Crawfish Festival and Fair (Breaux Bridge),
  226–27
Credit cards, 32
Creole Christmas, 27, 153
Creole Queen, 144, 202–3
Creoles, 5, 6, 8, 124, 138, 147, 205, 230
  cuisine of, 16, 17
Cruises, 48, 144, 202–3
Currency and exchange, 31–32, 35
Customs regulations, 31

Davis, Jefferson, 166
Decatur Street, 163–64
Degas, Edgar, 136, 158, 168, 174–75
Destrehan Manor (Destrehan), 210
Dewitt, Dom Gregory, 129
Dining customs, 16–17
Disabled travelers, 51
Dixieland jazz. *See* Jazz
Documents for entry into the U.S., 30–31
Donaldsonville, 214
Drinks, 18
Dueling Oaks, in City Park, 138

Embassies, 35–36
Emergencies, 36
Entertainment and nightlife, 192–203
Entry into the U.S., requirements for, 30–31
Esplanade Ridge, walking tour of, 173–76

Evangeline (Longfellow), 151, 222, 223, 224,
  234, 235
Evangeline Monument (St. Martinville), 234
Evangeline Oak (St. Martinville), 235
Excursion areas, 204–38
Expedite, Saint, 129

Famous and historical figures, 13–16. *See
  also specific figures*
Fashions, shopping for, 187–88
Fast facts, 34–38, 48–50
Faubourg Marigny, 45–46
Faulkner, William, 20, 165
Felicity United Methodist Church, 172
Ferries, 48
Festivals. *See* Annual events, festivals and
  fairs
Festivals Acadiens, 154–55
Food, 16–19, 224
  cooking lessons, 19
  dining customs, 16–17
  festivals, 154–55
  shopping for, 188
  vocabulary, 18–19
Football, 121, 156
  USF&G Sugar Bowl Classic, 25, 156
Foreign visitors, 30–40
Fountain, Pete, 14, 198
French Quarter, 2, 7, 8, 42, 43, 123–24
  accommodations in, 53–72
  bus tour of, 143–44
  entertainment in, 194–201
  historic buildings in, 131–34, 157–58,
      160–65
  organized walking tour of, 143
  restaurants in, 82–101
  shopping, 182
  voodoo tour, 136
  walking tour of, 157–65
French Quarter Festival, 26, 154
Frog Festival, Rayne, 156

Gallier Hall, 178
Gallier House Museum, 133–34, 163
Gambling, 7, 203, 205–6
Garden District, 43, 44, 124–25, 126
  restaurants in, 106–10
  tours of, 143
  walking tours of, 165–73
Gardens. *See also* Plantation houses
  Afton Villa Gardens (St. Francisville), 218
  Live Oak Gardens (New Iberia), 238
  Longue Vue Estate & Gardens, 139
  Rosedown Plantation and Gardens (St.
      Francisville), 217
  St. Anthony's Garden, 139
  Tabasco Sauce Factory and Jungle Gardens
      (Avery Island), 237
Gay men and lesbians, 50–51, 202
Geography, 3
Gift shops, 188–89
Golf, 138, 156
Gone With the Wind, 179, 230–31
Gottschalk, Louis Moreau, 14
Grau, Shirley Ann, 14, 20
Gray Line bus tours, 143–44, 209
Greater New Orleans Causeway, 127

Guesthouses, 52, 65–71, 79–80, 219
Gumbel, Bryant, 14
Gumbo, 18, 224
  festival, 27
  Mardi Gras, 152

Halloween, 27
Hat shop, 189
Haughery, Margaret, 136–37
Haunted houses, 161, 162–63
Hearn, Lafcadio, 14
Hellman, Lillian, 14
Hirt, Al, 15
Historical and cultural museums
  Acadian House Museum (St. Martinville),
    235
  Cabildo, 132, 165
  Confederate Museum, 134
  Gallier House Museum, 133–34, 163
  Germaine Wells Mardi Gras Museum, 82
  Historic New Orleans Collection–Museum/
    Research Center, 13, 158
  Jackson Barracks, 134
  Lafayette Museum, 230
  Musée Conti Wax Museum, 135
  New Orleans Historic Voodoo Museum,
    135–36
  New Orleans Pharmacy Museum, 136
  Old U.S. Mint, 133, 163
  Presbytère, 133, 164
  Rural Life Museum (Baton Rouge), 215
Historic buildings
  Archibald Bouleware House, 172
  Bank of Louisiana, 157–58
  Beauregard-Keyes House, 132
  Brulatour Court, 158
  Cabildo, 132, 165
  Court of Two Sisters, 158, 160
  Eagle Hall, 170
  826 St. Ann Street, 130–31
  Gallier Hall, 178
  Gallier House Museum, 133–34, 163
  Gilmour Parker House, 168
  House of Broel, 166
  Hugh-Wilson House, 172
  Jackson Barracks, 134
  John T. Moore, Jr., House, 171
  LaBranche House, 160
  Lafitte's Blacksmith Shop, 162, 200–201
  LaLaurie Home, 162–63
  Le Monnier Mansion, 160
  LePretre Mansion, 161
  Madame John's Legacy, 161–62, 206
  Merieult House, 158
  Musson-Degas House, 174–75
  Old Absinthe House, 131–32
  Old Town Praline Shop, 160
  Old Ursuline Convent, 133
  Old U.S. Mint, 133, 163
  Pitot House, 134, 176
  Plique-LaBranch House, 161
  Pontalba Apartments, 133, 164
  Presbytère, 133, 164
  Preservation Hall, 11, 160, 197
  Rillieux-Waldhorn House, 158
  Thierry House, 162
  Wedding Cake House, 179
  Widow Castanedo's House, 174

Historic New Orleans Collection–Museum/
  Research Center, 135, 158
History of New Orleans, 3–8
  books about, 20–21
  of Cajuns, 222–24
  of Mardi Gras, 146–49
Holidays, 36
Horse and carriage, 48, 145
Horseback riding, 156
Horse racing, 229
Hospitals, 49
Hostel, youth, 80
Houmas House (Darrow), 212–13

Information sources, 23, 42, 146, 151.
  See also Telephone numbers, useful
  Baton Rouge, 214
  Lafayette, 152, 155, 226, 228
Insurance, 31
Irish Channel, 44
Itineraries, 121–23

Jackson, Andrew, 1, 6, 132, 134, 139, 218
Jackson Barracks, 134
Jackson Square, 126
Jaxfest, 113, 182
Jazz, 7, 194. *See also specific musicians*
  books about, 21
  clubs, 11, 195–98
  history of, 8–10, 44
  museum: Old U.S. Mint, 133, 163
  New Orleans Jazz and Heritage Festival,
    26, 152–53
  recordings, 21–22
Jewelry stores, 189–90

Keyes, Frances Parkinson, 132, 210
King, Grace, 172
Krewe of Comus, 178
Krewe of Rex, 148

LaBranche House, 160
Lacombe, 112
Lafayette, 228–34
  accommodations in, 231–32
  Festivals Acadiens, 154–55
  Mardi Gras, 151–52
  restaurants in or near, 232–34
  sightseeing, 229–31
  tourist information, 152, 155, 226, 228
Lafitte, Jean, 1, 6, 162, 200, 226, 230, 238
Lafitte's Blacksmith Shop, 162, 200–201
Lafon, Thomy, 126–27
Lake Pontchartrain, 127–28
  restaurant, 111
LaLaurie Home, 162–63
Languages, 12–13
Late night/24-hour dining, 116–17
Latrobe, Benjamin H., 158
Laveau, Marie, 12, 128, 135
Layout of New Orleans, 42–43
Leather goods, shopping for, 190
Le Carpentier, Joseph, 132
Lee, Robert E., 178
Legal aid, 36
Le Petit Theatre du Vieux Carré, 194

LePretre Mansion, 161
Lewis, George, 15
Libraries, 49, 179
Liquor, 18
Liquor laws, 49
Live Oak Gardens (New Iberia), 238
Longfellow, Henry Wadsworth, 151, 222, 223, 224, 234, 235
Longfellow-Evangeline Commemorative Area, 235
Longue Vue Estate & Gardens, 139
Louisiana Children's Museum, 141–42
Louisiana Native Crafts Festival, 155
Louisiana Purchase, 6, 124, 132
Louisiana Superdome, 125, 156, 193–94
Lower Garden District. See Garden District
Loyola University, 180

Madame John's Legacy, 161–62, 208
Madewood (Napoleonville), 213
Magnolia Mound (Baton Rouge), 215
Maps, street, 120
Mardi Gras, 25, 146–52
   books about, 20
   Cajun, 151–52
   Germaine Wells Mardi Gras Museum, 82
   history of, 146–49
   Old U.S. Mint (museum), 133, 163
   parade, 149–50
   planning for, 150–51
   shopping for costumes, 187
Mardi Gras fountain, 127
Marmillion, Edmond, 210
Marsalis, Wynton, 15
Measurements, converting, 38–40
Metairie, 110–11, 128
Metairie Cemetery, 128
Military museums, 134
Mississippi River, 1, 3, 125
   cruises, 48, 144, 202–3
   ferry rides, 48
   steamboats on, 205–6
Mistick Krewe of Comus, 147
Money, 23–24, 31–32
Morton, Jelly Roll, 10, 15, 22
Municipal Auditorium, 193
Musée Conti Wax Museum, 135
Music, 8–11. See also Jazz
   blues, 195–98
   books about, 21
   Cajun, 198–99, 224–25
   Festival de Musique Acadienne, 155
   New Orleans Jazz and Heritage Festival, 26, 152–53
   piano bars, 201
   recordings, 21–22
   rock, 200
   world, 200
Myrtles, The (St. Francisville), 217–18

Natchez, 144
Native Americans, 4, 125, 127
Neighborhoods, 43–46
New Iberia, 236–38
New Orleans, Battle of, 1, 6, 132, 139, 163, 218
New Orleans Historic Voodoo Museum, 135–36

New Orleans Jazz and Heritage Festival, 26, 152–53
New Orleans Museum of Art, 136, 138
New Orleans Pharmacy Museum, 136
New Orleans Philharmonic Symphony Orchestra, 193
New Orleans Saints football team, 121, 156
Nottoway Plantation (White River), 215–16

Oak Alley (Vacherie), 212
Oakley Plantation (St. Francisville), 216–17
Observation deck, 137
Occult store, 190
Old Absinthe House, 131–32
Old French Market, 163
Old Ursuline Convent, 133
Old U.S. Mint, 133, 163
Oliver, King, 10, 22
Opera, 192
Ott, Mel, 15
Our Lady of Guadalupe International Shrine of St. Jude, 129

Packing for your trip, 27
Panoramas, 137, 201–2
Parks
   Audubon Park, 137–38, 180
   Chalmette National Historical Park, 139
   City Park, 138
   DeSoto Park, 176
   Longfellow-Evangeline Commemorative Area, 235
   Washington Artillery Park, 140
   Woldenberg River Park, 140
Parlange (New Roads), 216
Pastries, 114–16
Peoples, 8, 222–24. See also specific peoples
Percy, Walker, 15, 20
Performing arts, 192–94
Perfume, shopping for, 190–91
Peyehard, Antoine A., 158
Pharmacy Museum, New Orleans, 136
Photographic needs, 49
Piano bars, 201
Picnic fare, 117
Pipe shop, 191
Pitot House, 134, 176
Planning and preparing for your trip, 23–29
Plantation houses
   Asphodel (Jackson), 216
   Catalpa Plantation (St. Francisville), 217
   Chretien Point Plantation (Lafayette), 230–31
   The Cottage (St. Francisville), 218–19
   Destrehan Manor, 210
   history of, 206–8
   Houmas House (Darrow), 212–13
   Madewood (Napoleonville), 213
   Magnolia Mound (Baton Rouge), 215
   The Myrtles (St. Francisville), 217–18
   Nottoway Plantation (White River), 215–16
   Oak Alley (Vacherie), 212
   Oakley (St. Francisville), 216–17
   Ormond (Destrehan), 209–10
   Parlange (New Roads), 216
   Rosedown Plantation and Gardens (St. Francisville), 217

Plantation houses *(cont.)*
San Francisco (Reserve), 210–11
Shadows-on-the-Teche Plantation (New
Iberia), 237
Tezcuco (Darrow), 211–12
tours of, 209
Playground, 142
Pontalba, Joseph Xavier de, 62
Pontalba Apartments, 133, 164
Post office, 49
Pralines, 186–87
Presbytère, 133, 164
Preservation Hall, 11, 160, 197
Prudhomme, Paul, 17, 88
Psychic readings, 136, 190

Rainfall, average monthly, 25
Rayne Frog Festival, 156
Recordings, 21–22
Religious services, 49
Restaurants, 81–119
in Baton Rouge, 221
in Breaux Bridge, 227–28
in Burnside, 214
in Central Business District, 103–6
by cuisine, 117–19
in Donaldsonville, 214
downtown, 101–2
in the French Quarter, 82–101
in Lacombe, 112
Lafayette and environs, 232–34
Lake Pontchartrain, 111
in Metairie, 110–11
money-saving tips, 97
specialty dining, 113–17
in St. Martinville, 235–36
uptown, including the Garden District,
106–10
Reuther House, 175
Rice, Anne, 15, 20
Riverboats. *See* Steamboats
River Road, plantations along, 204–14
Rosedown Plantation and Gardens (St.
Francisville), 217
Rural Life Museum (Baton Rouge), 215

Sacred Heart Academy, 179
Saenger Theatre, 194
Safety, 32–33, 49–50, 124, 128–29
St. Alphonsus Church, 129
St. Anthony's Garden, 139
St. Francisville
accommodations in, 219–20
plantation houses, 216–19
St. Louis Cathedral, 164–65
St. Martin de Tours Church (St. Martinville),
234
St. Martinville, 234–36
St. Patrick's Church, 129
San Francisco (Reserve), 210–11
Shadows-on-the-Teche Plantation (New
Iberia), 237
Shopping, 181–91
Sightseeing, 120–80
for children, 141–42
itineraries, 121–23

Slavery, 7, 11, 205, 207
Spanish Fort, 127
Special events. *See* Annual events, festivals
and fairs
Sports, 156
Spring Fiesta, 26, 130, 153–54
Stanley, Henry Morton, 172–73
Steamboats, 205–6, 236
cruises, 48, 144, 202–3
Storey, William, 148
Story, Sidney, 7
Storyville, 7, 9, 44
books about, 20
Streetcars, 46–47
tour by, 177–80
Student travelers, 50
Superdome, 125, 156, 193–94
Swamp tours, 145, 229, 237

Tabasco Sauce Factory and Jungle Gardens
(Avery Island), 237
Taxes, 37
Taxis, 47
Telephone numbers, useful, 50
for concert/performance halls, 193
Telephones, 37
Temperatures, average monthly, 25
Tennessee Williams Literary Festival, 25–26,
154
Tennis, 156
Tezcuco (Darrow), 211–12
Theaters, 193–94
Theatre of the Performing Arts, 193
Thompson, Lydia, 147–48
Time, 38
Tipping, 50
Toilets, 38
Tourist information, 23, 42, 146, 151
Baton Rouge, 214
Lafayette, 152, 155, 226, 228
Tours. *See also* Walking tours
of the bayous, 145, 229, 237
by bus, 143–44, 209
of Cajun Country, 226, 236
of cemeteries, 129
by horse and carriage, 145
of plantation houses, 209
voodoo, 136, 143
Toy store, 191
Train travel, 28, 34, 42
Transportation, 46–48
Traveler's checks, 32
Traveling
to New Orleans, 28–29
to and within the U.S., 33–34
Tulane University, 156, 180
Twain, Mark, 1, 20, 172
Twelfth Night Revelers, 147

Universities
Louisiana State University, 127
Loyola University, 180
Tulane University, 156, 180
University of New Orleans, 156
University of Southwestern Louisiana
(Lafayette), 229

Vermilionville (Lafayette), 230
Voodoo, 11–12. *See also* Laveau, Marie
  New Orleans Historic Voodoo Museum, 135–36
  tour, 136, 143

Walker, Sara, 15
Walking tours
  Esplanade Ridge, 173–76
  French Quarter, 157–65
  Garden District, 165–73
  organized, 129, 142–43
  by streetcar, 177–80
Warehouse District, 43–44
Washington Artillery Park, 140

Weather, 24–25
West End, 127
White Castle, 215–16
Williams, Tennessee, 20, 55
  Literary Festival, 25–26, 154
Woldenberg River Park, 140
Women's Opera Guild Home, 168
Woodcrafts, shopping for, 191
World Trade Center of New Orleans, 137, 201–2

Young, Andrew, 15–16

Zoo, Audubon, 140
Zulu Social Aid & Pleasure Club, 148

ACCOMMODATIONS

Avenue Plaza Hotel (*M*), 76
Best Western Inn on Bourbon Street (*M*), 60
Bourbon Orleans Hotel (*M*), 60–61
Bourgoyne Guest House (*A*), 71
Chateau Motor Hotel (*M*), 61
Columns, The (*M*), 76–77
Dauphine Orleans Hotel (*E*), 54–55
Fairmont Hotel (*VE*), 72–73
Frenchmen, The (*M*), 61
French Quarter Maisonnettes (*G/I*), 67
Grenoble House (*G/E*), 65
Historic French Market Inn, The (*M*), 62
Holiday Inn–Chateau Lemoyne (*M*), 62
Holiday Inn Crowne Plaza (*E*), 75
Holiday Inn Downtown–Superdome (*M*), 77
Hotel de la Poste (*M*), 62
Hotel Inter-Continental (*VE*), 73
Hotel La Salle (*I*), 78–79
Hotel Maison de Ville (*E*), 55–56
Hotel Provincial (*I*), 64–65
Hotel St. Pierre (*M*), 63
Hotel Ste. Helene (*M*), 63
Hotel Villa Convento (*I*), 65
House on Bayou Road, The (*G/E*), 69–70
KOA New Orleans East (*CG*), 80
KOA New Orleans West (*CG*), 80
Lafitte Guest House (*G/M*), 65–66
Le Meridien Hotel (*VE*), 73–74
Le Pavillon Hotel (*M*), 77–78

Le Richelieu Motor Hotel (*M*), 63–64
Longpre House Hostel (*B*), 80
Maison Dupuy (*E*), 57–58
Mechling's Guest House (*G/M*), 70–71
Melrose Mansion (*G/VE*), 68–69
Monteleone Hotel (*E*), 58
Napoleon House (*A*), 71–72
New Orleans Guest House (*G/I*), 67–68
New Orleans Hilton Riverside & Towers Hotel (*E*), 75–76
Omni Royal Orleans (*VE*), 53–54
Parkview Guest House (*G/I*), 79–80
P. J. Holbrook's Olde Victorian Inn (*G/M*), 66–67
Place d'Armes Hotel (*M*), 64
Pontchartrain Hotel (*VE*), 74
Prince Conti Hotel (*M*), 64
Prytania Park Hotel (*M*), 78
Quality Inn Midtown (*I*), 79
Royal Sonesta (*E*), 58–59
St. Charles Inn (*I*), 79
St. Louis (*E*), 59
623 Ursulines (*G/I*), 68
Soniat House (*E*), 59–60
Sun and the Moon Bed and Breakfast (*G/I*), 68
Westin Canal Place (*VE*), 54
Windsor Court (*VE*), 74–75
YMCA International Hotel (*B*), 80

Excursion Areas

Barrow House Inn (St. Francisville, *M*), 219
Bois des Chenes Inn (Lafayette, *M*), 231
Cottage, The (St. Francisville, *M*), 219–20
Days Inn (Lafayette, *I*), 231
Hilton Baton Rouge (Baton Rouge, *M*), 220
Holiday Inn Central–Holidome (Lafayette, *I*), 231
Hotel Acadiana (Lafayette, *M*), 231–32

Lafayette Hilton and Towers (Lafayette, *M*), 232
Old Hotel Castillo Inn (La Place d' Evangeline) (St. Martinville, *I*), 235
Quality Inn (Baton Rouge, *I*), 220
St. Francis Hotel on the Lake (St. Francisville, *M*), 220
Sheraton Baton Rouge (Baton Rouge, *I*), 220–21

Key to abbreviations *A* = Apartment; *B* = Budget; *CG* = Campground; *E* = Expensive; *G* = Guest house; *I* = Inexpensive; *M* = Moderately priced; *VE* = Very expensive.

Now Save Money on All Your Travels by Joining FROMMER'S ™ TRAVEL BOOK CLUB

The World's Best Travel Guides at Membership Prices

FROMMER'S TRAVEL BOOK CLUB is your ticket to successful travel! Open up a world of travel information and simplify your travel planning when you join ranks with thousands of value-conscious travelers who are members of the FROMMER'S TRAVEL BOOK CLUB. Join today and you'll be entitled to all the privileges that come from belonging to the club that offers you travel guides for less to more than 100 destinations worldwide. Annual membership is only $25 (U.S.) or $35 (Canada and foreign).

The Advantages of Membership

1. Your choice of *three* free FROMMER'S TRAVEL GUIDES (any *two* FROMMER'S COMPREHENSIVE GUIDES, FROMMER'S $-A-DAY GUIDES, FROMMER'S WALKING TOURS *or* FROMMER'S FAMILY GUIDES—plus *one* FROMMER'S CITY GUIDE, FROMMER'S CITY $-A-DAY GUIDE *or* FROMMER'S TOURING GUIDE).
2. Your own subscription to **TRIPS AND TRAVEL** quarterly newsletter.
3. You're entitled to a **30% discount** on your order of any additional books offered by FROMMER'S TRAVEL BOOK CLUB.
4. You're offered (at a small additional fee) our **Domestic Trip-Routing Kits.**

Our quarterly newsletter **TRIPS AND TRAVEL** offers practical information on the best buys in travel, the "hottest" vacation spots, the latest travel trends, world-class events and much, much more.

Our **Domestic Trip-Routing Kits** are available for any North American destination. We'll send you a detailed map highlighting the best route to take to your destination—you can request direct or scenic routes.

Here's all you have to do to join:

Send in your membership fee of $25 ($35 Canada and foreign) with your name and address on the form below along with your selections as part of your membership package to **FROMMER'S TRAVEL BOOK CLUB, P.O. Box 473, Mt. Morris, IL 61054-0473.** Remember to check off your *three* free books.

If you would like to order additional books, please select the books you would like and send a check for the total amount (please add sales tax in the states noted below), plus $2 per book for shipping and handling ($3 per book for foreign orders) to:

FROMMER'S TRAVEL BOOK CLUB
P.O. Box 473
Mt. Morris, IL 61054-0473
(815) 734-1104

[ ] **YES.** I want to take advantage of this opportunity to join FROMMER'S TRAVEL BOOK CLUB.
[ ] **My check is enclosed.** Dollar amount enclosed_____*
     (all payments in U.S. funds only)

Name_____
Address_____
City_____ State_____ Zip_____
All orders must be prepaid.

To ensure that all orders are processed efficiently, please apply sales tax in the following areas: CA, CT, FL, IL, NJ, NY, TN, WA and CANADA.

*With membership, shipping and handling will be paid by FROMMER'S TRAVEL BOOK CLUB for the three free books you select as part of your membership. Please add $2 per book for shipping and handling for any additional books purchased ($3 per book for foreign orders).

Allow 4–6 weeks for delivery. Prices of books, membership fee, and publication dates are subject to change without notice. Prices are subject to acceptance and availability.

Please Send Me the Books Checked Below:

FROMMER'S COMPREHENSIVE GUIDES
(Guides listing facilities from budget to deluxe, with emphasis on the medium-priced)

	Retail Price	Code		Retail Price	Code
☐ Acapulco/Ixtapa/Taxco 1993–94	$15.00	C120	☐ Morocco 1992–93	$18.00	C021
☐ Alaska 1994–95	$17.00	C131	☐ Nepal 1994–95	$18.00	C126
☐ Arizona 1993–94	$18.00	C101	☐ New England 1994 (Avail. 1/94)	$16.00	C137
☐ Australia 1992–93	$18.00	C002	☐ New Mexico 1993–94	$15.00	C117
☐ Austria 1993–94	$19.00	C119	☐ New York State 1994–95	$19.00	C133
☐ Bahamas 1994–95	$17.00	C121	☐ Northwest 1994–95 (Avail. 2/94)	$17.00	C140
☐ Belgium/Holland/ Luxembourg 1993–94	$18.00	C106	☐ Portugal 1994–95 (Avail. 2/94)	$17.00	C141
☐ Bermuda 1994–95	$15.00	C122	☐ Puerto Rico 1993–94	$15.00	C103
☐ Brazil 1993–94	$20.00	C111	☐ Puerto Vallarta/ Manzanillo/Guadalajara 1994–95 (Avail. 1/94)	$14.00	C028
☐ California 1994	$15.00	C134			
☐ Canada 1994–95 (Avail. 4/94)	$19.00	C145	☐ Scandinavia 1993–94	$19.00	C135
☐ Caribbean 1994	$18.00	C123	☐ Scotland 1994–95 (Avail. 4/94)	$17.00	C146
☐ Carolinas/Georgia 1994–95	$17.00	C128	☐ South Pacific 1994–95 (Avail. 1/94)	$20.00	C138
☐ Colorado 1994–95 (Avail. 3/94)	$16.00	C143	☐ Spain 1993–94	$19.00	C115
☐ Cruises 1993–94	$19.00	C107	☐ Switzerland/ Liechtenstein 1994–95 (Avail. 1/94)	$19.00	C139
☐ Delaware/Maryland 1994–95 (Avail. 1/94)	$15.00	C136			
☐ England 1994	$18.00	C129	☐ Thailand 1992–93	$20.00	C033
☐ Florida 1994	$18.00	C124	☐ U.S.A. 1993–94	$19.00	C116
☐ France 1994–95	$20.00	C132	☐ Virgin Islands 1994–95	$13.00	C127
☐ Germany 1994	$19.00	C125	☐ Virginia 1994–95 (Avail. 2/94)	$14.00	C142
☐ Italy 1994	$19.00	C130			
☐ Jamaica/Barbados 1993–94	$15.00	C105	☐ Yucatán 1993–94	$18.00	C110
☐ Japan 1994–95 (Avail. 3/94)	$19.00	C144			

FROMMER'S $-A-DAY GUIDES
(Guides to low-cost tourist accommodations and facilities)

	Retail Price	Code		Retail Price	Code
☐ Australia on $45 1993–94	$18.00	D102	☐ Israel on $45 1993–94	$18.00	D101
☐ Costa Rica/Guatemala/ Belize on $35 1993–94	$17.00	D108	☐ Mexico on $45 1994	$19.00	D116
			☐ New York on $70 1994–95	$16.00	D120
☐ Eastern Europe on $30 1993–94	$18.00	D110	☐ New Zealand on $45 1993–94	$18.00	D103
☐ England on $60 1994	$18.00	D112	☐ Scotland/Wales on $50 1992–93	$18.00	D019
☐ Europe on $50 1994	$19.00	D115			
☐ Greece on $45 1993–94	$19.00	D100	☐ South America on $40 1993–94	$19.00	D109
☐ Hawaii on $75 1994	$19.00	D113	☐ Turkey on $40 1992–93	$22.00	D023
☐ India on $40 1992–93	$20.00	D010			
☐ Ireland on $45 1994–95 (Avail. 1/94)	$17.00	D117	☐ Washington, D.C. on $40 1994–95 (Avail. 2/94)	$17.00	D119

FROMMER'S CITY $-A-DAY GUIDES
(Pocket-size guides to low-cost tourist accommodations and facilities)

	Retail Price	Code		Retail Price	Code
☐ Berlin on $40 1994–95	$12.00	D111	☐ Madrid on $50 1994–95 (Avail. 1/94)	$13.00	D118
☐ Copenhagen on $50 1992–93	$12.00	D003	☐ Paris on $50 1994–95	$12.00	D117
☐ London on $45 1994–95	$12.00	D114	☐ Stockholm on $50 1992–93	$13.00	D022

FROMMER'S WALKING TOURS
(With routes and detailed maps, these companion guides point out the places and pleasures that make a city unique)

	Retail Price	Code		Retail Price	Code
☐ Berlin	$12.00	W100	☐ Paris	$12.00	W103
☐ London	$12.00	W101	☐ San Francisco	$12.00	W104
☐ New York	$12.00	W102	☐ Washington, D.C.	$12.00	W105

FROMMER'S TOURING GUIDES
(Color-illustrated guides that include walking tours, cultural and historic sights, and practical information)

	Retail Price	Code		Retail Price	Code
☐ Amsterdam	$11.00	T001	☐ New York	$11.00	T008
☐ Barcelona	$14.00	T015	☐ Rome	$11.00	T010
☐ Brazil	$11.00	T003	☐ Scotland	$10.00	T011
☐ Florence	$ 9.00	T005	☐ Sicily	$15.00	T017
☐ Hong Kong/Singapore/			☐ Tokyo	$15.00	T016
Macau	$11.00	T006	☐ Turkey	$11.00	T013
☐ Kenya	$14.00	T018	☐ Venice	$ 9.00	T014
☐ London	$13.00	T007			

FROMMER'S FAMILY GUIDES

	Retail Price	Code		Retail Price	Code
☐ California with Kids	$18.00	F100	☐ San Francisco with Kids		
☐ Los Angeles with Kids			(Avail. 4/94)	$17.00	F104
(Avail. 4/94)	$17.00	F103	☐ Washington, D.C. with		
☐ New York City with Kids			Kids (Avail. 2/94)	$17.00	F102
(Avail. 2/94)	$18.00	F101			

FROMMER'S CITY GUIDES
(Pocket-size guides to sightseeing and tourist accommodations and facilities in all price ranges)

	Retail Price	Code		Retail Price	Code
☐ Amsterdam 1993–94	$13.00	S110	☐ Montréal/Québec City 1993–94	$13.00	S125
☐ Athens 1993–94	$13.00	S114	☐ Nashville/Memphis 1994–95 (Avail. 4/94)	$13.00	S141
☐ Atlanta 1993–94	$13.00	S112	☐ New Orleans 1993–94	$13.00	S103
☐ Atlantic City/Cape May 1993–94	$13.00	S130	☐ New York 1994 (Avail. 1/94)	$13.00	S138
☐ Bangkok 1992–93	$13.00	S005	☐ Orlando 1994	$13.00	S135
☐ Barcelona/Majorca/ Minorca/Ibiza 1993–94	$13.00	S115	☐ Paris 1993–94	$13.00	S109
☐ Berlin 1993–94	$13.00	S116	☐ Philadelphia 1993–94	$13.00	S113
☐ Boston 1993–94	$13.00	S117	☐ San Diego 1993–94	$13.00	S107
☐ Budapest 1994–95 (Avail. 2/94)	$13.00	S139	☐ San Francisco 1994	$13.00	S133
☐ Chicago 1993–94	$13.00	S122	☐ Santa Fe/Taos/ Albuquerque 1993–94	$13.00	S108
☐ Denver/Boulder/ Colorado Springs 1993–94	$13.00	S131	☐ Seattle/Portland 1994–95	$13.00	S137
☐ Dublin 1993–94	$13.00	S128	☐ St. Louis/Kansas City 1993–94	$13.00	S127
☐ Hong Kong 1994–95 (Avail. 4/94)	$13.00	S140	☐ Sydney 1993–94	$13.00	S129
☐ Honolulu/Oahu 1994	$13.00	S134	☐ Tampa/St. Petersburg 1993–94	$13.00	S105
☐ Las Vegas 1993–94	$13.00	S121	☐ Tokyo 1992–93	$13.00	S039
☐ London 1994	$13.00	S132	☐ Toronto 1993–94	$13.00	S126
☐ Los Angeles 1993–94	$13.00	S123	☐ Vancouver/Victoria 1994–95 (Avail. 1/94)	$13.00	S142
☐ Madrid/Costa del Sol 1993–94	$13.00	S124	☐ Washington, D.C. 1994 (Avail. 1/94)	$13.00	S136
☐ Miami 1993–94	$13.00	S118			
☐ Minneapolis/St. Paul 1993–94	$13.00	S119			

SPECIAL EDITIONS

	Retail Price	Code		Retail Price	Code
☐ Bed & Breakfast Southwest	$16.00	P100	☐ Caribbean Hideaways	$16.00	P103
☐ Bed & Breakfast Great American Cities (Avail. 1/94	$16.00	P104	☐ National Park Guide 1994 (Avail. 3/94)	$16.00	P105
			☐ Where to Stay U.S.A.	$15.00	P102

Please note: if the availability of a book is several months away, we may have back issues of guides to that particular destination. Call customer service at (815) 734-1104.